Wireless Programming
with J2ME™

Wireless Programming with J2ME™

Cracking the Code™

Dreamtech Software Team

Hungry Minds™

Best-Selling Books • Digital Downloads • e-Books • Answer Networks •
e-Newsletters • Branded Web Sites • e-Learning

New York, NY ◆ Cleveland, OH ◆ Indianapolis, IN

Wireless Programming with J2ME™: Cracking the Code™

Published by
Hungry Minds, Inc.
909 Third Avenue
New York, NY 10022
www.hungryminds.com

Library of Congress Control Number: 2001093843

ISBN: 0-7645-4885-9

Printed in the United States of America

10 9 8 7 6 5 4 3 2 1

1B/QR/QS/QS/IN

Distributed in the United States by Hungry Minds, Inc.

Distributed by CDG Books Canada Inc. for Canada; by Transworld Publishers Limited in the United Kingdom; by IDG Norge Books for Norway; by IDG Sweden Books for Sweden; by IDG Books Australia Publishing Corporation Pty. Ltd. for Australia and New Zealand; by TransQuest Publishers Pte Ltd. for Singapore, Malaysia, Thailand, Indonesia, and Hong Kong; by Gotop Information Inc. for Taiwan; by ICG Muse, Inc. for Japan; by Intersoft for South Africa; by Eyrolles for France; by International Thomson Publishing for Germany, Austria, and Switzerland; by Distribuidora Cuspide for Argentina; by LR International for Brazil; by Galileo Libros for Chile; by Ediciones ZETA S.C.R. Ltda. for Peru; by WS Computer Publishing Corporation, Inc., for the Philippines; by Contemporanea de Ediciones for Venezuela; by Express Computer Distributors for the Caribbean and West Indies; by Micronesia Media Distributor, Inc. for Micronesia; by Chips Computadoras S.A. de C.V. for Mexico; by Editorial Norma de Panama S.A. for Panama; by American Bookshops for Finland.

For general information on Hungry Minds' products and services please contact our Customer Care department within the U.S. at 800-762-2974, outside the U.S. at 317-572-3993 or fax 317-572-4002.

For sales inquiries and reseller information, including discounts, premium and bulk quantity sales, and foreign-language translations, please contact our Customer Care department at 800-434-3422, fax 317-572-4002 or write to Hungry Minds, Inc., Attn: Customer Care Department, 10475 Crosspoint Boulevard, Indianapolis, IN 46256.

For information on licensing foreign or domestic rights, please contact our Sub-Rights Customer Care department at 212-884-5000.

For information on using Hungry Minds' products and services in the classroom or for ordering examination copies, please contact our Educational Sales department at 800-434-2086 or fax 317-572-4005.

For press review copies, author interviews, or other publicity information, please contact our Public Relations department at 317-572-3168 or fax 317-572-4168.

For authorization to photocopy items for corporate, personal, or educational use, please contact Copyright Clearance Center, 222 Rosewood Drive, Danvers, MA 01923, or fax 978-750-4470.

Hungry Minds™ is a trademark of Hungry Minds, Inc.

Credits

Acquisitions Editor
Chris Webb

Project Editor
Chandani Thapa

Technical Editor
Dr. K.V.K.K. Prasad

Media Development Specialist
Angela Denny

Permissions Editor
Laura Moss

Media Development Manager
Laura Carpenter VanWinkle

Project Coordinator
Nancee Reeves

Cover Design
Anthony Bunyan

Proofreader
Anne Owen

Indexer
Johnna VanHoose Dinse

Cover
Vault door image used courtesy of
Brown Safe Manufacturing
www.BrownSafe.com

Dreamtech Software India, Inc., Team

dreamtech@mantraonline.com
www.dreamtechsoftware.com

Dreamtech Software India, Inc., is a leading provider of corporate software solutions. Based in New Delhi, India, the company is a successful pioneer of innovative solutions in e-learning technologies. Dreamtech's developers have more than 50 years of combined software-engineering experience in areas such as Java, wireless applications, XML, voice-based solutions, .NET, COM/COM+ technologies, distributed computing, DirectX, Windows Media technologies, and security solutions.

About the Authors

Lead Author Team

Vikas Gupta, Co-founder and President. Vikas holds a B.E. in electronics, with a postgraduate diploma in sales and marketing and in publishing and printing studies. Actively engaged in developing and designing new technologies in wireless applications, e-learning, and other cutting-edge areas, he is also the Managing Director of IDG Books India (P) Ltd.

Avnish Dass, Co-founder and CEO. Avnish is a talented and seasoned programmer who has 15 years of experience in systems and application/database programming. Avnish has developed security systems, antivirus programs, wireless and communication technologies, and ERP systems.

Yashraj Chauhan, Sr. Software Developer. Yashraj has an advanced diploma in software development from IBM, with more than three years of experience in Java, XML, and C++, and is pursuing his Masters in computer science.

Other Contributors

Pankaj Kumar, Deepak Sharma, Gaurav Malhotra, Anil Kumar Singh, Bill Ray, a team of programmers of Dreamtech Software India, Inc. They contributed to the development of software in this book.

Acknowledgments

We acknowledge the contributions of the following people for their support in making this book possible:

John Kilcullen for sharing his dream and providing the vision for making this project a reality.

Mike Violano and **Joe Wikert** for believing in us.

V.K. Rajan and **Priti** for their immense help in coordinating various activities throughout this project.

To our parents and family and beloved country, India,
for providing an excellent environment
for nurturing and creating world-class IT talent.

Preface

Wireless devices are new entrants in the information technology arena. As wireless devices are compact and easy to handle, the focus of Information technology is rapidly shifting from PCs to PDAs, cellular phones, and pagers. The market for these devices has undergone a tremendous growth over the past few years. These devices are becoming increasingly sophisticated in response to the demand for using them to access the Net as well as computing devices. Moreover, these devices are paving the way for new business strategies.

Sun Microsystems fulfilled the aspirations of the Java Community by launching J2ME (Java 2 Micro Edition), which gave Java an edge over other programming tools in its performance on wireless devices. It was first introduced at the Java One Conference in 1999. The J2ME has two "design centers." Thus, this platform has two configurations and these are CLDC (Connected Limited Device Configuration) and CDC (Connected Device Configuration). This has to be kept in mind while talking about J2ME.

With an approach that is based on *configurations* and *profiles*, J2ME offers flexibility to the developer, which is of great significance for extremely diverse handheld and wireless devices. This approach makes it possible to provide as much functionality as the device has the potential to support. Added to this are the usual benefits of Java, such as portability across platforms, security, and the object–oriented character. This is why Java is predicted to be the most preferred language for the modern computing devices.

It may well be said that J2ME is still in the early stages of development. Two configurations have become available, but only a few of the proposed profiles are available as of now. This situation is bound to change as soon as the Micro Edition platform becomes more mature. Consequently, its use is also expected to increase considerably. Many leading companies have started releasing Java-enabled devices. This means that you can download Java applications even on your mobile phones and run them offline.

What this Book Covers

This book is based on the unique concept of cracking the code and mastering the technology. The technologies covered are J2ME (Java 2 Micro Edition) version 1.0.2 and the applications are also tested on version 1.0.3 Beta. The book is loaded with code, keeping theory to a minimum. All the applications for which the source code is given have been fully tested at Dreamtech Software Research Lab. The source code provided in the book is based on commercial applications developed by the software development company Dreamtech Software India Inc. Each program of an application is explained in a very detailed manner to provide the reader clear insight into the implementation of the technology in a real-world situation. At the end of the book, reference links are given so that the inquisitive reader can further explore the new developments that are taking place.

As J2ME is a new platform, not many books are available on this topic. There are some books that introduce you to the theory part of J2ME. This book, being a part of the Cracking the Code series, focuses more on developing applications. Here, only a brief introduction to J2ME has been given, with the major part of the book devoted to writing commercial-quality code. This is clear from the fact that, out of the 12 chapters in this book, six are actually projects. Another two are almost fully devoted to case studies. The idea here is to familiarize working professionals with the J2ME code. You can also see the practical differences between the Standard Edition and the Micro Edition by going through these projects and case studies.

It is assumed that the reader has a reasonable command over the Java language and has some experience in programming.

How the Book Is Organized

The book, as mentioned in the preceding section, consists of 12 chapters. The first five chapters dwell on theory, followed by six projects. The book ends with a chapter on the conversion of existing Java applications to their J2ME versions.

The first chapter provides a short overview of the Micro Edition platform. It introduces the basic building blocks of the platform, such as the CLDC, CDC, Foundation Profile, and MIDP. The J2ME virtual machines are also dealt with here. Significant features of J2ME, as compared to the Standard Edition, are pointed out. Related Java technologies such as Java Card, PersonalJava, and EmbeddedJava are mentioned in passing.

The second chapter discusses the programming techniques required for writing applications for small wireless devices. These devices may be severely constrained in terms of resources such as memory and processing power. This is why a new general approach has to be adopted, in addition to specific methods to take care of device-specific problems. This may be an important chapter for you if you are new to programming for small and wireless devices.

The third chapter is about a configuration — namely, CLDC. Configurations are the base on which profiles may be added. They provide the basic functionality common to devices of a particular category. You will find the following in this chapter:

◆ Introduction to the important classes that make up CLDC

◆ Procedure for installing CLDC (nothing much to explain there)

◆ Compiling, preverifying and running application written using J2ME CLDC

◆ Several case studies to illustrate the use of CLDC APIs

The fourth chapter explains the Mobile Information Devices Profile, or MIDP. The format of this chapter is the same as that of the previous chapter. You get an introduction to classes and the procedures of installing, compiling, preverifying, and running. Case studies are also presented to help you understand the APIs fully.

The fifth chapter is on J2ME and contains what is relevant to programming with J2ME. It deals with XML parsing. XML parsing is used in almost all the projects in the book. After the introduction, the reader is told about one of several available parser packages, namely kXML. Needless to say, this example of XML parsing is provided in the form of functioning code.

With the sixth chapter begins a series of projects. Chapter 6 is based on a project, or application if you please, called Online Testing Engine. It allows you to attempt tests online, using devices such as mobile phones. The application is a simple one, but it serves to illustrate the basic concept behind such applications. The project chapters follow the following format:

◆ Introducing the application

◆ Explaining the user interface

◆ Explaining the working of the application

◆ Complete source code with heavy commenting and line-by-line explanation

The seventh chapter is on a project called Online Ordering System. This project is an Ordering System for devices such as cell phones and pagers. You can check the stock available and place an order accordingly. The price of the order to be placed will also be calculated and displayed to you. This can be considered an m-commerce application that uses existing J2EE applications hosted on a server.

The eighth chapter is about a remote-control MP3 player application and is based on PersonalJava and can be used with devices such as Pocket PC. Though this application is written using PersonalJava, it can easily run on a CDC-based platform. It should be noted that, at the time of writing this application,

Personal Profile was not available, but it is known that PersonalJava will merge into J2ME as the Personal Profile. Therefore, this application can be considered a CDC-based application that uses Personal Profile. It also uses the Java Media Framework.

Chapter 9 is on a project called Peer-to-Peer Search Application. This application is a peer-to-peer searching tool for Palm devices. It allows you to search for files on particular system and displays the listing of the available files, somewhat like Napster. You can read a complete peer-to-peer application developed using J2SE and C# in the book *Peer-to-Peer Application Development* – Cracking the Code series, author Dreamtech Software Team.

Chapter 10 contains a project called Mobile Web Services. It is meant to provide services to the user that can be accessed from mobile devices. The project targets devices such as cell phones and similar services. The services the user gets are weather details, movie ticket booking, and news. This project uses XML very extensively.

Chapter 11 is devoted to writing a simple game for Palm devices. The game involves a stationary gun and a moving target. The user has to fire a limited number of bullets to hit the target. Points are awarded accordingly.

Chapter 12 deals with converting applications in which a great deal of effort has been put in by developers all around the world in developing Java applications. It is natural that some of these can be converted to work with handheld devices. The final chapter of the book explains how and to what extent this can be done. Some general guidelines to handle this process are provided.

As this is a code-heavy book with an introduction to the theory, we hope that it will help Java developers in adapting to the Micro Edition platform. Since entry-level material has been left out of the book, making the book smaller in size, you will find it easier to go through it even if you are short on time.

Who Should Read this Book

This book has been designed with some assumptions about the audience. This is necessary since the topic it deals with is somewhat advanced, and it is not possible to teach the Java language to the reader in the same book. Readers are expected to possess a basic knowledge of Java and preferably XML, too. Some experience in programming will definitely help.

The book will benefit people who want to or need to develop commercial-quality applications for devices such as PDAs, mobile phones, two-pagers, etc., using Java. The applications will have connectivity to the Internet and other networks if required. This is understandable because most of theses devices are mobile and use wireless communication.

"Example of --- file distribution, Device management,

— Put some codes together more!

Contents

Connected limited Device configuration (handwritten)

- J2 ME has 2 configurations

Chapter 1

An Overview of J2ME

This chapter presents the basics of J2ME and serves to enlighten the reader on the steps involved in programming with J2ME. It also provides the groundwork necessary for developing applications. J2ME has been compared with J2SE, and so some background is provided on J2ME virtual machines. We also mention, albeit not in detail, Java technologies of a similar nature.

Introduction

Java came to the limelight with the release of HotJava browser, which demonstrated the suitability of Java for the Internet. It established that dynamic and interactive Web pages could be created with Java. The craze for applets also caught up with its release. Subsequently, Netscape 2 for Windows became the first commercial browser to support Java 1.0. Java was at its maximum hype at this time, because it seemed to offer capabilities on the Web that weren't otherwise possible. The promise of cross-platform applications also added to Java's reputation.

Since then, Java has come a long way. Its acceptance is so widespread that you can find APIs for carrying out most of the things that can be done in other programming languages. From applets to RMI and from Servlets to speech APIs, you find everything under the Java umbrella. Perhaps this accumulation of tools providing all kinds of functionalities contributed to Sun Microsystem's decision to organize the Java family better.

Another reason for this could be the boom of nonconventional computing devices. These devices had actually started emerging before the birth of Java. In fact, the Java language itself was initially aimed at providing programming solutions for such devices. Computing was no longer restricted to servers or PCs. And the world of small devices spread far beyond organizers possessing 16K memory and toy processors. Newer devices not only had increased memory and processor power, but also were proliferating in shapes, sizes, display types and areas, input and output methods, and networking.

Sun Microsystems came up with the idea of dividing the Java universe into three separate platforms for different purposes. The domain of the three platforms was to be determined by the sizes for which they were meant. Thus the platform for conventional computing was called the *Java 2 Standard Edition* (*J2SE*) and that for enterprise applications and distributed computing became the *Java 2 Enterprise Edition* (*J2EE*).

The third platform was meant for the nonconventional consumer devices. These devices are characterized by some typical features, such as mobility, limited memory and processing power, incapability to access power from the mains (being battery powered), small display areas, and limitations and variety with respect to input and output methods. Of course, not all these features must be present on one device. One thing common to most of these devices is that they are all connected to some network, even if not always. The Java platform meant for these devices was called the *Java 2 Micro Edition* (*J2ME*). And this platform is what we focus on in this book.

What J2ME is about

Java 2 Micro Edition platform is not restricted to small devices. It has two *design centers*, depending on memory constraints. That's why this platform has two configurations: *CLDC* (*Connected Limited Device*

Configuration) and *CDC* (*Connected Device Configuration*). You need to keep this fact in mind while talking about J2ME. Whenever you're programming for a mobile phone, you are as much within the fold of the J2ME as you are if you're programming for a set-top box with almost as much computing power as a desktop system. But it is true that J2ME is more associated with small devices that have modest amounts of power and memory. Yet, when you program for devices such as set-top boxes, the difference between J2ME and J2SE narrows, and people who've been writing code for the standard edition feel quite at ease with J2ME. It is while writing code for devices such as mobile phones that the peculiarities of J2ME become relevant. We try to cover both design centers in this book, as far as possible.

The micro edition platform was conceived and designed in the form of layers (Figure 1-1). Each layer adds some functionality. The primary requirement is, of course, a virtual machine for running Java applications. These, together with the virtual machine, form part of the configuration. On top of this configuration resides a profile. The exact profile that can be added is dictated by the device and also by the configuration that is being used. But you're not restricted to one profile. You can add another profile on top of the first one. This cannot, however, be done arbitrarily — you cannot add any profile on top of profile.

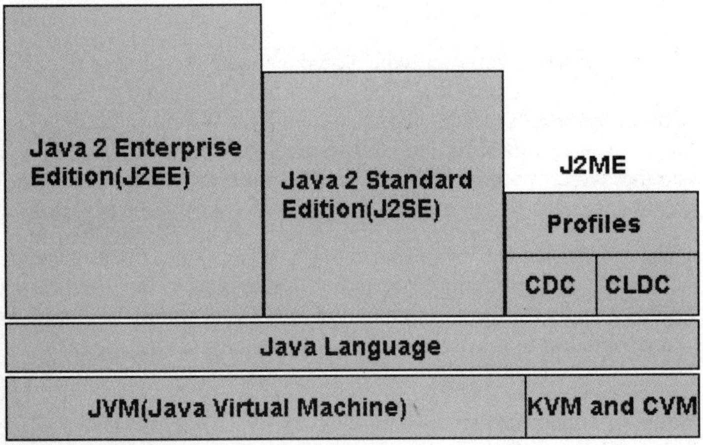

Figure 1-1: Java family

For the time being, we don't have many profiles to choose from: the profile released till recently was Mobile Information Device Profile. The newer Foundation Profile doesn't really match the concept of a profile because it has no libraries for providing user interface. Even after that day comes that we do have more choices, J2ME is not limited to Configurations and profiles, and we can also add optional packages over and above configurations and profiles.

Thus we may consider a *platform* as parts joined together to form a whole that suits the devices for which our applications are meant. Thus we find a great deal of flexibility in regard to implementing the programming model. Device manufacturers as well as independent vendors can provide their own versions of virtual machines if they follow the Java Virtual Machine Specification. If so, their virtual machines would be no less capable than those provided by Sun. Devices can be sold in Java-enabled condition, or they can be Java enabled later on by the user. Similarly, applications may be loaded onto the devices before the devices are sold, or the user may download them from the Web.

What J2ME offers

Java 2 Micro Edition complements technologies such as WAP, *cHTML* (*Compact HTML*), and i-Mode. It can do for small and limited devices what J2SE and J2EE did for desktop and server systems. Just as you can download and run an applet in a browser that supports HTML or XML, you can run a Spotlet or MIDlet in a browser that supports WML or I-Mode. Or you can run standalone J2ME applications on, say, a mobile phone, just as you can run standalone applications on a PC. And just as you can run an application that invokes a servlet residing on a server, you can run the same on a mobile phone or a set-top box. This is because the server side remains the same — you need to regard only the restrictions of the device. These applications can be games, navigation aids, applications interacting with databases, or anything permitted by the resources on the device. The idea of ubiquitous computing can be realized with this platform (Figure 1-2).

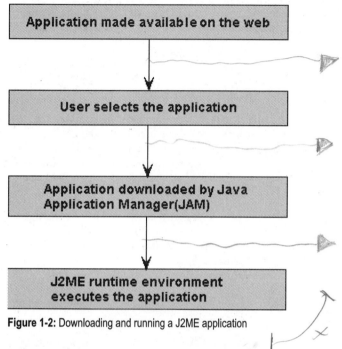

Figure 1-2: Downloading and running a J2ME application

J2ME Virtual Machines

The Java virtual machine used in the standard edition and the enterprise edition is meant for use only on desktop systems and servers. Its size renders it unfit for the small devices, which need a virtual machine with a very small footprint. These are devices such as the mobile phones, two-way pagers, PDAs or handheld devices, screen phones, smart phones, and so on. But J2ME also targets other devices that can accommodate a larger footprint but that still cannot use the conventional Java virtual machine in its original form. This category of devices includes set-top boxes, car navigation systems, handheld PCs, and so on.

In view of all these, two virtual machines were developed for the two design centers. The devices in the first category are supposed to use the smaller footprint *K Virtual Machine* (*KVM*), while those in the second category use the larger footprint *C Virtual Machine* (*CVM*).

The K Virtual Machine (KVM)

As you're probably aware by now, the KVM is a new, highly optimized Java virtual machine for resource-constrained devices. Appropriately, the K virtual machine is very small in size (about 40-80K), and every care has been taken to make it suitable for devices such as pagers, cell phones, and PDAs. Like any other Java virtual machine, it enables you to download and execute applications. Like applets, these applications provide a method for presenting dynamic content.

The KVM can run on any system that has a 16-bit/32-bit processor and 160-512K of total memory. As of now, the KVM has no support for certain features such as determinism, long and float data types, and so on. The design of KVM is based on some important considerations, including the small size to conserve as much space on the device memory as possible (both in terms of storage and runtime memory) and its capabilities to run on low-power processors, to enable partitioning of the VM, and to fulfill the Java assurance of portability. This last issue could have been a big problem, considering the diversity of small devices. There is actually no full portability, but porting is not very difficult because the KVM was implemented in C language.

Just as applets are written using the APIs available in the standard edition, these applications (spotlets, MIDlets, and more to come) are written using Java APIs available in CLDC, CDC, MIDP, Foundation Profile, and so on. And just as applets are run using the conventional JVM, these applications are run using the KVM.

We should note here that, when we talk of KVM, we mean the reference implementation of KVM provided by Sun. However, J2ME can use any VM that is written according to the Sun's Java Virtual Machine Specifications (JVMS) and can handle as much work as the K virtual machine.

The K Virtual Machine can theoretically run several profiles, but it cannot run quite perfectly all the profiles and APIs that aren't specifically designed for it, just as it cannot be used to run the CDC. It is basically meant for CLDC and, at present, for only one profile: MIDP. This means that applications written for the conventional JVM or even for CVM most probably cannot run on the KVM without some changes. But the converse is not true — applications written for KVM can easily run on the CVM or the normal JVM.

A more recent version of KVM (version 1.02) has some improved capabilities, such as a better garbage collector, debugging support with KDWP, a better preverifier, and so on. KDWP is a Debug Proxy (Debug Agent) tool. Debug proxy is tool that is interposed between a Java IDE (Integrated Development Environment) such as Forte and the KVM for debugging purposes. This version includes an implementation for Linux, too. Certain other bugs have been removed and the performance of the interpreter has been improved.

The C Virtual Machine (CVM)

The C Virtual Machine was required to provide additional functionality that our second-category devices could support but that KVM could not. Its capabilities come very close to that of the conventional virtual machine. You may wonder why it was necessary at all if it is almost as powerful as the normal JVM. Perhaps most important, these devices are meant to do (at least till now) very specific work. They are not supposed to be computing machines capable of doing all kinds of computing, as PCs do.

Many features that are not supported in KVM are supported in CVM. This is expected, because it is a full-featured virtual machine. Only a small portion of the functionality has been sacrificed to optimize it. It has not been used extensively till now, being introduced only recently, but Sun Microsystems claims that it has the following advantages over the K Virtual Machine:

♦ If CVM is used with a Real Time Operating System, it knows how to work with it using the real-time capabilities.

♦ The memory use in case of CVM is more efficient. This is achieved by making it more exact, reducing the garbage collection pause times, totally separating VM from the memory system, and so on.

♦ If you use CVM, you can directly map Java threads to native threads and run Java classes from read-only memory.

♦ It is easier to port CVM to newer platforms because, with CVM, you can use more than one porting option for processes that normally make porting difficult. Sun Microsystems says that it has tried to leave as little for porters as possible.

♦ Synchronization can be done with a small number of machine instructions, which increases the speed of synchronization.

- Besides dynamically loaded classes, CVM can be used with the so-called ROMable Classes. As a result, the virtual machine takes less time to start, fragmentation is reduced, and data sharing increases. This also means that you can execute bytecodes from ROM.

- Native threads are supported by CVM, and internal synchronization and exact garbage collection work with these.

- The footprint of CVM is only a little more than half that of JDK and about one sixth less than that of PersonalJava.

- All the VM specifications and libraries of JDK 1.3 are supported, including weak references, serialization, RMI, and so on.

- It is easier to add functionality to interfaces in the case of CVM.

[handwritten: CVM supports n-threads →]

Configurations

As already mentioned, configurations form the base of the J2ME platform. They provide the basic minimum functionality for a particular category of devices. This functionality is to be common to all devices in that category, irrespective of other factors. The very reason for dividing the platform into configurations and profiles is to serve this purpose. The devices targeted by J2ME, even those in the same category, are so diverse in terms of their capabilities that it would have been difficult, if not impossible, to implement the J2SE kind of model for them.

The whole platform had to be conceived in the form of layers, operating one on top of another. The base is formed by one configuration, over which you add one or more profiles. A *configuration* includes the virtual machine and the required basic minimum libraries. Because the devices can be broadly divided into two categories, two configurations were needed. These are the *Connected Limited Device Configuration* (*CLDC*) and the *Connected Device Configuration* (*CDC*). Their domains may overlap in some cases, because there isn't any definite border between the two. With some devices, it would be difficult to decide whether CLDC or CDC is the more suitable configuration. For example, some screen phones may have more resources which can be best explored by CDC-based applications where as some may not have enough resources to run the heavier CDC-based applications.

Configurations define the horizontal limits of the platform for a category or family of devices. They specify what parts of the Java language, what features of the Java virtual machine, and what core libraries are supported. As mentioned previously, you may sometimes have the option of using either of the two configurations, but you cannot use both simultaneously. You must choose one before you start running Java applications on the device. In fact, the manufacturer may have decided this for the user.

CLDC

The Connected Limited Device Configuration, or CLDC, has been designed for severely resource-constrained devices such as today's cell phones, PDAs, and so on. Therefore, it has everything optimized to a great extent. The virtual machine (KVM or any other similar implementation adhering to the specification) is small, and some of the Java language features are not supported. But the real difference is that the libraries available are very few in number. What this means is that you don't need to learn the basics again — what you learned about the standard edition suffices for the most part — but the libraries must be used with great care (Figure 1-3).

[handwritten: Shorten according to project aim.]　　*[handwritten: streaming]*

[handwritten: Down the line, mention intended profile, package, IDE, etc]

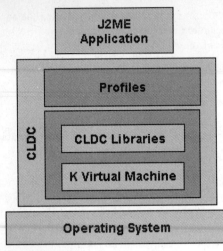

Figure 1-3: CLDC

Some of the main features of CLDC are as follows:

♦ Data types `long` and `float` are not supported. All the methods of J2SE inherited classes that use these data types have been removed.

♦ Several runtime exceptions are present, but the number of runtime errors has been reduced significantly for the classes inculded in CLDC. In fact, only the following three errors are available:

  • `java.lang.Error`

  • `java.lang.OutOfMemoryError`

  • `java.lang.VirtualMachineError`

  Other errors are handled in an implementation-specific manner.

♦ To make garbage collection simple, support for finalization is not provided. There is no `finalize` method in the `java.lang.Object` class.

♦ Java Native Interface (JNI) is not supported in CLDC. The purpose to eliminate-dependence such that the applications can be ported to any platform containing the virtual machine.

♦ You can use threads, but not thread groups or daemon threads.

♦ In the standard edition, you can mark objects for possible garbage collection. This cannot be done with CLDC. In other words, there is no support for weak references.

♦ Verification of classes to check whether the code is well-formed is done off-device — that is, on the desktop system on which the applications are developed. This is done by a tool called *preverifier*. You must do preverification explicitly after you compile your code.

♦ A different security model is used in CLDC, which is somewhat similar to the one used in browsers for downloaded applets. The reason is that the model used in the standard edition is too heavy for small devices, and the security needs of the connected devices are similar to those of the browsers.

There are only four packages available in CLDC. Most of the J2SE packages such as `java.lang.awt`, `java.lang.beans`, and so on have been dropped. CLDC contains only the following packages:

♦ `java.io`: Stripped-down version of the J2SE `java.io` package. It contains the classes required for data input and output using streams.

♦ `java.lang`: Stripped-down version of the J2SE `java.lang` package. It contains the classes that are basic to the Java language such as the wrapper classes for data types.

- `java.util`: Stripped-down version of the J2SE `java.util` package. It contains classes such as `Calender`, `Date`, `Vector`, and `Random`.

- `javax.microedition.io`: A newly introduced CLDC-specific class that defines the Generic Connection Framework. It contains the classes for handling all types of connections by using the same framework.

CDC

The Connected Device Configuration is designed for the devices of the second category. These devices, as we saw, are not as constrained as the CLDC targeted devices. CDC targets devices with 32-bit processor and 2MB+ memory. Consequently, this configuration can afford to provide many more features of the standard edition, both with respect to the Java language support and virtual machine support. In fact, it has full Java language and virtual machine support. And, more important, the number of APIs included in CDC is significantly higher than in CLDC. This means that you can have much more functionality in your application if you use CDC. You can do this, of course, only if the device permits (Figure 1-4).

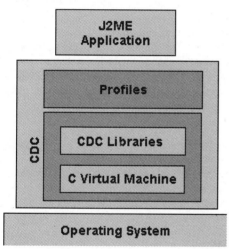

Figure 1-4: CDC

CDC gives you better networking support and a more flexible security mechanism. It does not contain the deprecated APIs of the standard edition. CDC must be used together with a profile called Foundation Profile, which we briefly introduce later in this chapter. On its own it cannot do much useful work. Some of the important features of this configuration are as follows:

- Full Java language and virtual machine support, according to the Java Language Specification and the Java Virtual Machine Specification.

- The interfaces between parts of the runtime environment, such the garbage collector, interpreter, and so on, are clearly defined so that it is easy to add new features to the virtual machine.

- Cleanup and shutdown of the virtual machine is efficient, freeing up all memory and stopping threads without any leaks.

Some other features have already been considered while discussing CVM. CDC contains the following packages, which are almost similar to those of the same names in the standard edition:

- `java.io`

- `java.lang`

- `java.lang.ref`

- `java.lang.reflect`
- `java.math`
- `java.net`
- `java.security`
- `java.security.cert`
- `java.text`
- `java.text.resources`
- `java.util`
- `java.util.jar`
- `java.util.zip`
- `javax.microedition.io`

Profiles

Configurations provide very little functionality — they just prepare the ground on which to add whatever you need. It is the profiles that give functionality, such as the graphical user interface. For example, if you have just CLDC installed on a device such as a PDA, you cannot create any user interface objects. No GUI is possible in your applications. For that, you need a profile. This is why Sun added a package called *KJava* with CLDC to enable testing and development, even if KJava is to be abandoned later. As a matter of fact, Sun Microsystems has provided tools for Palm development with its new wireless toolkit version 1.0.2 and the kit is based on CLDC and MIDP; there is no KJava now.

A profile may add other kinds of functionality, such as better networking support, database management, distributed computing, and so on. Like configurations, profiles may also be device-category specific. Some profiles may be useful for small devices, while others may be suitable for less-constrained devices. For example, MIDP and PDA Profile are used for mobile phones and PDA-like devices, respectively, on top of CLDC. On the other hand, Personal Profile is used for devices such as set-top boxes, on top of CDC.

Mobile Information Device Profile (MIDP)

CLDC can be used for writing applications for small devices. But it gives you very limited functionality. There is no way to provide a graphical user interface, unless you use KJava, which may become obsolete soon. For this and other reasons, it is necessary that you use some kind of profile if you want to build an effective application. The only profile so far available for small devices is the *Mobile Information Device Profile (MIDP)*. The most common mobile information devices are cell phones, so this profile is considered the profile for cell phones. Now that the Palm port has become available, it can be used for Palm devices also.

MIDP sticks to the CLDC approach of minimizing resource usage but provides ways to add reasonably a good user interface, given the constraints. It introduces a new application model in which every application is called a MIDlet and behaves somewhat like an applet. It can have three states: active, paused, and destroyed. The application manager software manages the lifecycle of the application. There is also a method to make data persistent.

The classes it contains in addition to those provided by the CLDC are as follows:

- `javax.microedition.midlet`: It is this package that defines the application model used in MIDP. It has a single class called MIDlet, with methods for enabling the application-managing software to create, pause, and destroy the application and perform some other tasks.

- `javax.microedition.lcdui`: This is the package responsible for providing the user interface. It includes classes such as those for creating user-interface elements (buttons, text fields, choice groups, gauges, images, and so on) and for handling events (listeners). This is basically a game-oriented user interface package, but can be used for other UI purposes.

- `javax.microedition.rms`: This package provides the capability to make data persistent. For this purpose, the main class that's included is the `RecordStore` class. In addition, there are interfaces for comparison, enumeration, filtering, and listening.

Foundation Profile

This profile is, in a way, just an extension of CDC. CDC APIs on the whole don't provide the functionality available in Java Standard Edition, therefore, to get the same functionality as the Java Standard Edition one has to use the APIs of Foundation Profile on top of CDC. Foundation profile acts as an extension to CDC to achieve Java 2 Standard Edition functionality. Profiles are normally supposed to add GUI functionality to the configurations, but Foundation Profile does not do this. There is no GUI package in this profile. Another peculiarity about this profile is that it is mandatory. You must use it along with CDC to prepare the ground for adding another profile. CDC, if combined with the Foundation Profile, adds up to complete the basic Java API set, as available in the standard edition. Refer to Figure 1-5 (Foundation Profile) to know in which layer the foundation profile comes. The only exception is the user interface — that is, there is no `java.awt` package.

The classes it contains, in addition to those provided by the CDC, are as follows:

- `java.security.acl`
- `java.security.interfaces`
- `java.security.spec`

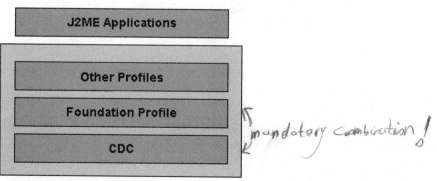

Figure 1-5: Foundation Profile

Other profiles

Apart from MIDP and Foundation Profile, no other profiles are formally available at the time of writing this chapter. But there has been something called *PersonalJava*, as you may well be aware. Because it uses a subset of the J2SE, it is comparable to the CDC-based segment of the J2ME platform. In fact, if you take care of certain things mentioned in the CDC-Foundation Profile porting guide, you can easily write applications that run on both the PersonalJava runtime environment and the CDC-based runtime environment. In other words, you can consider PersonalJava to be just another profile for CDC. This is why some people refer to it as the *PersonalJava Profile*. They are further justified in considering that it's soon to be formally merged with J2ME as the *Personal Profile*.

The profiles that are under development at present and may soon be available are as follows:

- Personal Profile
- PDA Profile
- RMI Profile

Getting Set to Program with J2ME

What are the prerequisites for taking up programming with J2ME? Where do we begin? We answer these questions in this section. The first thing you need is knowledge of the Java language. This book is, in fact, written for those who are already familiar with programming in Java. The libraries may be different depending on the configuration and profile that you use, but experience in using the libraries of the standard edition comes in handy even if you're using the new libraries. Moreover, if you move to CDC, you find many of the APIs present in J2SE.

If you know Java, you can start learning J2ME straightaway. To begin programming on this platform, you still need the Java Development Kit (JDK) installed — preferably, version 1.3. This kit can be downloaded from www.java.sun.com. You may already have it if you have been working with Java for a while.

The next thing that you need is a configuration. There are two options — CLDC or CDC. These can also be downloaded from the same site. To work with CLDC, your operating system must be Windows, Solaris, or Linux. For CDC, you need either VxWorks or Linux. Otherwise, you must port the configuration to your platform, which may prove a bit complicated.

If you want to work with profiles as well, you must download them, too. At present, only two profiles are available. These are the MIDP and the Foundation Profile. There is also PersonalJava, which is poised to become the Personal Profile. Even now, you can port your PersonalJava applications to J2ME, as explained in the CDC and Foundation Profile porting guide. Therefore, PersonalJava can be considered a part of the J2ME platform.

If you are going to work with MIDP, you can make the development process somewhat easier by downloading and installing the J2ME Wireless Toolkit, available from Sun's site as a free download. You can use it as is, or you can integrate it with Forte for Java. If you prefer the latter, you first must install Forte and then install the Wireless Toolkit, with the option for integrating selected.

The procedures for installing and using the configurations and profiles, as well as the toolkit mentioned in the preceding paragraph, are explained at the relevant places in this book.

Our First J2ME Application

We have talked about various configurations and profiles, but we haven't seen any code for the J2ME platform so far. To give you a feel of the J2ME code, we present here the first application of the book: a Hello application. We are not going to explain the code in Listing 1-1, because right now we are still acquainting ourselves with CLDC and MIDP, which are, respectively, the configuration and the profile used in this application. Just take a look at the following code and familiarize yourself with J2ME:

Listing 1-1: HelloFromJ2ME.java

```java
import javax.microedition.midlet.*;   // MIDP
import javax.microedition.lcdui.*;    //MIDP


/**
 * Our first application in J2ME
 */
public class HelloFromJ2ME extends MIDlet implements CommandListener {
```

```java
// Class String is from java.io, which is in CLDC...
 String s = "Hello From J2ME";
 private Command quit;  // The Quit button
 private Display ourDisplay;  // Declaring the display
 private Form ourForm = null;

 public HelloFromJ2ME() {
  ourDisplay = Display.getDisplay(this);
  quit = new Command("Quit", Command.SCREEN, 2);
 }


 /**
  * Creat a TextField and associate with it the quit button and the listener.
 */
 public void startApp() {
  ourForm = new Form("Our First");
  TextField ourField = new TextField("J2ME Application", s, 256, 0);

  ourForm.append(ourField);
  ourForm.addCommand(quit);
  ourForm.setCommandListener(this);
  ourDisplay.setCurrent(ourForm);
 }

 public void pauseApp() {
 }

 public void destroyApp(boolean unconditional) {
 }

 public void commandAction(Command c, Displayable s) {
  if (c == quit) {
  destroyApp(false);
  notifyDestroyed();
  }
 }
}
```

The output of the preceding code is shown in Figure 1-6.

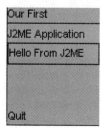

Figure 1-6: First J2ME application

RelatedJava Technologies

Java's association with limited devices is older than its J2ME initiative. For more than the last couple years, Java has been venturing into the realm of devices, which includes not only mobile phones and connected organizers, but smart cards as well. Even before J2ME became a platform and its constituents, such as CLDC and MIDP, made their appearance, technologies have propagated for more or less the same purpose for which J2ME is meant. These technologies also came forth from the Sun stable and were Java based. The more prominent ones among them are PersonalJava, EmbeddedJava, and JavaCard. PicoJava is a microprocessor dedicated to executing Java-based bytecodes without the need of an interpreter or Just-in-time compiler. PicoJava directly executes the Java virtual machine instruction set. As a result, Java software applications are up to three times smaller in code size and up to five times faster — thus reducing memory requirements — and are 20 times faster than Java interpreters running on standard CPUs.

Knowledge of these technologies is not mandatory for a J2ME programmer, but it serves to clarify the role of J2ME in the world of wireless programming. And because some of these technologies may be absorbed (in a modified form) into the J2ME fold in the future, many programmers working with them may choose to shift to the micro edition. Besides, there is the fact that many of the concepts used in J2ME are the same as those used in PersonalJava or EmbeddedJava. We find an analogy in that EJB existed before J2EE came into being, but now it is a part of the enterprise edition.

One more point to note here is that PersonalJava and EmbeddedJava have many things in common. Many tools are common to the two. Some tools work for both of them, such as javac, JavaCheck (a tool that checks whether applications and applets are compatible with a particular specification), JavaCodeCompact (a tool used to convert Java class files to C language source files so that they can be compiled into ROM format), and JavaDataCompact (a tool that's similar to JavaCodeCompact, except that, with JavaDataCompact, you can include HTML files, images, and sounds in the device ROM). This is one more reason why Java technologies dealing with connected and/or limited devices (other than PCs and servers, of course) should be brought under a common platform.

PersonalJava

PersonalJava has been in use for quite some time. It was meant to provide solutions for the same category of devices to which CDC-based J2ME is targeted — that is, devices such as Web phones, set-top boxes, and so on. You can use the same JDK for developing PersonalJava applications; the only thing to remember is that APIs not supported by it are to be avoided. Unlike the CDC-Foundation Profile, it has user-interface APIs in the form of AWT. This AWT is the java.awt package, which is inherited from J2SE.

To address the special needs of consumer devices, another method for adding GUI is provided. It comes as the *Truffle Graphical Toolkit*. Unlike AWT, which is meant for desktop display, this toolkit can be used to provide a customizable look and feel to targeted devices. You can test your application on the PersonalJava emulation environment.

The JDK-based APIs included in PersonalJava are as follows:

- `java.applet`
- `java.awt`
- `java.awt.datatransfer`
- `java.awt.event`
- `java.awt.image`
- `java.awt.peer`
- `java.beans`

- `java.io`
- `java.lang`
- `java.lang.reflect`
- `java.math`
- `java.net`
- `java.rmi`
- `java.rmi.dgc`
- `java.rmi.registry`
- `java.rmi.server`
- `java.security`
- `java.security.acl`
- `java.security.interfaces`
- `java.sql`
- `java.text`
- `java.text.resources`
- `java.util`
- `java.util.zip`

Some other APIs specific to PersonalJava are as follows:

- Double buffering
- Specifying component input behavior in mouseless environments
- Unsupported optional features
- Timer API

Java Card

Java Card technology has fewer chances of becoming part of the J2ME platform than the preceding two technologies. This technology, too, aims at providing programming tools for small devices with embedded processors. The devices it is concerned with are mostly smart cards, but other similar embedded devices can also avail this technology. The applications made using this technology are also called applets. You can call them *Java Card applets* or just *card applets* to differentiate them from normal applets. Although there are a number of differences between the standard edition and the Java Card technology, most of the basics remain the same.

Because we are talking about small cards the size of a business card (so that they can be carried in pockets), it is quite understandable that they are even shorter on resources than the small devices targeted by J2ME CLDC. Besides, this technology must deal with an even more varied diversity than J2ME does, because the number and varieties of smart cards used in the world is much more than the number of cell phones or pagers. This is why it was developed as a separate platform and is difficult to merge with J2ME.

Perhaps the difference that first strikes a Java programmer who is a newcomer to this technology is that the file system used is not the same as in the other Java technologies. Java Card does not use the class file format — it uses a new format called the *CAP* (Converted *AP*plet) file format. The Java Card system is made up of the following constituents:

- Java Card virtual machine
- Java Card converter
- A terminal installation tool
- An installation program to run on the card

The process involved in developing a card applet is as follows: First you write the applet on your desktop system, just as you write a normal applet or a MIDlet. After compiling it, you must test it by using a smart-card simulator. This step is similar to testing MIDlets on a cell-phone emulator. After you test and debug the applet, you are ready to install it on the device. For this, you first must create an `export` file that contains information about files being used by the applet. This is somewhat similar to creating `jad` files for MIDlets or MIDlet suites.

The next step is to convert the `class` and `export` files to CAP files. This is done by the converter mentioned in the preceding list. The converter may also automatically create `export` files. Then you copy these files to a card terminal — say, a PC to which a card reader is attached. The CAP files are loaded by an installation tool on the terminal, which then transfers the files to the device. Another installation tool on the device reads these files and brings them to a condition from which they can be run by the virtual machine. In other words, the virtual machine has lesser workload — there is division of labor between the installer and the VM. This division of labor reduces the size of both and adds modularity to the system. For clear view of the process, refer to Figure 1-7.

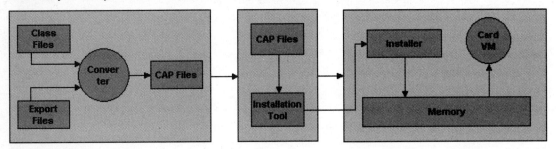

Figure 1-7: Java

Some other distinguishing features of the Java Card technology are as follows:

- Because smart cards almost always need some kind of authentication mechanism, very strong security is a must for this technology. This is partially achieved in Java by the verifier. Other methods may be used to further enhance security, but the Java Card specification leaves it to developers and users to enable flexibilty.

- There is also the provision of runtime environment security by techniques such as *applet firewall*. It basically isolates applets from one another.

- There is no support for dynamic class loading. To run applets on the card, you must mask them into the card during manufacturing or install them later as described previously.

- There is no security manager class in the Java Card API.

- Garbage collection and finalization are not possible in Java Card, nor are they required. Threads and cloning are also not supported.

- Access control is available, but some of the cases are not supported.

- The data types not supported are `char`, `double`, `float`, and `long`. The only numeric types supported are `byte` and `short`. The type `int` may be available in some implementations.

- Most of the Java core classes are not available in Java Card.

- ◆ The packages composing this platform are (presently) only four, as follows:
  - `java.lang`
  - `javacard.framework`
  - `javacard.security`
  - `javacardx.crypto`

On the whole, you must work harder to shift from the standard edition to Java Card than to the micro edition.

Summary

In this chapter, you are acquainted with J2ME and related technologies. We have tried to cover almost all related J2ME technologies available as of printing. J2ME is targeted for devices which are resource constrained; therefore, programming for these devices is also different from the programming done for desktop computers. Chapter 2 discusses the programming techniques involved for J2ME.

Programming Techniques for J2ME

Small devices, or *limited* devices as they are called, are designed for very specific purposes. These devices are typically characterized by limited processing speed and memory. Although their capabilities are being improved, at present they do not have the power of a server or even a desktop system. These devices differ from PCs not merely with regard to speed and processing power. It is not mandatory that they are interactive. Some of them may be wireless while others are wired. Generally the network to which devices are connected possess low bandwidths hence support low data rates and are constrained by their small size. These limitations do not apply to all of them as a rule. In fact each of these devices has its own specific attributes, which demand that each of them has to be programmed in a different way.

Constraints of J2ME Targeted Devices

Thus before attempting to program these devices using a platform such as J2ME, one has to consider the limitations of these devices and design the application accordingly. Let us consider in detail the constraints encountered by small devices before thinking of ways to deal with them. The major constraints that concern us are:

- The limited processing power and memory of these devices.
- The limitations in input/output mechanisms.
- Susceptibility to disconnection, low bandwidth, and the highly variable network conditions for devices connected to wireless networks.
- Most of these devices are mobile, which means that they change locations. This, in turn, implies dynamically changing network addresses.
- These devices depend on batteries for power.
- These devices have very limited display capabilities in terms of area, resolution, and so on.

We will discuss some of these in detail in following sections.

Limited processor speed

The performance of a processor is directly related to the power it consumes. Small devices are meant to be carried around and thus they cannot draw power from the mains. They have to depend on batteries for power. This applies to every mobile device, though not to those embedded in a static system.

Batteries have only a finite amount of energy stored in them. Hence, a device that depends on batteries for power should draw power at a low rate or else the batteries would not last long. Therefore, such devices have to use less powerful processors. Notebooks have processors as fast as desktop systems, and for this reason, their batteries drain out very soon. On the other hand, Palm handhelds can run for weeks on a couple of batteries or on internal rechargeable batteries.

Small devices have to employ central processing units that have been designed to consume low power, and which are consequently slower. The latest desktop systems, as of press time, have processor speeds in the range of 600 MHz to more than 1 GHz, whereas processors used for small devices may have speeds of the order of 20 MHz.

Small devices, as mentioned before, are used only for specific purposes and therefore have to be priced low. Fast processors cost more, and this is one more reason that small devices cannot afford to have fast processors. Because of the cost factor, even embedded and static systems may use slower processors.

The preceding considerations mean that small devices are usually slower than desktop systems and servers. So while developing applications for these devices, you should take care not to burden the processor. This is an important point to bear in mind while programming with J2ME.

Limited memory and storage

Only a few years back, it was not unusual to find PCs running on 4MB RAM. But things have changed, and today even 64MB RAM is considered low. Therefore, when compared to a PC, a typical PDA having 4 to 8MB of memory is definitely short on memory to an extent that affects programming capabilities.

This is more significant when you realize that this 4MB memory for a small device includes both the online memory available to store runtime application data and the offline storage capacity. If the entire RAM were 4MB, applications could easily be written for these devices using the same tools used in programming for PCs, compromising only on fancy functionality, which is not essential for small devices. Online memory is instantly available and might or might not be persistent. On the other hand, offline memory or storage is secondary and persistent. An example of such memory is the hard disk of your PC.

When you compare the RAM of a PC with that of a PDA, you will find that the ratio is around 64 to 4, which is significant but not so much so as to interfere with your programming. But there is no comparison to the total storage capacity of a desktop system and a small device (say, a PDA). Hard disks with 20GB capacity are seen as the lower limit for today's PCs. This difference in the total storage capacity is a key consideration in programming for small devices. One cannot use the usual tools or the same operating systems. Very few, if any, applications made for desktop systems can be used without change on small devices.

Nevertheless one fact cannot be overlooked — the difference in memory capacity is not forever. At least with some devices, the use of external memory sticks is narrowing it down. For instance, you can now download music from the Internet using your cell phone, store it on a memory stick, and play it whenever and wherever you like. Storage devices with up to even a few hundred MB of space are available. Such devices can be plugged into any device that has a compatible extension slot. You can use them with your PDA, and the total storage capacity of the small device goes up to a few hundred MB — though way behind 10GB of memory on a desktop computer and, a considerable advance over 4 or 8MB. In future, perhaps one can afford to ignore the memory aspect while writing an application for a mobile phone or a PDA. But for the time being, you have to take this into account.

Limited networking and bandwidth

Most small devices, whether they are pagers, mobile phones, PDAs, or set-top boxes, exchange or share information with some other device, desktop system, or server. In other words, they form a part of one or more networks. This network may be wired or wireless. A simple PDA may access data from a PC as well as offload data to it for faster computing. The data, which is shared by a small device and a big device, has to be kept up to date. The process by which this is done is known as *synchroni ation*. This is an automated process, and its objective is to avoid errors likely to occur in manually keeping the data up to date.

For transmission and reception of data, a device may use one or both of wired and wireless connections. For example, when a PDA is near the desktop, data synchronization with the desktop may be done by using a simple cable or a cradle, and when the PDA is not near the desktop, it may use wireless means, which may be infrared or radio-based. One way to classify devices is on the basis of network connection, under the categories of occasionally connected or always connected (or, more appropriately, always available). The former implies no permanent network connection, whereas the latter implies the capability to be always on the network, whether through a wire or without it. Generally, the throughput of an occasionally connected device is more than that of an always-available device. This is because the speed of basic serial connection is more than that of wireless communication. Speeds of both are, of course, increasing. Newer cradles that support Universal Serial Bus (USB) standard are faster, and the wireless communication is also becoming faster with the advent of Bluetooth and 3G.

The bandwidth of the network to which these devices are connected is normally limited. This limits the communication speed, and applications running consume more resources. The latency rate is also high which affects the performance of the application running on these devices. Also associated with this is the issue of cost of communication, especially of the wireless kind. The networking hardware also contributes to the cost of the device and the load on the power source — that is, the battery.

Wide variety of input/output methods

This variety is most evident when we consider the input/output methods employed by these devices. They are different for different devices. User interaction, which is the visible part of input/output, not only may be different but may even be totally absent in the case of some devices such as embedded systems, for which input/output may come from sensors. Also, the methods of input/output used in desktop systems are never possible with small devices because of the size factor.

Input methods

Handheld devices may or may not have a full keyboard and may or may not have a pointing/selection device. As an example, the data-ready mobile phone has only the following (see Figures 2-1 and 2-2):

♦ The usual keys found on a telephone, such as the digits 0-9, #, *, with alphabets marked on 2-9

♦ Arrow keys, may be just for up and down or left and right

♦ Some dedicated function keys or system keys

♦ One or more keys with programmable labels

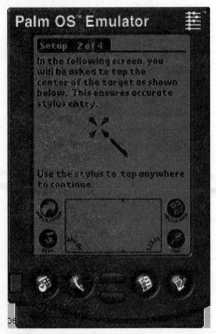

Figure 2-1: Palm top.

Alphanumeric pagers have even fewer keys. Item selection is accomplished through numbered lists or by using cursor keys to highlight a choice and then request an action on that item. Full 2-D cursor control through pointing devices such as touch pads, touch screens, or roller balls are rare. A full QWERTY keyboard is also not usual.

For personal digital assistants (for example, Palm V or Palm VII), the most common input device is the touch-sensitive screen, which may be monochrome or color (see Figures 2-1 and 2-2). These screens are usually used together with a writing or stroking device such as a pen or a stylus along with a handwriting-recognition software such as Graffiti (see Figure 2-2). A touch-sensitive screen has its own limitations. It is not very effective for text input. Therefore, if an application requires a lot of text input, it needs to be supplemented with a keyboard. Character recognition also demands processing power, which is in short supply in small devices. The keyboards used for these devices are usually scaled-down versions of full QWERTY keyboards, though full keyboards may sometimes be used as add-ons. Big keyboards increase the weight and size of the device and reduce some of its usefulness.

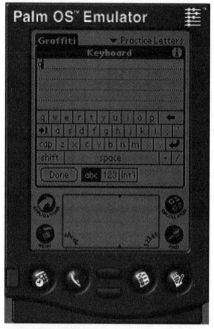

Figure 2-2: Palm keyboard.

In the future, work will be done to make voice recognition feasible on small devices. Still, voice recognition needs a lot of processing power and is available on some devices but only for voice dialing. Voice inputs are very limited in these devices and can't be a used as input devices. For this option to be used as a satisfactory input device, it needs a fare level of development and is in the processing stages. In the future, it may become the preferred input method for devices that cannot afford full keyboards.

Output methods

For most devices, the usual output method is a display screen (see Figure 2-3). It is nowhere near that of a PC in size. A typical display of a mobile device is capable of displaying 4-10 lines of text 12-20 characters wide and may be graphical (bitmapped) or text-only. At most, a small device (for example, a PDA) may have a screen that can display 20 lines of text. Apart from the size of the screen, these devices cannot display many fonts. Even simple bitmapped graphics cannot be taken for granted. Similar is the case with color support. A typical pager or a mobile rarely has color support. Even some PDAs do not have this capability (color support is given in Palm VII). This situation is set to change in a few years, and color capability will perhaps become the rule rather than the exception.

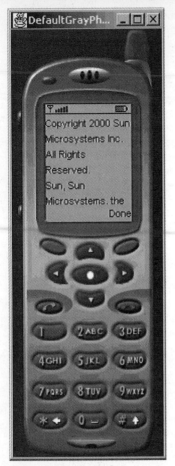

Figure 2-3: Mobile phone.

Some other simple output methods may also be used for denoting specific events or purposes. Indicator lights may alert the user about some hardware events such as network activity and power usage or software events such as message availability. These indicator lights can be programmed and can be controlled by an application.

Similarly, audio signals such as beeps and rings can indicate various hardware and software events. If the device has the capability, messages or music can be played back and voices can be synthesized. The vibrating battery of a mobile phone is also an output method. Infrared ports are also one way of communication between these devices where the communication takes place through infrared rays. For example, as soon as a device comes near another device, it may communicate with the second device by using infrared rays. The communication involves both input and output.

Size, shape, and weight

Small devices come in various sizes, shapes, and weights. For a comprehensive description of all these characteristics, a parameter called *form factor* is used. The purpose for which a particular device is to be used determines its form factor — that is, its size, shape, and weight. A mobile phone should be so designed that it can be carried in a pocket and can be operated with one hand. The same applies to a pager (see Figure 2-4). A Palm organizer should fit into one hand so that its stylus can be used with the other. A wireless handheld device may need to fit in a belt holster, just like a pager.

Figure 2-4: Two-way pager.

The importance of form factor is not limited to the characteristics it refers to. It also influences the choice of input and output methods. Input methods such as keyboards and output methods such as display screens are dependent on the form factor. The type, size, and location of batteries also depend on the form factor. A device that needs to be thin and light may have to be designed with rechargeable batteries. Hardware needed for various purposes such as wireless communication may affect the form factor. So, before starting to write applications for a small device, it is useful to consider how this factor affects your application.

Rapid changes in the world of small devices

Apart from diversity, there is another factor that is not a limitation but affects the development of applications for these devices in general and, hence, needs consideration. It is that such devices are changing more rapidly than desktop systems. Every day, a new device with a different set of features comes up. Operating systems, protocols, methods of transferring data, user interfaces, display, and so on are all changing. This is a period of transition for these devices. They are not luxuries anymore; they have become necessities. The world of small devices will take a long time to stabilize.

Operating systems for mobile devices

The operating systems for mobile devices in the past were developed in-house by device manufacturers such as Nokia, Ericsson, and Motorola. However, the product life cycle of devices such as mobile phones has become short. Due to this, it became necessary that some elements in the product development phase be outsourced — operating systems being one of them.

Some of the main operating systems for these devices are:

- Symbian with its EPOC operating system.
- Microsoft with Pocket PC (formerly Windows CE).
- Palm with its Palm operating system.

Symbian/EPOC

In mid 1998, Nokia, Ericsson, Motorola and Psion Software teamed up to form Symbian for developing the software and hardware standards for the next generation of wireless smart phones and terminals. The operating system for Symbian is EPOC, which has already been developed and incorporated into palmtop computers such as the Psion Series 5. Industry leaders such as Sony, Sun, Philips and NTT DoCoMo have joined the Symbian alliance and licensed EPOC.

Microsoft Pocket PC (Formerly Windows CE)

Pocket PC incorporates a subset of the Win32 Application Programming Interface (API) that is used by software developers to develop desktop PC applications. This means that there are no new programming languages to be learnt to develop an application on CE. Microsoft plans to integrate Windows CE into household items such as refrigerators and toasters. In Chapter 8 we develop a project for PocketPC using Personal Java.

Palm OS

Palm holds about three quarters of the global handheld computing market. Major Palm partners include IBM which developed WorkPad PC. Other Palm OS (Operating System) licensees include Handspring, OmniSky, and Nokia. You can develop J2ME applications for Palm using CLDC and Kjava APIs. Refer to Chapter 3 wherein we develop some case studies for Palm OS.

Programming Techniques to Counter the Limitations

Now that we are aware of the constraints associated with the devices targeted by J2ME, we can try to find ways to overcome them. The answers to our problem originate from the consideration of two facets: the limitations of the devices and the features of the J2ME platform. Note that, with regard to the constraints as well as the solutions, we refer mainly to the first category of devices mentioned in the first chapter — that is, those that are targeted by CLDC and associated profiles such as MIDP. CDC targeted devices are likely to have more resources, and programming for them will not be drastically different from that for desktop systems. Anyway, let us first consider ways around the limitations of devices.

Do not overload the processor

We have seen that the processor speeds for small devices are significantly less than those for PCs. This means that our applications will have to be light on the processors. This in turn means that, while writing an application, we have to avoid unnecessary load on the processor. If you are used to developing applications for desktop systems or servers, you may not be aware of unnecessary processing. With a high power processor, this is not a serious issue, but while working with a constrained device, this has to be handled carefully.

One example of such optimizations can be the use of arrays where normally you would use objects such as `Strings`, `StringBuffers`, `Vectors`, and `HashTables`. Arrays are usually faster than these objects. This would, of course, apply in certain conditions, not all. For example, if you just want to map keys to values, it would be preferable to go for arrays rather than `HashTables`. Another way to optimize is to specify the initial size of `HashTables` or `Vectors` as near to their expected size as possible. This will save the processing needed to grow these objects when new elements are added to them. The moral of the story is to use arrays directly whenever possible.

Conserve memory to the maximum extent

Since the memory budget available on CLDC targeted devices is small, you have to restrict the size of the application to within this budget so that the application runs comfortably without affecting performance. The following points will help in this regard:

- ◆ **Use proper data types:** Do not use larger data types than needed. If the size of your variable is almost certain to keep within the size of `short`, do not use `long`.

- ◆ **Keep the runtime memory limit in mind:** As pointed out earlier, the memory on a small device such as PDA includes both the dynamic runtime memory and the static storage (see Figure 2-5). So, even if the total memory is 8MB, the runtime memory may just be 256K. It is this 256K in which the application and the operating system and so on will have to run. In other words, your runtime memory budget is even more limited.

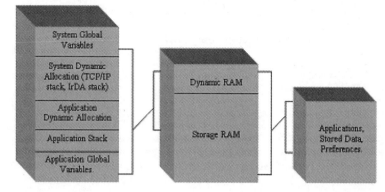

Figure 2-5: Data storage structure.

♦ **Make your applications small:** Besides conserving runtime memory, you have to keep the size of your application in accordance with the storage available. To achieve this, you can package your application in the form of a JAR archive. Other tools that remove unnecessary information from a file may also be used to cut down the size of the application.

♦ **Use of scalar types:** Whenever you declare an object, it is allocated space on the runtime heap. To reduce consumption of runtime memory, try to declare as few objects as possible. This can be achieved by using scalar types such as `int`, `short`, and so on in place of object declaration.

♦ **Do not hold on to resources when not needed:** Resources such as files, network connections, and so on should not be kept up when they are not in use. Perform necessary cleanup operations yourself (such as assigning null value to objects when they are no longer needed) rather than depending on the garbage collector or the host environment.

♦ **Recycle objects:** Once an object has been declared, it occupies some space on the runtime memory. Thus, if you can recycle some of your objects, you save on this space.

♦ **Allocate objects as and when needed:** This can reduce the load on memory. To use this technique, you have to check whether the object reference is null or not.

♦ **Avoid creating objects inside loops:** If you create objects inside a loop, a new object will be created for every iteration of the loop, and it will have memory reserved for it. This will thus cause wastage of memory space for limited memory devices, since most of these objects are not going to be used later and will be out of scope. Moreover, the garbage collector will spend time and resources in dealing with these objects. To avoid these, you can first create an array and then loop through the indices of this array. In fact, this technique can be used for other kinds of optimizations, too. For example, you can try to avoid calling a method inside a loop.

♦ **Check the memory usage:** Before concluding that everything possible has been done to conserve memory, it would definitely help if there were a way to find out how much total memory is being actually used and how much of it is being used by a particular object. There is a procedure for this. The class `java.lang.Runtime` has methods `freeMemory` and `totalMemory`. The method `freeMemory` can be used to find out how much memory is presently free. The memory is measured in bytes. The method `totalMemory`, as you can guess, returns the amount of total memory available. To find the memory used by an object, you can use the `freeMemory` method before and after the object is instantiated. Then you just have to find the difference between the two values returned. One more method of use in this regard is the `currentTimeMillis` in `java.lang.System` class that gives you the time taken to execute a method. Like the freeMemory method just discussed, here, too, you have to use it before and after the method is called.

♦ **Catch the OutMemoryError:** If after all of the previous, the system runs out of memory, you should ensure that your application has an exit route available if the problem cannot be solved. You might be able to resolve such a crisis by releasing resources, but if you can't, at least show the user a message and allow the application to be closed. Manage this yourself instead of leaving it to the operating system.

Pass the load to the server

Since the processor power and the memory are both in short supply on these devices, one way to ease the load on the device is to make the server do as much work as possible. Use the device only to perform the functions that the server cannot do. For example, if you want to make available an address book to the user, it will have to be available offline as you cannot expect the user to connect to the server every time he wants to use or see his address book. But if there is some task that can be done only when the user is connected, you can safely make the server do it. One task that has to be done on the device itself is the user interface part. The server can do most other computing.

Avoid using string concatenation

Strings can be built in Java by using string concatenation. But this is not an efficient approach. Every time a string concatenation is used, a StringBuffer object is created. Its append method is called to add one part to the other. Then you get the final string when its toString method is called. All these are done automatically. Doing this inside a loop will imply creating a large number of objects. If you write the code yourself for doing this instead of directly using string concatenation, you can significantly improve the performance of this operation.

Give the garbage collector light work

You cannot depend as safely and surely on the CLDC garbage collector as in J2SE. Make sure that you do not leave so much work for it so as to overload it. You should not allocate objects at a speed with which the garbage collector cannot catch up. If you do so, your application might slow down. The memory that is once taken up by the execution engine may not be returned to the system, even when the garbage collector has caught up with it.

Another very simple technique is to set the object references to null when you no longer need them.

Use exceptions sparingly

Java has extensive support for exceptions. You can use resources better if you restrict the use of exceptions. Another point is that specific exceptions should be used as far as possible. If you use general exceptions, all specific exceptions would have to be checked to find out which type a particular exception is. Using specific exceptions will save this work.

Use local variables

When loops are used, class members are called repeatedly. The execution of the program can be made faster by using local variables instead of class members. The value of the class member can be assigned to a temporary variable on the stack. This value can then be used in place of the class member. The same applies to arrays also.

Make your suite light

It may often be necessary to use third-party libraries. For example, you may need an XML parser to parse the XML thrown by the server, as was the case with most of the projects included in this book. When you have to do this, it is better to include only those classes in your JAR package that are actually being used instead of shipping the whole library or set of libraries. This will mean some more work for you, but it will reduce the size of your application. We have used Kxml parser and included only some of the classes provided in the `org.kxml.*` package instead of the whole as the device is memory constrained and has less processing power. We didn't do it because our applications are not so heavy as to require the use of such strategy, and also because the version of this parser that we have used is the lightest one.

Managing with the limited features of J2ME

J2ME, especially the part based on CLDC, does not have the functionality anywhere near that of J2SE. So to provide the user with an effective application, you have to make very efficient use not only of the resources available on the device, but also of the features provided by J2ME. You can do so by virtue of the following techniques.

Plan your application well

Before you start coding, it will be worthwhile if you spend some time planning your application to ensure that it makes optimal use of both the resources and the features available. This is true for all programming, but perhaps more so for J2ME. Planning will allow you to weed out those parts that cause nonoptimal computing. Moreover, it will also help you in achieving better results from the same classes.

Use GUI classes optimally and creatively

Since one of the computing tasks that cannot be transferred to the server is the graphical user interface, you have to design it in such a way that the basic functionality is achieved without putting much load on the resources of the device. For example, you will have to do away with most of the images, which are supported to a very limited extent. In making optimal use of images, you may have to seek the help of an artist so that images can be made attractive without affecting performance.

Optimizing the GUI part will have the advantage that your application will seem to be faster than it may actually be, because GUI is what the user sees. Be sure that the application responds to the user's actions fast enough and that processing doesn't freeze the GUI as far as possible. The user's patience is likely to be less for applications being run on small and mobile devices as compared to applications meant for PCs.

Use the server's functionality

Transferring work to the server is important not only from the point of view of reducing the consumption of resources on the device, but also for utilizing the functionality on the server. After all, the server has the full JDK installed on it. You can use the classes in the Standard Edition to do the work in a Micro Edition application. This synergy between the client device and the server will enhance the potential of your application.

Use low-level UI APIs in MIDP

The APIs relating to GUI in MIDP are of two categories. One is aimed to achieve portability, while the other is capable of providing device specific functionality. The first can be considered high-level APIs, while the second can be considered low-level APIs. If your application doesn't need a fancy GUI, there is no point in using the high-level APIs, which are somewhat heavier. But if you are aiming to achieve extra functionality, and the device you are targeting is not too short on memory or other resources, you can go for the high-level APIs. You may want to do this if you are aiming for a look that is comparable to that of a desktop application.

Some of the high-level APIs are briefly introduced in Chapter 4. You can refer to that chapter for more details, but here we'll consider some points about these classes. To show 2-D graphics in your application, you can use the `Graphics` class. With this class, you can draw lines, arcs, rectangles, images, and such on the display. The shapes drawn can be filled with any color of your choice if that color is supported by the device. The color model used in these classes is a 24-bit model. There are 8 bits each for colors red, green, and blue. Of course, not every device can render such variety of colors on the display. This means that mapping of requested colors to available colors will occur, that is, if an application uses colors that a device doesn't support, the device will map to those colors that are supported by the device.

You can display fairly good-looking images on small devices by using the low-level APIs. This can be done by using the drawImage method of the Graphics class. It has the following signature:

```
public void drawImage(Image img, int x, int y, int anchor);
```

The last parameter refers to anchor points used in several of the GUI classes. These are used to ensure that the processing needed to position an object properly on the display is reduced.

Another feature in these APIs that can be of much help in improving the look of your application is the Font class. The letters used on small devices are usually displayed with the same font. You certainly don't get the variety you can have on a desktop, but at least you can select one out of a few choices. The number may increase in the future. You can also specify the style and size of the font, in addition to its face name. A Font object is created in the following way:

```
Font myFont = Font.getFont(Font.FACE_SYSTEM, Font.STYLE_ITALIC,
    FONT.SIZESMALL);
```

The three parameters are the face, style, and size, respectively.

Use SyncML for data synchronization

Small and mobile devices are meant to make data and services available anywhere, even while you are moving from one place to another. This requires that the data that the device is accessing should be the latest. For this, you may need to synchronize the data between all the places where it is located. Normally, if you want to make data synchronization possible with every platform, you will have to add many things to your MIDlet suite, because not all servers will support the synchronization technology used. You can avoid this by using the SyncML protocol for data synchronization. SyncML has the advantage that it is an industry standard for data synchronization . What is even more important is that it can be used with MIDP and support for it will increase in the future. For more details on SyncML, refer to http://www.syncml.org.

Summary

After completing this chapter, the reader should be acquainted with the techniques involved in programming for J2ME. These considerations in this chapter are important and should be taken into account while programming for J2ME to develop a quality software for resource constrained devices. In Chapter 3, we will start programming in CLDC and Kjava used for Palm application development. We will discuss the APIs and implement them with some case studies.

Chapter 3

CLDC API and Reference Implementation

Although this chapter is on CLDC, we also take up the Kjava API, which is used to enable CLDC on a Palm device. The Kjava API has some extra functionality for adding user interface components to J2ME applications. This API may be absent in future releases of CLDC. It is a temporary arrangement by Sun Microsystems to allow development and testing of CLDC applications.

CLDC specification 1.0 lays down the guidelines to which any implementation of CLDC has to adhere. Sun has developed its own reference implementation of this configuration, but vendors are free to provide their own. In this chapter, we take up only Sun's implementation. It can be downloaded for free from www.sun.com/software/communitysource/j2me/.

Version 1.0 of the reference implementation provided by Sun can be run as is here on Windows and Solaris platforms. You can also run it on Palm devices, but for that you will have to download a "Palm overlay" and unzip it into the directory in which CLDC is installed. A newer version of CLDC, numbered 1.0.2, is available for Linux as well, in addition to Windows and Solaris.

The CLDC API consists of only four packages: java.io, java.lang, java.util, and javax.microedition.io. The first three are subsets of similar packages in J2SE and are covered very briefly. The fourth package is new and is unique to the micro edition.

Core Packages

The three core packages in the CLDC implementation are discussed in this section.

java.lang package

This package has the classes that are fundamental to the Java language. These classes define the data types, basic exceptions, and so on. Many classes that are not required in J2ME are absent. Two interfaces — Cloneable and Comparable — are not included. Some classes, such as those for Float and Double data types, are absent. There is no ClassLoader. Several exceptions present in J2SE, such as NoSuchFieldException, are not there in CLDC. The interfaces, classes, and exceptions that are part of the CLDC and thus define the Java language in Java 2 Micro Edition platform are listed in the section, "Brief introduction to commonly used packages."

java.io package

This package for providing data input and output through data streams has two interfaces (DataInput and DataOutput) and several input and output stream as well as reader and writer classes, similar to the Java 2 Standard Edition. In addition, there are several I/O exceptions. Because of the limited input/output capabilities of the mobile devices, this package provides limited functionality as compared to the java.io package in Java Standard Edition. Most of the classes are absent in this package. For data input and output, you don't have the option of using serialization or file systems. Whatever is present is used in almost the same way as in the standard edition.

java.util package

This package contains the utility classes for such things as generating random numbers, creating time zone objects, implementing growable array of objects, enumeration, and so on. As compared to the Java 2 Standard Edition, J2ME has only seven classes and one interface left.

Brief introduction to commonly used packages

As mentioned previously, these packages are the same as in J2SE. The difference is that the classes included in these packages are fewer, keeping only those methods that are suitable to small devices. In the following paragraphs, we will discuss the most commonly used classes of these packages, with code snippets to illustrate their use. For more details, you can refer to the documentation. Like in J2SE, all the classes are inherited from the `class` object. You can refer to Figures 3-1 and 3-2 to get a view of the hierarchy of the important classes in the CLDC APIs.

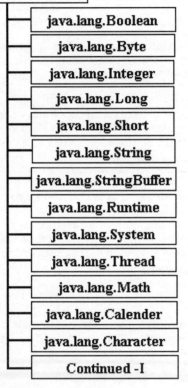

Figure 3-1: CLDC Class Hierarchy – I.

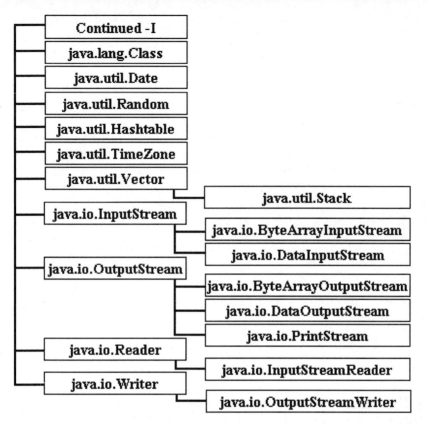

Figure 3-2: CLDC Class Hierarchy – II.

Basic data types

All the basic data types available in the J2SE platform are present in CLDC, with the exception of `float` and `double`. These two have been left out due to the limitations of small devices, as discussed in Chapter 2. The syntax for using these data types is the same as in J2SE — for example:

```
int i; // declares a variable of the type int
char a; // declares a variable of the type char
boolean b; // declares a variable of the type boolean
byte t; // declares a variable of the type byte
      // etc.
```

Comparison with J2SE java.lang package

This package is just a stripped-down version of the `java.lang` package in J2SE. Since they are used in the same way, we simply give the comparison of the two editions in terms of constructors and methods present:

♦ **Boolean:** Only one constructor is available — that which takes a Boolean value. Methods `getBoolean` and `valueOf` are not available.

♦ **Byte:** Only one constructor is left in CLDC — one that takes a string value is not present. Methods `compareTo`, `decode`, `doubleValue`, `floatValue`, `intValue`, `longValue`, `shortValue`, and `valueOf` are not present.

♦ **Character:** Less than one third of the methods are not present compared to J2SE.

- **Integer:** Methods `compareTo`, `decode`, `doubleValue`, `floatValue`, and `getInteger` are not present.

- **Long:** Constructor with string value as an argument is not present. Methods `byteValue`, `compareTo`, `decode`, `doubleValue`, `floatValue`, `getLong`, `intVlaue`, `shortValue`, `toBinaryString`, `toHexString`, `toOctalString`, and `valueOf` are absent.

- **Object:** As in J2SE, this is the root of the class hierarchy. But it doesn't have methods `clone` and `finalize`.

- **Runtime:** This class instance allows the application to interact with the java runtime environment (virtual machine) which is responsible for running the application. Only these methods are available in CLDC: `exit`, `freeMemory`, `gc`, `getRuntime`, and `totalMemory`.

- **Short:** Only constructor is the one that takes a `short` value. The methods available are: `equals`,`hashCode`, `parseShort`, `shortValue`, and `toString`.

- **String:** These methods are not available: `compareTo (Object o)`, `compareToIgnoreCase`, `copyValueOf`, `equalsIgnoreCase`, `intern`, `lastIndexOf (String sr)`, `lastIndexOf (String sr, int fromIndex)`, `regionMatches (int toffset, String other, int ooffset, int len)`, `toLowerCase(Locale locale)`, `toUpperCase(Locale locale)`, `valueOf (double d)`, and `valueOf (float f)`.

- **StringBuffer:** There is no constructor that takes an `int` value. Methods `replace` and `substring` are also not present.

- **System:** Only these methods are available in the CLDC version: `arrayCopy`, `currentTimeMillis`, `exit`, `gc`, `getProperty`, and `identityHashCode`.

- **Thread:** Methods included in CLDC are `activeCount`, `currentThread`, `getPriority`, `isAlive`, `join`, `run`, `setProperty`, `sleep`, `start`, `toString`, and `yield`.

The syntax for using these classes is the same as in J2SE, but since some of the constructors are absent, they can't be used. For example, you will still use the `StringBuffer` class as:

```
StringBuffer sb = new StringBuffer(5); // Declares a StringBuffer with
// no characters and an initial capacitiy of 5 characters.
```

Similarly, `Thread` and `String` will be used as:

```
Thread t= new Thread(); // Declares an object of the type Thread
String s = new String(); // Declares an object of the type String
```

Comparison with J2SE java.io package

In the stripped-down version of the `java.io` package, the number of classes is reduced, but otherwise there is no difference. The methods and the syntax are the same. The classes present in the CLDC version are:

- `InputStream`
- `ByteArrayInputStream`
- `DataInputStream`
- `Reader`
- `InputStreamReader`
- `OutputStream`
- `ByteArrayOutputStream`
- `DataOutputStream`
- `Writer`

◆ `OutputStreamWriter`

◆ `PrintStream`

Comparison with J2SE java.util package

The same thing about the package being a stripped-down version of the J2SE goes for this package, too. The comparison of the two editions is as follows:

◆ **Enumeration:** It has the same two methods as in the J2SE — `hasMoreElements` and `nextElement`.

◆ **Calendar:** Only the constructor without parameters is available. The other one, which takes time zone and locale as the parameters, is absent. A lot of methods are also absent. The available methods are `after`, `before`, `equals`, `get`, `getInstance`, `getTime`, `getTimeInMillis`, `getTimeZone`, `set`, `setTime`, `setTimeInMillis`, and `setTimeZone`.

◆ **Date:** Two constructors are present — one without any parameters and another that takes the parameter date as a `long` value. Methods available are: `equals`, `getTime`, `hashCode`, and `setTime`.

◆ **Hashtable:** One constructor is empty and the other takes initial capacity as integer value as the parameter. These methods are absent: `clone`, `containsValue`, `entrySet`, `equals`, `hashCode`, `keySet`, `putAll`, and `values`.

◆ **Random:** The same two constructors as in J2SE are present, but only four methods remain: `next`, `nextInt`, `nextLong`, and `setSeed`.

◆ **Stack:** Both the constructor and the methods are the same as in the standard edition.

◆ **TimeZone:** Methods available are `getAvailableIDs`, `getDefault`, `getID`, `getOffset`, `getRawOffset`, `getTImeZone`, and `useDaylightTime`.

◆ **Vector:** Since there is no `Collections` class in CLDC, the constructor that takes a collection as an argument is not available. Methods absent are `add`, `addAll`, `clear`, `clone`, `containsAll`, `equals`, `get`, `hashCode`, `remove`, `removeAll`, `removeRange`, `retainAll`, `set`, `subList`, `toArray`, and `trimToSize`.

Generic Connection Framework

This is the only new package in CLDC. It includes the classes that facilitate establishing connections. CLDC couldn't afford to use the J2SE kind of connections as the devices for which CLDC is used are very resource constrained and J2SE connections need a lot of resources. For this reason, a new framework was designed, called the Generic Connection Framework. These classes are related to I/O and network connectivity. The functionality they provide is the same as the `java.io` and `java.net` packages of J2SE. The difference is that it doesn't depend on the specific capabilities of the device. Generic Connection Framework is based on the concept that all network and input/output communication can be abstracted. This is why there is only one class `Connector` but there are eight interfaces in this package. To view the hierarchy of interfaces which are part of `javax.microedition.io` package, refer to Figure 3-3. All these are listed below:

◆ `Interface Connection`

◆ `Interface ContentConnection`

◆ `Interface Datagram`

◆ `Interface DatagramConnection`

◆ `Interface InputConnection`

◆ `Interface OutputConnection`

◆ `Interface StreamConnection`

- Interface StreamConnectionNotifier
- Class Connector

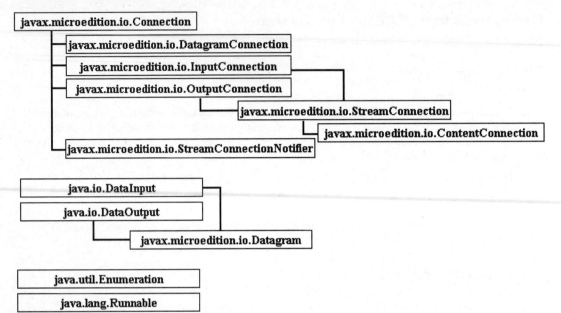

Figure 3-3: CLDC Interface Hierarchy.

Class connector is the only class in the package and is used to open a connection with the open method. The parameter string describing the target conforms to the URL format as described in RFC 2396. This takes the general form:

```
{scheme}:[{target}][{params}]
```

Where {scheme} is the name of a protocol such as http, {target} is the name of the target device to which the connection is to be made. Similarly, {param} are the parameters required to establish the connection. The methods available are listed below:

- open
- openDataInputStream
- openDataOutputStream
- openInputStream
- openOutputStream

The following code block shows how this class and its methods can be used:

```
InputStream input;
Input = Connector.openInputStream("testhttp://www.s-cop.com/userlist.asp");
```

The preceding code opens a connection to a URL named www.s-cop.com/userlist.asp   and requests the server to execute an ASP named userlist.asp. Notice the use of testhttp   instead of http. This becomes necessary because CLDC 1.0 does not have implementation for any of the standard protocols. Sun has implemented a protocol called testhttp   for testing and development purposes.

```
     try
       {
  // A Socket connection is made on a port with the Listener
       socket =
              (StreamConnection)Connector.open("socket://127.0.0.1:7070",
                         Connector.READ_WRITE,true);

  // If the socket is null then the connection is not established.
       if (socket != null)
         {
       System.out.println("Connection is established to localhost on port
7070...");
         }

  //  Opening the Input and Output Streams to the Socket.

       socket_inputstream = socket.openInputStream();
       socket_outputstream = socket.openOutputStream();
         }
       catch(IOException ae)
         {
       System.out.println("Couldn't open socket:");
         }
```

This code block opens a socket connection to a URL named 127.0.0.1 at a port 7070. Read/write access is provided to the client. Input/output streams are also obtained from the connection using the methods of the interface StreamConnection (openInputStream and openOutputStream). These methods return streams which are used for communication.

Kjava API

This API, which is composed of the com.sun.kjava package, is officially not part of the CLDC but has been included with the reference implementation release of CLDC to allow development and testing of CLDC applications. CLDC doesn't have any user interface classes. This is where Kjava comes in. It has the GUI classes such as Bitmap, TextField, and so on, which make development of interactive applications possible (to view all the classes with the hierarchy structure refer to Figure 3-6 and Figure 3-7). But it should be noted that this is only a stopgap arrangement. It may change in future releases or may be absent altogether. Remember that adding GUI components is something that is supposed to be done with a profile, at least in case of CLDC. When you want to actually deploy your applications, you may have to substitute the Kjava GUI components with those of a profile, such as the PDA profile when it is available (it is under development at present).

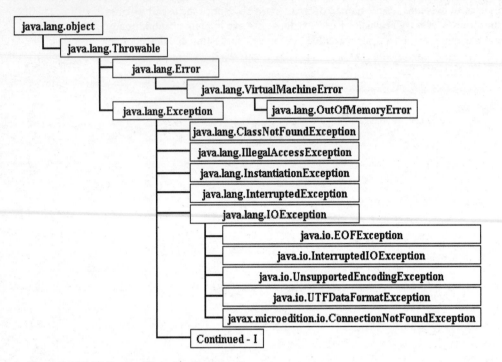

Figure 3-4: CLDC Error and Exception Hierarchy – I.

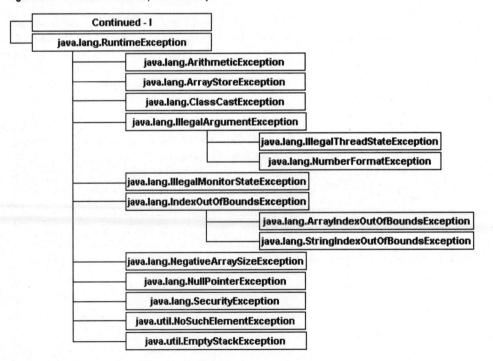

Figure 3-5: CLDC Error and Exception Hierarchy – II.

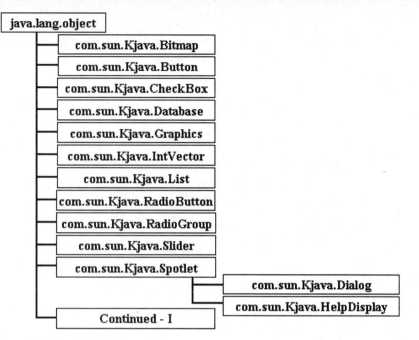

Figure 3-6: Kjava API's Hierarchy – I.

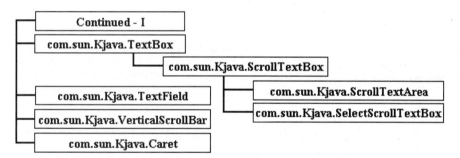

Figure 3-7: Kjava API's Hierarchy - II.

Very recently, Sun Microsystems has come up with MIDP for Palm. This means that if you want to use CLDC on Palm, you can do so by using MIDP for Palm. In that case, Kjava will no longer be needed. If we are still including Kjava in this chapter, it is because it is included in the CLDC release. Moreover, MIDP has some extra functionality in addition to having the GUI classes. The GUI classes, too, are more advanced than in Kjava. Therefore, in our opinion, if you want to get an idea of how CLDC works, first try your hand on CLDC with Kjava. When you have explored it enough, you can move on to MIDP.

In this section, we briefly explain the GUI classes provided in the Kjava package. Kjava includes the following classes:

- ♦ Spotlet
- ♦ Graphics
- ♦ HelpDisplay
- ♦ TextBox
- ♦ TextField
- ♦ Button

- CheckBox
- RadioButton
- RadioGroup
- ScrollTextBox
- Database
- List
- Slider
- Bitmap
- Caret
- Dialog
- IntVector
- SelectScrollTextBox
- ValueSelector
- VerticalScrollBar

Brief introduction to commonly used classes

In this section, we will be explaining some of the most commonly used classes. Their use is illustrated with code examples.

Spotlet

All applications made using CLDC and Kjava have to extend this class. This is the only way you can make an executable application unless you decide to use MIDP. The application you write can consist of more than one spotlet, but only one spotlet can be activated at one time. This class is used for event handling callbacks, registering the application, and so on. *Registering* means giving focus to the spotlet. And only the spotlet with focus will have callbacks.

```
public class First extends Spotlet
{
 First()
{
register(NO_EVENT_OPTIONS);
}
 public void penDown(int x, int y)
{
 // Handling the pen strokes
}
public void keyDown(int x, int y)
{
 // Handling the key pressed
}
}
```

In the preceding code block, the application named First is declared. It is inherited from the class Spotlet, so, therefore, it has to extend this class. It is registered with NO_EVENT_OPTION, which means the spotlet is made current and will not be unregistered on pressing normal keys. However, if the system keys (five keys for Palm devices) are pressed, then the spotlet is unregistered.

The system keys are the five keys through which the Palm device is being operated. The five keys are used to invoke different applications in the Palm device and there are two additional keys for up and down scrolling. The first key from the left is to set the date and time. The second key is for the phone book, the third key is for up and down scrolling, the fourth key is for Address book and the last key is for Memo Pad.

Graphics

This is the basic class used to draw objects on the display, almost in the same way as in the standard edition. For drawing the object, it uses the following methods:

- getGraphics
- drawLine
- drawRectangle
- drawBorder
- borderType
- drawString
- setDrawRegion
- resetDrawRegion
- copyRegion
- copyOffScreenRegion
- clearScreen
- drawBitmap
- playSound

Use of some of these methods is shown below with code examples. First, we look at initialization of a variable of the Graphics class and at clearing the drawing region by calling the appropriate functions of the Graphics class, namely resetDrawRegion() and clearScreen():

```
graphics = Graphics.getGraphics();
graphics.resetDrawRegion();
graphics.clearScreen();
```

If you want to display a String (the title of the graphic) at a specified position, you can use the drawString method of the Graphics class:

```
graphics.drawString("Target Practice",35,10);
```

To draw a rectangle without rounded corners, you will write:

```
graphics.drawRectangle(initial_position_bullet,72,15,5,Graphics.GRAY,0);
```

And to draw a circle, you can use the same method with the corner radius parameter equal to half the square's width:

```
graphics.drawRectangle(initial_position_bullet,72,4,4,Graphics.GRAY,2);
```

Seems familiar, doesn't it?

Button

No need to explain this class. Just have a look at the following code:

```
// Declaring button variables.
    private Button play;
...
```

```
/*
 * Initializing the button object 'play', placing it on the screen
 *at the appropriate position and then painting (drawing it).
 */
    play = new Button("Play Now",10,140);
    play.paint();
```

For event handling of this button, the code will look like this:

```
    public void penDown(int x, int y)
    {
      if(play.pressed(x,y))
      {
    // Write your code here.

      }
}
```

TextField

Now we consider how the class TextField can be used. It, too, is similar in use to the TextField class in J2SE:

```
// Declaration of a TextField named choicefield

private TextField choicefield;
```

After declaring the TextField, we initialize it with proper parameters. These parameters specify the String label for the TextField, its position in terms of coordinates, and its width and height. To allow the text to be entered in only the uppercase, we have to call the setUpperCase method with the parameter true. Next we give it the focus by calling the setFocus method:

```
choicefield = new TextField("Option:",10,145,50,10);
choicefield.setUpperCase(true);
choicefield.setFocus();
```

To make the TextField visible on the screen, we use the paint method, as in J2SE:

```
choicefield.paint();
```

Now we determine whether the TextField has the focus or not. If it has, we call the handleKeyDown method, which in turn calls spotlet's keyDown method:

```
if(choicefield.hasFocus()) {
choicefield.handleKeyDown(x);
}
```

Finally, after the user has completed entering text, we remove the focus from the TextField by calling the loseFocus method. We also remove the caret by using the killCaret method:

```
choicefield.loseFocus();
choicefield.killCaret();
```

RadioButton and RadioGroup

Let us now look at the use of classes RadioButton and RadioGroup. First, we initialize a RadioGroup of the name level. All the radio buttons belonging to level will be placed in this RadioGroup. As usual with radio buttons, only one of the buttons can be selected at a time:

```
private RadioGroup level = new RadioGroup(2);
```

```
    private RadioButton simple = null;
    private RadioButton difficult = null;
```

Now we initialize the `RadioButton` objects "`simple`" and "`difficult`", placing them on the screen at the appropriate positions and then drawing them:

```
  simple = new RadioButton(85,45,"Simple");
// Initially this button is to be kept selected. Therefore, a method
// setState is called, which is passed a parameter 'true', which will take
//care of this.
  simple.setState(true);
  simple.paint();

/**
 *  Initializing the RadioButton object 'Difficult', placing it
 * on the screen at the appropriate position and then drawing it.
 */

difficult = new RadioButton(85,60,"Difficult");
difficult.paint();
```

The radio buttons have to be added to the `RadioButton` group, so that only one of the buttons will be selected at a particular instant of time:

```
  level.add(simple);
  level.add(difficult);
```

If a radio button is selected, the appropriate variable associated with that radio button is assigned that value. For example, if the radio button of the label Simple is selected, then the variable `label_information` is given the value "`simple`". This is done by calling the method `handlePenDown`:

```
    else if (simple.pressed(x,y))
    {
      level_information = "simple";
              simple.handlePenDown(x,y);
    }
    else if (difficult.pressed(x,y))
    {
      level_information = "difficult";
              difficult.handlePenDown(x,y);
    }
```

HelpDisplay

The class `HelpDisplay` is provided in Kjava to give the user some information about how to use the application or to display simple text for whatever purpose the developer thinks this class can be used. The following code initializes a `HelpDisplay` object with parameters being the text to be shown, the class to be called, and event options:

```
// Call to the class HelpDisplay to display the help text.
  (new HelpDisplay(helpText,"TargetPractice",
    NO_EVENT_OPTIONS)).register(NO_EVENT_OPTIONS);
```

ScrollTextBox

If the text that the user enters does not fit in the display area, you will have to use the `ScrollTextBox`. We show here an example of declaring and then initializing a `ScrollTextBox` named `first`. The parameters supplied are the initial text, the position in terms of coordinates, and the size (width and height):

```
private ScrollTextBox first;
    // initializing the ScrollText Box..
 first = new ScrollTextBox(textx,0,0,150,140);
 first.paint();
```

Now we define handling for the event that occurs when the user places the pen on the display. It is similar to clicking the mouse on a PC. The difference is that we are using the penDown method:

```
public void penDown(int x, int y) {
if (first.contains(x,y))
first.handlePenMove(x,y);
}
```

Similarly, we define event handling for movement of the stylus, just as we do for movement of mouse. We will be using the penMove method here:

```
public void penMove(int x, int y) {
if (first.contains(x,y))
first.handlePenMove(x,y);
}
```

Database

If you want to develop any nontrivial application, you can't avoid using some form of database. The problem is that CLDC had to have a very small footprint and the devices also don't have much space for databases. So, some optimal method of using very limited functionality databases has to be used. This is why Kjava has a class called Database that just acts as an interface with the database manager on the Palm OS. We show here the way to use this class:

```
// Declaration
Database dbg;

// Initializing the Database by creating the name of the
//  Database, the creator id(cid) and the table id(tid)..
String nameing = "data_base";
int cid = 0x4B415754;
int tid = 0x44425370;
dbg = new Database (tid,cid,Database.READWRITE);
// Creating the Database...
Database.create(0,nameing,cid,tid,false);
}  // end Constructor..
```

As you can see, a Database object is first declared and then initialized with table id (tid), creator id (cid) and the mode as the parameters. The mode is set to READWRITE so as to allow both reading from and writing to the database. The database is actually created by calling the create method. This method takes the following parameters:

- int cardNo: the card number
- java.lang.String name: name of the database
- int cID: creator ID
- int tID: table ID
- boolean resDB

To set the content of the database, we use the method setRecord:

```
dbg.setRecord(ij,data);
```

And to read a database record into a byte array, we use the `getRecord` method:

```
byte[] data = dbg.getRecord(1);
```

The method for adding a record to the database is, predictably, `addRecord`.

TextBox

This class serves a similar purpose as the `TextField` class, but you will prefer it when you want the text in it to look graceful even when the width of the text is more than the display area. This is because a `TextBox` will not break words. The text will not be wrapped to the following lines. Following is a code block showing the use of this class:

```
TextBox Text;
Text = new TextBox("Text To be Displayed",10,10,120,120);
Text.paint();
```

Installation of CLDC

When you download the CLDC reference implementation from Sun's site, you get a ZIP archive that can run on Windows, Solaris, and Linux. To install it, you just have to unzip the archive into any directory of your choice. There is no setup program. But you should have JDK installed on your computer before you try to run CLDC applications.

Version 1.0 of CLDC was available in one archive, which also has non-CLDC classes in the `com.sun.kjava` package. With this, you could develop and test applications on your desktop system. But if you needed to run these applications on a Palm device, you had to install a Palm overlay that was available in a separate archive. In the new 1.02 version, the Kjava API has been taken out of the CLDC archive and is added to the Palm overlay. In other words, now you have to download both CLDC and the Palm overlay, even if you have to run applications only on the desktop system.

For installing version 1.02, you first unzip the CLDC in any directory and then unzip the Kjava overlay in the `j2me_cldc` directory that was created while you were unzipping the CLDC archive. Note that you have to unzip with the overwrite option selected.

The CLDC archive and the Kjava overlay include the following:

♦ Compiled CLDC and non-CLDC (Kjava) classes in the `bin\api` directory.

♦ KVM interpreter and preverification tool (in the `bin` directory) and their complete source code (in the `tools\preverifier` directories).

♦ Complete documentation for all the classes (both CLDC and non-CLDC) in HTML format as well as PDF format. The release notes and the CLDC 1.02 specification are also included.

♦ Source code for Java Application Manager (JAM) and JavaCodeCompact (JCC) tool. A sample implementation of the application management software is included.

♦ The source code of the KDWP Debug Proxy (also known as Debug Agent) implementation in the `tools\kdp` directory. It is a tool that can be interposed between a Java development environment (such as Forte) and the KVM.

♦ Sample applications in the `samples` and `bin\samples` directories.

This reference implementation of the CLDC is meant for device manufacturers, developers, or those who want to port the KVM to a platform other than Windows, Solaris, Palm, or Linux. It includes all that is needed to build the complete reference implementation on Windows, Solaris, Palm, or Linux. Some parts of the KVM are optional, and if you are ambitious enough, you can compile your own KVM to experiment with various optional features.

Compiling, preverifying, and running applications

After you write an application, you will have to compile it — just as in J2SE. But there is an additional stage of preverifying the compiled files before actually running them. For this, a preverify tool is provided, as mentioned previously. The CLDC reference implementation also has many sample applications which you can try preverifying and running. The procedure for compiling, preverifying, and running is explained in the following sections.

Compiling

On Windows platform, the command used to compile an application is:

```
javac -g:none -bootclasspath
       %cldc_root%\bin\common\api\classes
-classpath %cldc_classpath% -d %classfile_dir% %1%.java
```

The options used in the preceding command are:

- ◆ -g:none: For no debugging information. If you want debugging information, you can use just –g or –g:{lines,vars,source}.
- ◆ -bootclasspath: For overriding the location of bootstrap class files.
- ◆ %cldc_root%\bin\api\classes: The directory where CLDC class libraries are located. If you use %cldc_root%, you will have to give a command line argument for this directory. You may avoid this by giving the full path where you unzipped the CLDC libraries.
- ◆ -classpath: For giving the path to the user class files.
- ◆ %cldc_classpath%: The location of the user class files. Again, you may avoid giving the command line argument by giving the full path. If you want to use files from more than one directory, they can be specified by separating them with semicolons.
- ◆ -d: For specifying the directory where you want to store your compiled class files.
- ◆ %classfile_dir%: The location of the compiled class files. You may give the full path or use command line argument.
- ◆ %1%.java: The file(s) you want to compile.

Preverifying

After compiling, you can preverify the compiled class files by using the following command:

```
%cldc_root%\bin\win32\preverify -d %preverified_dir%
-classpath %cldc_classpath%;%cldc_root%\bin\common\api\classes
%classfile_dir%
```

Needless to say, this and the other commands that follow have to each be entered as a single line on the console. The options used in this command are explained here:

- ◆ %cldc_root%\bin\win32\preverify: This is the command for the preverify tool, along with the directory in which it is located. Instead of using command line argument, as here, you can give the absolute path.
- ◆ -d: The option to use if you want the preverified files to be stored in a particular directory.
- ◆ %preverified_dir%: The directory in which preverified class files are to stored. It is recommended that you make it the same as that for compiled files.
- ◆ %classfile_dir%: The directory where the compiled class files are located.

Running

Once preverification has been done, you are ready to run the application. For this, the command will be something like this:

```
%cldc_root%\bin\win32\kvm -classpath
%preverified_dir%;%cldc_classpath%;%cldc_root%\bin\common\api\classes %1%
```

Explanations of the options are given here:

- ♦ %cldc_root%\bin\win32\kvm: The command to run the KVM along with the path where KVM is located.
- ♦ -classpath: The option for specifying the location of preverified files.
- ♦ %1%: The main class file that you want to run.

Making a Batch file

To simplify compiling, preverifying, and running applications, you can combine all three commands into a batch file. An example of such a batch file called RUN.BAT is given here:

```
javac -g:none -bootclasspath C:\j2me_cldc\bin\api\classes;
       -classpath  C:\j2me_cldc\bin\api\classes;
       C:\cldccasestudies\CaseStudy;
       -d C:\cldccasestudies\CaseStudy
       C:\cldccasestudies\CaseStudy\%1%.java
c:\j2me_cldc\bin\preverify -d C:\cldccasestudies\CaseStudy
       -classpath C:\j2me_cldc\bin\api\classes;
       C:\cldccasestudies\CaseStudy
c:\j2me_cldc\bin\kvm -classpath
       C:\j2me_cldc\bin\api\classes;
C:\cldccasestudies\CaseStudy %1%
```

Note that all these commands are for CLDC version 1.0. For version 1.02, you will have to add to the classpath the directory where Kjava libraries are stored.

Case Studies

Now that we have become familiar with the CLDC API and the new classes, and so on, in it, we can try our hands at programming with this basic constituent of the J2ME platform. In this section, we are going to practically use some of the important CLDC classes to do some routine tasks such as building parts of the user interface. Since CLDC by itself doesn't have much functionality, we will use it along with the Palm overlay — that is, the Kjava API — to demonstrate how CLDC can be used. This will be done with the help of some case studies. Each of these case studies is aimed at performing some common programming task. These case studies are in the form of spotlets, which can be compiled and run to see the results. The concept of spotlet is introduced in the com.sun.kjava package, of which the former is a class.

TextField_Spotlet

In any interactive application, one of the most basic requirements is that the user should be able to enter text. This can be met by providing a text box in which the user clicks and starts typing. We provide such a text box in this case study. After entering the text, the user clicks the button labeled OK and is shown the text entered. Of course, typing and clicking may not really be the actions an actual user will perform, because PDAs don't usually have a mouse and a keyboard. But whatever the pointing and text entering mechanism, the logic remains the same.

Since we are using the Palm overlay, we have to import the com.sun.kjava package. A text field is declared using the TextField class of Kjava. As you can see, the drawing part is similar to an applet — everything is finally put on the screen using the paint method. Note the use of register method of the spotlet class, which makes the spotlet the focus of event handling. Other methods from the Kjava API are penDown and keyDown, which are for clicking and typing, respectively. They belong to the spotlet class. Methods like setFocus, setUpperCase, pressed, and so on, belong to the TextField class. To see the output, refer to Figure 3-8.

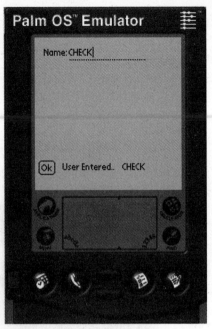

Figure 3-8: Output TextField_Spotlet.

Listing 3-1: TextField_Spotlet.java

© 2001 Dreamtech Software India Inc.
All rights reserved

```
1) import com.sun.kjava.*;
2)
3) /**
4) * A program that gives the user a feel of GUI
(specially
5) * text fields and buttons).
6) */
7)
8) public class TextField_Spotlet extends Spotlet {
9) // Declaring the variables...
10) private Button ok_button = null;
11) public TextField tf_textfield = null;
12) Graphics gr = Graphics.getGraphics();
13)
14) public TextField_Spotlet(){
15) register(NO_EVENT_OPTIONS);
16)// Clearing the drawing area...
17)  gr.clearScreen();
18)// Initializing text fields and buttons...
```

```
19)  ok_button = new Button("Ok",5,130);
20)  tf_textfield = new 21)TextField("Name",10,10,110,110);
22)  ok_button.paint();
23)  tf_textfield.setUpperCase(true);   // Accepts
         only upper case
24)  tf_textfield.setFocus();
25)  // Sets the focus so that the cursor blinks
26)  tf_textfield.paint();
27) }
28)
29) public void penDown(int x, int y) {  // Handling
     events...
30)  if(ok_button.pressed(x,y)) {
31)    gr.drawString("User Entered..",30,130);
32)    gr.drawString(tf_textfield.getText() + "
         ", 95,130);
33)  }
34) }
35)
36) public void keyDown(int x) {
37)  if(tf_textfield.hasFocus()){
38)    tf_textfield.handleKeyDown(x);
39)  }
40) }
41)
42) public static void main(String args[]) {
43)// Call to the main function...
44)  new TextField_Spotlet();
45) }
46)}
```

ScrollTextBox_Spotlet

The next spotlet shows a list of items, which are too numerous to fit within the display screen. We provide a scroll bar to allow the user to see all the items. When the user presses the OK button, the application is closed. This is done by using the ScrollTextBox class of the Kjava API. Note that the penDown method is still there, but instead of keyDown, we have to use the penMove method. We have used here the pressed, handlePenDown, and handlePenMove methods of the ScrollTextBox class. To see the output, refer to Figure 3-9.

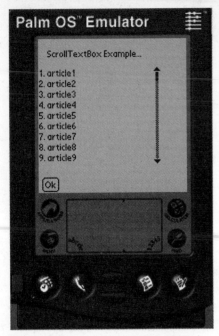

Figure 3-9: Output ScrollTextBox_Spotlet.

Listing 3-2: ScrollTextBox_Spotlet.java

```
1)import com.sun.kjava.*;
2)
3)public class ScrollTextBox_Spotlet extends Spotlet {
4) private Button bt = new Button("Ok",5,145);
5) public ScrollTextBox stb;
6) Graphics gr = Graphics.getGraphics();
7)
8)
9) public ScrollTextBox_Spotlet(){
10)  register(NO_EVENT_OPTIONS);
11)  gr.clearScreen();
12)  bt.paint();
13)  gr.drawRectangle(0,0,160,80,0,1);
14)  gr.drawString("ScrollTextBox 15)Example...",10,10);
16) String temp = "1. article1\n2. article2\n3.
     article3\n4.
17) article4\n5. article5\n6. article6\n7.
     article7\n8.
18) article8\n9. article9\n10. article10\n11.
     article11\n12. article12\n13.
19) article13\n14.
     article14\n15. article15\n16.
20) article16\n17.
21)   article17\n";
22)
23)// initailizing the scrolltextbox with string temp...
24)  stb = new ScrollTextBox(temp,1,30,130,100);
```

```
25)  stb.paint();
26)  }
27)
28) public void penDown(int x, int y)    {
29) // Handling the Events.....
30)  if (bt.pressed(x,y)) {
31)    System.exit(0);
32)  }
33)  if (stb.contains(x,y)) {
34)    stb.handlePenDown(x,y);
35)  }
36) }
37)
38) public void penMove(int x, int y) {
39)  if (stb.contains(x,y)) {
40)    stb.handlePenMove(x,y);
41)  }
42) }
43)
44) public static void main(String args[]){
45)   new ScrollTextBox_Spotlet();
46) }
47) }
```

HelpDisplay_Spotlet

Users who get your applications may not be sure how to use them. Even simple applications have to provide some sort of help for new users. In the case of fast-evolving small devices, which run faster-evolving applications, providing a Help feature is even more relevant. This spotlet illustrates how you can add instructions for using your application. For this, you simply use the HelpDisplay class. The user is shown some Help text, and when he presses the **Done** button, he is returned to the screen from which he asked for help. To see the output, refer to Figure 3-10 and Figure 3-11.

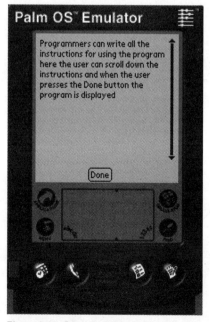

Figure 3-10: Output HelpDisplay_Spotlet -I.

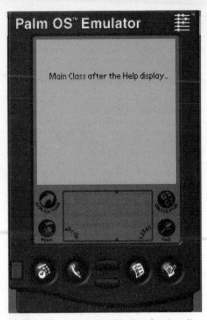

Figure 3-11: Output HelpDisplay_Spotlet - II.

Listing 3-3: HelpDisplay_Spotlet.java

```
1)import com.sun.kjava.*;
2)/**
3) * A program that gives the reader a feel of how help
   displays are to be
4) * used in a program. Help displays are helpful in
   giving the
5) * user instructions as to how the program is to be
   used...
6)*/
7)public class HelpDisplay_Spotlet extends Spotlet {
8) public static void main(String args[]){
9)  String helpText = "Programmers can write all
        the instructions
10)   for using the program here the user can
             scroll down
11)   the instructions and when the user presses
            the Done button the program is displayed";
12)
13)/**
14) * Help display is being initialized here the first
    argument tells the
15) * text to be displayed, the second argument mentions
    the class which
16) * is to be run after the user presses the DONE
    button, the third
17) * argument tells about the events in which we are
    interested. After
18) * the help display is shown and the DONE button is
```

```
        pressed,
19) * the class name(2nd argument) is registered and its
    events are taken
20) * into consideration...
21)*/
22)
23)  (new 25)HelpDisplay(helpText,"HelpDisplay_Spotlet",
24)  NO_EVENT_OPTIONS)).register(NO_EVENT_OPTIONS);
25) }
26)
27) public HelpDisplay_Spotlet(){
28)  Graphics gr = Graphics.getGraphics();
29)  gr.clearScreen();
30)  gr.drawString("Main Class after the Help
        display..", 15,35);
31) } }
32)}}
```

CheckRadio_Spotlet

The capability of the user to make choices from a given list is another part of an interactive application. Two ways of doing this are through radio buttons (for selecting only one element) and check boxes (for making more than one choice). This spotlet shows how this can be done with CLDC and Kjava. The user is shown four radio buttons, out of which he has to choose one. Two check boxes are also shown, out of which one or both can be selected. On pressing the OK button, the choices made by the user are displayed. Note the use of the if statement for controlling event handling. To see the output, refer to Figure 3-12.

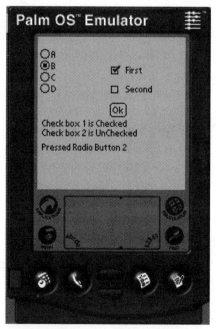

Figure 3-12: Output CheckRadio_Spotlet.

Listing 3-4: CheckRadio_Spotlet.java

```
1)import com.sun.kjava.*;
2)
3)/**
4) * A program that gives the user a feel of GUI
            (specially check boxes and
5) * radio buttons.
6)*/
7)
8)public class CheckRadio_Spotlet extends Spotlet {
9) private Button ok_button = null;
10) private CheckBox cb1_checkbox = null;
11) private CheckBox cb2_checkbox = null;
12) private RadioGroup radiogroup = new RadioGroup(4);
13) private RadioButton rb1_radiobutton = null;
14) private RadioButton rb2_radiobutton = null;
15) private RadioButton rb3_radiobutton = null;
16) private RadioButton rb4_radiobutton = null;
17) private String str1 = "";
18) private String str2 = "";
19) boolean checked_1 = false;
20) boolean checked_2 = false;
21)
22) Graphics gr = Graphics.getGraphics(); // Initialzing
       the graphic
23)
24) public CheckRadio_Spotlet(){
25)  register(NO_EVENT_OPTIONS);
26)
27)// Initializing the buttons, the check boxes and the
     radio buttons
28)  ok_button = new Button("Ok",80,70);
29)  cb1_checkbox = new CheckBox(80,30,"First");
30)  cb2_checkbox = new CheckBox(80,50,"Second");
31)  rb1_radiobutton = new RadioButton(4,14,"A");
32)  rb2_radiobutton = new RadioButton(4,26,"B");
33)  rb3_radiobutton = new RadioButton(4,38,"C");
34)  rb4_radiobutton = new RadioButton(4,50,"D");
35)  gr.clearScreen();  // Clear the drawing area
36)
37)// Adding the radio buttons in a group so that only
   one can be clicked
38)// at a time
39)  radiogroup.add(rb1_radiobutton);
40)  radiogroup.add(rb2_radiobutton);
41)  radiogroup.add(rb3_radiobutton);
42)  radiogroup.add(rb4_radiobutton);
43)
44)// Putting (painting the various GUI components on the
     drawing area
45)  cb1_checkbox.paint();
46)  cb2_checkbox.paint();
47)  ok_button.paint();
```

```
48)
49)   rb1_radiobutton.paint();
50)   rb2_radiobutton.paint();
51)   rb3_radiobutton.paint();
52)   rb4_radiobutton.paint();
53) }
54)
55) public void penDown(int x, int y) {
56)
57) // Event handling routines...
58)   if(ok_button.pressed(x,y)) {
59)     if (checked_1)
60)       str1 = "Check box 1 is Checked     ";
61)     else
62)       str1 = "Check box 1 is UnChecked";
63)     gr.drawString(str1,5,85);
64)     if (checked_2)
65)       str2 = "Check box 2 is Checked     ";
66)     else
67)       str2 = "Check box 2 is UnChecked";
68)     gr.drawString(str2,5,95);
69)   }
70)
71)   if(cb1_checkbox.pressed(x,y)) {
72)     checked_1 = !checked_1;
73)     cb1_checkbox.handlePenDown(x,y);
74)   }
75)
76)   if(cb2_checkbox.pressed(x,y)) {
77)     checked_2 = !checked_2;
78)     cb2_checkbox.handlePenDown(x,y);
79)   }

80)   if(rb1_radiobutton.pressed(x,y)) {
81)     gr.drawString("Pressed Radio Button 1",
        5,110);
82)     rb1_radiobutton.handlePenDown(x,y);
83)   }
84)
85)   if(rb2_radiobutton.pressed(x,y)) {
86)     gr.drawString("Pressed Radio Button 2",
        5,110);
87)     rb2_radiobutton.handlePenDown(x,y);
88)   }
89)
90)   if(rb3_radiobutton.pressed(x,y)) {
91)     gr.drawString("Pressed Radio Button 3",
        5,110);
92)     rb3_radiobutton.handlePenDown(x,y);
93)   }
94)
95)   if(rb4_radiobutton.pressed(x,y)) {
96)     gr.drawString("Pressed Radio Button 4",
        5,110);
97)     rb4_radiobutton.handlePenDown(x,y);
98)   }
```

```
99) }
100)
101 public static void main(String args[]){
102)   new CheckRadio_Spotlet();
103) }
104)}
```

HttpCheck_Spotlet

Any device that is to be connected to a network should be able to access files from another system on that network. The most common way of doing this is presently through an HTTP connection. Any J2ME application you make for a PDA may have to use files placed on a Web server. In CLDC, this is done by using the Connector class. This is the class that holds the methods used to create all connection objects.

Here we first create a text file called check1.txt and place it on a server. The user is shown a scroll text box and a button labeled Fetch. When the user presses this button, the contents of the file are displayed in the scroll text box. The file on the server is fetched with the help of OpenDataInputStream method of the Connector class. It takes the URL of the file to be fetched as the argument. Since the connection framework of CLDC is still in the development stage, you have to use test as the prefix before the actual URL of the file. To see the output, refer to Figures 3-13 and 3-14.

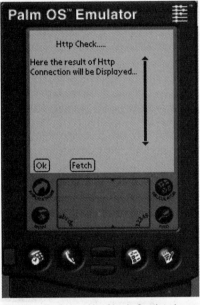

Figure 3-13: Output HttpCheck_Spotlet - I.

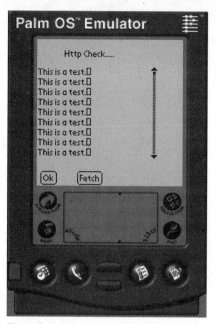

Figure 3-14: Output HttpCheck_Spotle – II.

Listing 3-5: HttpCheck_Spotlet.java

```
1)import java.io.*;
2)import javax.microedition.io.*;
3)import com.sun.kjava.*;
4)
5)/**
6) * A program to show how http connections work on CLDC.
   The user is
7) * given the feel of http connections by a simple GUI
   program. In this
8) * program the users have one scroll text box where the
   result of file read
9) * will be displayed, the user when presses "Fetch" the
   contents of the
10) * field "check1.txt" are sent via network..  (The
   user is required to
11) * create check1.txt on the server directory...).
12)*/
13)
14)public class httpcheck_spotlet extends Spotlet {
15) private Button bt = new Button("Ok",5,145);
16) private Button fetch = new Button("Fetch",45,145);
17) public ScrollTextBox stb;
18) DataInputStream dos;
19) byte [] b= new byte[32];
20) byte [] c = new byte[15000];
21)
22) Graphics gr = Graphics.getGraphics();
23)
```

```
24) public httpcheck_spotlet(){
25)   register(NO_EVENT_OPTIONS);
26)   gr.clearScreen();
27)   gr.drawString("Http Check.....",30,10);
28)   bt.paint();
29)   fetch.paint();
30)   gr.drawRectangle(0,30,160,80,0,1);
31)   String temp = "Here the result of Http
      Connection will
32)    be Displayed...";
33)
34)// Initailizing the scroll text box with string
    temp...
35)   stb = new ScrollTextBox(temp,1,30,130,100);
36)   stb.paint();
37)   try {
38)    dos = 39)Connector.openDataInputStream("testhttp://
40)      127.0.0.1/check1.txt");
41)   }
42)   catch (IOException e) {
43)   }
44) }
45)
46) public void penDown(int x, int y) { // Handling the
      events...
47)   if(bt.pressed(x,y)) {
48)     try {
49)       dos.close();
50)     }
51)     catch (IOException e) {
52)       System.out.println( e );
53)     }
54)     System.exit(0);
55)   }
56)
57)   if (fetch.pressed(x,y)) {
58)     int count;
59)     int total = 0;
60)     try {
61)     while ((count = dos.read(b,0,32)) > 0) {
62)         for (int i = 0;i<count;i++) {
63)                 c[total]  = b[i];
64)                 total++;
65)         }
66)     }
67)     }
68)     catch (IOException e) {
69)     }
70)
71)     String str  = new String(c, 0 ,total);
72)     stb = new ScrollTextBox(str,1,30,130,100);
73)     stb.paint();
74)   }
75)
76)   if (stb.contains(x,y))
77)     stb.handlePenDown(x,y);
```

```
78) }
79)
80) public void penMove(int x, int y) {
81)   if (stb.contains(x,y))
82)   stb.handlePenMove(x,y);
83) }
84)
85) public static void main(String args[]){
86)   new httpcheck_spotlet();
87) }
88)}
```

Server

The data on a device such as a PDA needs to be frequently synchronized with the data on a desktop or server system. For this, you need a listener on the desktop or server system, which will respond to the request from the client — that is, the PDA. This is not a J2ME application, but we have used it because, without it, the next spotlet can't be run. You can see that the java.net package has been imported, which is a part of the standard edition.

Listing 3-6: Server.java

```
1) import java.io.*;
2) import java.net.*;
3)
4) public class server {
5) public static void main(String args[]) {
6)   try {
7)     ServerSocket server_soc = new ServerSocket(5555);
8)     Socket sc;
9)     sc = server_soc.accept();
10)    BufferedReader br = new BufferedReader (new
InputStreamReader(sc.getInputStream()));
12)    PrintWriter pw = new PrintWriter (new BufferedWriter(
14)      new OutputStreamWriter(
15)      sc.getOutputStream())),true);
16)    while (true) {
17)      String str = br.readLine();
18)      pw.println("Response from the Server-" +str);
19)    }
20)  }
21)
22)  catch(Exception ae) {
23)  }
24) }
25)}
```

Socket_Check

Another way of transferring data from one device to another is through socket connections. In this case study, we give an example of how this can be done. The user is given a text field in which he enters some text. On pressing the OK button, the contents of the text field are transferred via the socket connection to a server socket. The server reads the text and responds to the client socket. A message is shown indicating that the connection has been established. Whatever the user types in the text field is redirected to the client and is shown on the screen.

We open the socket connection by using the StreamConnection interface of the javax.microedition.io package. You can also see the use of many other CLDC classes and methods in this spotlet.

To run this spotlet, first make sure that your Server.class class file is not in the folder in which you have the Socket_Check.class file (because when you preverify the application you will get an error as the Server.class is a Java Standard Edition program). You then have to start the server by typing **java server** at the command prompt. On pressing the Exit button, both the spotlet and the server are closed. To see the output, refer to Figures 3-15 and 3-16.

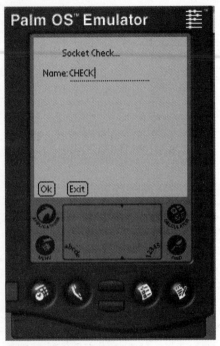

Figure 3-15: Output Socket_Check - I.

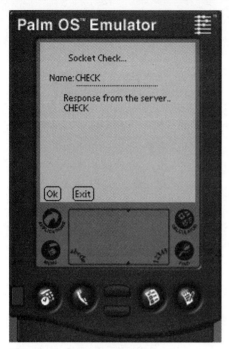

Figure 3-16: Output Socket_Check – II

Listing 3-7: Socket_Check.java

```
1)import com.sun.kjava.*;
2)import java.lang.*;
3)import java.io.*;
4)import javax.microedition.io.*;
5)
6)/**
7) * A program to show how Sockets work on CLDC. The user is given the
8) * feel of socket connections by a simple GUI program in this program. The
9) * users have one text field, the user enters the text on the text field and
10) * press OK the contents of the text field are sent via network over to some
11) * server socket which is running (use "server.java" in this case present
12) * in "..\serverforsocket\server.java" run it using the command "java
13) * server"). The server then reads the message and responds back to the same
14) * message to the client socket which will show the message on the spotlet..
15)*/
16)
17)public class socket_check extends Spotlet {
18) InputStream is;
19) OutputStream os;
20) StreamConnection socket = null;
21)
22)// Initialzing the various GUI components
23) private Button bt = new Button("OK",5,145);
24) private Button bt1 = new Button("Exit",35,145);
25) public TextField tf = new 26)TextField("Name",10,30,110,110);
27)
```

```
28) Graphics gr = Graphics.getGraphics();
29)
30) public socket_check(){
31)   register(NO_EVENT_OPTIONS);
32)   gr.clearScreen();
33)   gr.drawString("Socket Check...",30,10);
34)   bt.paint();
35)   bt1.paint();
36)   gr.drawRectangle(0,20,160,80,0,1);
37)   tf.setUpperCase(true);
38)   tf.setFocus();
39)    tf.paint();
40)
41)// Initializing the socket connections
42)   try {
43)     socket = (StreamConnection)Connector.open(
44)     "socket://127.0.0.1:5555", 45)                    Connector.READ_WRITE,
true);
46)    if (socket != null) {
47)      System.out.println("Connection is established to
49)      localhost on port 5555...");
50)    }
51)
52)// Opening the input and output streams...
53)     is = socket.openInputStream();
54)     os = socket.openOutputStream();
55)   }
56)   catch(IOException ae) {
57)     System.out.println("Couldn't open socket 58)         to
59)     127.0.0.1 :5555... Either server is not 60)         started
61)      (start it from ../serverforsocket/
62)     using the
63)      command java server ) or port is 64)                already in
65)                use.... "  );
66)     System.exit(0);
67)   }
68) }
69)
70) public void penDown(int x, int y) {
71)   if(bt.pressed(x,y)) {
72)     try {
73)         os.write((tf.getText()+"\n").getBytes());
74)      StringBuffer sb = new StringBuffer();
75)
76)      int b;
77)      while ((b=is.read()) != 13) {
78)          sb.append((char)b);
79)      }

80)     gr.drawString(sb.toString(), 55,50);
81)     sb.delete(0,sb.capacity());
82)   }
83)    catch (IOException aer) {
84)      System.out.println(aer);
85)    }
86)   }
```

```
87)
88)  if (bt1.pressed(x,y)) {
89)    try {
90)      socket.close();
91)    }
92)    catch (IOException e) {
93)      System.out.println( e );
94)    }
95)    System.exit(0);
96)  }
97) }
98) public void keyDown(int x) {
99)  if(tf.hasFocus()) {
100)    tf.handleKeyDown(x);
101)  }
102) }
103)
104) public static void main(String args[]){
105)   new socket_check();
106)   }
107)}
```

No practical interactive application can avoid using databases. This final spotlet of the chapter shows how databases can be created and accessed by using CLDC. Strictly speaking, we are adding database functionality by using not just CLDC, but the Kjava API. This is because CLDC in itself doesn't have database functionality.

This spotlet faces a problem. Although a database is being created and accessed successfully, when you try to add a new record to the database, it overwrites the existing record, even when you use the `addRecord` method of the `Database` class. We find a way around this problem in the project on CLDC later in the book in Chapter 6.To see the output, refer to Figures 3-17 and 3-18.

Figure 3-17: Output Database_Check - I.

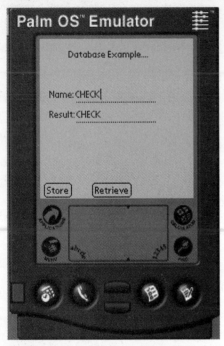

Figure 3-18: Output Database_Check - II.

Listing 3-8: Database_Check.java

© 2001 Dreamtech Software India Inc.
All rights reserved

```
1)import com.sun.kjava.*;
2)
3)public class database_check extends Spotlet {
4)
5)// Declaring the variables...
6) private Button ok_button = null;
7) private Button get_button = null;
8) public TextField tf_textfield = null;
9) public TextField tf1_textfield = null;
10)
11) Database dbg;
12)
13) Graphics gr = Graphics.getGraphics();
14
15) public database_check() {
16)  register(NO_EVENT_OPTIONS);
17)
18)// Clearing the drawing area....
19)  gr.clearScreen();
20)  gr.drawString("Database Example....",30,10);
21)
22)// Initializing textfields and Buttons.........
23)
24)  ok_button = new Button("Store",5,145);
25)  get_button = new Button("Retrieve",55,145);
26)
```

```
27)   tf_textfield = new 28)          TextField("Name",10,50,110,20);
29)   tf1_textfield = new 30)         TextField("Result",10,70,110,20);
31)
32)   ok_button.paint();
33)   get_button.paint();
34)
35)   gr.drawRectangle(0,30,160,80,0,1);
36)   // Draw a rectangular area so that
37)   //  textfield can be drawn.
38)
39)   tf_textfield.setUpperCase(true); // Accepts
              only upper case
40)   tf_textfield.setFocus();
41)   // Sets the Focus so that the cursor blinks
42)
43)   tf_textfield.paint();
44)   tf1_textfield.paint();
45)
46)// Database initialization.....
47)   String name = "check";
48)   int cid = 0x4B415754;
49)   int tid = 0x44425370;
50)
51) dbg = new Database
52) 52)        (tid,cid,Database.READWRITE);
53)
54)   if (dbg.isOpen()){
55)     Database.create(0,name,cid,tid,false);
56)   }
57)   else {
58)     Database.create(0,name,cid,tid,false);
59)   }
60) }
61)
62) public void penDown(int x, int y)    {
63)
64)// Handling events...
65)   if(ok_button.pressed(x,y)) {
66)     byte[] data = 67)              (tf_textfield.getText()+"?").getBytes();
68)     dbg.addRecord(data);
69)   }
70)   if(get_button.pressed(x,y)) {
71)     byte[] data = dbg.getRecord(65535);
72)     String temp = new String(data);
73)     temp = 74)             temp.substring(0,temp.indexOf("?"));
75)     tf1_textfield.setText(temp);
76)   }
77) }
78)
79) public void keyDown(int x) {
80)   if(tf_textfield.hasFocus()){
81)     tf_textfield.handleKeyDown(x);
82)   }
83) }
84)
85) public static void main(String args[]){
```

```
86)  new database_check();
87) }
88)}
```

Summary

This chapter gives you a feel for programming mobile devices and the restrictions in terms of resources for mobile devices. This chapter is groundwork for the next chapter in the book as we have six unique projects in this book. One should be well conversant with the APIs before going on to these chapters. Chapter 4 concentrates on MIDP. It's an important chapter as we have two MIDP-based projects in this chapter.

Chapter 4

MIDP-MIDlet Implementation with Case Studies

This chapter takes up the reference implementation provided by Sun for the profile that it designed for devices such as mobile phones. To make the reader familiar with what the reference implementation covers, the APIs are briefly dealt with. Examples of developing applications with this implementation are given in the form of case studies.

Sun's reference implementation of Mobile Information Device Profile for Windows comes in the form of a zip file named `j2me_midp-1_0-ea1-win.zip`, which is available for free download from Sun's site. Once you possess it, you are ready to program using MIDP, although for testing purposes, it is better if you also have the J2ME Wireless Toolkit. We will be learning how to use the toolkit later in this chapter.

The release of MIDP provided by Sun includes the following:

♦ The MIDP API in the form of a jar file called `midp.jar` in the directory `midp-ea1\lib`.

♦ A device emulator, which can be run by executing the file `midp.exe` (in the directory `midp-ea1\bin`). With this emulator you can test your applications for cell phone and pager.

♦ A preverifying tool, which is also in the directory `midp-ea1\bin`.

♦ Complete documentation in the `midp-ea1\docs` directory.

♦ Several sample MIDlets (*games:* Sokoban, Puzzle tiles, ManyBalls; *utilities:* Color chooser, Property inspector, Graphics sampler, HttpTest; *applications:* Auction demo, Stock tracker) in the form of a jar archive named `examples.jar`, in the directory `midp-ea1\lib`, and their source code in the directory `midp-ea1\src\example`.

♦ A `makefile` that includes targets that will launch demonstration programs or can be used to actually build and run your own applications.

You can find additional information about the runtime environment and basic instructions for building your own MIDlet applications in the `docs` directory. The HTML documentation includes both the MIDP and the CLDC. To unpack the `javadoc` files, you have to unzip the documentation bundle.

```
J2ME_MIDP+CLDC-1_0-EA1-DOCS-*.zip.
```

MIDlets and MIDlet States

The application model used in MIDP is different from that used in CLDC. In CLDC, you could make the application by using the `main()` method, as in J2SE standalone applications, or you had to use the KJava model. The problem with the first approach is that there was no way to provide user interface capabilities. And the second approach relies on something that is itself transitory and may not be available in future.

To solve these problems, MIDP uses an application model based on MIDlets. These MIDlets are somewhat similar to applets. Every MIDP application is a MIDlet, and every MIDlet extends the class `javax.microedition.midlet.MIDlet`. Also, like an applet, it has to necessarily implement some methods. These methods are `startApp`, `pauseApp`, and `destroyApp`. As you can guess from their names, they are meant to allow the application management software to manage the lifecycle of the MIDlet. A MIDlet, during its lifecycle, can be in any of the following states (usually in the same order):

- **Loaded:** Occurs when the MIDlet has been created using the `new` keyword. This state can occur only once per instance of a MIDlet. In case of an exception, the MIDlet is destroyed.

- **Paused:** Occurs when the MIDlet has been initialized but is not holding any shared resources.

- **Active:** Occurs after it has been initialized and is functioning normally. This state is entered into after the paused state.

- **Destroyed:** Occurs when the MIDlet is destroyed and all the resources are released.

MIDlet Suites

Just as J2SE classes can be packaged together into a single JAR file, so, too, can MIDlets. When this is done, the JAR file is called a *MIDlet suite*. A MIDlet suite is created if the MIDlets need to share code or data. The MIDlets in the suite can share the resources in the JAR file, i.e., it can call another MIDlet in the JAR file. Moreover, MIDlets in different suites cannot interact directly. This provides security around the MIDlet suite instead of around each MIDlet.

The name, version, and creator of the MIDlet suite are all identified by entries in the manifest. These entries also describe the minimum configuration and profile versions required. The following are the MIDlet manifest attributes:

- **MicroEdition-Configuration:** The name and version of the J2ME configuration required to run the MIDlet suite. (Optional)

- **MicroEdition-Profile:** The name and version of the J2ME profile required to run the MIDlet suite. (Compulsory)

- **MIDlets:** The name, icon, and main class of each MIDlet in the suite. (Compulsory)

- **MIDlet-Data-Size:** The minimum number of bytes of persistent storage that the MIDlet requires to run. The default is zero. (Optional)

- **MIDlet-Description:** A description of the MIDlet suite. (Optional)

- **MIDlet-Icon:** The path of PNG file within the JAR file, used by the application management software to identify the MIDlet suite. (Optional)

- **MIDlet-Info-URL:** A URL describing the MIDlet suite in detail. (Optional)

- **MIDlet-Name:** The name of the MIDlet suite. (Compulsory)

- **MIDlet-Vendor:** The vendor of the suite. (Compulsory)

- **MIDlet-Version:** The version number of the suite in the format *XX.YY* or *XX.YY.ZZ*. (Compulsory)

MIDP API

The MIDP API consists of the following packages:

- **Core packages (`java.io`, `java.lang`, `java.util`):** These form the base on which CLDC and MIDP stand.

- **`javax.microedition.lcdui`:** A User Interface API for Mobile Information Devices such as cell phones.

- ♦ **javax.microedition.rms:** To provide a mechanism for MIDlets to persistently store data and later retrieve it.

- ♦ **javax.microedition.midlet:** This package defines Mobile Information Device Profile applications and the interactions between the application, as well as the environment in which the applications run.

- ♦ **javax.microedition.io:** A package that provides networking support based on the Generic Connection Framework from the Connected Limited Device Configuration.

The core packages are the same as in CLDC. Their purpose is to define the Java language as used in CLDC and MIDP and provide means of input/output and some utilities for writing applications. We have briefly discussed these in Chapter 3. Here we will focus on packages specific to MIDP. But before that, we should take note of the difference in one of the common packages. The java.util package in MIDP has two classes that are not present in CLDC. These are Timer and TimerTask classes. The first represents a task that can be scheduled for one-time or for repeated execution, and the second provides a facility for threads to schedule tasks for future execution in a background thread.

Application Lifecycle Package

The package named javax.microedition.midlet is to MIDP what the Applet package is to the Standard Edition. It is included primarily for defining how MIDP applications should be organized and how they should interact with their environment. This is why it has only one class, called MIDlet.

Like an applet, a MIDlet is an application. Every MIDP application has to extend this class so that the application management software can control the application. It is also necessary because the properties from the application descriptor have to be obtained and state changes have to be notified and requested. As we saw earlier in MIDlets and MIDlet States section in this chapter, there are methods to create, start, pause, and destroy a MIDlet. The possibility for a MIDlet to have several states is important because it allows several applications to be run at the same time. Apart from the inherited methods, this class has the following methods:

- ♦ startApp
- ♦ pauseApp
- ♦ destroyApp
- ♦ notifyDestroyed
- ♦ notifyPaused
- ♦ getAppProperty
- ♦ resumeRequest

To get a better idea of the use of this class and its methods, look at the following code that represents a skeleton MIDP application:

```
import javax.microedition.midlet.*;
import javax.microedition.lcdui.*;

/**
 * Skeleton Application illustrating the use of MIDlet Class..
 */
public class first extends MIDlet implements CommandListener {

 private Command quit;  // The Quit button
 private Display ourDisplay;  // Declaring the display

// Initialize the Display and place system controls in the Constructor..
```

```
public first()
{
 ourDisplay = Display.getDisplay(this);
 quit = new Command("Quit", Command.SCREEN, 2);
}


/**
 * Initialize all the classes to be used in the program here (startApp())..
 */
public void startApp()
{

  ...
  ...


}



// If the Application needs to be paused temporarily.
 public void pauseApp()
 {

  ...
  ...


 }
// Clean up when the application is destroyed..

 public void destroyApp(boolean unconditional)
 {

  ...
  ...


 }

// Event handling routine..

 public void commandAction(Command c, Displayable s)
 {
    if (c == quit)         // If Quit button is pressed..
     {
            notifyDestroyed(); // Call the destroyApp method..
     }
 }
}
```

User Interface Package

Unlike the CLDC API, MIDP has its own GUI package, as it is a profile. This package is the `javax.microedition.lcdui`, which is optimized for devices such as cell phones, two-way pagers, etc. It wasn't possible to use the AWT package for MID devices since it is too heavy for these devices. Besides, there is no mouse on such devices to exploit the potential of AWT. A new package was therefore required. This package is basically a game-oriented one, although it can be used for other purposes. It has been designed in such a way that both portability and device-specific functionality can be achieved to a great extent. The former is ensured by using abstraction and the latter by including features that may not be available on all devices.

The user interface model used in MIDP is built around screens. A MIDlet has a `Display`, on which an object of `Displayable class` can be shown. There can be two kinds of such class objects — `Canvas` and `Screen`. While the `Canvas` class is meant for low-level UI objects for displaying graphics (using the `Graphics` class) and taking care of inputs, the `Screen` class provides a set of the most commonly used UI objects such as `TextField`, `List`, `TextBox`, `ChoiceGroup`, `StringItem`, etc. The `Screen` class also has a subclass called `Form`, to which `Items` (`StringItem`, `ImageItem`, `TextField`, `DateField`, `Gauge`, and `ChoiceGroup`) can be added.

The classes available in the MIDP user interface package are:

- `Alert`
- `Canvas`
- `ChoiceGroup`
- `Command`
- `DateField`
- `Display`
- `Displayable`
- `Font`
- `Form`
- `Gauge`
- `Graphics`
- `Image`
- `ImageItem`
- `Item`
- `List`
- `Screen`
- `StringItem`
- `TextBox`
- `TextField`
- `Ticker`

And the interfaces present in this package are:

- `Choice`
- `CommandListener`
- `ItemStateListener`

We will be explaining the more commonly used among these in this section.

Interface CommandListener

In MIDP, event handling is based on the listener model. Every `Displayable` object needs one (and only one) listener. `CommandListener` is a listener for high-level events. Like other listeners, it is registered using the method `Displayable.setCommandListener`. It has only one method called `commandAction`, which we have used in the following code block:

```
// Implementing the interface...
public class TextFieldCheck extends MIDlet implements CommandListener {

// Declaring Buttons and initializing them to null...
 Command ok = null;
 Command quit = null;

// Handling the event.

public void commandAction(Command c, Displayable d) {
// Event handling for the Button
  if ( c == ok )
  {
     // Code for tasks to be done on OK button press...
  }
  if ( c == quit )
  {
     // Code for tasks to be done on Quit button press...
  }
 }
```

Alert Class

This class is used to show a message, warning, or other information to the user for a specified period of time or until the user cancels it. It can contain strings, images, etc., and can also handle events, like any other screen. The methods available for this class are:

- getDefaultTimeout
- getTimeout
- setTimeout
- appendString
- appendImage
- appendItem
- insertItem
- deleteItem

Following is a code block showing the use of Alert class and some of its methods:

```
// Popping an Alert...
// Parameters..
// 1. Title of the Alert..
// 2. Text of Alert.
// 3. Image if required.
// 4 Type of Alert (INFO, WARNING,ERROR, CONFIRMATION, ALARM).


Alert alert = new Alert ("Warning", "You have entered Wrong serial number",
                         null, AlertType.WARNING);
// Making this alert a Modal alert..
     alert.setTimeout(Alert.FOREVER);
// or else...
// Making this alert disappear after certain milliseconds..
     alert.setTimeout(10);
```

ChoiceGroup Class

This class provides us a way of adding UI components that may be selected by the user. It is possible to create components that can be selected, either one or more at a time. In other words, both radio buttons and check boxes can be created using this class. Which one will be created depends on the value of the choiceType parameter. If it is EXCLUSIVE, we will get check boxes, and if it is MULTIPLE, we will have radio buttons. The methods provided for this class are implementations of methods in the interface Choice:

- appendElement(String stringElement, Image imageElement)
- deleteElement(int index)
- getImage(int i)
- getSelectedFlags(boolean[] selectedArray_return)
- getSelectedIndex()
- getSize()
- getString(int i)
- insertElement(int index, String stringElement, Image imageElement)
- isSelected(int index)
- setElement(int index, String stringElement, Image imageElement)
- setSelectedFlags(boolean[] selectedArray)
- setSelectedIndex(int index, boolean selected)

Let us look at the use of this class for creating radio buttons:

```
// Declaring Form and ChoiceGroup objects and initializing them to null...
Form ui_holder = null;

ChoiceGroup radiobutton_type = null;

String[] name = {"a","b","c"};
Image[] img = null;

// Initialize the ChoiceGroup..
// Parameter 1 ---    Title
// Parameter 2 ---    Type of ChoiceGroup (Exclusive for RadioButtons)
// Parameter 3 ---    Label of the radio buttons displayed
// Parameter 4 ---    Images for the radio button label if required

radiobutton_type = new ChoiceGroup("Choices..",ChoiceGroup.EXCLUSIVE,name,img);

// Adding the ChoiceGroup to the Form...
ui_holder.append(radiobutton_type);

// Event Handling..
// To get the String of the selected radio button...
radiobutton_type.getString(radiobutton_type.getSelectedIndex());
```

Now we create a group of check boxes with the same class, just changing the choiceType parameter:

```
// Declaring Form and ChoiceGroup objects and initializing them to null...
Form ui_holder = null;
ChoiceGroup checkbox_type = null;
```

```
String[] name1 = {"d","e","f"};
Image[] img = null;

checkbox_type = new ChoiceGroup("Choices..",ChoiceGroup.MULTIPLE,name1,img);

ui_holder.append(checkbox_type);

checkbox_type.isSelected(i)
```

Command Class

MIDP has no `Button` class. Instead, a class called `Command` is used to create UI objects that behave almost like buttons. Only the label, that is, the name of the command, priority of the command, and so on, are contained in a `Command`. What the `Command` object will actually do is specified in the `CommandListener` attached to the screen on which the object is placed.

The parameters required to be passed while instantiating a `Command` object are:

♦ Label for the Command button.

♦ Position of Command button.

♦ Priority of the command over other commands.

The third parameter (if it is used as the number of the accelerator key) works as follows: If the user presses the central button (hot key) of the cell phone, all the commands listed will be shown; the user can then scroll to the label of the button he or she wishes to use, or the user can press the serial number of the button to choose that particular button.

There is only one method available for this class. This method is `toString`, which returns a string representation of the object. See the following code to see how button-like objects can be created using this class:

```
Form ui_holder = null;

// Declaring Command objects and initializing them to null...
 Command ok = null;
 Command quit = null;
// Instantiating the Form...
 ui_holder = new Form("User Interface - TextField");
...
 ok = new Command("Ok",Command.SCREEN,3);
 quit = new Command("Quit",Command.SCREEN,2);

// Adding Command Button to the Form
   ui_holder.addCommand(ok);
   ui_holder.addCommand(quit);
...
  // Invoking Action Listener
 ui_holder.setCommandListener(this);

 public void commandAction(Command c, Displayable d) {
// Event handling for the Button
 if ( c == ok )
 {
 ...
 }
 if ( c == quit )
 {
```

```
   ...
  }
}
```

Display Class

This class represents the display of the device. To show a user interface object on the device, you first have to declare the display, get it, and then make it current with the object supplied as the parameter to the setCurrent method. The methods specific to this class are enlisted:

♦ getDisplay

♦ isColor

♦ numColors

♦ getCurrent

♦ setCurrent

Let us see the use of this class in the following code block:

```
// Declaring Form object and initialzing it to null...
  Form ui_holder = null;

// Declaring variable for Display class and initializing as null...
  private Display display = null;

// Getting the Display unique to this MIDlet...
  display = Display.getDisplay(this);

/*
 * Making the Display Current so that it can show
 * the Form.
 */

  display.setCurrent(ui_holder);
```

Form Class

LCDUI package contains a Form class. A Form is a kind of Screen on which other UI objects can be added. You can instantiate a Form object with either just a string title or a string title and an array containing the Items to be added to Form. The methods available are:

♦ appendItem

♦ appendString

♦ appendImage

♦ insertItem

♦ deleteItem

♦ setItem

♦ getItemAt

♦ getSize

♦ setItemStateListener

In the following code snippet, we create a Form and initialize it to null. This Form is given a string title. Then we add a TextField to this Form by calling the append method:

```
// Declaring the form...
Form myform = null;
...
// Declaring the Display and initializing it as null...
private Display show = null;
...
// Getting the Display unique to this MIDlet...
show = Display.getDisplay(this);
// Initializing the form with a string title...
myform = new Form("User Interface - TextField");
// Declaring and initializing a TextField...
tx = new TextField("MyField","Type here...",70,0);
// Adding the TextField to the form...
myform.append(tx);
// Showing the form, which is a Displayable object, on the screen...
show.setCurrent(myform);
```

Gauge Class

Sometimes you want to use a bar graph indicating progress of some process or for use in a game. The class Gauge serves this purpose. It can be both interactive and noninteractive, depending on the need of the application. What determines this fact is the Boolean value of the second parameter taken by the constructor of this class. The methods for this class are:

♦ setValue

♦ getValue

♦ setMaxValue

♦ getMaxValue

In the following code block, we create a Form and add to it a Gauge with the interactive parameter specified as true. In other words, the bar graph created will be of interactive type:

```
private Display display = null;
Form ui_holder = null;
...
// Declaring variable for the Gauge class...
Gauge gaugeUI;
...
display = Display.getDisplay(this);
...
ui_holder = new Form("User Interface - Gauge ");
gaugeUI = new Gauge("Values..",true,10,0);
ui_holder.append(gaugeUI);
...
display.setCurrent(ui_holder);
...

// Event handling for the OK button..
if ( c == ok ) {
int i = gaugeUI.getValue();

display.setCurrent(ui_holder);
}
...
```

Graphics Class

The `Graphics` class in MIDP is somewhat like the class of the same name in the standard edition. It provides fairly good functionality for displaying 2-D graphics on constrained devices. Many of the methods of this class are similar to those of the `Graphics` class in J2SE. (However, as expected, some methods have been dropped since they are not relevant here. Some new methods have also been introduced, keeping in mind the characteristics of mobile devices. We briefly describe those methods that are present and point out the differences from their J2SE versions:

♦ **translate:** To translate the origin of the graphics context to the point (x, y) relative to the current coordinate system.

♦ **getTranslateX:** A new method to get the X coordinate of the translated origin of this graphics context.

♦ **getTranslateY:** Also a new method to get the Y coordinate of the translated origin of this graphics context.

♦ **getColor:** To determine the current color. It returns an integer in the form 0x00RRGGBB.

♦ **getRedComponent:** Another new method to determine the red component of the current color. It returns an integer value in the range 0-255.

♦ **getGreenComponent:** A similar method to find out the green component of the current color.

♦ **getBlueComponent:** To find out the blue component of the current color.

♦ **getGrayScale:** This one is also a new method, like the preceding three. It can be used to determine the current grayscale being used for all subsequent rendering operations. For color values, this returns the brightness of the color.

♦ **setColor:** A variation of the J2SE method, with two constructors instead of just one. It can be used to specify the current color in RGB values. All subsequent rendering operations will use this specified color. In one constructor, the red, green, and blue values are passed as three parameters (with values in the range 0-255). In the second constructor, only one parameter is used to specify RGB values in the format 0x00RRGGBB.

♦ **setGrayScale:** Like `getGrayScale`, it is a new method. It specifies the current grayscale to be used for all subsequent rendering operations. For color displays, this method sets the color for all subsequent drawing operations to be of gray color equivalent to the value passed in this method. This value is in the range 0-255.

♦ **getFont:** To get the current system font.

♦ **setFont:** To specify the font for all subsequent text-rendering operations.

♦ **getClipX:** A variation of the `getClip` method of J2SE. It returns the X offset of the current clipping area, relative to the point from which the coordinate system starts for this graphics context. Separating the `getClip` operation into two methods returning integers is more performance- and memory-efficient than one `getClip()` call returning an object.

♦ **getClipY:** Same as the preceding, but for returning the Y offset of the current clipping area.

♦ **getClipWidth:** This method is a variation of `getClipBounds` method. It returns the width of the current clipping area.

♦ **getClipHeight:** This returns the height of the current clipping area.

♦ **clipRect:** This method is the same as in J2SE, being used with the following constructor:

```
clipRect(int x, int y, int width, int height)
```

♦ **setClip:** To set the current clip to the rectangle specified by the given coordinates. Rendering operations have no effect outside the clipping area. Only one constructor is available, with the following signature:

```
setClip(int x, int y, int width, int height)
```

♦ **drawLine:** Same as in J2SE. Draws a line between the coordinates (x1,y1) and (x2,y2) using the current color. Its signature is:

```
drawLine(int x1, int y1, int x2, int y2)
```

♦ **fillRect:** Same as in J2SE. It fills the specified rectangle with the current color. The signature is:

```
fillRect(int x, int y, int width, int height)
```

♦ **drawRect:** Same as in J2SE. It draws the outline of the specified rectangle using the current color. The resulting rectangle will cover an area of width + 1 pixels by height + 1 pixels. The width and height have to be nonnegative. The signature is:

```
drawRect(int x, int y, int width, int height)
```

♦ **drawRoundRect:** Same as in J2SE. It draws the outline of the specified rounded corner rectangle using the current color. The signature is:

```
drawRoundRect(int x, int y, int width, int height,
int arcWidth, int arcHeight)
```

♦ **fillRoundRect:** Same as in J2SE. Fills the specified rounded corner rectangle with the current color. The signature is of the form:

```
fillRoundRect(int x, int y, int width, int height,
int arcWidth, int arcHeight)
```

♦ **fillArc:** Same as in J2SE. Fills a circular or elliptical arc covering the specified rectangle. The signature is:

```
fillArc(int x, int y, int width, int height,
int startAngle, int arcAngle)
```

♦ **drawArc:** Same as in J2SE. Draws the outline of a circular or elliptical arc covering the specified rectangle.

```
drawArc(int x, int y, int width, int height,
int startAngle, int arcAngle)
```

♦ **drawString:** Slightly different from the J2SE version. It draws the specified String   using the current font and color. There is an additional parameter for the anchor point for positioning the text. The String to be drawn should be at least one character long. The (x,y) position is the position of the anchor point. The signature is:

```
drawString(String str, int x, int y, int anchor)
```

♦ **drawSubstring:** A new method that draws a part of the specified String using the current font and color. The (x,y) position is the position of the anchor point. The parameters to be passed are:

  • the String to be drawn
  • zero-based index of first character in the substring
  • length of the substring
  • the x coordinate of the anchor point
  • the y coordinate of the anchor point
  • the anchor point for positioning the text

The method can throw java.lang.ArrayIndexOutOfBoundException.

- **drawChar:** A new method in addition to the `drawChars` method. It draws only the specified character using the current font and color. You have to specify the character, the x and y positions of the anchor point, and the anchor point itself.

- **drawChars:** A method similar to that in J2SE, but with an additional parameter for the anchor point. It draws the specified characters using the current font and color. The signature is:

```
drawChars(char[] data, int offset, int length, int x,
int y, int anchor)
```

- **drawImage:** A simplified version of `drawImage` methods in J2SE. Only one constructor is available. It draws the specified image by using the anchor point. The image can be drawn in different positions relative to the anchor point by passing the appropriate position constants. The signature of this method is:

```
drawImage(Image img, int x, int y, int anchor)
```

Class List

This class is used to add selectable objects to the UI of your application. It is quite similar in nature and behavior to the `ChoiceGroup` class in J2SE. One of the differences is that the `choiceType` parameter can have an additional value `IMPLICIT`, which allows handling of events generated by the user selecting a choice. The methods used with this class are also just the implementations of the methods in the interface `Choice`:

- `getSize`
- `getString`
- `getImage`
- `appendElement`
- `insertElement`
- `deleteElement`
- `setElement`
- `isSelected`
- `getSelectedIndex`
- `getSelectedFlags`
- `setSelectedIndex`
- `setSelectedFlags`

We use the List class here to create menu of choices. Just as action is taken when you select an item in the menu, selecting a choice item in the `List` will notify the application:

```
// Declaring a variable of the type List..
List menu = null;
// Initializing the variable ...
// Parameter 1 --- Label of the List.
// Parameter 2 --- List Type IMPLICIT. (Selection by scrolling)

  menu = new List("Various Options..",List.IMPLICIT);

// Adding the List Items..
// Parameter 1 --- Label.
// Parameter 2 --- Image if required.

  menu.append("TextField",null);
```

```
  menu.append("Ticker",null);
  menu.append("Alert",null);

// Adding action Listener to the List..

  menu.setCommandListener(this);

// Making it the current Display.

  display.setCurrent(menu);

// Handling the events on the List.
 public void commandAction(Command c, Displayable d)
{
   List down = (List)display.getCurrent();
   switch(down.getSelectedIndex()) {
   case 0: System.out.println ("Text Field...");
           break;
   case 1: System.out.println ("Ticker...");
           break;
   case 2: System.out.println("Alert...");
           break;
}
}
```

Class StringItem

This class can be used to add `Strings` to a `Form`, just as `ImageItem` could be used to add `Images`. You have to specify the label of the item and the text to be added:

- ◆ `getText`
- ◆ `setText`

A simple use of the `StringItem` class is shown here:

```
// Declaring variable for StringItem class.
StringItem string_item = null;
// Initializing the variable

// parameter 1 .. Label to be displayed
// parameter 1 .. Text along with the Label.

string_item = new StringItem("User Entered ..", "");


// Adding String item to the form (place holder)
ui_holder.append(string_item);


// Changing the Textual context of the StringItem

  string_item.setText(textcheck.getString());
```

Class TextField

This is a class to represent a standard text field so that the user can enter text into it. The parameters required are the label, the initial text, the maximum size, and the input constraints. The concept of input constraints is common to TextField and TextBox. These constraints are meant to restrict the user's input so that only that input that is relevant to the purpose of the TextField is allowed. For example, if the NUMERIC constraint is used on a TextField, the implementation has to ensure that only numerals can be entered.

The constraints can be any of the following:

- TextField.ANY: User is allowed to enter any text.
- TextField.EMAILADDR: User is allowed to enter e-mail address.
- TextField.PASSWORD: Text entered is invisible.
- TextField.PHONENUMBER: For entering telephone numbers in the proper format.

The methods you can use with this class are:

- getString
- setString
- getChars
- setChars
- getSize
- setSize
- getConstraints
- setConstraints

In the following code, we add a TextField to a Form:

```
// Declaring a variable of the type TextField
 TextField textcheck = null;

 textcheck = new TextField("Enter the Text Here..","",50,0);

// Adding TextField to the form (place holder)
  ui_holder.append(textcheck);

// Event Handling..

public void commandAction(Command c, Displayable d) {
// Event handling for the Button
  if ( c == ok )
  {
    System.out.println(textcheck.getString());
  }
 }
```

Class TextBox

This class creates an object that is similar to a TextField object, but one difference is that a TextBox is not an Item that has to be added to a Form. Rather, it is a component that can be directly added to a Screen. The methods available are:

- getString
- setString
- getChars

- ◆ setChars
- ◆ getSize
- ◆ setSize
- ◆ getConstraints
- ◆ setConstraints

Following is some code that creates a `TextBox` object named `ourBox`, with some initial text:

```
String s = "Hello From J2ME";
...
private Display ourDisplay;  // Declaring the display
private Form ourForm = null;
...
ourDisplay = Display.getDisplay(this);
...
ourForm = new Form("Our First");
TextBox ourBox = new TextBox("J2ME Application", s, 256, 0);
ourForm.append(ourBox);
...
ourForm.setListener(this);

ourDisplay.setCurrent(ourForm);
```

Class Ticker

The class `Ticker` provides a way to show some horizontally scrolling text on the display, somewhat like a marquee in HTML. The text `String` is passed as parameter. Its methods are:

- ◆ setString
- ◆ getString

It is not very difficult to use this class, as you can see from the following code:

```
// Initializing the Ticker.
// Parameter 1  ..  Text For the Ticker.

ui_ticker = new Ticker("..This is an Example of a Ticker User Interface..");

// Adding Ticker to the Form.
  ui_holder.setTicker(ui_ticker);
```

Persistence Package

The Mobile Information Device Profile gives you a mechanism to persistently store data and later retrieve it. This persistent storage mechanism is modeled after a simple record-oriented database and is called the Record Management System. The package it is contained in is named `javax.microedition.rms`. The only class in this package is the `RecordStore` class. In addition, there are four interfaces. These interfaces and their methods are listed as follows:

- ◆ **RecordComparator:** To compare and sort record in the `RecordStore`. It has only one method: `Compare`.

- **RecordEnumeration:** To maintain the sequence of records and to iterate over them during sorting or searching operations. Its methods are:
  - numRecords
  - nextRecord
  - nextRecordId
  - previousRecord
  - previousRecordId
  - hasNextElement
  - hasPreviousElement
  - reset
  - rebuild
  - keepUpdated
  - isKeptUpdated
  - destroy
- **RecordFilter:** To check whether a given record meets some condition. It can be used for searching or for creating subsets of RecordSets. The only method available is matches.
- **RecordListener:** This is the interface that can be used for listening to events generated when records are changed, added, or deleted. The methods it has are:
  - recordAdded
  - recordChanged
  - recordDeleted

Class RecordStore

The only class of this package – it is used to represent a collection of records in a device database. These records remain persistent even when another MIDlet is started or even when the device is rebooted or the battery is changed. Following are some points to note when dealing with record stores using MIDP:

- You can manipulate only the MIDlet suite's own record stores. There is no way to share records between MIDlets in different suites.
- In accordance with the Java convention, record store names are case sensitive and may consist of any combination of up to 32 unicode characters. They have to be unique in a given MIDlet suite.
- If you use more than one thread in a MIDlet, you have to coordinate this access yourself.
- Records are uniquely identified within a given record store by their recordId, which is an integer value and is used as the primary key. The recordId of the first record created in a record store will be 1.
- The record store keeps track of an integer representing a version. This version number is incremented for each operation that changes the contents of the record store.

The methods available with this class are:

- openRecordStore
- closeRecordStore
- listRecordStores
- deleteRecordStore
- getName

- getVersion
- getNumRecords
- getSize
- getSizeAvailable
- getLastModified
- addRecordListener
- removeRecordListener
- getNextRecordID
- addRecord
- deleteRecord
- getRecordSize
- getRecord
- setRecord
- enumerateRecords

In the following code block, we define a method called read_record, which reads the contents of an XML file and then adds the parsed values to a RecordStore. For this, it calls another method record_add defined after the read_record. This method is used in our Mobile Web Services project in Chapter 10. Most of the code here is to handle the reading and parsing of the XML file contents, but it may help you in getting an idea about the practical use of RecordStore class. You will be able to understand the following code if you also refer to Chapter 10 briefly. The RecordStore class gives you many methods for managing the device database. We have used only a few of these, but once you are able to use these, it may be easier to use others. For an even better illustration of the use of this class, see the case study named *AddressBook* later in this chapter.

```
void read_record()
 {
   int k, id;
   String state = "", data = "";
   boolean founditem = false, foundstate = false;
 try
   {
   /*  Opens RecordStore for insertion of records */
   recordStore = RecordStore.openRecordStore("addresses", true);
     }
   catch(RecordStoreException rse)
   {
       rse.printStackTrace();
     }

// Start of XML handling part...
   do
   {
    try
    {
     /* Events generated by the parser while parsing XML file */

     event = parser.read ();

     /* Type of event generated while parsing XML File */
     if(event.getType()==Xml.START_TAG)
```

```
      {
        StartTag stag = (StartTag)event;
        if(stag.getName().equals("weather"))
        {
         founditem = true;
        }
        if(stag.getName().equals("state"))
        {
         foundstate = true;
        }
      }
      if(event.getType()== Xml.TEXT)
      {
       TextEvent tevent = (TextEvent)event;
       if(foundstate)
       {
        state =  tevent.getText();
        data = data+"?"+state;
        foundstate = false;
       }
       else
       {
        data = data+"?"+ tevent.getText();
       }
      }

      if(event.getType()==Xml.END_TAG)
      {
       EndTag etag = (EndTag)event;
       if(etag.getName().equals("weather"))
       {
       data = data+"?";
       founditem = false;
// End of XML handling part

       /* Calling the method for insertion of record into the database */
       id = record_add(data);

       /* insertion of record into the hashtable */

       htable.put((Object)state, Integer.toString(id));

       data = "";
      }
     }
    }
...
   }
  while (!(event instanceof EndDocument));
  try
  {
   /*  Closes  RecordStore after insertion of records */
         recordStore.closeRecordStore();
  }
  catch(RecordStoreException rse)
  {
```

```
  rse.printStackTrace();
 }


}
```

The method `record_add` defined next is meant to add records to a store, as the name suggests:

```
/* Function for record addition...*/
int record_add(String data)
{
 int i = 0;
 try
 {
  byte b[] = data.getBytes();
  i = recordStore.addRecord(b,0, b.length);
 }
 catch (RecordStoreException rse)
 {
        rse.printStackTrace();
 }
 return i ;
}
```

The method given next deletes the whole `RecordStore`:

```
/* Method for deletion of records from the Recordstore   */
void deleterecords()
{
 try
 {
  System.out.println(" Test Before Delete ");
  recordStore.deleteRecordStore("addresses");
  System.out.println(" Test After Delete ");
 }
 catch (RecordStoreException rse)
 {
        rse.printStackTrace();
 }

}
```

Exceptions in Persistance Package

The exceptions in this package are listed as follows:

- `InvalidRecordIDException`
- `RecordStoreException`
- `RecordStoreFullException`
- `RecordStoreNotFoundException`
- `RecordStoreNotOpenException`

Installation of MIDP and Running Applications

Installation of MIDP is as simple as that of CLDC. You just have to download the zip archive and unzip it in any directory of your choice. After that, you are ready to run the sample applications shipped along with the MIDP Early Access Release. These are mainly games and simple MIDlets to make you familiar with the use of basic features of MIDP. Of course, you should have JDK1.3 installed on your system if you want to compile the source code. The tool to be used for running applications is the simulator provided in the form an executable named `midp.exe`. If you just go to the directory containing this tool and type **midp** at the command prompt, the simulator will start, although it will not run any application. For that, you have to give it the location of the libraries you click the Open Project button and select the application you want to run.

The sample applications are in the form a JAR archive. If you are using Windows 95/98/2000, you can make a `run.bat` file, as given in the following code, to run these applications. Doing this will open a menu showing the list of applications. Note that `sokoban.zip` is the archive in which boards for various levels of the Sokoban game have been stored.

run.bat

```
@echo off

rem This file runs the example.jad/jar file in the emulator.
set CLASSPATH=lib\midp.jar;lib\examples.jar;
        src\example\sokoban\sokoban.zip
bin\midp -descriptor run.jad
```

When you write your own applications, you can change the classpath according to the directory where you store your source files.

For compiling and preverifying, you can add commands to the batch file listed in the preceding code. The commands will be similar to those used in CLDC; you just have to use relevant classpaths. Note that the MIDP APIs are available in the JAR archive `midp.jar`. You can extract these if you like. In order to give you a better idea about the whole process of compiling, preverifying, jarring, jadding (jadding is creating an application descriptor which is required by the midp.exe to execute the application), and running MIDlets and MIDlet suites, we are giving in the following section the code for a longer sample batch file.

This file takes a command line argument called `%name%` that signifies the name of your application, in this case, the sample MIDlets. We have used the same name for the directory in which the source files, the manifest (`example.mf`), the application descriptor (`example.jad`), and the JAR archive (`example.jar`) are placed. If you want different names for these files and directories, you can use more command line arguments, but a single name is more convenient if you are careful about the directories and the classpath. The benefit of using such a batch file is that it gives you the option of executing or skipping each command. This way, you can try to fix things in one of the commands by just skipping the rest.

Obviously, the name of the batch file and also its content — except the Java files — are not case sensitive. Also, the indented lines are a continuation of the preceding lines — that is, if you type them on the console, you have to type them without pressing the Enter key. Before being able to run applications, you have to prepare the manifest and the application descriptor, describing the MIDlet. The contents of these will include attributes mentioned MIDlet Suites section earlier in this chapter.

Some other things should be noted with respect to the commands used in the batch file. Unlike previous files, we are compiling, verifying, jarring, and jadding the source files given in the `src` directory. Earlier, we had just used the JAR archive provided with the release. This seems to create a problem in the preverifying tool (`preverify.exe`) in Windows 98 (which was tried) in that it is unable to do its job on specifying `midp.jar` in the classpath. One workaround tried was to unjar the MIDP API and specify the name of the directory in the classpath — only for preverification, because there is no problem in compiling or running with the JAR file. Also, the preverifying tool in the MIDP release was replaced with the one that came with the J2ME Wireless Toolkit. It worked as far as preverifying goes, but the emulator crashed sometimes while running the sample MIDlets.

sample.bat

Code for sample.bat is described here:

```
@echo off
rem This file compiles, preverifies, and runs the sample
        applications in the emulator.

set name=%1
shift
if "%name%"=="" goto :abort

echo Creating directories...

mkdir tmpclasses
mkdir classes
mkdir res

choice /c:ync /t:n,10 Do you want to compile?
if errorlevel 2 goto skipcompile

echo Compiling source files...

rem Replace or change classpaths according to the locations on your disk...

javac -bootclasspath lib\midp.jar -d tmpclasses
        -classpath tmpclasses src\%name%\*.java
javac -bootclasspath lib\midp.jar -d tmpclasses
        -classpath tmpclasses src\%name%\lcdui\*.java
javac -bootclasspath lib\midp.jar -d tmpclasses
        -classpath tmpclasses src\%name%\manyballs\*.java
javac -bootclasspath lib\midp.jar -d tmpclasses
        -classpath tmpclasses src\%name%\sokoban\*.java
javac -bootclasspath lib\midp.jar -d tmpclasses
        -classpath tmpclasses src\%name%\stock\*.java
javac -bootclasspath lib\midp.jar -d tmpclasses
        -classpath tmpclasses src\%name%\tiles\*.java

:skipcompile
choice /c:ync /t:n,10 Do you want to preverify?
if errorlevel 2 goto skippreverify

echo Verifying class files...
bin\preverify -classpath lib;tmpclasses -d classes tmpclasses

:skippreverify
choice /c:ync /t:n,10 Do you want to do jarring?
if errorlevel 2 goto skipjarring

echo Jarring verified class files...
jar cmf %name%.mf %name%.jar -C classes .

echo Jarring resource files...
jar umf %name%.mf %name%.jar -C res .

:skipjarring
choice /c:ync /t:n,10 Do you want to run the applications?
```

```
if errorlevel 2 goto skiprun

set CLASSPATH=lib\midp.jar;%name%.jar
bin\midp -classpath lib\midp.jar;%name%.jar;
        src\example\sokoban\sokoban.zip -descriptor %name%.jad
goto rundone

:skiprun
echo Skipping run.
goto rundone

:abort
echo Aborting now. Give application name to be run.

:rundone
```

example.jad

Code for example.bat is described here:

```
MIDlet-Name: SunSamples
MIDlet-Version: 1.0
MIDlet-Vendor: Sun Microsystems, Inc.
MIDlet-Description: Sample suite from MIDP early access workspace.
MicroEdition-Profile: MIDP-1.0
MicroEdition-Configuration: CLDC-1.0
MIDlet-1: Sokoban, /icons/Sokoban.gif, example.sokoban.Sokoban
MIDlet-2: Tickets, /icons/Auction.gif, TicketAuction
MIDlet-3: Colors, /icons/ColorChooser.gif, example.Color
MIDlet-4: Stock, /icons/Stock.gif, example.stock.StockMIDlet
MIDlet-5: Tiles, /icons/Tiles.gif, example.tiles.Tiles
MIDlet-6: ManyBalls, /icons/ManyBalls.gif, example.ManyBalls
MIDlet-7: Sampler, /icons/App.gif, Sampler
MIDlet-8: Properties, /icons/App.gif, example.PropExample
MIDlet-9: HttpTest, /icons/App.gif, example.HttpTest
```

You can also run MIDlet suites from a browser by configuring them to recognize the MIME type. For example, you can add the following types to Netscape Communicator. Then, if you open the application descriptor — say, `example.jad` — the browser will run it for you. At least this is what Sun's documentation says. When this was tried on Windows 98 with Netscape, either there was no response or the system halted. With IE, the system did not halt but the browser did nothing.

```
Description: MIDP app descriptor
MIME Type: text/vnd.sun.j2me.app-descriptor
Extension: jad
Application: D:\DTP\J2ME\Download\j2me_midp-1_0-ea1-win\midp-
   ea1\bin\midp.exe -transient file://%1
```

J2ME Wireless Toolkit

You may be wondering at this stage whether it is not possible to do compilation, etc., without having to bother with giving classpaths and writing a batch file. There is indeed a much easier way to do all this with J2ME Wireless Toolkit. It provides you three ways of developing your applications:

♦ With KToolbar, you can perform, build, and run operations using a simple graphical user interface.

- With J2ME Wireless Module — a plug-in for Forte for Java —you can use the development environment of Forte while developing J2ME applications.

- You also have the option to operate from command line if you don't like to work with graphical user interfaces or if you want to do something so advanced that it needs special options to be specified at the command line.

Note that this toolkit is meant for MIDP only and not for other profiles — not so far, at least.

You download the J2ME Wireless Toolkit from Sun's product page just as you can download CLDC and MIDP implementations. You will, of course, need JDK before you can use it. If you want to use it with Forte, you will also need to download Forte for Java from Sun's site from the URL `http://www.sun.com/forte/ffj/ce`. A newer version of this toolkit, numbered 1.0.1, is now available. As far as an ordinary user will be able to make out, it just has the design of its emulated devices changed.

J2ME Wireless Toolkit includes everything you need to develop applications. It includes the preverifier, the MIDP libraries, MIDP documentation, an emulator to run MIDlets, and even the sample applications that are available with MIDP release. Moreover, to perform build and run operations from command line, batch files are provided.

There are in fact several emulators included with the toolkit. The emulator gives you the choice to test your applications on a default gray phone, default color phone, minimum phone, and even a pager. The emulator also supplies runtime logging of various events, including method tracing, garbage collection, class loading and exceptions thrown. Thus you can trace the execution of an application. The limitations of the emulator are that it does not emulate the application management and speed of execution. The latter means that the application may execute at a different speed on the actual device for which it is meant.

Operation of the KToolbar is quite simple. It can be started from the Start button on Windows. You have to first create a new project and give it a name, as well as specify the MIDlet class name. After this, a directory will be created with the same name as the one you give for the project. It will contain three subdirectories (`bin`, `res`, and `src`). You then have to put the source code you wrote in the `src` directory. When you hit the Build button, the application will be compiled and preverified. To run it, you have to just hit the Run button. Before running the application, you can choose the device on which you want to see it run. There are four choices, as mentioned previously.

For more information about this toolkit, you can read the user guide included in the download.

MIDP for Palm

MIDP is now not restricted to mobile phones and pagers. You can even use it on Palm devices. This means that Palm devices can now take advantage of this profile instead being restricted to a configuration (CLDC) and a temporary arrangement such as KJava for providing a user interface. Sun has released its implementation of MIDP for Palm OS, which allows you to convert MIDlets into `prc` files so that they can run on Palm devices.

This release, too, is available for download from Sun's site in the form of a zip archive. This can be unzipped into any directory — say, the same one in which you unzipped MIDP. On unzipping, a subdirectory (`midp4palm`) will be formed, which contains the following:

- Java Manager executable file

- Test applications

- Demo applications and games

- A sample multi-application bundle

- Utilities

Files converted by this implementation can be run on any device running Palm OS 3.5 or later and with at least 4 MB of total memory. The release has some limitations:

♦ There is a limit of around 20K pixels on the maximum size of image. A typical maximum image size is 200 by 98 pixels.

♦ There is a known problem in Palm OS 3.5 with the HTTP Post command. If you are not connected to the palm.net site, the command will send only the HTTP headers, not the Post data. As a workaround, use HTTP's Get command instead of Post whenever possible.

We will be looking at how to use this release when we discuss J2ME implementations for Palm devices later in the book. Figures 4-1 through 4-8 detail class hierarchy.

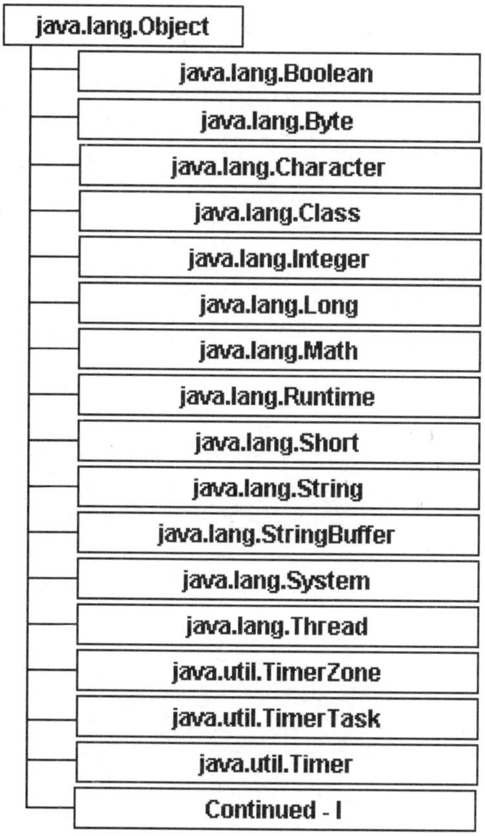

```
java.lang.Object
    ├── java.lang.Boolean
    ├── java.lang.Byte
    ├── java.lang.Character
    ├── java.lang.Class
    ├── java.lang.Integer
    ├── java.lang.Long
    ├── java.lang.Math
    ├── java.lang.Runtime
    ├── java.lang.Short
    ├── java.lang.String
    ├── java.lang.StringBuffer
    ├── java.lang.System
    ├── java.lang.Thread
    ├── java.util.TimerZone
    ├── java.util.TimerTask
    ├── java.util.Timer
    └── Continued - I
```

Figure 4-1: MIDPClass Hierarchy - I.

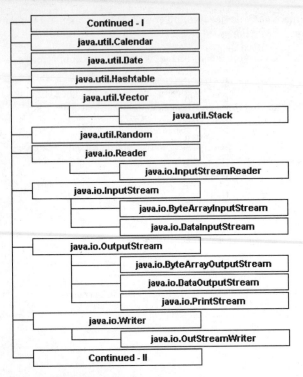

Figure 4-2: MIDPClass Hierarchy - II.

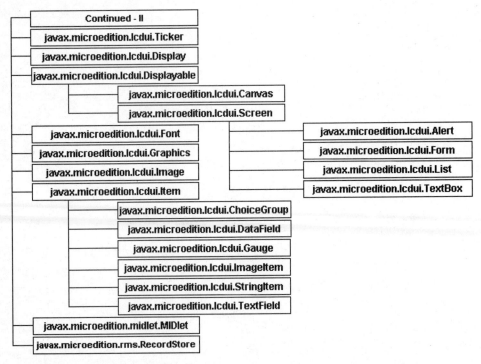

Figure 4-3: Output MIDPClass Hierarchy - III.

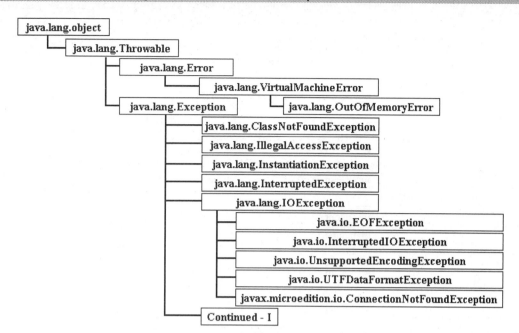

Figure 4-4: MIDP Error and Exception Hierarchy - I.

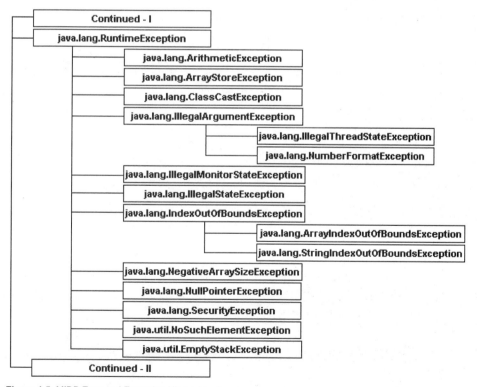

Figure 4-5: MIDP Error and Exception Hierarchy - II.

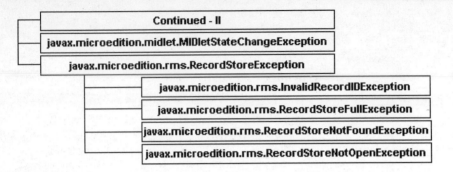

Figure 4-6: MIDP Error and Exception Hierarchy - III.

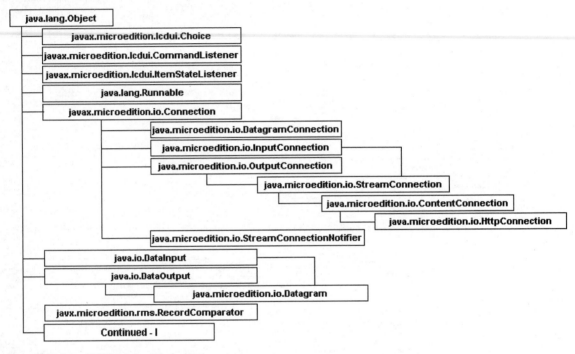

Figure 4-7: Output MIDP Interface Hierarchy - I.

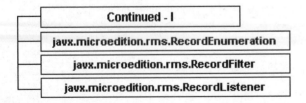

Figure 4-8: MIDP Interface Hierarchy - II.

Case Studies

This section is on case studies developed using MIDP APIs. The case studies covers important GUI classes and also makes use of HTTP connection.

TextFieldCheck

Our first example of an MIDP application is a simple MIDlet to demonstrate the use of a `TextField`. You can use it in several classes and methods that are required in most MIDlets. These include, especially, the class MIDlet (which has to be used in every MIDlet) and the methods of this class for managing the life cycle of a MIDlet (such as `startApp`, `pauseApp`, and `destroyApp`). You can run this application in J2ME Wireless Toolkit as explained previously. On starting the MIDlet, the user sees a screen displaying the name of the MIDlet. On selecting it, the user is shown a `TextField` in which he can enter any text. After he has done this, he can press the OK button. Upon this, a message is displayed that the user has successfully entered whatever was required refer to Figure 4-9 to view the Output. Of course, the "button" is just a label above the actual button of the mobile phone. The top-right button is used as an OK button, and the top-left button is used as an Exit button.

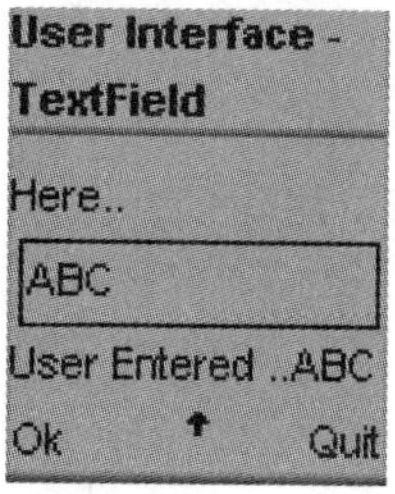

User Interface - TextField

Here..

ABC

User Entered ..ABC

Ok   ↑   Quit

Figure 4-9: Output TextFieldCheck.

To add the UI component `TextField`, we first create a `Form` in this MIDlet and then add the component to it. In addition to the `TextField`, there are buttons on this form to allow the user to indicate that he has finished typing in the `TextField` and to allow him to quit. These buttons are created by implementing the class `Command`. For event handling, `CommandListener` is used. We have to implement this interface to define what will be the behavior of the application when the user presses the button. This is done by using a simple `if` block.

Note that in using the `pauseApp` and `destroyApp` methods, all items have to be assigned `null` values.

Listing 4-1: TextFieldCheck.java

```java
import javax.microedition.midlet.*;
import javax.microedition.io.*;
import javax.microedition.lcdui.*;

/** A program to demonstrate how a TextField works on a handheld
 * device. The program gives a feel of how a TextField works by
 * putting the text taken from a TextField on to the StringItem.
 */


public class TextFieldCheck extends MIDlet implements
        CommandListener {

  // Declaring variable for Display class.
        private Display display = null;
```

```java
        // Declaring variable for StringItem class.
        StringItem string_item = null;

// Declaring variable for Form class.
Form ui_holder = null;

// Declaring variables for Buttons in the UI.
Command ok = null;
Command quit = null;

        // Declaring variable for the TextField.
TextField textcheck = null;

public TextFieldCheck() {

  // Initializing the Display
    display = Display.getDisplay(this);
    // Initializing the Buttons
    ok = new Command("Ok",Command.SCREEN,3);
    quit = new Command("Quit",Command.SCREEN,2);
  }

public void startApp(){
  ui_holder = new Form("User Interface - TextField");

  // Initializing the Form
  textcheck = new TextField("Enter the Text Here..","",50,0);

  string_item = new StringItem("User Entered ..", "");

  // Adding TextField to the form (place holder)
  ui_holder.append(textcheck);

// Adding Stringitem to the form (place holder)
ui_holder.append(string_item);

// Adding Command Button to the Form
  ui_holder.addCommand(ok);

            // Adding Command Button to the Form
            ui_holder.addCommand(quit);

  // Invoking Action Listener
  ui_holder.setCommandListener(this);

 /*
 * Making the Display Current so that it can show
 * the Form.
 */
display.setCurrent(ui_holder);
  }

  public void pauseApp() {
    string_item = null;
    ui_holder = null;
    textcheck = null;
```

```
  }

  public void destroyApp(boolean condition) {
    string_item = null;
    ui_holder = null;
    textcheck = null;

    // Destroy the form...
    notifyDestroyed();
  }

  public void commandAction(Command c, Displayable d) {
// Event handling for the Button
    if ( c == ok ) {
      string_item.setText(textcheck.getString());
    }
    if ( c == quit ) {
      destroyApp(true);
    }
  }
} // End of TextFieldCheck class.
```

LabelUI

The next MIDlet is about putting some text on the screen to serve as a label. This is done here in two ways. First, a string `User Interface - Label` is passed as parameter to a `Form` named `ui_holder`. Then another string `A simple Label...` is added to the `Form` by calling the `append` method. The first string can be considered the title and the second can be the description as shown in Figure 4-10.

```
User Interface -
Label

A simple Label..
Example of a String
Item....Hello World
Label
       ◆       Ok
```

Figure 4-10: Output LabelUI.

In the second way of doing a similar thing, two strings are passed as parameters to a `StringItem`, the first of which serves as a label for the second. Then this `StringItem` is added to the `Form`, again by calling the `append` method. There is an `OK` command so that the user can indicate that he has completed viewing the text.

Again note that all items have to be assigned `null` values in `pauseApp` and `destroyApp` methods.

Listing 4-2: LabelUI.java

```
import javax.microedition.midlet.*;
import javax.microedition.io.*;
import javax.microedition.lcdui.*;

/** A program to demonstrate how Labels work on a handheld
 * device. The program gives a feel of both types of
 * Labels, i.e. a standard Label and a StringItem.
 */
```

```
public class LabelUI extends MIDlet implements
        CommandListener {

        // Declaring variables for Display class.
 private Display display = null;

 // Declaring variables for StringItem class.
 StringItem string_item = null;

 // Declaring variables for Form class.
 Form ui_holder = null;

 // Declaring variables for Buttons.
 Command ok = null;

 public LabelUI() {
   // Initializing the Display
display = Display.getDisplay(this);
ok = new Command("Ok",Command.SCREEN,3);
 }

 public void startApp() {
// Initializing the Form.
   ui_holder = new Form("User Interface - Label");

// Adding a simple label to the Form.
   ui_holder.append("A simple Label...");
string_item = new StringItem("Example of a String
Item....", "Hello World Label");

// Adding StringItem to the form (place holder).
   ui_holder.append(string_item);

// Adding Command Button to the Form.
ui_holder.addCommand(ok);

// Invoking Action Listener..
ui_holder.setCommandListener(this);

/* Making the Display Current so that it can show
 * the Form.
 */
   display.setCurrent(ui_holder);
 }

 public void pauseApp() {
   string_item = null;
   ui_holder = null;
 }

 public void destroyApp(boolean condition) {
   string_item = null;
   ui_holder = null;

// Destroy the form.
```

```
        notifyDestroyed();
            }

    public void commandAction(Command c, Displayable d) {

    // Event handling for the Button.
      if ( c == ok ) {
        destroyApp(true);
      }
    }
} // End of LabelUI class.
```

ChoiceGroupUI

This MIDP application shows how you can put the equivalent of radio buttons and check boxes on the UI of a MIDlet. The class responsible for both these in MIDP is ChoiceGroup. It is only the value of the parameter choiceType that determines whether the ChoiceGroup elements will act as radio buttons or check boxes. The three types of ChoiceGroups are EXCLUSIVE, MULTIPLE, or IMPLICIT.

The label for the whole ChoiceGroup is set by passing the value of the label parameter as Choices. Text labels for the elements of a ChoiceGroup are added by passing the stringElements parameter with a value equal to a string array containing the labels. Since in this case we wanted no images, we have set the value of the imageElements as null. All the elements are added to the Form by calling the append method as before.

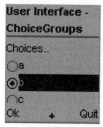

Figure 4-11: Output ChoiceGroupUI - I.

Figure 4-12: Output ChoiceGroupUI – II.

When the user makes his choices and presses the OK button, the commandAction is used for event handling. For this event handler, if blocks and a for loop are used. As a result of this, the user is shown a message reporting the choices made by him as shown in Figure 4-11 and Figure 4-12. He can get out of the application by pressing the Quit button.

Listing 4-3: ChoiceGroupUI.java

```
import javax.microedition.midlet.*;
import javax.microedition.io.*;
import javax.microedition.lcdui.*;
```

```java
/** A program to demostrate how a ChoiceGroup works on a
 * handheld device.
 */

public class ChoiceGroupUI extends MIDlet
        implements CommandListener {

        // Declaring variable for the Display class.
 private Display display = null;

        // Declaring variables for the ChoiceGroup.
 ChoiceGroup radiobutton_type = null;
        ChoiceGroup checkbox_type = null;

        // Declaring variables for the StringItem class.
 StringItem string_item1 = null;
        StringItem string_item2 = null;

        // Declaring variables for the Form class.
 Form ui_holder = null;

        // Declaring variables for Buttons.
 Command ok = null;
        Command quit = null;

        String[] name = {"a","b","c"};
 String[] name1 = {"d","e","f"};

 Image[] img = null;
 boolean[] values = null;

 public ChoiceGroupUI() {
// Initializing the Display.
  display = Display.getDisplay(this);

// Initializing the Button.
 ok = new Command("Ok",Command.SCREEN,3);
quit = new Command("Quit",Command.SCREEN,2);
}

 public void startApp() {
// Initializing the Form.
  ui_holder = new Form("User Interface - ChoiceGroups");

  // Initializing the Choice groups.
  radiobutton_type = new ChoiceGroup("Choices..",
ChoiceGroup.EXCLUSIVE,name,img);
  string_item1 = new StringItem("User Clicked   ","");

  checkbox_type = new ChoiceGroup("Choices..",
ChoiceGroup.MULTIPLE,name1,img);

// Getting the values the user clicked.
  string_item2 = new StringItem("User Clicked   ","");

// Adding StringItem to the form (place holder).
```

```
   ui_holder.append(radiobutton_type);
   ui_holder.append(string_item1);
   ui_holder.append(checkbox_type);
   ui_holder.append(string_item2);

// Adding Command Button to the Form.
   ui_holder.addCommand(ok);
   ui_holder.addCommand(quit);

   // Invoking Action Listener.
   ui_holder.setCommandListener(this);

/* Making the Display Current so that it can show
 * the Form.
 */
   display.setCurrent(ui_holder);
 }

 public void pauseApp() {
   string_item1= null;
   string_item2= null;

   ui_holder = null;
   radiobutton_type = null;
   checkbox_type = null;
 }

 public void destroyApp(boolean condition) {
   string_item1= null;
   string_item2= null;

   ui_holder = null;
   radiobutton_type = null;
   checkbox_type = null;

// Destroy the form.
   notifyDestroyed();
 }

 public void commandAction(Command c, Displayable d) {
// Event handling for the Button.
   if ( c == ok ) {
     String temp = "";
 string_item1.setText(
radiobutton_type.getString(
radiobutton_type.getSelectedIndex()));
     for (int i=0;i<3 ;i++ ) {
       boolean val1 = checkbox_type.isSelected(i);
       if (val1) {
         temp = temp+name1[i];
       }
     }
     string_item2.setText(temp);
   }
   if ( c == quit ) {
     destroyApp(true);
```

```
   }
  }
} // End of TextFieldCheck class.
```

TickerUI

This is a simple MIDlet, showing the use of the `Ticker` class. It basically shows the user some scrolling text — somewhat like a marquee in HTML. The `Ticker` has to be passed some string as the parameter. This string will be shown scrolling horizontally on the screen as in Figure 4-13. But before it happens, you have to call the `setTicker` method and pass the name of the `Ticker` object as an argument to this method. Note that we are not using the `append` method as we did in previous examples. There is an OK button for the user to indicate that the user has had enough of the `Ticker`.

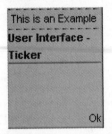

Figure 4-13: Output TickerUI.

Listing 4-4: TickerUI.java

```java
import javax.microedition.midlet.*;
import javax.microedition.io.*;
import javax.microedition.lcdui.*;

/** A program to demostrate how a "Ticker" works on a
 * handheld device.
 */

public class TickerUI extends MIDlet
        implements CommandListener {

// Declaring variables for Display class.
 private Display display = null;

// Declaring variables for Form class.
Form ui_holder = null;

// Declaring variables for Buttons.
Command ok = null;

// Declaring variables for Ticker in the UI.
 Ticker ui_ticker = null;
 public TickerUI() {
// Initializing the Display.
   display = Display.getDisplay(this);

// Initializing the Command Button.
 ok = new Command("Ok",Command.SCREEN,3);
 }

 public void startApp() {
```

```
// Initializing the Form.
ui_holder = new Form("User Interface - Ticker");

// Initializing the Ticker.
 ui_ticker = new Ticker("..This is an Example of a
Ticker User Interface..");

// Adding Ticker to the Form.
   ui_holder.setTicker(ui_ticker);

// Adding Command Button to the Form.
ui_holder.addCommand(ok);

// Invoking Action Listener.
ui_holder.setCommandListener(this);

/* Making the Display Current so that it can show
 * the Form.
 */
   display.setCurrent(ui_holder);
}

 public void pauseApp() {
  ui_holder = null;
  ui_ticker = null;
 }

 public void destroyApp(boolean condition) {
  ui_holder = null;
  ui_ticker = null;

// Destroy the form.
notifyDestroyed();
 }

 public void commandAction(Command c, Displayable d) {
// Event handling for the Button.
  if ( c == ok ) {
   destroyApp(true);
  }
 }
} // End of TickerUI.
```

MenuCheck

Now we present a more advanced application. This is a very useful MIDlet, since it shows how a menu can be created with MIDP. The class used for this is List. Just as in the case of ChoiceGroup, there can be three types of Lists: IMPLICIT, EXCLUSIVE, and MULTIPLE. We use the first variety here, as this will perhaps be the most used in applications. For this variety, we don't have to attach application-defined commands — it is enough to register CommandListener that is called when the user makes a selection.

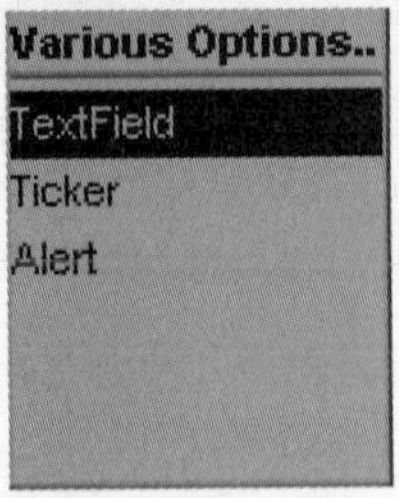

Various Options..

TextField
Ticker
Alert

Figure 4-14: Output MenuCheck - I.

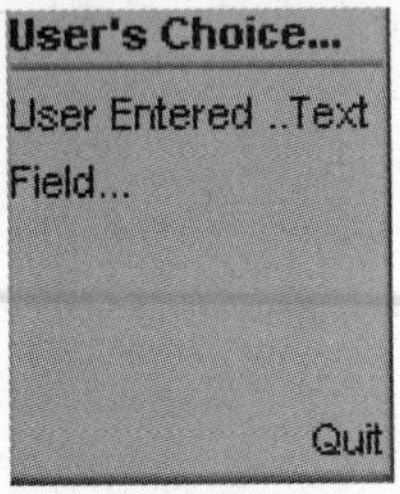

User's Choice...

User Entered ..Text
Field...

Quit

Figure 4-15: Output MenuCheck - II.

We begin building a menu by adding elements to a List by calling the append method. The other important thing to do is to implement the commandAction method of the CommandListener class. We do this by using the switch block to determine what the user will get when he selects an entry on the menu. In our case, the user sees a message (as in Figure 4-15) describing the selection he made. Needless to say, there is a Quit button here as well, since we don't want to lock in the user.

Listing 4- 5: MenuCheck.java

```java
import javax.microedition.midlet.*;
import javax.microedition.io.*;
import javax.microedition.lcdui.*;

/** A program to check how a Menu works on a handheld.
 * The program gives a taste of how a Menu works by adding
 * various Alerts and TextFields on to it.
 */


public class MenuCheck extends MIDlet
        implements CommandListener {
 private Display display = null;
 Command ok = null;
 Command quit = null;
 List menu = null;
 Form ui_form = null;
 StringItem si = null;

 public MenuCheck() {
             // Initializing the Display…
   display = Display.getDisplay(this);
   quit = new Command("Quit",Command.SCREEN,2);
 }

 public void startApp() {
   menu = new List("Various Options..",List.IMPLICIT);
```

```
menu.append("TextField",null);
menu.append("Ticker",null);
menu.append("Alert",null);

menu.setCommandListener(this);

display.setCurrent(menu);

ui_form = new Form("User's Choice...");
si = new StringItem("User Entered ..", "");
ui_form.append(si);

// Adding Command Button to the ui_form.
ui_form.addCommand(quit);

// Invoking Action Listener
ui_form.setCommandListener(this);
}

public void pauseApp() {
 menu = null;
}

public void destroyApp(boolean unconditional) {
 menu = null;
 notifyDestroyed();
}

public void commandAction(Command c, Displayable d) {
          // Event handling for the Button
  if ( c == quit ) {
    destroyApp(true);
  }
  else {
    List down = (List)display.getCurrent();
switch(down.getSelectedIndex()) {
case 0: si.setText("Text Field...");
break;
case 1: si.setText("Ticker...");
break;
case 2: si.setText("Alert...");
break;
    }
 display.setCurrent(ui_form);
  }
}
} // End of MenuCheck.
```

AddressBook

This is perhaps the most advanced application in this chapter. In a way, this MIDlet is an extension of the MenuCheck MIDlet. It doesn't just show some message when the user makes a selection. Rather, it goes on to add some real functionality by allowing the user to add records to an address book, search them, delete them, and moreover, to quit the application.

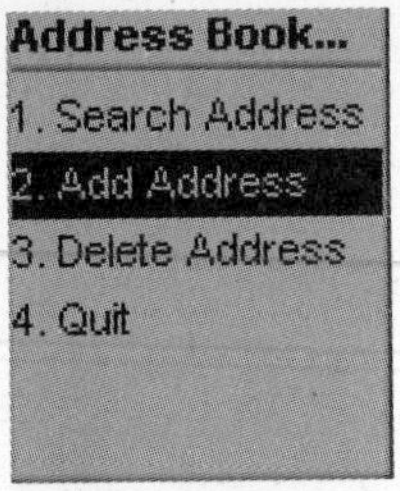

Address Book...
1. Search Address
2. Add Address
3. Delete Address
4. Quit

Figure 4-16: Output AddressBook - I.

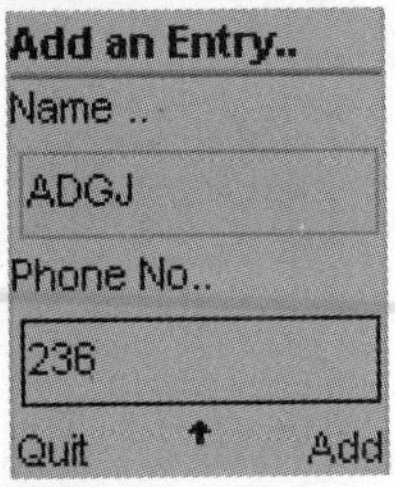

Add an Entry..
Name ..

ADGJ

Phone No..

236

Quit ↑ Add

Figure 4-17: Output AddressBook - II.

The menu is created in the same way as previously by using the `List` class and adding elements to it by calling the `append` method see Figure 4-16. This `List` is again of `IMPLICIT` type.

For adding entries to an address book (or for searching for and deleting them), you need to use database capability. This is where MIPD's persistence package and its `RecordStore` class are relevant. A `RecordStore` is opened by calling its `openRecordStore` method. Records are added to it by calling the `addRecord` method. When the user selects Add Address on the menu, he gets two `TextFields` in which he can type his name and telephone number, respectively as shown in Figure 4-17. The `getString` method is used on these `TextFields` to get the text user types. You can also see the use of `ByteArrayOuputStream`, `DataOutputStream`, and the `writeUTF` method.

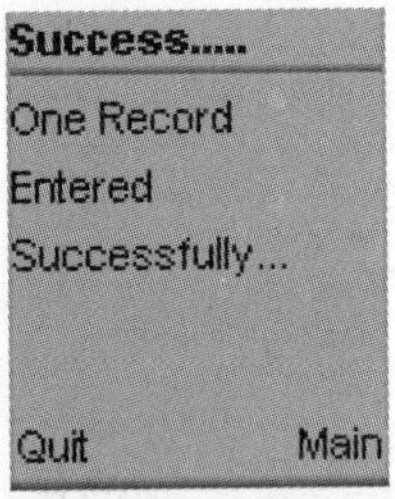

Success.....
One Record
Entered
Successfully...

Quit Main

Figure 4-18: Output AddressBook - III.

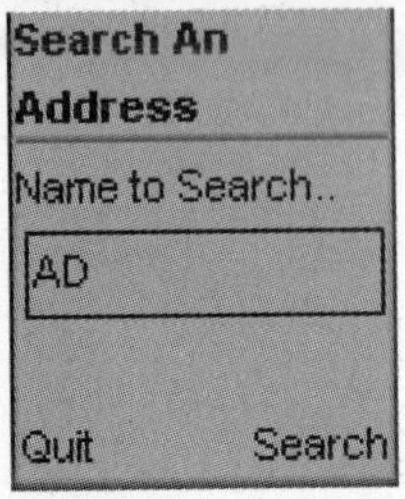

Search An
Address
Name to Search..

AD

Quit Search

Figure 4-19: Output AddressBook - IV.

For searching records, `enumerateRecords` method is used (Figure 4-19 shows how to search the record and Figure 4-20 displays the search results), along with `while` and `if` blocks. For deleting records(refer to Figures 4-21 and 4-22), `deleteRecord` method is used, in addition to the enumerateRecords method. Don't forget that nextRecord method makes you capable of going to the next record while enumerating.

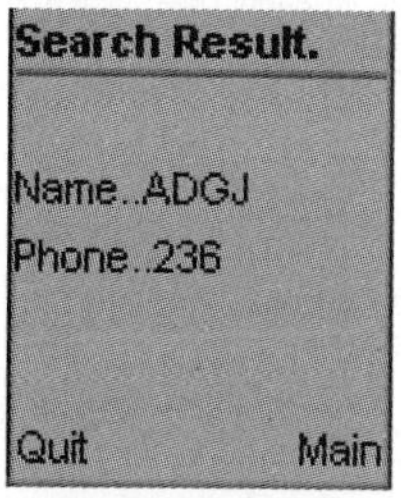

Search Result.

Name..ADGJ
Phone..236

Quit   Main

Figure 4-20: Output AddressBook - V.

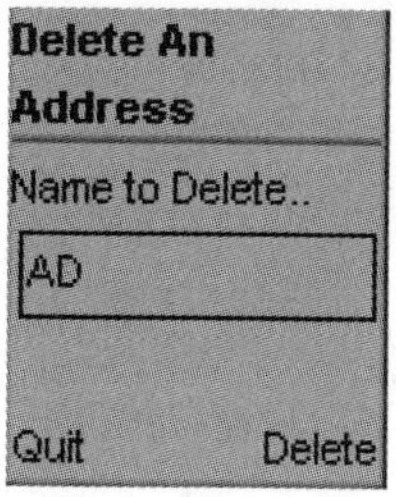

Delete An
Address

Name to Delete..

AD

Quit   Delete

Figure 4-21: Insert caption here Output AddressBook - VI.

Finally, calling the closeRecordStore method of the RecordStore class closes the database. But before proceeding to the next MIDlet, take note of the exceptions and try...catch blocks, as well as the switch block that is used for event handling in case of the main menu.

Delete Result..

The Record is not
Listed...

Quit   Main

Figure 4-22: Insert caption here Output AddressBook - VII.

Listing 4- 6: AddressBook.java

```java
import javax.microedition.midlet.*;
import javax.microedition.io.*;
import javax.microedition.lcdui.*;
import javax.microedition.rms.*;
import java.util.Enumeration;
import java.util.Vector;
import java.io.*;


/** A program to demonstrate how databases work on a handheld device
 * by creating an address book where you can add, search and
 * delete number/addresses.
 */

public class AddressBook extends MIDlet
        implements CommandListener {
```

```java
private Display display = null;
Command search = null;
Command quit = null;
Command delete = null;
Command addnow = null;
Command mainmenu = null;

// Declaring a Menu(List)
    List menu = null;
    Form ui_form = null;
StringItem si = null;

// TextField for storing the name...
TextField name = null;
TextField phone = null;

    // Declaring a RecordStore (Database)...
RecordStore recordStore = null;

public AddressBook() {
  display = Display.getDisplay(this);
  quit = new Command("Quit",Command.SCREEN,3);
  search = new Command("Search",Command.SCREEN,2);
  delete = new Command("Delete",Command.SCREEN,2);
  addnow = new Command("Add",Command.SCREEN,2);
  mainmenu = new Command("Main",Command.SCREEN,2);

// Initializing the Record Store
 try {
recordStore = RecordStore.openRecordStore(
"addresses", true);
}
catch(RecordStoreException rse) {
rse.printStackTrace();
}
}

 public void startApp() {
  menu = new List("Address Book...",List.IMPLICIT);
  menu.append("1. Search Address",null);
  menu.append("2. Add Address",null);
  menu.append("3. Delete Address",null);
  menu.append("4. Quit",null);

  menu.setCommandListener(this);
  display.setCurrent(menu);
 }

  // GUI for the Search Screen...
  void searchScreen() {
  ui_form = new Form("Search An Address");

  name =  new TextField("Name to Search..","",50,0);
  ui_form.append(name);

  ui_form.addCommand(search);
```

```
  ui_form.addCommand(quit);

  // Invoking Action Listener…
  ui_form.setCommandListener(this);

  display.setCurrent(ui_form);

 }

      // GUI for the Addition Screen...
 void addScreen() {
  ui_form = new Form("Add an Entry..");

  name =  new TextField("Name ..","",50,0);
  ui_form.append(name);

  phone =  new TextField("Phone No.. ","",50,0);
  ui_form.append(phone);

ui_form.addCommand(addnow);
ui_form.addCommand(quit);

  // Invoking Action Listener…
  ui_form.setCommandListener(this);

  display.setCurrent(ui_form);
 }

      // GUI for the Delete Screen...
 void deleteScreen() {
  ui_form = new Form("Delete An Address");

  name =  new TextField("Name to Delete..","",50,0);
  ui_form.append(name);

  ui_form.addCommand(delete);
  ui_form.addCommand(quit);

  // Invoking Action Listener…
  ui_form.setCommandListener(this);

  display.setCurrent(ui_form);
 }

 public void pauseApp() {
  menu = null;
 }

 public void destroyApp(boolean unconditional) {
  menu = null;
  notifyDestroyed();
 }

 public void commandAction(Command c, Displayable d) {
// Event handling for the Button…
  if ( c == quit ) {
```

```
    try {
                            close();
    }
    catch (RecordStoreException rse) {
                            rse.printStackTrace();
    }
    destroyApp(true);
  }
  else if (c == search) {
            // When Search button is pressed (search_add is called)
    String temp_search = name.getString();
    search_add(temp_search);

  }
  else if (c == mainmenu) {
  // To return to Main Menu...
      startApp();
  }
  else if (c == delete) {
  // When delete button is pressed (delete_add) is called
    String temp_delete = name.getString();
    delete_add(temp_delete);
  }
  else if (c == addnow) {
            // When add button is pressed (address_add) is called
    String temp_name = name.getString();
    String temp_phone = phone.getString();

    address_add(temp_name, temp_phone);
  }
  else {
    List down = (List)display.getCurrent();
    switch(down.getSelectedIndex()) {
      case 0: searchScreen();break;
      case 1: addScreen();break;
                    case 2: deleteScreen();break;
      case 3: destroyApp(true);break;
    }
  }
}

void search_add(String address) {
 // Function for searching...
  String temp = " ";
  String phone_number;
  String person_name;
  int size = address.length();
  try {
    RecordEnumeration re =
recordStore.enumerateRecords(
null, null, false);
  ui_form = new Form("Search Result.");

    while(re.hasNextElement()) {
String name1 = new String(re.nextRecord());
try {
```

```
person_name = name1.substring(
2,name1.indexOf("?"));
    }
    catch (Exception ef) {
    person_name = "check";
    }
     String check_name =
person_name.substring(0,size);
    if (check_name.equals(address)) {
      try {
       phone_number = name1.substring(
name1.indexOf("?")+1);
    }
     catch (Exception e) {
      phone_number = "";
    }
     temp = temp +"\nName.."+
person_name+"\nPhone.."+
phone_number;
    }
  }
  if (temp.equals(" ")) {
  temp = "The required address not found...";
  }
  ui_form.append(temp);

  ui_form.addCommand(quit);
  ui_form.addCommand(mainmenu);

  // Invoking Action Listener...
  ui_form.setCommandListener(this);

  display.setCurrent(ui_form);
  }

  catch (RecordStoreNotOpenException rsnoe) {
          rsnoe.printStackTrace();
  }

  catch (InvalidRecordIDException irid) {
irid.printStackTrace();
  }
  catch (RecordStoreException rse) {
rse.printStackTrace();
  }
 }

 void delete_add(String address) {
  // Function for deletion....
    String temp = " ";
  String phone_number;
  String person_name;
  int i = 1;
  int del_id = 0;
  try {
  RecordEnumeration re =
```

```
recordStore.enumerateRecords(
null, null, false);
   ui_form = new Form("Delete Result..");

    while(re.hasNextElement())    {
         String name1 = new String(re.nextRecord());
      try {
        person_name = name1.substring(
2,name1.indexOf("?"));
      }
      catch (Exception ef) {
    person_name = "check";
      }
      if (person_name.equals(address)) {
     del_id  = i;
      }
   i++;
   }
    if (del_id != 0) {
     recordStore.deleteRecord(del_id);
      temp = "One Record Deleted Successfully...";
     }
     else {
    temp = "The Record is not Listed...";
   }
   }
   catch(Exception e) {
   }

   ui_form.append(temp);

   ui_form.addCommand(quit);
   ui_form.addCommand(mainmenu);

   // Invoking Action Listener…
   ui_form.setCommandListener(this);

   display.setCurrent(ui_form);
 }

 void address_add(String address, String phone) {
   // Function for address addtion...
   String data = address+"?"+phone;
// ? (to distinguish between name and phone number

   ByteArrayOutputStream baos = new ByteArrayOutputStream();
   DataOutputStream outputStream =
new DataOutputStream(baos);
   try {
    outputStream.writeUTF(data);

   byte[] b = baos.toByteArray();

    recordStore.addRecord(b,0, b.length);

    ui_form = new Form("Success.....");
```

```
    ui_form.append("One Record Entered
Successfully...");
    ui_form.addCommand(quit);
ui_form.addCommand(mainmenu);

    // Invoking Action Listener…
  ui_form.setCommandListener(this);

    display.setCurrent(ui_form);
    }
    catch (IOException ioe) {
ioe.printStackTrace();
    }

    catch (RecordStoreException rse) {
rse.printStackTrace();
    }
  }

public void close() throws RecordStoreNotOpenException,
RecordStoreException {
recordStore.closeRecordStore();
}
} // End of AddressBook.
```

TestHTTP

We end the chapter by showing how connectivity can be established with a MIDlet. It is done by using the HttpConnection interface and Connector class of javax.io package. We first open an HTTP connection by using the open(url) method and then calling the openInputStream method on this connection in order to allow reading data from it by using the read(data) method. The file to be read is passed as a URL to the connection. Both the connection and the input stream are closed by calling the close method. This final part is done inside a finally block to release all the resources. It is a simple MIDlet, but a useful one. To see the output refer to Figure 4-23.

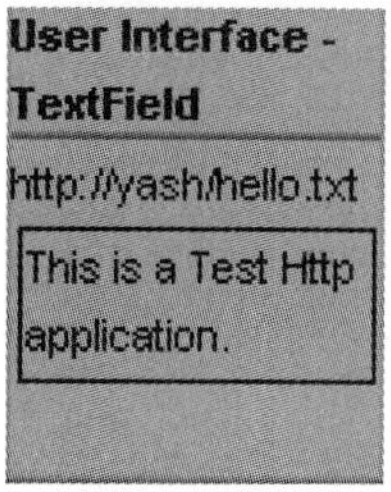

User Interface - TextField

http://yash/hello.txt

This is a Test Http application.

Figure 4-23: Output TestHTTP.

Listing 4-7: TestHTTP.java

```
import java.io.*;
import javax.microedition.lcdui.*;
import javax.microedition.io.*;
import javax.microedition.midlet.*;
/** This is a program to test HTTP connection using MIDP. This
 * class reads a text file from an http URL and displays
 * the content in a TextFeild.
 */
```

```java
public class TestHTTP extends MIDlet {
 String url = "http://yash/hello.txt";
 HttpConnection con = null;
 InputStream ins = null;
 String str = null;
 TextField tx = null;
 Form myform = null;
 private Display show = null;
 public TestHTTP() {
  try {
   try {
                        con = (HttpConnection)Connector.open(url);
    ins = con.openInputStream();
   }
   catch(IOException ex) {
    ex.printStackTrace();
   }

   int i = (int)con.getLength();

   byte[] data = new byte[i];
   if(i>0) {
    try {
     int actual = ins.read(data);
    }
    catch(IOException ex) {
     ex.printStackTrace();
    }

    str = new String(data);

   }

   show = Display.getDisplay(this);
   myform = new Form("User Interface - TextField");
   tx = new TextField(url,str,70,0);
   myform.append(tx);
   show.setCurrent(myform);
   System.out.println(str + "hello");
  }
  finally {
   try {
    if(con != null)
     con.close();
    if(ins != null)
     ins.close();
   }
   catch(IOException ex) {
    ex.printStackTrace();
   }
   str = null;
   tx = null;
  }
 }

 public void startApp() {
```

```
    new TestHTTP();
}

public void pauseApp() {
}

public void destroyApp(boolean b) {}
}
```

Summary

This chapter gives you a feel for programming mobile devices and a sense of the restrictions in terms of resources for mobile devices. This chapter is groundwork for the six unique projects in this book. You should be well conversant with the APIs before going on to these chapters. Chapter 5 concentrates on XML parsing using kxml parser for J2ME. This is an important chapter as we have four project chapters that have extensive use of XML.

Handling and Parsing XML in J2ME

Java is a cross-platform application development environment. J2ME is the edition of Java used for handling micro devices such as cell phones and PDAs. The code written in Java is portable across various platforms. Besides this, transferability of the data across platforms is also required. XML is used to provide portable data formats, which can be used by various application development environments.

Brief Overview of XML

XML may be described as a metalanguage, a language that defines other languages. With the help of XML, the user can define his own tags. Since the tag description is also in XML, the description can be understood by every platform making the data portable. Since XML allows the user to create a new language with new tags, it allows the data to be stored in any format. In fact, it is basically used to describe the way information is stored. XML can provide much better browser capabilities using CSS and XSL style sheets. Once the tags have been defined in XML, it is quite easy to use this data in any XML software.

In XML, DTD (Document Type Definition) is used to define the structure and type of tags used by the program code. DTD defines the names of the tags, their placement, and their relationship with one another. The DTD definition follows the SGML tag-declaration rules. Sometimes, this definition of tags becomes the part of the document containing the tags. In that case, the document is called a *DTDLess* code. The XML DTD, or Schema, can also be used to define the contents of the XML document.

XML is a format-specific language; it first reads the data definition, understands it, and stores it in the memory before taking up the document to execute the functioning of the tags defined. To render the data format understandable by the application defined in the DTD requires special software called *parsers*.

Structure of XML

An XML document is just like an HTML document, having the new tags defined in the Schema, or the DTD. The first line is used for declaring the version of the XML; and the second line indicates the name of the DTD to be used by the document. These constitute the *XML Prolog*.

The XML Prolog is written as:

```
<?xml version="1.0"?>
<!DOCTYPE  shop SYSTEM "shopfile.dtd">
```

Further, the document will have the structure of the HTML body, in which tags will be used as per their structure, and nesting will be defined in the DTD:

```
<shoplist>
<itemname> Computer </itemname>
 <price> $500        </price>
 <qty> 2    </qty>
 <memory> 1.2MB </memory>
</shoplist>
```

The declaration of these tags will be defined in shopfile.dtd as shown in Listing 5-1:

Listing 5-1: shopfile.dtd

```
1)<!ELEMENT  shop(shoplist)+>
2)<!ELEMENT shoplist(itemname,price,qty,memory)+>
3)<!ELEMENT itemname (#PCDATA)>
4)<!ELEMENT price (#PCDATA)>
5)<!ELEMENT qty (#PCDATA)>
6)<!ELEMENT memory (#PCDATA) #REQUIRED>
```

The preceding declaration explains the functionality of the tags as follows:

- Line 1: The tag group shop contains the main container tag shoplist. The plus (+) indicates that a shoplist can occur several times in shop.
- Line 2: The shoplist tag contains itemname, price, qty, and memory.
- Line 3: The itemname tag contains character data.
- Line 4: The price tag contains character data.
- Line 5: The qty tag contains character data.
- Line 6: The memory tag contains character data and is mandatory.

The preceding example declares an external DTD. The following example in Listing 5-2 illustrates an embedded DTD.

Listing 5-2: shopfile.xml

```
<?xml version="1.0"?>
<!DOCTYPE shop[<!ELEMENT  shop(shoplist)+>
<!ELEMENT shoplist(itemname,price,qty,memory)+>
<!ELEMENT itemname (#PCDATA)>
<!ELEMENT price (#PCDATA)>
<!ELEMENT qty (#PCDATA)>
<!ELEMENT memory (#PCDATA) #REQUIRED>

<shoplist>
 <itemname> Computer </itemname>

 <price> $500      </price>
 <qty> 2     </qty>
 <memory> 1.2MB </memory>
</shoplist>
```

The other special symbols used to define tags are:

- #FIXED: Defines the fixed value of an element.
- #IMPLIED: Specification of default value.
- ID: Defining ID.
- ENTITY: Pointing to external data.
- |: OR (EITHER).

- ◆ +: ONE OR MORE.
- ◆ *: ZERO OR MORE.
- ◆ ?: OPTIONAL.
- ◆ EMPTY: Defines an empty tag.
- ◆ ANY: indicates that it can contain any element.

XML Schema

We have just seen that only ELEMENT is used to define the type of tag in DTD. To define further types for the tags for the validation of the datatypes inserted in between the tags, XML Schemas are used. The Schemas are written as an XML file so that the need for the processing software to read the XML declaration syntax is obviated. XML Schema is a complete language used to define and describe the classes for the XML document. It contains the type declarations such as byte, integer, date, sequence, and so on. It also allows derived data-type declarations from the basic data types available in the language. It is the function of the XML Schema to define the relationship between the XML document, namespaces, and DTDs. These Schemas are also used to check the validity of the XML document.

XML Parsing

XML parsing refers to the concept of translating the tag definition and executing the document with the new tags so that the user or the application development environment can understand the data stored in the document. The special software required for this is called a *parser*.

A parser is software that parses an XML document on the basis of XML tags. The parser recognizes the XML tag on the basis of parameters passed to it and gets the text associated with the tag (refer to Listing 5-1). This is accomplished by interpreting and translating the definition of tags contained in a DTD.

There are two categories of parsers:

- ◆ Validating parsers
- ◆ Nonvalidating parsers

In order to understand these types, it is required to know the meaning of *valid* and *well-formed* documents. A *valid XML document* is a document that is compliant to the DTD which is associated with the XML document. The DTD can be written in the same XML document (embedded) or it can be specified as a link. A valid document has to be well-formed. While you're defining tags in a DTD, their inter-relationships are also defined. A *well-formed document* is one in which all the tags adhere to the relationships defined in the DTD. Some of the rules to be followed by well-formatted documents are:

- ◆ All the tags used in the document have to be balanced by including start and end tags.
- ◆ All the essential attributes defined in the DTD should be present.
- ◆ The attribute values have to be given within quotes.
- ◆ The container and containing tags must be strictly as per the DTD, or the Schema.
- ◆ Markup characters such as < or & cannot be present alone. If required, they have to be used as &lt, &amp, etc.
- ◆ All empty tags should end with />.

It is the function of the parser to check for the preceding rules.

Based on the XML documents we have discussed above, there are two types of XML parsers, one for parsing valid XML documents and the other one for non-valid XML documents.

♦ **Nonvalidating parser:** These parsers check only to determine whether the document is well-formed or not; in other words, the parser performs only the syntactical verification of the DTD in a document, which is why it is known as a nonvalidating parser. All the parsers discussed in this chapter are nonvalidating parsers, since J2ME cannot support XML document validations. So to run the code and to check the execution, validating parsers will also be required, along with these parsers.

♦ **Validating parser:** These parsers compile DTD and execute the tag declaration to generate the output in the user readable form.

XML parsers available for KVM

There can be different kinds of parsers for KVM. The parsers discussed in the following sections work on KVM. We will be discussing just the functionality of the parsers. kXML will be discussed in detail in the kXML section.

♦ **Pull parsers:** In these parsers, first the data is read and then it is parsed from the definition. The parsing can be done in recursive functions in order to translate the tree structure of the document.

♦ **Push parsers:** These parsers process the data definition before processing the document. The complete tree structure is created in the memory before the actual processing of the XML document starts. In this case, the complete DOM tree is generated in the memory even without the need of doing so.

kXML

This is the most important and popularly used XML parser for KVM. This is a combination of the pull parser and the XMLWriter, which is used for writing XML. It contains a WAP Binary XML (WBXML), which is used for transmitting XML documents over wireless communication channels. For this, it has support for Wireless Markup Language. It does contain a special kDOM, which is a Document Object Model replacement for kXML. It is simpler and manages the space more efficiently than Document Object Model. It compiles and works in the Mobile Information Device environment without any modifications. It is present in de.kxml.parser package. Its functionality is defined in the `Parser` class.

TinyXML

This is a nonvalidating push parser, which compiles the entire DOM tree into the memory and then parses the entire XML document in one go. It needs modifications to the source code to run on Mobile Information Device. The main feature of the TinyXML is that it follows only a few specific encoding types: ASCII, UTF-16, UTF-16BE, and UTF-8. The encoding type has to be specified in the XML Prolog. If the type specified in the XML Prolog is not of the encoding ASCII, UTF-16, UTF-16BE, and UTF-8,the TinyXML parser will not parse the XML document and will throw an exception.

NanoXML

This is another parser for KVM, which works on push-parsing technology. It has a specific feature for modifying a document and writing the modified document back onto the stream. Since this feature is not very useful for MID at present, this parser does not have any major use or popularity. However, once this feature is accepted in the MID specifications, it will be an important parser for wireless communication.

Working with kXML

XML has support for various packages. We have used the kXML minimum version, which uses a zip file named kxml-min. This version has only the org.kxml.io and the org.kxml.parser package with `Attribute` class, `PrefixMap` class, and XML class. The minimum version of kXML parser is for KVM, which is for most resource constraint devices, which is why only the necessary classes are given in the minimum version. The packages not present in this minimum version are:

- org.kxml.kdom
- org.kxml.wap

Let's discuss the classes and packages present in the minimum version of kXML parser, as we will be using this version.

- **Attribute class:** This class represents the attribute of a tag. When you call the `StartTag.getAttribute` method, it returns an object of type `Attribute` that is the attribute of that tag. This class has four methods. Of these, the `getname( )` method returns the name of the attribute of the tag. You can also get the value of the attribute by calling its `getvalue( )` method. The `tostring( )` method will give the string representation of the `Attribute` object.
- **XML class:** This class represents XML data. This class is used by the parser. All the methods in this class are static. It has some fields, which are used by the parser, such as START-TAG, TEXT, END-TAG, etc.
- **PrefixMap class:** This class represents the PrefixMap of the tag. When you call the `StartTag.getPrefixMap( )` method, it returns an object of `getPrefixMap`. This class has three methods: the `getNamespace( )` method, which returns the namespace of this prefix, the `getPrefix( )` method, which returns the string representation of prefix, and the `PrefixEnumeration( )` method.

org.kxml parser package

This package contains classes related to parsing XML data. Let us discuss these classes one by one:

- **AbstractXml Parser:** This class is an abstract class. All XML parser classes extend this class. To start parsing data, you have to call the `read( )` method of this class. This method generates an object of `ParserEvent` class. All the other methods are used by the parser. For details of the methods, refer to the help provided with this package.
- **Xml Parser:** This class extends `AbstractXmlParser` class. The constructor of this class needs a reader class object, from which it starts reading the XML data and, while parsing it, simultaneously generates the parser events. This class inherits all the methods of `AbstractXmlParser` class. For details of the methods, refer to the help provided with this package.
- **ParseEvent Class:** This is an abstract class, which represents the events generated by the parser while parsing the XML data.
- **StartTag class:** This class extends `ParseEvent` class. The object of this class is generated when the parser finds the starting of a tag — for example:

```
<?xml version="1.0"?>
<  Hello> Hello How are you
</Hello>
```

While parsing the preceding XML, when the parser comes across the `<Hello>` tag, it will generate a `StartTag` event. The `getname( )` method of this class will return `Hello`, which is the name of the tag. For details of using this tag, refer to the case study in this chapter.

- **TextEvent class:** This class also extends `ParseEvent` class. The object of this class is generated when the parser finds some text associated with the tag. For example, in the preceding XML, when the parser comes across `Hello How are you`, it will generate a text event. The `getText( )` method of this class will return `Hello How are you`, which is the text of the tag.
- **EndTag class:** This is a subclass of the `ParseEvent` class. The object of this class is generated when the parser finds the end of a tag. For example, in the XML given in the `StartTag` class, when the parser comes across the `</Hello>` tag, it will generate an `EndTag` event. The `getName( )` method of this class will return `Hello`, the name of the end tag.

♦ **EndDocument:** This is a sub-class of the `ParseEvent` class. The object of this class is generated when the parser finds the end of a document — that is, the end of an XML file.

org.kxml.io package

This package contains classes for writing XML data. Let us discuss these classes one by one:

♦ **AbstractXmlWriter:** This class is a base class for `XmlWriter` class and provides functionality for the `XmlWriter` class. This class has methods which are used for writing XML documents; the methods like `attribute()`, `endTag()`, and `startTag()` are used to create XML documents.

♦ **LookAheadReader:** This class is like a reader class, but there is a `peek()` function in this class that shows the next character; this class also doesn't throw `IOException`.

♦ **XmlWriter:** This class gets its functionlity from `AbstractXmlWriter` class. This class has `checkpending()`, `close()`, and `write(char c)`, other than the methods inherited from `AbstractXmlWriter` class.

Application

This application will illustrate XML parsing by defining `subject ID` and `subjectname` tags, parsing the data, displaying the parsed data on the screen, and reading the data.

Structure of the application

The application is made up of two files:

♦ **`XmlCaseStudy.java`**: The main file that reads and parses the data.

♦ **`result_screen.java`**: This is used to display the output on the screen.

Functioning of the application

The first file, `XmlCaseStudy.java`, defines the packages, classes, buttons, and so on., to read and parse the data. Once the data is parsed, the result is given to a second file, `result_screen.java`, which displays it on the screen.

Application description

The code listings for the two programs are given in Listings 5-3 and 5-4.

Listing 5-3: XmlCaseStudy.java

© 2001 Dreamtech Software India, Inc.
All Rights Reserved.

```
/**
 *  Basic packages used by various classes.
 *
 */
1.  import java.io.InputStream;
2.  import java.util.Hashtable;
3.  import java.util.Enumeration;
4.  import com.sun.kjava.*;
5.  import java.lang.*;
6.  import javax.microedition.io.*;
7.  import java.io.*;
/**
 *  Packages used by the XML parser...
```

```
 *
 */
8.  import org.kxml.*;
9.  import org.kxml.io.*;
10. import org.kxml.parser.*;
/**
 *  Declaring a class XmlCaseStudy. This class is responsible for
 * reading the file  and parsing it. Then it displays a screen
 * which contains the parsed results.
 */

11. public class XmlCaseStudy extends Spotlet
12. {

/**
 *   declaring the variables used by the parser..
 *
 */

13. AbstractXmlParser xmlparser;
14. ParseEvent event;
15. DataInputStream din;
16. String result_string = "";

/**
 *  Declaring the GUI components
 *
 */

17. private Button bt = new Button("Ok",70,145);
        // Gui Components (Button)
18. private Button exit = new Button("Exit",35,145);
        // Gui Components (Button)

/**
 *   main Class which calls the Class XmlCaseStudy.
 *
 */

19. public static void main(String args[])throws Exception
20. {
21. XmlCaseStudy casestudy = new XmlCaseStudy();
22. }
23. public XmlCaseStudy()
24. {
/**
 *  Getting the Graphics and redrawing the screen.
 *
 */

25. Graphics graphics = Graphics.getGraphics();
26. graphics.resetDrawRegion();
27. graphics.clearScreen();

/**
```

```
 *   Painting the title on the screen.,
 *
 */

28.  graphics.drawString("XML case Study..",25,10);
29.  graphics.drawString("Press OK to fetch XML file and Parse it",5,40);

/**
 *  Registering the Spotlet and painting the GUI components.
 *
 */

30.  register(NO_EVENT_OPTIONS);
31.  bt.paint();
32.  exit.paint();
33.  }
34.  public void penDown(int x, int y)
35.  {

/**
 *  When Ok is pressed unregister the spotlet, call the startReading
 *  class to read the XML file then call the XML parser which will
 * parse the file and store the results in a string which is passed
 * as a parameter to another class which displays the result.
 */

36.  if(bt.pressed(x,y))
37.  {
38.  unregister();
39.  startReading();
40.  parseData();
41.  new result_screen(result_string);
42.  }
43.  else

/**
 *   Exit the program
 *
 */

44.  {
45.  System.exit(0);
46.  }
47.  }
48.  public void startReading()
49.  {
50.  try
51.  {

/**
 *   Read the file and pass to the XML parser..
 *
 */

52.  din = Connector.openDataInputStream("testhttp://pankaj/books.xml");
53.  xmlparser = new XmlParser(new InputStreamReader(din));
```

```
54.    }
55.    catch(IOException e)
56.    {
57.    System.out.println("Exception Occurred while reading");
58.    }
59.    }
60.    void parseData()
61.    {
62.    do
63.    {
64.    try
65.    {
66.    event = xmlparser.read ();

/**
 *  Start Tag is encountered.. and Appended to a string.
 *
 */

67.    if(event.getType()==Xml.START_TAG)
68.    {
69.    StartTag stag = (StartTag)event;
70.    String name = stag.getName();
71.    result_string = result_string + "Start "+name + "\n";
72.    }

/**
 *  text between tags is encountered and appended to the String.
 *
 */

73.    if(event.getType()== Xml.TEXT)
74.    {
75.    TextEvent tevent = (TextEvent)event;
76.    String name = tevent.getText();
77.    name = name.trim();
78.    result_string = result_string +"Value  "+name + "\n";
79.    }

/**
 *  End Tag is encountered.. and Appended to a string.
 *
 */

80.    if(event.getType()== Xml.END_TAG)
81.    {
82.    EndTag end_tag = (EndTag)event;
83.    String name = end_tag.getName();
84.    result_string = result_string + "End  "+name + "\n";
85.    }
86.    }
87.    catch(IOException ex)
88.    {
89.    System.out.println("Exception occured");
90.    }
91.    }
```

```
92.  while (!(event instanceof EndDocument));
93.  System.out.println("**** END OF DOCUMENT ****"); // End od document is
     reached.
94.  }
95.  }
```

Code description

♦ Lines 1-7: Basic packages used by various classes.

♦ Lines 8-10: Packages used by the XML parser.

♦ Lines 11-12: Declaring a class XmlCaseStudy. This class is responsible for reading the file and parsing it. Then it displays a screen, which contains the parsed results.

♦ Lines 13-16: Variable declaration to be used within this code.

♦ Lines 17-18: Declaration of GUI components.

♦ Lines 19-22: Declaration of constructor of XmlCaseStudy class to run the Java application is encoded here.

♦ Lines 25-27: Getting the graphics and redrawing the screen.

♦ Lines 28-29: Painting the title on the screen.

♦ Lines 30-33: Registering the spotlet and painting the GUI components.

♦ Lines 36-42: When OK is pressed, this code unregisters the spotlet, calls the startReading class to read the XML file and then calls the XML parser, which will parse the file and store the results in a string that is passed as a parameter to another class, which will display the result.

♦ Lines 43-46: To exit from the program.

♦ Lines 48-66: For reading the file and passing it to the XML parser. The code block serves to open the file and catch the exception if the file is not found. Opens and displays the file on the screen if found.

♦ Lines 67-72: This if condition is true if the Start tag is encountered and the name of the tag is passed to the String variable called name. The name is appended in another String variable result_string.

♦ Lines 73-79: It reads the data as a string and trims it till the end tag is encountered. The string is appended to the String variable.

♦ Lines 80-95: Checks for the end tag in the loop and catches any exception encountered. It checks for the end of the document, and when this is done, the message is printed on the screen.

Output

Figures 5-1 and 5-2 give the user a sense of the look of DTD and XML files.

Figure 5-1: The starting screen.

Listing 5-4: result_screen.java

```
/**
 *  Basic packages used by various classes..
 *
 */
1.  import com.sun.kjava.*;

/**
 *  Decalaring a class result_screen which is responsible for
 *  showing the results in the ScrollTextBox
 */

2.  public class result_screen extends Spotlet
3.  {

/**
 *  Declaring the GUI components
 *
 */

4.  Button exit = new Button("Exit", 80,145);
5.  ScrollTextBox result_box;
6.  result_screen(String result)
7.  {

/**
 *  Getting the Graphics and redrawing the screen.
 *
 */

8.  Graphics graphics = Graphics.getGraphics();
9.  graphics.resetDrawRegion();
10. graphics.clearScreen();
/**
 *  Painting the title on the screen.,
 *
 */

11.  graphics.drawString("Result of parsing",25,2);

/**
 *  Registering the Spotlet and painting the GUI components.
 *
 */

12.  result_box = new ScrollTextBox(result,10,20,120,120);
13.  exit.paint();
14.  result_box.paint();
15.  register(NO_EVENT_OPTIONS);
16.  }
17.  public void penDown(int x, int y)
18.  {
```

```
/**
 *  Exit the program
 *
 */

19.  if (exit.pressed(x,y))
20.  {
21.  System.exit(0);
22.  }
23.  else if (result_box.contains(x,y))
24.  result_box.handlePenMove(x,y);
25.  }
          // declaration of the penMove function

26.  public void penMove(int x, int y)
27.  {
28.  if (result_box.contains(x,y))
29.  result_box.handlePenMove(x,y);
30.  }
31.  }
```

Code description

♦ Line 1: Basic packages used by various classes.

♦ Line 2: Declaring a class `resultscreen` that is responsible for showing the results in the `ScrollTextBox`.

♦ Lines 4-6: Declaration of the GUI components to display on the screen.

♦ Lines 8-10: Getting the graphics and redrawing the screen.

♦ Lines 12-18: Registering the spotlet and painting the GUI components.

♦ Lines 19-25: Exit the program.

♦ Lines 26-30: Declaration of `penmove` function.

Output

Figure 5-2 shows the output screen.

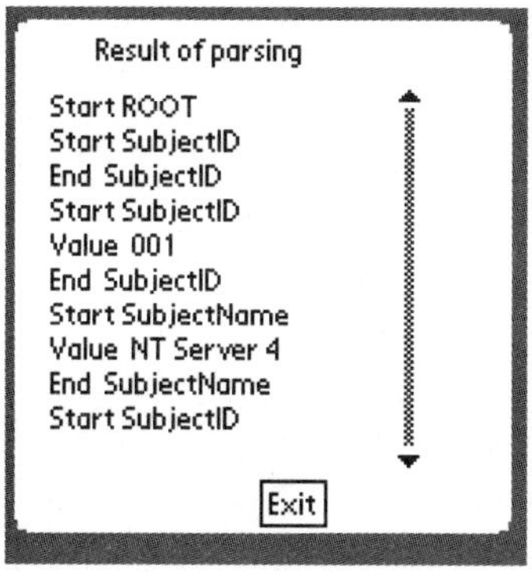

Figure 5-2: The output screen.

Summary

This chapter serves to give the reader an overview of the parsers available for XML to be used with J2ME. The XML parsers are small, since the memory and other resources are limited in the case of wireless devices.

Some of the common XML browsers are:

- kXML
- NanoXML
- TinyXML
- WBXML

More details of these browsers can be found at the following links:

- **kXML:** `http://kxml.enhydra.org/`
- **NanoXML:** `http://nanoxml.sourceforge.net/`
- **TinyXML:** `htttp://gibaradunn.srac.org/tiny/`
- **WBXML:** `http://trantor.de/wbxml/`

We have discussed the kXML parser and the main classes and methods for handling the wireless devices. Further details of these classes can be obtained from `http://kxml.enhydra.org/`.

The example given in the application section of this chapter illustrates the usage of some of the classes discussed in the text. The application presented takes the data from the file, parses it, and displays the output on the screen.

Chapter 6

Project 1: Online Testing Engine

That Internet has made it possible to do many things remotely and is now a fact of life. You can buy things, play games, chat with anybody sitting anywhere in the world, and do innumerable other things. One of the areas where the Net can play a very positive role is education. Examinations are an important part of education. There are applications to manage these exams. This is what our first full-blown application of this chapter does.

This Testing Engine application is called TestManager. It allows the user to take exams remotely. Many such applications are available. The specialty of this application is that it works on a Palm device; In other words, you don't need a PC to take exams. Since you can do it on a PDA, theoretically there is no need to sit in one place for the whole duration of the exam. However, whether the examination authorities who may potentially use such an application allow you to move around during the period of the exam is another matter.

Our TestManager uses CLDC and Kjava – it is basically a spotlet. In addition, it makes use of ASP and a third-party XML parser to read XML output from ASP scripts. We can divide the project into two parts: the server side and the client side. On the server side, we have ASP scripts and an MS Access database. On the client side, we have Java (J2ME) classes, including those of the parser.

User Interface

The main class of TestManager is named, not surprisingly, TestManager. It contains the GUI components that the user sees on the screen, such as scroll text box, buttons, text fields, etc. When the application is started, the user sees a Welcome screen. He can proceed from here by pressing the OK button, or if he changes his mind, he can quit the application by pressing Exit. If he wants to go on and presses OK, he sees a scroll text box showing the topics on which he can test his knowledge. He enters the serial number of one of the topics and presses the OK button. He is presented with the first question on that topic, picked randomly from the database. There are three buttons on the screen labeled Next, Prev, and Review. He can decide on attempting a question by entering the serial number of the option he thinks is correct. Or he can leave the question unanswered and go to the next question by pressing Next. In the same way, he can tackle more questions. At any stage during the test, he can see the status of the test by pressing the Review button. If he does this, the number of questions attempted, number of correct and wrong answers, and the number of unattempted questions are displayed. On this Review screen, he can decide whether the test is too tough for him and quit the test by pressing Exit. Otherwise, he can get back to the test by pressing OK. Moreover, while answering the question, he can even go back to the previous question by pressing the Prev button.

On completing the test, he can see the final result. Results are given in terms of how many questions were answered correctly, how many were unattempted, how many remain unanswered (that is, were read but not attempted), and how many were answered but were wrong. The test also has one "history sheet," where the user can see a chronological summary of all the tests and the results.

Running the Project

To run this application, you can create a `run.bat` file with the following entries:

```
javac -g:none -bootclasspath c:\j2me_cldc\bin\api\classes;        -classpath
c:\j2mecldc\bin\api\classes;
    -d c:\testmanager *.java
c:\j2mecldc\bin\preverify -d c:\testmanager
  -classpath c:\j2me_cldc\bin\api\classes; c:\testmanager
c:\j2mecldc\bin\kvm -classpath

c:\j2mecldc\bin\api\classes;c:\testmanager %1%
```

Here it is assumed that the CLDC has been installed in the `c:\j2mecldc` directory and the `TestManager` project has been installed in the `c:\testmanager` directory. The complete source code for the project is given in the TestManager.java, MainScreen.java, QuestionParser.java, Books.asp, and TestFile.asp sections in the chapter. You can also copy it from the CD to run it. However, you should have Personal Web Server (or any other Web server) installed and running for testing this application. Moreover, you will have to copy the ASP files in the root directory of the server.

How It Works

The project includes the following files:

♦ `TestManager.java`: The main Java (CLDC) file.

♦ `MainSreen.java file`: Contains four inner classes named `NextScreen`, `Results`, `ResultScreen`, and `TestHistory`.

♦ `QuestionParser.java`

♦ A third-party XML parser

♦ `Books.asp`

♦ `TestFile.asp`

♦ `MaintenanceSoft.mdb`: MS Access database, where topics, questions, results, etc., are stored.

The topics on which the user can test his knowledge, questions on these topics, options for these questions, and the answers are stored on the server in the MS Access file named `MaintenanceSoft.mdb`. The MaintenanceSoft.mdb file has three tables: MainData, QuestionData, and AnswerData. These tables store all the data related to the Test for table structure of the given tables refer to Figures 6-1, 6-2, and 6-3. The MainData table shown in Figure 6-1 contains the name of the subjects on which tests are available.

The QuestionData table as shown in Figure 6-2 stores details related to the questions. The information like the QuestionId, the QuestionText, and the NoOfChoices for that Question are stored in this table.

The AnswerData table as shown in Figure 6-3 stores details related to the answer of a particular question. The information like the QuestionId to which this answer is associated the ChoiceNo field stores the no of choices the AnswerText field stores the content of the answer, Correct field stores the correct option to this answer etc.

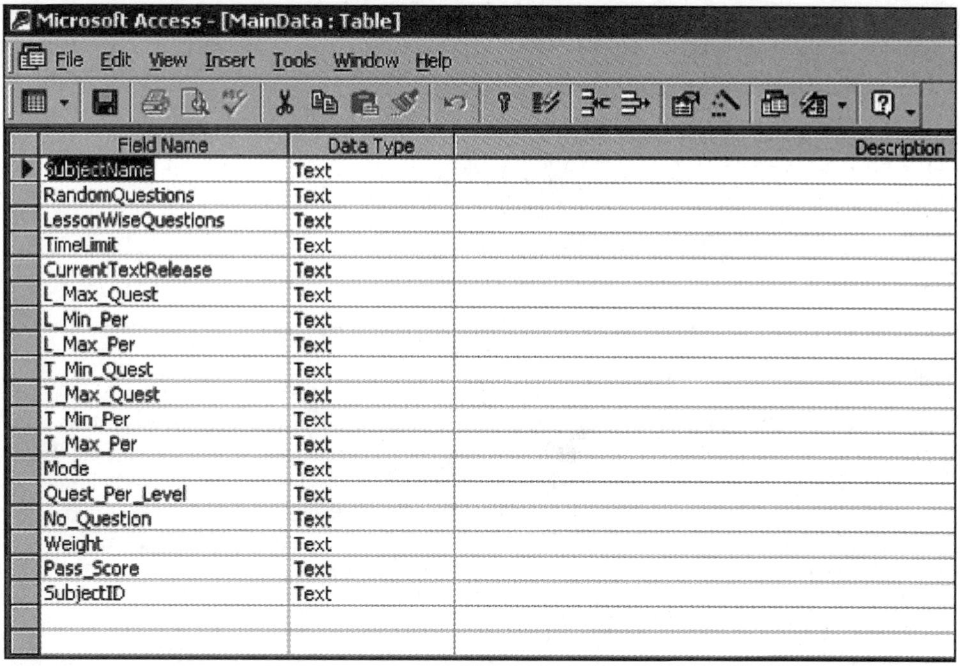

Field Name	Data Type	Description
SubjectName	Text	
RandomQuestions	Text	
LessonWiseQuestions	Text	
TimeLimit	Text	
CurrentTextRelease	Text	
L_Max_Quest	Text	
L_Min_Per	Text	
L_Max_Per	Text	
T_Min_Quest	Text	
T_Max_Quest	Text	
T_Min_Per	Text	
T_Max_Per	Text	
Mode	Text	
Quest_Per_Level	Text	
No_Question	Text	
Weight	Text	
Pass_Score	Text	
SubjectID	Text	

Figure 6-1: MainData Table.

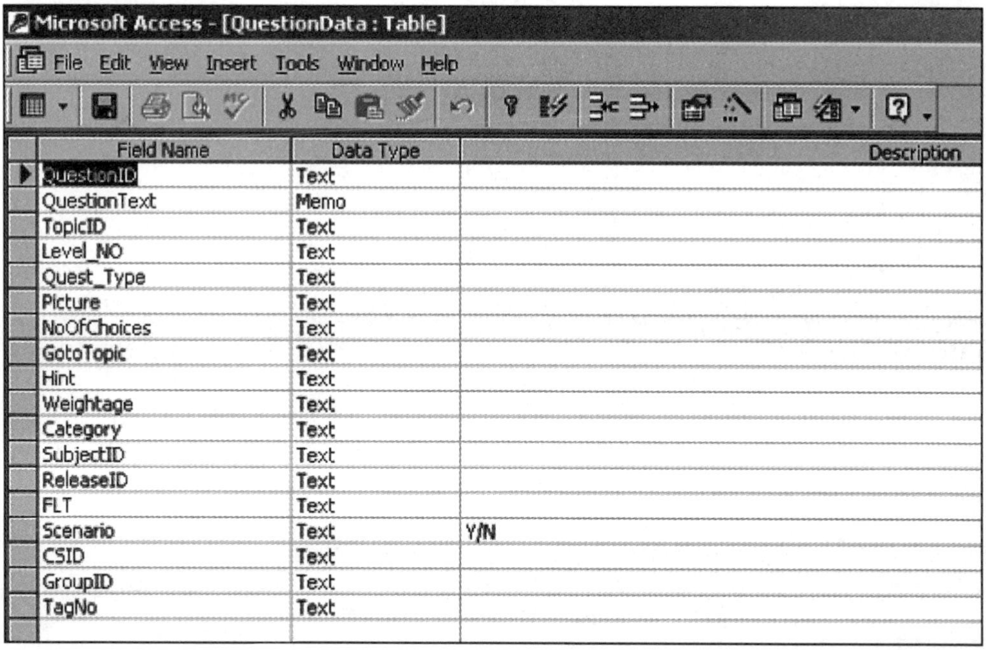

Field Name	Data Type	Description
QuestionID	Text	
QuestionText	Memo	
TopicID	Text	
Level_NO	Text	
Quest_Type	Text	
Picture	Text	
NoOfChoices	Text	
GotoTopic	Text	
Hint	Text	
Weightage	Text	
Category	Text	
SubjectID	Text	
ReleaseID	Text	
FLT	Text	
Scenario	Text	Y/N
CSID	Text	
GroupID	Text	
TagNo	Text	

Figure 6-2: QuestionData Table.

Microsoft Access - [AnswerData : Table]

File Edit View Insert Tools Window Help

Field Name	Data Type	Description
QuestionID	Text	
ChoiceNo	Text	
AnswerText	Memo	
Correct	Text	
SubjectID	Text	
ReleaseID	Text	

Figure 6-3: AnswerData Table.

On starting the application (Figure 6-4), a request is sent to the ASP file kept on the server, to which the ASP responds by reading the database of topics and sending the list of the topics in XML format. The XML parser reads this list, and it is shown in a scroll text box to the user. It is stored on the Palm device in a Palm database. When the user selects a topic for the exam, the ASP file reads the database on questions, picks up questions at random on the selected topic, and returns these to the client in XML format. The XML parser again reads these and then shows them to the user.

Welcome to the Test Manager..

Ok Exit

Figure 6-4: Welcome Screen.

The flow of the program is shown in the flow chart and is explained as follows:

- Executing the Java class file `TestManager` starts the application. It causes the ASP file `http://host/books.asp` to read the topics stored in the MS Access file and return them in XML format.

- The XML parser parses the XML and stores the result in a Palm database on the PDA.

- The class `MainScreen` is called, which creates the GUI components and displays the text parsed from XML (the list of topics) on the scroll text box as shown in Figure 6-5.

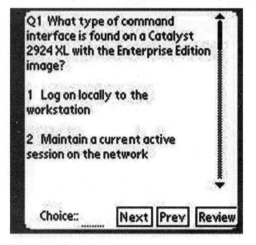

Figure 6-5: List of topics.

♦ The user enters the serial number of the test he wants to attempt and presses OK. At this, class `QuestionParser` is called. The choice is passed as a parameter to an ASP file called `TestFile.asp` as a search string. A file of the same name is created. For example, if the user entered 1, a file `001.xml` would be generated.

♦ The parser again parses the XML which contains data related to the test ie the questions their choices and the correct choice of the respective question are stored in a database.

♦ An inner class of `MainScreen`, named `NextScreen`, is now called. It creates the new GUI components and displays the first question as shown in Figure 6-6.

Figure 6-6: Question Screen.

♦ Now the user has the option to press one out of these three buttons: Next, Prev (Previous), or Review.

♦ If the user presses one of the first two buttons, a function `critical` is called, which displays either the next question or the previous one, depending on the user's choice.

♦ When Next is pressed, the correct answer of the question is matched with the answer selected by the user and, accordingly, one out of these four options is stored: Correct, Wrong, Unanswered, and Unattempted. This goes on till all the questions are answered.

♦ If the user presses the Review button mentioned previously, an inner class of `MainScreen`, named `Result`, is called. A tentative result of the test up to that time is displayed on the screen. The user sees three buttons labelled OK, Exit, and Result as shown in Figure 6-7.

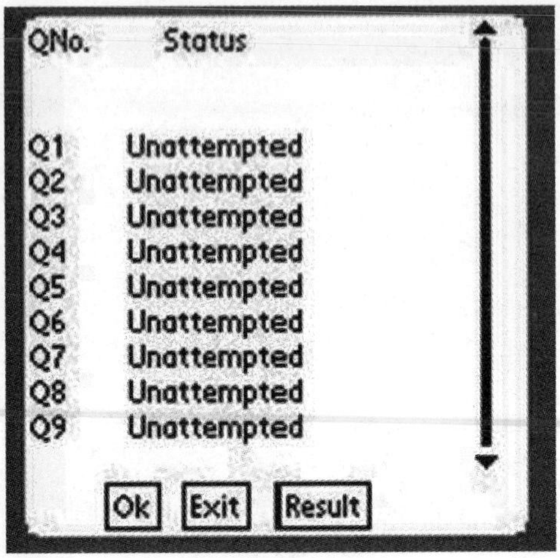

QNo.	Status
Q1	Unattempted
Q2	Unattempted
Q3	Unattempted
Q4	Unattempted
Q5	Unattempted
Q6	Unattempted
Q7	Unattempted
Q8	Unattempted
Q9	Unattempted

Ok   Exit   Result

Figure 6-7: Review Screen.

♦ If the user presses the Exit button, the application is closed.

♦ If the user presses the OK button, a function named `critical` is called. This function moves back to the question where the user pressed the Review button.

♦ If the user decides to quit the test, he can press the Result button. At this, the class `NextScreen` is called, which tells the user the details of the test as shown in Figure 6-8. It presents the results in terms of the following:

Result Screen...

Examination	:2
Date	:2.4.2001
Questions Asked	:5
Correct Answers	:1
Your Score	:1

Exit   History

Figure 6-8: Result Screen.

- Name of the test
- Date on which the test is being taken
- Questions asked
- Correct answers to the questions asked
- Score in the test

- Required minimum score to clear the test
- The final result

♦ At this point, the user sees two buttons labelled Exit and History. If he or she presses the Exit button, the application is closed. In case he or she presses the History button, a class named TestHistory is called, which provides the information about the tests taken by the user so far as shown in Figure 6-9. This information includes:

- Names of the tests
- Dates on which they were taken
- Questions
- Correct answers
- The current status

♦ The application can now be closed by pressing the Exit button.

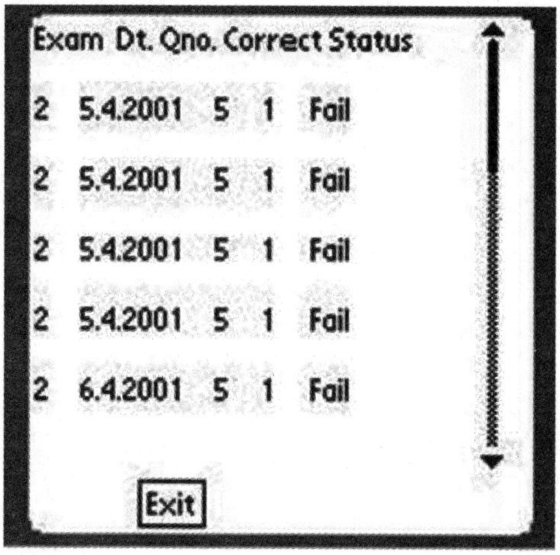

Exam	Dt.	Qno.	Correct	Status
2	5.4.2001	5	1	Fail
2	5.4.2001	5	1	Fail
2	5.4.2001	5	1	Fail
2	5.4.2001	5	1	Fail
2	6.4.2001	5	1	Fail

Exit

Figure 6-9: History Screen.

TestManager flow chart

Figures 6-10 through 6-12 are flow charts for TestManager.

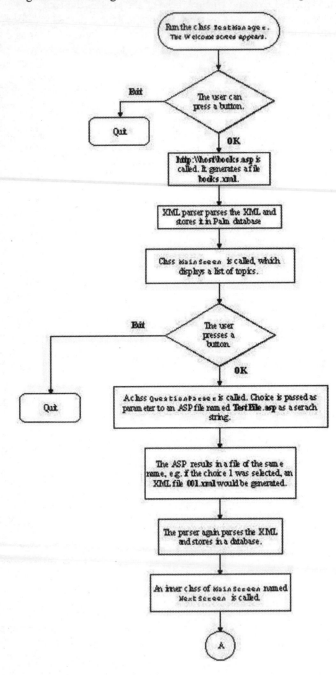

Figure 6-10: Flow Chart-I.

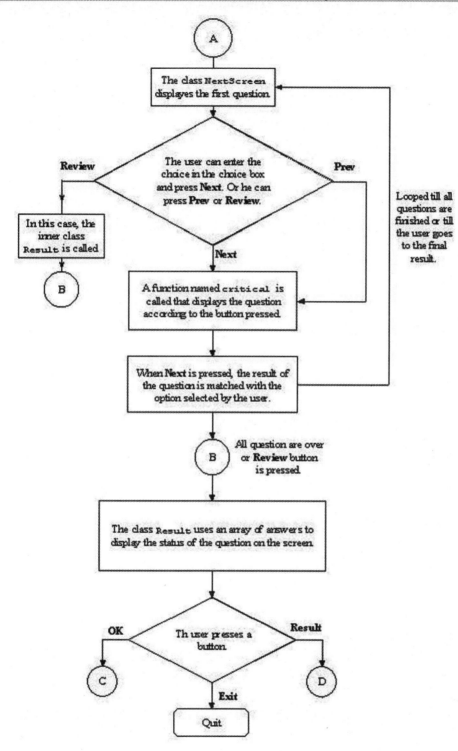

Figure 6-11: Flow Chart - II.

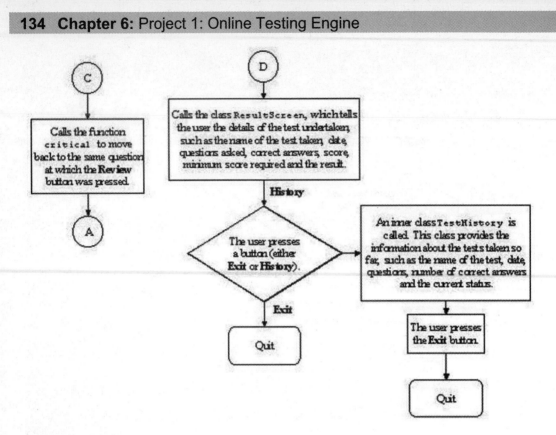

Figure 6-12: Flow Chart - III.

TestManager.java

This is the main class of the `TestManager`. It starts the `TestManager` with a welcome screen and when the user presses the "OK" button it calls an XML parser and stores the results provided by the parser in the palm Database. This class calls the QuestionParser class internally.

Listing 6-1: TestManager.java

© 2001 Dreamtech Software India, Inc.
All rights reserved.

```
1)  import java.io.InputStream;
2)  import java.util.Hashtable;
3)  import java.util.Enumeration;
4)  import com.sun.kjava.*;
5)  import java.lang.*;
6)  import javax.microedition.io.*;
7)  import java.io.*;
8)  import java.util.*;
9)  import org.kxml.*;
10) import org.kxml.io.*;
11) import org.kxml.parser.*;
12) /* This is the main class of the testmanager. It starts the testmanager  with
    a welcome screen... when the user presses the "Ok" button it calls an XML
    parser and stores the results provided by the parser in the palm Database...
13) */
14) public class TestManager extends Spotlet {
```

```
15) // temporary variables used for storing the results in
16) // Database..
17) boolean subject_id = false;
18) // temporary variables used for storing the results in
19) // Database..
20) boolean subject_name = false;
21) // temporary variables used for storing the results in
22) // Database..
23) boolean root_flag = false;
24) int ij = 1;
25) int ijk = 0;
26) String name1 = "";
27) Database dbg;
28) // An Object of the class AbstractXmlparser(xml parser).
29) AbstractXmlParser xmlParser;
30) // An Object to record the events generated by the xml
31) // parser.
32) ParseEvent event;
33) // InputStream initialization...
34) DataInputStream dos;
35) DataInputStream din;
36) // Declaration of buttons...and textBoxes.
37) private Button bt = new Button("Ok",85,145);
38) private Button exit = new Button("Exit",110,145);
39) private TextBox message = new TextBox("Welcome to the Test
40) Manager..",10,10,130,50);
41) // Main Class...
42) public static void main(String args[])throws Exception {
43) /**
44)  * Call to the Parser to generate the list of possible  tests from
45) * the site
46) */
47) TestManager CallParser = new TestManager();
48) /**
49) * GUI for the topic list screen...
50) */
51) }
52) // Constructor for the Testmanager Class..
53) public TestManager()
54) {
55) // No other events should interfere
56) register(NO_EVENT_OPTIONS);
57) //Put the textbox, the buttons(Ok and Exit on to the GUI.
58) bt.paint();
59) exit.paint();
60) message.paint();
61) // Initializing the Database by creating the name of the
62) //  Database, the creator id(cid) and the table id(tid)..
63) String nameing = "data_base";
64) int cid = 0x4B415754;
65) int tid = 0x44425370;
66) dbg = new Database (tid,cid,Database.READWRITE);
67) // Creating the Database...
68) Database.create(0,nameing,cid,tid,false);
69) }  // end Constructor..
70) // Handling the events... fired on the buttons..
```

```
71) public void penDown(int x, int y) {
72) // If "Ok" is pressed..
73) if(bt.pressed(x,y))
74) {
75) unregister(); // unregister the Spotlet..
76) // Call the start function
77) start();
78) // Call the parseData function to get/store the
79) // results in the Database..
80) parseData();
81) // After storing the results call the main_screen
82) // class which pertains to the main testing portion...
83) new main_screen();
84) }
85) else // If "Exit" is pressed..
86) {
87) System.exit(0);
88) }
89) }
90) // The start function helps in sending the request to the
91) // central server to get the list of all the tests
92) // currently present. Then the Stream is passed on to
93) // the xmlparser for parsing...
94) public void start()
95) {
96) try {
97) din =
98) Connector.openDataInputStream("testhttp://www.s-cop.com/books.asp");
99) din.close();
100) dos = Connector.openDataInputStream("testhttp://www.s-cop.com/books.xml");
     xmlParser = new XmlParser(new InputStreamReader(dos));
101) }
102) catch(IOException e) {
103) System.out.println( "gh" );
104) }
105) }
106) // This function is used to generate all the callbacks..
107) // and storing them in Database...
108) void parseData() {
109) do {
110) try {
111) event = xmlParser.read ();
112) // If start tag then set the flags for SubjectId
113) // and SubjectName..
114) if(event.getType()==Xml.START_TAG) {
115) StartTag stag = (StartTag)event;
116) String name = stag.getName();
117) root_flag = true;
118) if (name.equals("SubjectID")) {
119) subject_id = true;
120) }
121) else if (name.equals("SubjectName")) {
122) subject_name = true;
123) }
124) }
125) // Store the text in the database using delimiters.
```

```
126) if(event.getType()== Xml.TEXT) {
127) TextEvent tevent = (TextEvent)event;
128) String name = tevent.getText();
129) name = name.trim();
130) if ((subject_id)&&(root_flag))
131) name1 = name1+"è"+name+"è";
132) else if ((root_flag)&&(subject_name))
133) name1 = name1+name+"\n";
134) }
135) // When End tag is encountered reset all the flags and
136) // add a record onto the database...
137)         if(event.getType()== Xml.END_TAG) {
138)    EndTag end_tag = (EndTag)event;
139)   String name = end_tag.getName();
140)    if (name.equals("ROOT")) {
141) root_flag = false;
142) name1 = name1 +"ì";
143) byte[] data = name1.getBytes();
144) dbg.setRecord(ij,data);
145) ij++;
146) name1 = "";
147) }
148) else if (name.equals("SubjectID")) {
149) subject_id = false;
150) }
151) else if (name.equals("SubjectName")) {
152) subject_name = false;
153) }
154) }
155) }
156)    catch(IOException ex) {
157)   System.out.println("Exception occured");
158) }
159) }
160) while (!(event instanceof EndDocument));
161) System.out.println("**** END OF DOCUMENT ****");
162) // When the end of the document is encountered store
163) // in the first record of the database the total
164) // number of records..
165) String stre = ""+ij;
166) byte[] data2 = stre.getBytes();
167) dbg.setRecord(ijk,data2);
168) }
169) }
```

Code explanation

♦ Lines 1-8: The code between these lines pertains to the inclusion of the basic packages used by various classes in the project, such as `java.util.*` for vectors and enumerations and `java.io.*` for input and output.

♦ Lines 9-11: The code between these lines pertains to the inclusion of the packages required by the various classes in the XML parser.

♦ Line 14: The code here pertains to declaring the main class of the online Testing Engine. It starts the `TestManager` with a welcome screen. Subsequently, when the user presses the OK button, it calls an XML parser and stores the results provided by the parser in the Palm database.

◆ Lines 17-27: The code between these lines pertain to declaring the temporary variables used for storing the results.

◆ Lines 29-32: Declares the variables for the XML parser and parse event (where the callbacks after the parsing will be stored).

◆ Lines 34-39: Declares the variables for the `DataInputStream` — for reading the ASP, for buttons (OK and Exit), for textbox (message), etc.

◆ Lines 42-51: This is the main program that indicates the starting of the Online Testing Application by calling the class `TestManager`.

◆ Line 56: The code here pertains to making the spotlet the current spotlet. The system keys can cancel the spotlet any time.

◆ Lines 58-60: The code here pertains to painting the buttons and the textbox on to the screen.

◆ Lines 63-68: Initializing the database by creating the name of the database, the creator- idis cid and the table-id is tidand subsequently creating the database.

◆ Lines 73-84: The code between these lines pertains to the action taken when the user presses the OK button.

  • 75: The spotlet is unregistered thereby making way for the next spotlet.

  • 77: The code here pertains to calling a function `start  ()`, which is used to send a request to the server.

  • 80: A function `parseData()` is called in which the results of parsing are stored.

  • 83: After storing the results, a call is made to a user-defined class, `main_screen`, which pertains to the main testing portion.

◆ Lines 85-88: The code between these lines is used when the user presses the button Exit. When the button is pressed, the application is closed, and control is returned to the OS.

◆ Lines 94-105: The code here pertains to sending an ASP request to the server to get a list of all the available tests. This request is made using the class `Connector` of the CLDC's `javax.microedition.io` package. The server returns an XML file. The XML stream is then directly passed on to the parser, which parses the XML file.

◆ Lines 108-168: The code between these lines pertains to an important function `parseData`. This is the function in which the XML parser sends the callbacks. The callbacks are identified accordingly by using the functions (whether the element obtained is the start tag or end tag, etc).

  • 118-119: If the tag encountered is `SubjectID`, the corresponding flag — that is, `subject_id` — is made true.

  • 121-122: If the tag encountered is `SubjectName`, the corresponding flag — that is, `subject_name` — is made true.

  • 130-133: If the flags (`subject_id` and `root_flag`) are true, the text obtained between the nodes is stored in a string variable of the name `name1`, separated by a predetermined delimiter (`ALT + 232`). Similarly, if the flags (`subject_name` and `root_flag`) are true, the text obtained between the nodes is appended to the variable `name1`.

  • 137-152: When the end of the XML document is obtained, all the flags are made false, and the data in the variable name is appended by a last delimiter (`ALT+237`) and then finally converted into a byte array and stored into the Palm database created earlier.

  • 165-167: When the end of the XML document is reached, the total number of records are counted and stored in the first recording place of the Palm database.

MainScreen.java

This class pertains to the `TestManager`'s screen. This class shows all the number of tests available at a particular instant of time. When the user presses a choice, then a request is made to the central server to generate that test based on the choice made. The test generated is in XML format and is sent to the parser, after which the first question is shown to the user.

Listing 6-2: MainScreen.java

```java
1)  import com.sun.kjava.*;
2)  import java.lang.*;
3)  import javax.microedition.io.*;
4)  import java.io.*;
5) import java.util.*;
6) /* This screen pertains to the main testmanager's screen. On this screen all
      the tests available at a particular instant of time are shown..When the user
      presses a choice then a request is made to the central server to generate
      that test' s XML file and and send it to the parser and then show the first
      question to the user..
7)  */
8)  public class MainScreen extends Spotlet {
9)  /**
10) * Global Data.... which is used in all the classes..
11) */
12) static int op = 1;
13) static int serialno = 1;
14) static String answer[][] = new String[50][2];
15) static Database database;
16) static String exam_code = "";
17) static String exam_name = "";
18) static String total_number = "";
19) /* this is a static function and therefore initialized only
       once. It is used to maintain the History of the Test
       taken by the user...
20) */
21) static void entry(String str) {
22) String previous = "";
23) byte[] data_prev;
24) try {
25) data_prev = database.getRecord(65535);
26) previous = new String(data_prev);
27) }
28) catch(Exception e) {
29) previous = "?";
30) }
31) try {
32) database.deleteRecord(65535);
33) }
34) catch (Exception e) {
35) }
36) previous = previous+str+"?";
37) byte[] enter = previous.getBytes();
38) database.addRecord(enter);
39) }
```

```
40) /**
41) * Data for the TestManager...
42) */
43) // GUI Components ie two buttons namely "Ok", "Exit",
44) // A choice field..
45) private Button bt = new Button("Ok",85,145);
46) private Button exit = new Button("Exit",110,145);
47) private TextField choicefield;
48) String strp = "";
49) Database dbg; // DataBase variable...
50) private ScrollTextBox first;s
51) String choose[] = new String[150];
52) String choose_text[] = new String[150];
53) int qno = 1;
54) // Initializing Graphics...
55) Graphics gr = Graphics.getGraphics();
56) // Constructor for the Class MainScreen
57) public MainScreen()
58) {
59) // Registering the Spotlet
60) register(NO_EVENT_OPTIONS);
61) // initializing the TextField and putting the cursor
62) // on to the focus..
63) choicefield = new TextField("Option:",10,145,50,10);
64) choicefield.setUpperCase(true);
65) choicefield.setFocus();
66) String textx = " ";
67) /*  Call to an important function is made known as Reading
       this function reads the database created and puts the
       results in a proper format onto the ScrollTextBox also
       stores the result in a 2-D Array...
       It returns a String which is put onto the
       ScrollTextBox...
68) */
69) textx = reading();
70)    // initializing the ScrollText Box..
71) first = new ScrollTextBox(textx,0,0,150,140);
72) /* Putting the ScrollTextBox, Buttons (Ok, Exit) and the
73) TextField on the Screen..
74) */
75) bt.paint();
76) exit.paint();
77) first.paint();
78) choicefield.paint();
79) /* Initializing the Database by creating the name of the
       Database, the creator id(cid) and the table id(tid)..
    This Database is used to maintain the History of the
    Tests undertaken by the user…
80) */
81) String name = "history";
82) int cid = 0x4B415755;
83) int tid = 0x44425371;
84) database = new Database (tid,cid,Database.READWRITE);
85) // Creating the databse…
86) Database.create(0,name,cid,tid,false);
87) }
```

```
88) /**
89)  Event to query the database. It Reads the Database generated by the
     testmanager.class and stores the result in a 2-D array and also stores in a
     string in proper format as this screen is used for Display to the user all
     the available tests at a particular instant of time..It reads the Database
     with the help of delimiters and whereever it encounters those delimiters it
     stroes the result..
90) */
91) public String reading() {
92) /* Opening the Database by providing the same name,
93) cid(creator id) and Tid (table id)
94) */
95) String nameing = "data_base";
96) String str22 = " ";
97) int cid = 0x4B415754;98)  int tid = 0x44425370; 90)// initializing the
Database in a READONLY mode..
99) dbg = new Database (tid,cid,Database.READONLY);
100) byte[] data = dbg.getRecord(1);
101) String questiontext = new String(data);
102) String puttext = "";
103) char kg = 'a';
104) /* the process of reading is as follows..from the database the record
     containing the subject number and subject name is  chosen and read character
     by character when a delimiter is found then the contents of string buffer
     are stored in an array and also appended at the end of string the
     stringbuffer is emptied..this process is continued till the last delimiter
     is encountered.At that instant the string is returned to the calling
     program..
105) */
106) int iq = 1;
107) int county = 0;
108) StringBuffer sb = new StringBuffer();
109) while (kg != 'ì') {
110) kg = questiontext.charAt(iq);
111) if(kg != 'è')
112) sb= sb.append(kg);
113) else {
114) county++;
115) int check = county / 2;
116) int rem = county - check*2;
117) if (rem == 1) {
118) choose[qno] = sb.toString();
119) puttext = puttext+ qno+ ".      ";
120) }
121) else {
122) puttext = puttext + sb.toString() + "\n";
123) choose_text[qno] = sb.toString();
124) qno++;
125) }
126) sb.delete(0,sb.capacity());
127) }
128) iq++;
129) }
130) dbg.close();
131) return(puttext);
132) }
```

```
133) /**
134)  * Event handling for various buttons on the Class Main          Screen
135)  * which is first screen.
136)  */
137) public void penDown(int x, int y) {
138) if(bt.pressed(x,y)) // When "Ok" is pressed..
139) {
140) // Unregister the events of the Spotlet
141) unregister();
142) // Get the Choice entered by the user and store it in the variable str3.
143) String str3 = choicefield.getText();
144) // Disable the cursor of the choicefield.
145) choicefield.loseFocus();
146) // The array in which test serial no. is maintained along with the
     testnumber is referenced to get the testnumber on the basis of str3(Integer
     value)
147) strp =  choose[Integer.parseInt(str3)];
148) exam_name = choose_text[Integer.parseInt(str3)];
149) exam_name = exam_name.substring(0,exam_name.length()-1);
150) strp = strp.substring(0,3);
151) exam_code = str3;
152) strp = strp+".xml";
153) // That exam name is passed on to the question parser to generate an xml
     file of the same name.
     QuestionParser parser= new QuestionParser(strp);
154) // A function is called to send the request ..
154) parser.start1();
155) // parsedata is called to parse the XML file generated in response to the
     request..
156) parser.parseData();
157) // After parsing the database will be generated and a class(inner) is called
     of the name nextscreen()
159) new NextScreen();
160) }
161) // Handling events…
162) if(exit.pressed(x,y))  // When exit button is
163) pressed..
164) {
165) System.exit(0);
166) }
167) if (first.contains(x,y))
168) first.handlePenMove(x,y);
169) }
170) public void penMove(int x, int y) {
171) if (first.contains(x,y))
172) first.handlePenMove(x,y);
173) }
174) // Event for the textfield..
175) public void keyDown(int x)
176) {
177) if(choicefield.hasFocus()) {
178) choicefield.handleKeyDown(x);
179) }
180) }
181) /**
182)  * Class for displaying the next screen which shows the appropriate
```

```
183) * test after the user has made a choice.
184) */
185) public class NextScreen extends Spotlet {
186) /**
187) * GUI components for the screen...
188) */
189) private ScrollTextBox text;
190) private TextField choice = new TextField("Choice:",10,145,50,20);
191) private Button bt1 = new Button("Next",70,145);
192) private Button bt2 = new Button("Review",130,145);
193) private Button bt3 = new Button("Prev",100,145);
194) /**
195) * Database initialization for generating questions during the tests.
196) */
197) // The database is generated by a given name , cid(creator id), (Table
     id)tid..
198) String strp = "not";
199) String nameing = "www.s-cop.com";
200) int cid = 0x4B425754;
201) int tid = 0x44445370;
202) // Database is initialized in read/write mode..
203) Database dbg1 = new Database
204) (tid,cid,Database.READWRITE);
205) String str22;
206) // Initializing the Graphics
207) Graphics gr1 = Graphics.getGraphics();
208) NextScreen()  // Next Screen Constructor..
209) {
210) // Registering the spotlet
211) register(NO_EVENT_OPTIONS);
212) gr1.resetDrawRegion();
213) gr1.clearScreen();
214) // The Database generated by the questionParser.java is run, the first
     record is read to get the total number of questions..
215) byte[] data1 = dbg1.getRecord(0);
216) str22 = new String(data1);
217) str22 =str22.substring(0,str22.indexOf("?"));
218) gr1.resetDrawRegion();
219) gr1.clearScreen();
220) // A function called critical is called which is responsible for generating
     the questions
221) critical(serialno);
222) // Call to generate the questions according to the format...
223) }// End of the constructor..
224) /**
225) * To generate questions after querying the database...
226) */
227) // The function critical takes the argument the question to be generated..
228) public void critical(int jk)
229) {
230) // Register the spotlet..
231) register(NO_EVENT_OPTIONS);
232) gr1.resetDrawRegion();
233) gr1.clearScreen();
234) choice.setUpperCase(true);
235) choice.setFocus();
```

```
236) choice.setText("");
237) // Query the database on the record index.. and put the data in question
     text..
238) byte[] data = dbg1.getRecord(jk);
239) String questiontext = new String(data);
240) String puttext = "";
241) char kg = 'a';
242) /* the process of reading is as follows..from the database the record is
     chosen and read character by character when a delimiter is found then the
     contents of string buffer are  appended at the end of string also if the
     option has correct answer then the 2-D array is initialized with serial
     number of the option and answer[questionno][1] = "u" is also set, the
     stringbuffer is emptied..this process is continued till the last delimiter
     is encountered.At that instant the string is returned to the calling
     program..
242) */
243) int iq = 1;
244) int county = 0;
245) StringBuffer sb = new StringBuffer();
246) while (kg != 'ì') {
247) kg = questiontext.charAt(iq);
248) if(kg != 'è')
249) sb= sb.append(kg);
250) else {
251) county++;
252) if (county == 1) {
253) puttext = "Q"+serialno + "   ";
254) }
255) if ((county ==2)||(county ==5)||(county ==8)||
256) (county == 11)||(county ==14)||(county ==17)||
257) (county ==20)||(county == 23)||(county == 26))
258) puttext = puttext + sb.toString() + "    ";
259) else if ((county ==3)||(county ==6)||(county ==9)||
260) (county == 12)||(county ==15)||(county ==18)||
261) (county ==21)||(county == 24)||(county == 27)) {
262) String gfd = sb.toString();
263) if ((gfd.equals("Y")) && (county == 3)) {
264) answer[serialno][0] = "1";
265) answer[serialno][1] = "U";
266) }
267) else if ((gfd.equals("Y")) && (county == 6)) {
268) if (answer[serialno][0] != null)
269) answer[serialno][0] = 266)answer[serialno][0]+","+"2";
270) else
271) answer[serialno][0] = "2";
272) answer[serialno][1] = "U";
273) }
274) else if ((gfd.equals("Y")) && (county == 266)9)) {
275) if (answer[serialno][0] != null)
276) answer[serialno][0] =
277) answer[serialno][0]+","+ "3";
278) else
279) answer[serialno][0] = "3";
280) answer[serialno][1] = "U";
281) }
282) else if ((gfd.equals("Y")) && (county == 266)12)) {
```

```
283) if (answer[serialno][0] != null)
284) answer[serialno][0] =
285) answer[serialno][0]+","+"4";
286) else
287) answer[serialno][0] = "4";
288) answer[serialno][1] = "U";
289) }}
290) else if ((gfd.equals("Y")) && (county == 266)15)) {
291) if (answer[serialno][0] != null)
292) answer[serialno][0] = 266)answer[serialno][0]+","+"5";
293) else
294) answer[serialno][0] = "5";
295) answer[serialno][1] = "U";
296) }
297) else if ((gfd.equals("Y")) && (county == 18)) {
298) if (answer[serialno][0] != null)
299) answer[serialno][0] = answer[serialno][0]+","+"6";
300) else
301) answer[serialno][0] = "6";
302) answer[serialno][1] = "U";
303) }
304) else if ((gfd.equals("Y")) && (county == 21))
305) {
306) if (answer[serialno][0] != null)
307) answer[serialno][0] = 300)answer[serialno][0]+","+"7";
308) else
309) answer[serialno][0] = "7";
310) answer[serialno][1] = "U";
311) }
312) else if ((gfd.equals("Y")) && (county == 24))
313) {
314) if (answer[serialno][0] != null)
315) answer[serialno][0] = 300)answer[serialno][0]+","+"8";
316) else
317) answer[serialno][0] = "8";
318) answer[serialno][1] = "U";
319) }
320) else if ((gfd.equals("Y")) && (county == 27))
321) {
322) if (answer[serialno][0] != null)
323) answer[serialno][0] = 300)answer[serialno][0]+","+"9";
324) else
325) answer[serialno][0] = "9";
326) answer[serialno][1] = "U";
327) }
328) }
329) else
330) puttext = puttext + sb.toString() + "\n\n";
331) sb.delete(0,sb.capacity());
332) }
333) iq++;
334) }
335) // The text returned is put on the scrolltextbox initialized below..
336) text = new ScrollTextBox(puttext,0,0,150,130);
337) bt1.paint();
338) // Painting various GUI components on the screen...
```

```
339) bt2.paint();
340) // Painting various GUI components on the screen...
341) bt3.paint();
342) 343)    text.paint();
344) // Painting various GUI components on the screen...
345) choice.paint();
346) }
347) /**
348) * Event handling for the GUI components.
349) */
350) public void penDown(int x, int y) {
351) if(bt1.pressed(x,y))   // When next is pressed
352) {
353) // When next is pressed then the choice entered by the user is taken and
     added to answer[][1] set against the serial number of the question.
354) // The serial no. is advanced..checked if it is not the last number if not
     then again critical function is called to generate the bnext question..else
     if the serial number is the last serial then a class(inner) result is
     called..(by giving total number of questions and the state as parameter)
355) String stre = choice.getText();
356) answer[serialno][1] = stre;
357) serialno++;
358) if (serialno < Integer.parseInt(str22))
359) critical(serialno);
360) else {
361) choice.loseFocus();
362) gr1.clearScreen();
363) new Results(str22,1);
364) }
365) }
366) if(bt2.pressed(x,y)) // If review button is pressed
367) {
368) // then a class(inner) result is called..(by giving total number of
     questions and the state (0) as parameter)
369) choice.loseFocus();
370) gr1.clearScreen();
371) new Results(str22,0);
372) }
373) if(bt3.pressed(x,y)) // If prev button is pressed..
374) {
375) // Check whether the question is not the first question itself.. if not then
     decrease the serial number
   by one  and again call the critical function..
376) if(serialno != 1)
377) {
378) choice.loseFocus();
379) gr1.clearScreen();
380) serialno--;
381) answer[serialno][0] = "";
382) answer[serialno][1] = "U";
383) critical(serialno);
384) }
385) }
386) if (text.contains(x,y))
387) text.handlePenDown(x,y);
388) }
```

```
389) public void keyDown(int x) {
390) if(choice.hasFocus()){
391) choice.handleKeyDown(x);
392) }
393) }
394) public void penMove(int x, int y) {
395) if (text.contains(x,y))
396) text.handlePenMove(x,y);
397) }
398) } // End of Class NextScreen
399) /**
400) * Class responsible for handling results at intermediate stage...
401) */
402) public class Results extends Spotlet {
403) /**
404) * Local variables for GUI components used in this screen...
405) */
406) private ScrollTextBox stb;
407) private Button ok;
408) private Button end;
409) private Button result;
410) String total_num ="" ;
411) String str;
412) // Initializing the Graphics.
     Graphics gr2 = Graphics.getGraphics();
413) Results(String str22, int state) {  //  Constructor...
414) gr2.clearScreen();
415) // registering the Spotlet
416) register(NO_EVENT_OPTIONS);
417) total_num = str22;
418) // A String str is first initialized with question no and sttus text..
419) str = "QNo." + "              "  + "Status" + 400)"\n\n\n";
420) // A Loop is executed from 1 to the total number of questions and
answer[loop][0] is mapped with answer[loop][1] and accordingly the message is
appended to the string variable str.(correct,wrong,unanswered,unattempted)
421) for(int i = 1;i<serialno;i++) {
422) if (i<=9) {
423) if (answer[i][0].equals(answer[i][1]))
424) str = str +"Q" +i+"             "+"Correct"+ 400)"\n";
425) else if (answer[i][1].equals(""))
426) str = str +"Q" +i+"             400)"+"Unanswered"+ "\n";
427) else
428) str = str +"Q" +i+"             "+"Wrong"+ "\n";
429) }
430) else {
431) if (answer[i][0].equals(answer[i][1]))
432) str = str +"Q" +i+ "             "+"Correct"+ "\n";
433) else if (answer[i][1].equals(""))
434) str = str +"Q" +i+ "             400)"+"Unanswered"+ "\n";
435) else
436) str = str +"Q" +i+ "             "+"Wrong"+ "\n";
437) }
438) }
439) for(int yu = serialno;yu<Integer.parseInt(str22);yu++)
440) {
441) if (yu<=9)
```

```
442) str = str +"Q" +yu+ "            "+"Unattempted"+ "\n";
443) else
444) str = str +"Q" +yu+ "            "+"Unattempted"+ "\n";
445) }
446) // The str variable is then put on to a ScrollTextBox
447) stb = new ScrollTextBox(str,0,0,150,140);
448) stb.paint(); // The Scroll Textbox is then painted on to the    window.
449)  // Three Buttons are also initialized..
450) ok = new Button("Ok",25,145);
451) end = new Button("Exit",50,145);
452) result = new Button("Result",80,145);
453) if(state ==0)
454) ok.paint();
455) end.paint();
456) result.paint();
457) }// End Constructor results.
458) // Event handling...
459) public void penDown(int x, int y)
460) {
461) if(ok.pressed(x,y)) // When Ok button is pressed.
462) {
463 )unregister(); // Unregister the Spotlet..
464) new NextScreen(); // Call the nextscreen class.
465) // When Ok button is pressed then if the result screen was pressed before
     the test is completed then
     the control reaches back to the question..
466) }
467) if(end.pressed(x,y)) // If end button is pressed..
468) {
469) System.exit(0);
470) }
471) if(result.pressed(x,y))  // If result button is pressed
472) {
473) // Unregister the Spotlet..
474) unregister();
475) /**
476) * Call to the class that shows the final result
477) */
478) new ResultScreen(total_num);
479) }
480) if (stb.contains(x,y))
481) stb.handlePenDown(x,y);
482) }
483) public void penMove(int x, int y) {
484) if (stb.contains(x,y))
485) stb.handlePenMove(x,y);
486) }
487) } // End of Results class...
488) /**
489) * Class that shows final result of the test
490) */
491) public class ResultScreen extends Spotlet {
492) /**
493) * Local variables used for GUI components...
494) */
```

```
495) // This class shows the final result ie the name of the test the date of
     test taking.., the total number of questions, the total number of correct
     answers, the required score. And the status.. along with it,it has two more
     buttons exit and history..
496) private Button exit;
497) private Button history;
498) private ScrollTextBox stb;
499) Calendar cal;
500) // Initialize the graphics..
501) Graphics gr23 = Graphics.getGraphics();
502) ResultScreen(String total_num) // Constructor of the Result Screen.
503) {
504) // Clear the drawing region
505) gr23.resetDrawRegion();
506) gr23.clearScreen();
507) // register the Spotlet..
508) register(NO_EVENT_OPTIONS);
509) // Calendar for getting the Date.
510) cal =Calendar.getInstance();
511) String current_date;
512) total_number = total_num;
513) int question_asked = Integer.parseInt(total_num) - 1;
514) String questions = ""+question_asked;
515) int year = cal.get(Calendar.YEAR);
516) int date = cal.get(Calendar.DAY_OF_WEEK);
517) int month = cal.get(Calendar.MONTH)+1;
518) current_date = date+"."+month+"."+year;
519) String exam_name1 = exam_name;
520) int number = 0;
521) // Check the number of correct answers and store the number in the variable
     number..
522) for(int i=1;i<Integer.parseInt(total_num);i++){
523) if(answer[i][0].equals(answer[i][1]))
     number++;
524) }
525) // Calculate the required score..
526) int required_score = (75*question_asked)/100;
527) String status = "";
528) //Calculate the status on the basis of the required score..
529) if (number<required_score)
530) status = "Fail";
531) else
532) status = "Pass";
533) String printtext;
534) // Append all this information in a string
535) printtext..
536) printtext = "                Result Screen... \n\n";
537) printtext = printtext + "Examination          :
538) "+exam_name+"\n\n";
539) printtext = printtext + "Date                 :
540) "+date+"."+month+"."+year+"\n\n";
541) printtext = printtext + "Questions Asked      :
542) "+question_asked+"\n\n";
543) printtext = printtext + "Correct Answers      :
544) "+number+"\n\n";
545) printtext = printtext + "Your Score           :
```

```
546) "+number+"\n\n";
547) printtext = printtext + "Required Score          :
548)"+required_score+"\n\n";
549) printtext = printtext + "Result                  :
550) "+status+"\n\n";
551) // Initialize the ScrollTextBox With printtextbox
552) stb = new ScrollTextBox(printtext,0,0,150,140);
553) exit = new Button("Exit",35,145);
554) history = new Button("History",60,145);
555) stb.paint();// paint the GUI components.
556) exit.paint();// paint the GUI components.
557) history.paint();// paint the GUI components.
558) String entry_string = exam_name1+">"+current_date+
559) ">"+questions+">"+number+">"+status+">";
560) // Initialize a variable of the name entry_string with all the information
      collected and pass it as a parameter to the function entry so as to make an
      entry in the history database.
561) entry(entry_string);
562) }
563) public void penDown(int x, int y) { // Event handling....
564) if(exit.pressed(x,y)) // If exit button is pressed
565) {
566) System.exit(0);
567) }
568) if (history.pressed(x,y))    // When history Button is pressed.
569) {
570) // Unregister the Spotlet..
571) unregister();
572) // Call the class(inner) test_history which will display all the test given
      so far..
573) new test_history();
574) }
575) if (stb.contains(x,y))
576) stb.handlePenDown(x,y);
577) }
578) public void penMove(int x, int y) {
579) if (stb.contains(x,y))
580) stb.handlePenMove(x,y);
581) }
582) }   // End of ResultScreen class
583) // This class maintains the History of all the tests taken  by the user
584) public class TestHistory extends Spotlet {
585) private Button exit; // Declaring button
586) private ScrollTextBox stb;   // Declaring ScrollTextBox
587) // Initializing the graphics..
588) Graphics gr23 = Graphics.getGraphics();
589) String data_string[] = new String[5];
590) String printtext = "Exam  Dt. Qno. Correct Status \n\n";
591) String final_text = " ";
592) TestHistory() // Constructor of the Class TestHistory..
593) {
594) // Reset the drawing region
595) gr23.resetDrawRegion();
596) // Clear the drawing region
597) gr23.clearScreen();
598) // registering the Spotlet..
```

```
599) register(NO_EVENT_OPTIONS);
600) // To maintain history a database of the name"database" was opened in the
    main_screen constructor..It is then queried to get the history information..
601) byte[] data = database.getRecord(65535);
602) String temp_data = new String(data);
603) int temp = 1;
604) StringBuffer sb = new StringBuffer();
605) String intermediate;
606) while (temp != temp_data.length()){
607) while (temp_data.charAt(temp)!='?') {
608) sb.append(temp_data.charAt(temp)); temp++;
609) }
610) if (temp_data.charAt(temp)=='?') {
611) intermediate = sb.toString();
612) sb.delete(0,sb.capacity());
613) // Function display is called..
614) display(intermediate);
615) temp++;
616) }
617) }
618) final_text = printtext + final_text;
619) // initialize the scrolltextbox..
620) stb = new ScrollTextBox(final_text,0,0,150,140);
621) exit = new Button("Close",35,145);
622) // Putting the ScrollTextBox on the Screen
623) stb.paint();
624) // Putting the ExitButton on the Screen
625) exit.paint();
626) }
627) void display(String str) {
628) StringBuffer sb_display = new StringBuffer();
629) int r = 0;
630) int temp = 0;
631) // The delimiter's used are " > " and until the delimiter is encountered the
    characters generated will be put on to a stringbuffer and when the
    delimitter is obtained then then it is put onto  an array..
632) while (temp != str.length()){
633) while (str.charAt(temp)!='>') {
634) sb_display.append(str.charAt(temp));
635) temp++;
636) }
637) if (str.charAt(temp)=='>')   {
638) data_string[r] = sb_display.toString();
639) sb_display.delete(0,sb_display.capacity());
640) temp++;
641) r++;
642) }
643) }
644) String data_temp = "";
645) for (int y= 0;y<5;y++) {
646) data_temp = data_temp + data_string[y] + "       ";
647) }
648) // Later that array is displayed..
649) final_text = final_text+data_temp + "\n\n";
650) }// End Constructor.. Test_history..
651) // Handling events on buttons
```

```
652) // If close button is pressed then the control goes back to the result
     screen..
653) public void penDown(int x, int y) { // Event handling...
654) if(exit.pressed(x,y)) {
655) new ResultScreen(total_number);
656) }
657) // For handling scrolling down action..
658) if (stb.contains(x,y))
659) stb.handlePenDown(x,y);
660) }
661) // For handling pen move..
662) public void penMove(int x, int y) {
663) if (stb.contains(x,y))
664) stb.handlePenMove(x,y);
665) }
666) }  // End of the inner class
667) } // End of Class MainScreen
```

Code explanation

♦ Lines 1-5: The code contained in these lines pertains to the inclusion of the basic packages used by various classes in the project, such as `java.util.*` for vectors and enumerations and `java.io.*` for input and output.

♦ Line 8: The most important class of the online Testing Engine `MainScreen` is declared here. A list of all the tests available at a particular instant of time is shown. When the user makes a choice, a request is made to the central server to generate the XML file for that test, send it to the parser, and then show the first question to the user.

♦ Lines 12-18: The declarations of the static data variables, which are used by all the inner classes of the `MainScreen`, are encoded in these lines. These include examination code (exam_code), examination name (exam_name), and total number of questions in a test (`total_number`).

♦ Lines 21-39: The static function `entry` is declared here. This function is used to maintain a history of the tests taken by the user.

  • 25: The data is stored in a specific position on the database — that is, record number 65535.

  • 26: The earlier data is retrieved from the location.

  • 32: The old data is deleted from the location.

  • 36: The new entry is added to the database location.

♦ Lines 45-47: The button variables `bt` and `exit` are initialized and a Textfield variable `choicefield` is declared.

♦ Line 60: The code here pertains to making the spotlet the current spotlet. The system keys can cancel the spotlet at any time.

♦ Lines 63-65: These lines initializes the `TextField` and put the cursor onto the focus.

♦ Line 69: A call to an important function is made known as `reading()`. This function reads the database created and puts the results in a proper format onto the `ScrollTextBox` and also stores the result in a 2-D array. It returns a String, which is put onto the `ScrollTextBox`.

♦ Lines 71-78: These are for initializing the `ScrollTextBox` variable of the name `first` and painting the buttons and the `ScrollTextBox` onto the screen.

♦ Lines 81-86: These are for initializing the database by creating the name of the database, the cid (creator id), and the tid(table id). This database is used to maintain the history of the tests undertaken by the user.

- Lines 91-132: The code in these lines pertains to the declaration of a function `reading()`, which is used for reading the database generated earlier and storing the results in the appropriate format. It reads the database generated by the `testmanager.class` and stores the result in a 2-D array, and it also stores it in a String in proper format, as this screen is used to display to the user all the available tests at a particular instant of time. The function `reading()` reads the database with the help of delimiters, and wherever it encounters these delimiters, it stores the result.

  - 106-131: These lines encode the process of reading from the database. The process is as follows: From the database, the record containing the subject number and subject name is chosen and read character by character. When a delimiter is found, the contents of the string buffer are stored in an array and also appended at the end of the String. The string buffer is emptied, and this process is continued till the last delimiter is encountered, and then the String is returned to the calling program.

- Lines 138-161: These represent the action taken when the user presses the OK button.

  - 141: The spotlet is unregistered, thereby making way for the next spotlet.

  - 143-149: The choice entered by the user is taken, and the array in which the test serial numbers are maintained along with the test number is referenced to get the test number on the basis of the number entered by the user.

  - 152: An XML extension (`.xml`) is appended to the filename returned by the array.

  - 153-157: The filename is passed on to a class `QuestionParser` to generate the XML file of the same name. The class is responsible for sending a request to the server, using an ASP for which it uses a function `start1().`. The server sends response in XML data which is parsed and stored in the Palm Database using function `parsedata()`.

  - 159: After the parsing, another inner class, `NextScreen`, is called, which is responsible for displaying the questions to the user along with the choices for each question.

- Lines 162-166: These correspond to the event of the user pressing the Exit button. When the button is pressed, the game is closed and control is returned to the OS.

- Line 185: The code here pertains to declaring an inner class of `MainScreen` (`NextScreen`). Here on the screen, the first question of the test selected by the user is displayed — that is, the test-taking procedure is started.

- Lines 189-193: The GUI components of the class that are to be displayed on the screen are declared. These lines contain a variable of the class `ScrollTextBox`, a variable of `TextField`, and three variables of the button type (`Next`, `Prev`, and `Review`)

- Lines 198-204: The database is initialized in read/write mode.

- Line 211: This code is for making the spotlet the current spotlet. The system keys can cancel the spotlet at any time.

- Lines 212-213: The code represents initializing the variable of the graphics class and clearing the drawing region by calling the appropriate functions of the graphics class — namely, `resetDrawRegion()` and `clearScreen()`.

- Line 221: An important function, `critical`, is called, which is used to generate the questions one after the other.

- Lines 228-346: These lines indicate the declaration of the function `critical`. The function `critical` takes an integer value as argument which is a question number that will be shown to the user.

  - 238: The code queries the database on the record index and put the data in the question text.

  - 242-328: The code between these lines represents the reading of a particular question from the database. The process of reading is as follows: From the database, the record is chosen and read character by character. When a delimiter is found, the contents of the string buffer are appended at the end of String; also, if the option has the correct answer, the 2-D array is initialized with the serial number of the option, and `answer[questionno][1] = "u"` is also set, and the string buffer is emptied. This process is continued till the last delimiter is encountered. At that instant, the String is returned to the calling program.

- 336: The String is put onto the `ScrollTextBox` for display.

- 337-345: The various GUI components are painted onto the screen.

♦ Lines 351-365: These lines encode the event executed when the button Next is pressed. When Next is pressed, the choice entered by the user is taken and added to a two dimentional array `answer[][1]`. The first value to the array is a `serialnumber` of the question the `serialnumber` is checked in case the `serialnumber` is not last number a function named `critical` is called to generate the next question. If the serial number is the last serial, a `class` Results is called (by giving the total number of questions and the state as a parameter).

♦ Lines 366-372: This code is executed when the button Review is pressed.

- 369 - 370: The `TextField`'s caret is killed and the graphics is redrawn.

- 371: An inner class `Results` is called (by giving total number of questions and the state `(0)` as parameters).

♦ Lines 373-385: The code contained in these lines is executed when the button Prev is pressed.

- 376-384: A check is made to see whether the current question is the first question or not. If the current question displayed is the first question, nothing is done; otherwise, the `serialno` variable is decremented by one and passed on to the function `critical`.

♦ Line 402: The code here is for declaring the inner class `Results`, which is responsible for handling the results at an intermediate stage.

♦ Lines 406-411: Various variables (`Button`, `ScrollTextBox`, etc.) are being declared.

♦ Lines 414-416: The code makes the spotlet the current spotlet, besides initializing the variable of the graphics class and clearing the drawing region by calling the appropriate functions of the graphics class — namely, `resetDrawRegion()` and `clearScreen()`.

♦ Line 419: A String `str` is first initialized with question number and status text.

♦ Lines 421-445: A Loop is called from 1 to the total number of questions, and `answer[loop][0]` is matched with `answer[loop][1]` and, accordingly, the message is appended to the String variable `str` (`correct`, `wrong`, `unanswered`, `unattempted`, etc).

♦ Lines 447: The String variable `str` is then put onto a `ScrollTextBox`.

♦ Lines 450-452: Three buttons of the label (Ok,Exit and Result) are also initialized and placed at appropriate positions on the screen.

♦ Lines 461-466: The code between these lines pertains to the situation when the OK button is pressed.

- 463: The spotlet is unregistered, thereby making way for the next spotlet.

- 464: The class `NextScreen` is called, meaning that the control returns to the screen where the user had pressed the Review button.

♦ Lines 467-470: The code between these lines is used when the user presses the button Exit. When the button is pressed, the Test is closed and the control is returned to the OS.

♦ Lines 471-479: The code between these lines is used when the user presses the button Result.

- 474: The spotlet is unregistered, thereby making way for the next spotlet.

- 478: A call is made to another inner class, which shows the final result of the test (`ResultScreen`).

- Line 491: The code here pertains to declaring an inner class of the MainClass (ResultScreen). This class is responsible for showing the final result — that is, the name of the test, the date of taking the test, the total number of questions, the total number of correct answers, the required score, and the status along with it. It has two more buttons, Exit and History.

- Lines 496-498: Declaration of the various GUI components used in the display of the class ResultScreen, such as buttons (Exit and History) and ScrollTextBox.

- Lines 505-508: The code between these lines pertains to making the spotlet the current spotlet, initializing the variable of the graphics class, and clearing the drawing region by calling the appropriate functions of the graphics class — namely, resetDrawRegion() and clearScreen().

- Lines 509-518: From the Calendar object, the date is constructed.

- Lines 522-524: A Loop is used, which checks the total number of correct answers.

- Lines 534-550: All the information — that is, the name of the test, the test-taking date, the score scored, the minimum score required to pass, and the status of the text — is appended to a String.

- Line 552: The String is then displayed in a ScrollTextBox.

- Lines 555-557: The GUI components are then painted onto the screen.

- Lines 564-567: The code between these lines is used when the user presses the button Exit. When the button is pressed, the application is closed and the control is returned to the OS.

- Lines 568-574: The code between these lines is used when the user presses the button History.

  - 571: The spotlet is unregistered, thereby making way for the next spotlet.

  - 573: A new class, test_history, is called, which will display a record of all the tests taken by the user so far.

- Line 584: A class is declared (test_history), which is used to maintain the history of all the tests taken by the user so far.

- Lines 595-599: The code between these lines pertains to making the spotlet the current spotlet, initializing the variable of the graphics class, and clearing the drawing region by calling the appropriate functions of the graphics class — namely, resetDrawRegion() and clearScreen().

- Lines 601-612: The database is checked to get the history information.

- Line 649: The history information is then passed on to the ScrollTextBox for display.

- Lines 653-656: If the Close button is pressed, the control returns to the Results screen.

QuestionParser.java

When the user, after seeing all the available tests, selects a test to give, a request is made to the server to generate that test by calling an ASP of the name test.asp and passing it a parameter bookid = choice selected. The ASP then generates an XML file of the same name; the XML file is then passed on to the XML parser, which parses the XML; and the callbacks generated by the XML parser are stored in the Database.

Listing 6-3: QuestionParser.java

© 2001 Dreamtech Software India Inc.
All rights reserved.

```
1)   import java.io.InputStream;
2)   import java.util.Hashtable;
3)   import java.util.Enumeration;
4)   import com.sun.kjava.*;
```

```
5)  import java.lang.*;
6)  import javax.microedition.io.*;
7)  import java.io.*;
8)  import java.util.*;
9)  import org.kxml.*;
10) import org.kxml.io.*;
11) import org.kxml.parser.*;
12) public class QuestionParser  {
13) // temporary variables used for storing the results in
14) // Database..
15) boolean question_flag = false;
16) boolean question_id = false;
17) boolean question_text = false;
18) boolean option_id = false;
19) boolean text_id = false;
20) boolean correct_id = false;
21) int ij = 1;
22) int ijk = 0;
23) String name1 = "";
24) Database base;
25) String filename = "";
26) // Object of the Class AbstractXmlParser(Xml Parser Used)
27) AbstractXmlParser xmlParser;
28) // Object of the Class ParseEvent used to store all the callbacks..
29) ParseEvent event;
30) // InputStream to be used to request the Server..
31) InputStream dos;
32) InputStream din;
33) // Constructor of the class QuestionParser.. it takes as a
34) // parameter the file name to be generated..
35) public QuestionParser(String file)
36) {
37) filename = file;
38) // Initializing the Database of the name, creator id and
39) // table id
40) String nameing = "data_base";
41) int cid = 0x4B415754;
42) int tid = 0x44425370;
43) // Initialize the Database in read/write mode..
44) base = new Database (tid,cid,Database.READWRITE);
45) // Create the Database of the given name with creator
46) // id and table id..
47) Database.create(0,naming,cid,tid,false);
48) }
49) // start1 method of the class questionparser is called
50) // which helps in generating the request to the server and
51)  // passing the file generated by the server onto the
52) xmlparser for parsing...
53) public void start1() {
54) try {
55) String temp  =
56) filename.substring(0,filename.indexOf("."));
57) // Generating the request
58) din =
59) Connector.openInputStream("testhttp://www.s-cop.com/testfile. 60)
 asp?bookid="+temp);
```

```
61)    din.close();
62) // Creating the inputstream from the file generated..
63)    InputStream dos =
64) Connector.openInputStream("testhttp://www.s-cop.com/"+filename);
65) // Passing the inputstream to the xml parser
66) xmlParser = new XmlParser(new 20)InputStreamReader(dos));
67) }
68) catch(IOException e) {
69) System.out.println( "gh" );
70) }
71) }// This is the function on which when the parser parses the data then it put
the callbacks on this function..
73) void parseData() {
74) do {
75) try {
76) event = xmlParser.read ();
77) // If start_tag is found.. then identify it as a question tag, option_tag,
   correct_tag,or option _text and accordingly the corresponding flag is set
   true…
78) if(event.getType()==Xml.START_TAG)
79) {
80) StartTag stag = (StartTag)event;
81) String name = stag.getName();
82) if (name.equals("question")) {
83) question_flag = true;
84) }
85) else if (name.equals("questiontext")) {
86) question_text = true;
87) }
88) else if (name.equals("optionno")) {
89) option_id = true;
90) }
91) else if (name.equals("correct")) {
92) correct_id = true;
93) }
94) else if (name.equals("text")) {
95) text_id = true;
96) }
97) }
98) if(event.getType()== Xml.TEXT)
99) {
100) // When the text of the tags is encountered then after checking for the
   appropriate tag they are stored in a String variable called name after
   applying the delimiters..
101) TextEvent tevent = (TextEvent)event;
102) String name = tevent.getText();
103) name = name.trim();
104) if ((question_text)&&(question_flag))
105) name1 = name1+"è"+name+"è";
106) else if ((question_flag)&&(option_id))
107) name1 = name1+name+"è";
108) else if ((question_flag)&&(correct_id))
109) name1 = name1+name+"è";
110) else if ((question_flag)&&(text_id))
111) name1 = name1+name+"è";
112) }
```

```
113) if(event.getType()== Xml.END_TAG)
114) {
115) // When the End tag(question) is encountered the respective flag is reset
     and the the name (variable )is stored in the databse.. else if for all the
     tags only the respective flags are reset.
116) EndTag end_tag = (EndTag)event;
117) String name = end_tag.getName();
118) if (name.equals("question")) {
119) question_flag = false;
120) name1 = name1 +"ì";
121) byte[] data = name1.getBytes();
122) base.setRecord(ij,data);
123) ij++;
124) name1 = "";
125) }
126) else if (name.equals("questiontext")) {
127) question_text = false;
128) }
129) else if (name.equals("optionno")) {
130) option_id = false;
131) }
132) else if (name.equals("correct")) {
133) correct_id = false;
134) }
135) else if (name.equals("text")) {
136) text_id = false;
137) }
138) }
139) }
140) catch(IOException ex) {
141) System.out.println("Exception occured");
142) }
143) }
143) while (!(event instanceof EndDocument));
144) // When the end of document is reached, to the first record of the database
     a number is added. This number denotes the total number of records present..
146) System.out.println("**** END OF DOCUMENT ****");
147) String stre = ""+ij+"?";
148) byte[] data2 = stre.getBytes();
149) base.setRecord(ijk,data2);
150) }
151) }
```

Code explanation

◆ Lines 1-8: The code here pertains to the inclusion of the basic packages used by various classes in the project, such as `java.util.*` for vectors and enumerations and `java.io.*` for input and output.

◆ Lines 9-11: These encode the packages required by the various classes in the XML parser.

◆ Line 12: This signifies declaring another important class of the online Testing Engine (`QuestionParser`). It sends a request to the server to generate a test on the basis of the test number of the test passed to it as a parameter. It then parses the XML response sent by the server and stores the result of the parsing in a Palm database.

◆ Lines 15-20: Various Boolean flags used in parsing are initialized to false.

- Lines 27-29: Declaring variables for the XML parser and parse event (where the Callbacks after the parsing will be stored).

- Lines 31-32: Declaring the variable for the `DataInputStream` (for reading the ASP).

- Lines 40-47: Initializing the database by creating the name of the database, the `cid`(creator- id), and the `tid`(table id) and then creating the database.

- Lines 53-70: The code pertains to the declaration of the method `start1`. This method helps in generating the request to the server and passing the file generated by the server onto the XML parser for parsing.

- Lines 73-151: The function `parseData` is encoded here. This is the function by which the XML parser sends the Callbacks. The Callbacks are identified accordingly by using the functions (whether the element obtained is the start tag or end tag, etc.).

- Lines 82-83: If the tag encountered is `question`, the corresponding flag — that is, `question_flag` — is made true.

- Lines 85-86: If the tag encountered is `questiontext`, the corresponding flag — that is, `questiontext_flag` — is made true.

- Lines 88-89: If the tag encountered is `optionno`, the corresponding flag — that is, `option_id` — is made true.

- Lines 91-92: If the tag encountered is `correct`, the corresponding flag — that is, `correct_id` — is made true.

- Lines 94-95: If the tag encountered is `text`, the corresponding flag — that is, `text_id` — is made true.

- Lines 100-112: In these lines of code XML parser throws a `TextEvent` when it encounters text associated with a tag.The text is extracted and stored in a String variable name with delimiter(ALT+232).

- Lines 116-139: When the end tag (`question`) is encountered, the respective flags are reset and the name (`variable`) is stored on the database.

- Lines 147-149: When the end of the XML document is reached , the total number of records are counted and stored in the first recording place of the Palm database.

Books.asp

This asp file is requested for the list of topics available on which the test can be given. The asp file sends query to the database and generates XML data to be sent as response to the client.

Listing 6-4: Books.asp

```
 1  <%@ Language=VBScript %>
 2    <?xml version="1.0"?>
 3    <ROOT>
 4    <%
 5    Dim conn,objrs,objrs1,sql1,tsql,count
 6    set conn = Server.CreateObject("ADODB.Connection")
 7    conn.ConnectionString="DRIVER={Microsoft Access Driver (*.mdb)};"&_
 8    "DBQ=c:\Shared\MaintenanceSoft.mdb"
 9    conn.Open
10    Set objrs = Server.CreateObject("ADODB.Recordset")
11    Set objrs1 = Server.CreateObject("ADODB.Recordset")
12    objrs.CursorType = adOpenStatic
```

```
13  objrs1.CursorType = adOpenStatic
14  tsql = "SELECT DISTINCT(SubjectID) from QuestionData order by
15  SubjectID"
16  objrs.Open tsql,conn
17  Function changequote(tmpstring)
18  tmpstring = REPLACE(tmpstring,"<","&lt;")
19  tmpstring = REPLACE(tmpstring,">","&gt;")
20  tmpstring = REPLACE(tmpstring,"""" ,"&quot;")
21  tmpstring = REPLACE(tmpstring,"&","&amp;")
22  changequote = tmpstring
23  End Function
24  while not(objrs.EOF)
25  subid = objrs.Fields("SubjectID")
26  sql1 = "SELECT SubjectName from MainData where SubjectID='" & subid & "'"
27  objrs1.Open sql1,conn
28  while not(objrs1.EOF)
29  subjecttext = objrs1.Fields("SubjectName")
30  stext = changequote(subjecttext)
31  %>
32  <SubjectID><%Response.Write (objrs.Fields("SubjectID"))%>
33    </SubjectID>
34  <SubjectName><%Response.Write stext %>
35   </SubjectName><%
36  objrs1.MoveNext
37  wend
38  objrs1.Close
39  objrs.MoveNext
40  wend
41  conn.Close
42       set conn=Nothing
43  %>
44  </ROOT>
```

Code explanation

♦ Line 5: Variables are declared here.

♦ Lines 6-9: An ADODB connection object with name conn is created here, which is used to establish the connection with MaintenanceSoft database on the MS-Access. A connection object represents an open connection to a data source. Here ADODB connection object is used to establish a connection with MS-Access. A connection object is needed to acces data using data environment and will represent a connection to a database residing on server that is used as a data source.

♦ Lines 10-13: The new instances of the ADODB recordset are created here and have names objrs,objrs1 and set their CursorType as adopenstatic . A cursor type is way to cache data on the client machine and to provide local scrolling, filtering and sorting capabilities. Adopenstatic is a static copy of a set of records and can be used to find data or generate reports, in this changes by other users are not visible).

♦ Lines 14-16: A SQL query is defined in the variable tsql which is selecting distinct subjectID from the QuestionData table. Then selected record will be opened in the objrs recordset.

♦ Lines 17-23: Function changequote is defined here. This function stores the passed parameter's value in the tmpstring variable. Then this function calls the REPLACE function to replace the escape sequeces like "<", ">", "&", """ into "<", ">", "&", """ respectively in the tmpstring and then returns the resulted string.

♦ Lines 24-40: An XML is generated on the base of the records selected in the objrs recordset. A SQL query is defined in the variable sql1 which is selecting SubjectName from the MainData table where SubjectID is equal to the SubjectIDs selected in the objrs recorset. Then selected records are opened in the objrs1 recordset. Then selected SubjectID and SubjectName will be displayed in the XML format.

- ◆ Lines 41-42: The instance of the connection which is created in the beginning of the file, are going to be closed and destroyed here. These lines help in closing the connection "conn" created earlier and set it to null value.

TestFile.asp

This asp file is requested for the test questions on the basis of topics given as parameter given to this asp. The asp file sends a query to the database and generates a set of questions with choices and answers in XML data to be sent as responses to the client.

Listing 6-5: TestFile.asp

© 2001 Dreamtech Software India Inc.
All rights reserved.

```
 1   <%@ Language=VBScript %>
 2   <html>
 3   <body>
 4   <%
 5   bookid = Request.QueryString("bookid")
 6   Dim conn,i,objrs,objrs1,tsql,tsql2,questionarr(),boolvalue
 7   set conn = Server.CreateObject("ADODB.Connection")
 8   conn.ConnectionString="DRIVER={Microsoft Access Driver
 9   (*.mdb)};" &_
10   "DBQ=c:\inetpub\wwwroot\MaintenanceSoft.mdb"
11   conn.Open
12   Set objrs = Server.CreateObject("ADODB.Recordset")
13   Set objrs1 = Server.CreateObject("ADODB.Recordset")
14   Set objrs2 = Server.CreateObject("ADODB.Recordset")
15   objrs.CursorType = adOpenStatic
16   objrs1.CursorType = adOpenStatic
17   objrs2.CursorType = adOpenStatic
18   boolvalue = FALSE
19   tsql = "SELECT QuestionID from QuestionData where SubjectID='" & bookid &
 "' order by QuestionID"
20   objrs.Open tsql,conn
21   Set fso Server.CreateObject("Scripting.FileSystemObject")
22   fname = bookid & ".xml"
23   Set MyFile=fso.CreateTextFile("c:\inetpub\wwwroot\" & fname)
24   MyFile.WriteLine("<?xml version='1.0'?><ROOT>")
25   Function changequote(tmpstring)
26   tmpstring = REPLACE(tmpstring,"<","&lt;")
27   tmpstring = REPLACE(tmpstring,">","&gt;")
28   tmpstring = REPLACE(tmpstring,"'","&apos;")
29   tmpstring = REPLACE(tmpstring,"""","&quot;")
30   tmpstring = REPLACE(tmpstring,"&","&amp;")
31   changequote = tmpstring
32   End Function
33   while not(objrs.EOF)
34   if boolvalue = FALSE Then
35   ReDim Preserve questionarr(0)
36   questionarr(0) = objrs.Fields("QuestionID")
37   boolvalue = TRUE
```

```
38  else
39  ReDim Preserve questionarr(UBound(questionarr) + 1)
40  questionarr(UBound(questionarr)) =    objrs.Fields("QuestionID")
41  end if
42  objrs.MoveNext
43  wend
44  objrs.Close
45  maxno = Int(UBound(questionarr))
46  if (maxno<30) then
47  num = maxno
48  else
49  num= 30
50  end if
51  i = 0
52  while(i<num)
53  Randomize()
54  MyValue = Int((maxno * Rnd) + 0)
55  qid = questionarr(MyValue)
56  tsql2 = "SELECT QuestionID,ChoiceNo,AnswerText,Correct,SubjectID,ReleaseID
from AnswerData where SubjectID='" & bookid & "' and QuestionID='" & qid & "'
and ChoiceNo <> '0' order by choiceNo"
57  objrs1.Open tsql2,conn
58  tsql3 = "SELECT QuestionText from QuestionData where QuestionID = '" & qid
& "'"
59  objrs2.Open tsql3,conn
60  qtext = objrs2.Fields("QuestionText")
61  qtext = changequote(qtext)
62  MyFile.WriteLine("<question><questionid>")
63  MyFile.WriteLine(qid & "</questionid>")
64  MyFile.WriteLine("<questiontext>")
65  MyFile.WriteLine(qtext & "</questiontext>")
66  objrs2.Close
67  while not(objrs1.EOF)
68  cno = objrs1.Fields("ChoiceNo")
69  correct = objrs1.Fields("Correct")
70  text = objrs1.Fields("AnswerText")
71  text = changequote(text)
72  MyFile.WriteLine("<optionno>" & cno & "</optionno>")
73  MyFile.WriteLine("<correct>" & correct & "</correct>")
74  MyFile.WriteLine("<text>" & text &"</text>")
75  objrs1.MoveNext
76  wend
77  MyFile.WriteLine("</question>")
78  i = i + 1
79  objrs1.Close
80  wend
81  MyFile.WriteLine("</ROOT>")
82  conn.Close
83  set conn = Nothing
84  %>
85  </body>
86  </html>
```

Code explanation

♦ Line 5: Variables are declared here.

♦ Line 6: This line initializes the value of variable bookid with the value of query string variable "bookid" retrieved from client.

♦ Lines 7-11: An ADODB connection object with name conn is created here, which is used to establish the connection with MaintenanceSoft database on the MS-Access. A connection object represents an open connection to a data source. Here ADODB connection object is used to establish a connection with MS-Access. A connection object is needed to acces data using data environment and will represent a connection to a database residing on server that is used as a data source.

♦ Lines 12-17: The new instances of the ADODB recordset are created here and having names objrs,objrs1,objrs3 and set their CursorType as adopenstatic. (A cursor type is a way to cache data on the client machine and to provide local scrolling, filtering, and sorting capabilities. Adopenstatic is a static copy of a set of records can be used to find data or generate reports, in this changes by other users are not visible).

♦ Line 18: The value of variable boolvalue is set to false here.

♦ Lines 19-20: A SQL query is defined in the variable tsql which is selecting the QuestionID from the QuestionData table where SubjectID is equal to the value of bookid variable. Then selected record will be opened in the objrs recordset.

♦ Line 21: This line creates a FileSystem object fso.

♦ Line 22: This line sets the name of the xml filename in the fname variable.

♦ Line 23: A new xml file is created by fso object here.

♦ Lines 25-32: Function changequote is defined here. This function stores the passed parameter's value in the tmpstring variable. Then this function calls the REPLACE function to replace the escape sequences like "<", ">", "&", """ into "<", ">", "&", """ respectively in the tmpstring and then returns the resulting string.

♦ Lines 33-43: An array questionaire is creating here and its elements are set with the values of QuestionIDs selected in the objrs recordset.

♦ Line 45: This line sets the value of maxno variable with the upperlimit of the questionaire variable.

♦ Lines 46-50: Value of the num variable set with the value of max if the value of max if less than 30, otherwise it is set to 30.

♦ Lines 52-80: A random number between 1 to 30 is generated here using the Rnd function. And on the basis of this random number a record is picked up from the database to be written in the above created xmlfile in the xml format.

♦ Lines 82-83: The instance of the connection which is created in the beginning of the file is going to be closed and destroyed here. These lines help in closing the connection "conn" created earlier and set it to null value.

Summary

This chapter was the first full-blown application developed using J2ME for Palm devices; there are five more such applications described in the coming chapters which will make the reader conversant with J2ME technology. We have another application based on CLDC and Kjava APIs in Chapter 11. You can go to Chapter 11 directly if you are interested in developing a game for Palm devices, as Chapter 11 is based on developing a game using CLDC and Kjava APIs. In Chapter 7, we will develop an application using MIDP APIs.

Project 2: Online Ordering System

Even as e-commerce becomes popular, m-commerce is taking its place: handling business on the move is the new mantra. Anybody with anything to sell or any business proposal wants to make it available via mobile devices. Because J2ME is meant for these devices, we believe it very relevant to present an example of a J2ME application that enables you to do business on, say, a mobile phone. We've already built a CLDC application in Chapter 6, so we now turn to MIDP. This is certainly appropriate, considering mobile phones remain the most common small devices and are growing at the fastest rate.

We call this application `OrderManager`. It enables the user to place an order by using a cell phone. A customer may place an order merely after viewing a list of available items, which is what he can do on a cell phone. But still the application is useful if it makes the user aware of the products a supplier offers and, as a result, the user decides to order while on the move. This application presents the opportunity to place such an order. If the ordering option isn't available in such a scenario, the customer's impulse may subside or he may opt for another supplier.

`OrderManager` uses the Mobile Information Device Profile (MIDP) of the J2ME platform, along with JSP and a third-party XML parser. We can also divide the application into two parts: server side and client side. Because the J2ME classfile is on the mobile phone, the client side is what interests us here.

User Interface

The main class of the project is named `OrderManager`. It contains the GUI components and displays the list of items and the stock available. It receives the quantity being ordered, calculates the total amount of the order as well as the cost, and updates the database by calling a JSP script. It has an inner class named `GetData`, which opens a URL and reads XML data on the fly. This class calls a JSP script, which queries the database and generates XML data about the item, quantity available, and the cost. It uses a Java-based XML parser to parse XML data.

On starting the application, the user sees a screen displaying the items and their available quantities. He can select an item by pressing Enter. On this, a text field appears in which the quantity to order can be entered. He can press the Save button so that the quantity is saved. Or he can go back to the list of items by pressing the Back button. He can order as many items as he wants and can even change the quantity of an item previously selected. At the end, he can quit by pressing the Exit button.

Running the Application

For running this application, you should have the J2ME Wireless Toolkit installed, as we explained in Chapter 4 on MIDP. You can run it without the toolkit, but it is much simpler to compile, preverify, and run with the toolkit, since the toolkit has a GUI which is easy to operate and you don't have to mess around with classpaths. The steps involved for running the application would be:

1. Start KToolbar of the J2ME Wireless Toolkit from the Start menu.
2. Begin a new project by clicking New Project.
3. Enter a name for the project — say, **OrderManager**.

4. Enter the name of the main MIDlet class, which is also named `OrderManager`.
5. Click Create Project.
6. Copy the source code for the project in the preceding directory.
7. Now come back to the KToolbar and click the Build button.
8. Once the project is successfully compiled and preverfied, click the Run button.

You should have a server running at the time that you follow the preceding steps, and JSP file should be stored in the root directory of the server.

How It Works

The project includes the following files:

◆ `OrderManager.java`: The main file, which also includes an inner class called `GetData`.

◆ `sql_xml.jsp`: The JSP script that returns data from the database.

◆ `sql_order_mon.jsp`: The JSP script, which updates the database according to the order placed.

◆ A third-party XML parser.

`OrderManager` demonstrates the way in which a J2ME application can be used in concert with an existing J2SE or J2EE application. The supplier may already have a J2SE or J2EE application for receiving orders from customers sitting in front of their PCs. This means there is already an application running for receiving requests and sending response. In the present case, this is done by using Java Server Pages. The items and their quantities available are stored in a database on the server. Let's go through the database table structure which stores the data on the server. There are three tables in the database, namely stock_mast table,Order Table, and Status Table.

The table stored in Figure 7-1 is `stock_mast` table. The field `item_code` stores information related to the code of the item, field `quantity` stores information about the quantity of item available, and the field `unit_price` stores information about the per unit price of the item.

Alter Table - dba.stock_mast						
Column Name	Data Type	Width	Dec	Null	Default	
→ item_code	char	20		No	(None)	
quantity	numeric	11	2	Yes	(None)	
unit_price	numeric	11	2	Yes	(None)	

Figure 7-1: Stock table.

The table shown in Figure 7-2 is the `order` table that stores information related to the order placed. This field `order_id` stores information related to the order id, field `order_date` stores information about the date on which the order was placed, field `item_code` stores information about the item ordered, field `quantity` stores information about the quantity ordered and the field `rate` stores information about the amount or the total price of order.

Alter Table - dba.order						
Column Name	Data Type	Width	Dec	Null	Default	
→ order_id	numeric	5	0	No	(None)	
order_date	date			No	(None)	
item_code	varchar	10		No	(None)	
quantity	numeric	10	2	No	(None)	
rate	numeric	10	2	No	(None)	

Figure 7-2 Order table.

The table shown in Figure 7-3 is the Status table that stores information about the status of the order.

Column Name	Data Type	Width	Dec	Null	Default
→ order_id	numeric	5	0	No	(None)

Figure 7-3: Status table.

There are two JSP scripts — one reads the database and displays the list of items and their quantities, and the other saves the values of quantities ordered by the customer to the database. The J2ME application does the rest. The control flow of the project is explained in the following paragraphs and is also shown in the flow chart:

The application is started (Figure 7-4) by executing the Java `classfile OrderManager`.

Choose One:

OrderManager

About

Figure 7-4: Launch Application screen.

The inner class `GetData` is called, which in turn calls a JSP script named `sql_xml.jsp`. This JSP reads the database, where items and their quantities are stored, and returns the item code, quantity available, and the unit price of the item in XML format.

The XML data is parsed in the `parseData` method of the `GetData` class by using a third-party XML parser. It is simultaneously stored in vectors.

After the data has been completely parsed, the values of the items stored (quantity and price) are returned.

At this point, the list of items is displayed, showing quantity and item codes in Figure 7-5.

Items

V0102	10
V0202	50
V0203	30
V0204	100
V0207	90

Exit   Total

Figure 7-5: Item Details screen.

The user can either press the Total button or select an item (see Figure 7-5).

If he selects an item, the next screen is displayed with a text field in which the quantity to order can be entered as shown in Figure 7-6. After entering the quantity, the user can press either the Back button or the Save button as shown in Figure 7-7. If the former, he is returned to the list of items. If the latter, the quantity entered is saved. The user presses the Back button to go back to the list, which will display the screen shown in Figure 7-5.

Entry Form

Enter Quantity

Back

Figure 7-6: Enter Quantity Screen - I.

Entry Form

Enter Quantity

65

Back

Figure 7-7: Enter Quantity Screen - II.

If the user presses the Total button shown in Figure 7-5, a new screen appears that displays the total amount ordered per item and the total order shown in Figure 7-8. The user can press either the Back button or the OK button. If he presses the former, he is returned to the list shown in Figure 7-5. If he presses the OK button, a JSP script, `sql_order_mon.jsp`, is called, values is passed as parameters, and the database is updated to store the ordered values.

View Total

V0102   6500

Total   6500

Back   OK

Figure 7-8: Total Order screen.

Now the user can press the Exit button to quit the application. This button is present on earlier screens, too, so the user could have quit at any stage, even without ordering anything. If the user presses the OK button without entering anything, an error screen is displayed for some amount of seconds (in our case, 5000 milliseconds — see Figure 7-9).

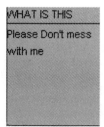

WHAT IS THIS

Please Don't mess
with me

Figure 7-9: Error screen.

A flow chart for OrderManager is shown in Figure 7-10.

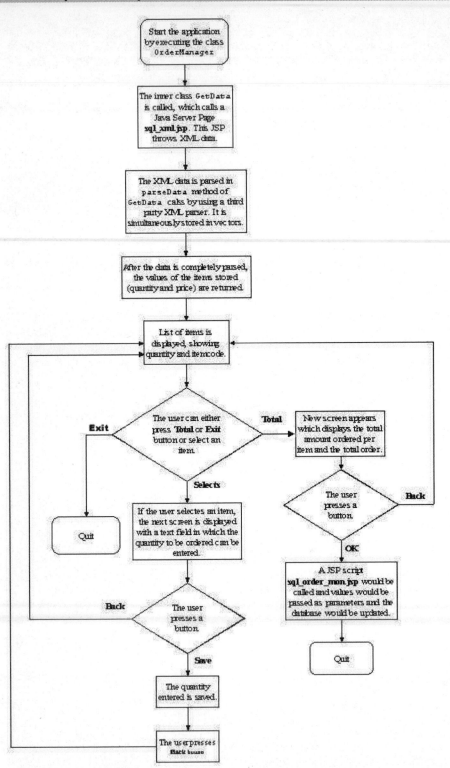

Figure 7-10: Flow OrderManager.

OrderManager.java

This is the only java file in this application. All the functionality related to this application is handled by OrderManager class. There is an inner class GetData to this class. The GetData class handles sends request to the server for item details and handles XML parsing.

Listing 7-1: OrderManager.java

© 2001 Dreamtech Software India, Inc.
 All rights reserved

```
1.    import javax.microedition.midlet.MIDlet;
2.
3.    import javax.microedition.lcdui.CommandListener;
4.    import javax.microedition.lcdui.Command;
5.    import javax.microedition.lcdui.Displayable;
6.    import javax.microedition.lcdui.Display;
7.    import javax.microedition.lcdui.List;
8.    import javax.microedition.lcdui.Form;
9.    import javax.microedition.lcdui.Command;
10.   import javax.microedition.lcdui.TextField;
11.   import javax.microedition.lcdui.StringItem;
12.   import javax.microedition.lcdui.Alert;
13.   import javax.microedition.lcdui.AlertType;
14.
15.   import java.io.InputStream;
16.   import java.io.IOException;
17.   import java.io.InputStreamReader;
18.
19.   import org.kxml.*;
20.   import org.kxml.parser.XmlParser;
21.   import org.kxml.parser.*;
22.
23.   import java.util.Vector;
24.   import java.util.Hashtable;
25.   import java.util.Enumeration;
26.
27.   import javax.microedition.io.HttpConnection;
28.   import javax.microedition.io.Connector;
29.
30.   import java.lang.String;
31.
32.   /**
33.    * This class Displays the  User Interface for this Project. It displays
34.    * the list of items available with the stock of every item. Accepts the
Quantity
35.    * to be Ordered and Calculates the total Amount of Order based on the
Quantity
36.    * Ordered.And updates the Database by calling a JSP passing ITEMCODE,
QUNATITY ORDERED
37.    * TOTAL AMOUNT as parameters.
38.    */
39.   public class OrderManager extends MIDlet implements CommandListener
40.   {
41.    /* This vector will contain Item Code  */
42.    private Vector vitem = null;
43.    /* This Vector will contain Item Quantity  */
```

```
44.    private Vector vquantity = null;
45.    /* This Vector will contain Item Price */
46.    private Vector vrate = null;
47.
48.    /* This Class GetData is an internal class and returns Item Code with
Quantity and Rate */
49.    private GetData gdata = null;
50.
51.    /* Declaring variables for Display class.  */
52.    private Display displaylist = null;
53.
54.    /* Declaration of List which will Display the Items with Quantity  */
55.    private List items = null;
56.    /* Declaration of Form  */
57.    private Form entryform = null;
58.    private Form displayform = null;
59.
60.    private String itemselect = null;
61.    /* This Command is a backcommmand  */
62.    private Command backcommand = null;
63.    /* This command is to view the total  */
64.    private Command totalcommand = null;
65.    /* This command is to place an order  */
66.    private Command okcommand = null;
67.    /* This command again displays the list of items with the quantity  */
68.    private Command goback = null;
69.    /* This command quits the application */
70.    private Command exit = null;
71.    /* This TextFeild is to get the quantity to be ordered  */
72.    private TextField enter = null;
73.    /* This Hashtable contains entries of itemcode and the quantity ordered.
The key
74.    is the itemcode.  */
75.    private Hashtable htable = null;
76.    /* This HttpConnection object connects to the web server and updates the
database by
77.    placing an order  */
78.    private HttpConnection connection = null;
79.
80.    /* Constructor Called  */
81.    public OrderManager()
82.    {
83.     /* This will get the Display Object  */
84.     displaylist = Display.getDisplay(this);
85.
86.     /* Declarations   */
87.     items = new List("Items",List.IMPLICIT);
88.     items.setCommandListener(this);
89.     htable = new Hashtable();
90.     backcommand = new Command("Back",Command.BACK,1);
91.     goback = new Command("Back",Command.BACK,1);
92.     totalcommand = new Command("Total",Command.SCREEN,1);
93.     okcommand = new Command("OK",Command.SCREEN,1);
94.     exit = new Command("Exit",Command.EXIT,1);
95.    }
96.
```

```
97.     /* This method is called when the application starts  */
98.     public void startApp()
99.     {
100.         /* Gdata Instantiated  */
101.         gdata = new GetData();
102.         /* GetData parseData method called. This method parses XML  */
103.         gdata.parseData();
104.         /* GetData returnItem method returns vector object containing Item
list  */
105.         vitem = gdata.returnItem();
106.         /* This line trims  white spaces from the vector vitem  */
107.         vitem.trimToSize();
108.         /* GetData returnStock method returns Vector object containing Stock
list(availabel
109.         item quantity  */
110.         vquantity = gdata.returnStock();
111.         /* Trims empty spaces from Vector  */
112.         vquantity.trimToSize();
113.         /* GetData returnPrice method returns Vector object containing Price
list  */
114.         vrate = gdata.returnPrice();
115.         /* Trims empty spaces from Vector  */
116.         vrate.trimToSize();
117.         /* For loop starts
118.         This for loop runs until there are values in Vector
vitem(vitem.size() give the size
119.         of the vector)  */
120.         for(int i=1;i<=vitem.size();i++)
121.         {
122.                 /* In this line List append method is called and the itemcode
and the quantity
123.                 available are added to the list  */
124.                 items.append((String)vitem.elementAt(i-1) +"    "+
(String)vquantity.elementAt(i-1),null);
125.         }
126.         /* this line will display the list containing the items  */
127.         displaylist.setCurrent(items);
128.         /* List is registered for totalcommand and commands other than Select
command have to be
129.         registered with the List class object by calling its addCommand
method  */
130.         items.addCommand(totalcommand);
131.         /* List is registred for exit command */
132.         items.addCommand(exit);
133.         /* entryform instantiated. A TextFeild will be added to this
form(Form  behaves like
134.         containers in the JAVA Standard Edition  */
135.         entryform = new Form("Entry Form");
136.         /* entryform is registered with backcommand  */
137.         entryform.addCommand(backcommand);
138.         /* entry form registered for receiving command  */
139.         entryform.setCommandListener(this);
140.         /* displayform is instantaited. This will display the total amount of
order with item code  */
141.         displayform = new Form("View Total");
142.         /* displayform registered for receiving command  */
```

```
143.        displayform.setCommandListener(this);
144.        /* displayform is registered with goback command  */
145.        displayform.addCommand(goback);
146.        /* displayform is registered with okcommand  */
147.        displayform.addCommand(okcommand);
148.    }
149.
150.    /**
151.    * This method is called whenever a user presses a button or a command is
given on any
152.    * of the Items. The two parameters are Command object and the displayable
object
153.    */
154.    public void commandAction(Command c, Displayable d)
155.    {
156.        int totalbill = 0;
157.        int a = 0;
158.        /* The code in this if condition is executed
159.         when an item is selected in the list)  */
160.        if(c == List.SELECT_COMMAND)
161.        {
162.            /* This line of code gets the String value of the List item
selected by calling the
163.            getString(). List getSelectedIndex() returns the index of the
item selected which
164.            is passed as an argument to the getString().  */
165.            String str = items.getString(items.getSelectedIndex());
166.            int i = str.indexOf(" ");
167.            /* This line will get only the item value from str(str
contains item as well as its
168.            quantity)  */
169.            itemselect = str.substring(0,i);
170.            /* TextFeild instantaited  */
171.            enter = new TextField("Enter
Quantity","",5,TextField.NUMERIC);
172.            /* The code in if block cleares the entryform(deletes the
items in the entryform)  */
173.            if((entryform.size() > 0))
174.            {
175.                entryform.delete(0);
176.            }
177.            /* This line adds items to the entryform.  TextFeild entered
is added to the
178.            entryform  */
179.            entryform.append(enter);
180.            /* The entryform is displayed  */
181.            displaylist.setCurrent(entryform);
182.        }
183.
184.        /* The code in this if condition is executed when back command on the
entryform
185.        is generated(i.e when  user presses the Back button.  */
186.        if(c == backcommand)
187.        {
188.            /*The code in the if block is executed only when the user
enters some value in the
```

```
189.                 Textfeild  */
190.                 if(!(enter.getString().equals("")))
191.                 {
192.                         /*Two values are put in htable(HashTable)the first one
is itemselect which is the
193.                         itemCode and the second one is quantity the user
entered to be ordered. Both the values are
194.                         String values  */
195.                         htable.put(itemselect,enter.getString());
196.                 }
197.                 /* the back command again displays the List  */
198.                 displaylist.setCurrent(items);
199.         }
200.
201.        /* The code in this if condition is executed when total command on
the List
202.        is generated(i.e when  user presses the Total button  */
203.        if(c == totalcommand)
204.        {
205.                 String str;
206.                 /* This is a StringItem declaration  */
207.                 StringItem sitem;
208.                 /* This for loop will run until the end of HashTable.
htable.keys() returns an
209.                 Enumeration of Objects in the HashTable e.hashMoreElements
returns True if there
210.                 are more elements.  */
211.                 for (Enumeration e = htable.keys(); e.hasMoreElements();)
212.                 {
213.                         /* The e.netElement() returns an Object with which
hkey is initialized  */
214.                         Object hkey = e.nextElement();
215.                         /* The vitem.indexOf() method returns an integer value
which is the index of the
216.                         Object in this vector.The argument to this method is a
String value which is the
217.                         item code and indexitem is initialized with this
integer value.  */
218.                         int indexitem = vitem.indexOf((String)hkey);
219.                         /* htable.get(hkey) method returns the object
associated with this key
220.                         in the hashtable. So, it returns the quantity ordered
for this item code  */
221.                         int quan = Integer.parseInt((String)htable.get(hkey));
222.                         /* vrate.elementAt() returns an Object. This object is
the rate of the item whose index
223.                         value is indexitem. This is typecast to String.
parseInt method parses this string
224.                         into int value and initializes to rate.  */
225.                         int rate =
Integer.parseInt((String)vrate.elementAt(indexitem));
226.                         /* The total will contain the amount of the each item
ordered which is quan*rate
227.                         (Quantity*Rate)  */
228.                         String total = new String();
229.                         total = total.valueOf(quan*rate);
```

```
230.                              /* This String contains the hkey(Item Code)and the
total value of that item code
231.                      to be displayed to the user   */
232.                      str = ((String)hkey) +"        " + total;
233.                      /*The str is passed as an argument to the Constructor
of StringItem which will
234.                       display the value in str   */
235.                      sitem = new StringItem("",str);
236.                      /* sitem is added in displayform    */
237.                      displayform.append(sitem);
238.                      /* totalbill is the total amount of order */
239.                      totalbill+=(quan*rate);
240.              }
241.          /* This str contains total amount of order   */
242.          str = "Total"+"          "+totalbill;
243.          /* str passed to StringItem */
244.          sitem = new StringItem("",str);
245.          /* added to displayform   */
246.          displayform.append(sitem);
247.          /* This will display the displayform containing the items
ordered and total
248.              */
249.          displaylist.setCurrent(displayform);
250.      }
251.      /* The code in this if condition is executed when goback command on
the displayform
252.      is generated(i.e when  user presses the Back button)   */
253.      if(c == goback)
254.      {
255.              /* displayform.size() returns an int value indicating the
Number of objects in the
256.              displayform   */
257.              int noofobjects = displayform.size();
258.              /* This while loop runs until there are objects in the
displayform.The code in this
259.              while loop deletes the objects from the displayform.This code
behaves like  clear
260.              screen command*/
261.              while(noofobjects > 0)
262.              {
263.                      /*Displays the object at this position.In Form class
the position of objects starts
264.                      from 0 and deleting a item will make other items shift
upward.ie if you delete an item
265.                      at 0th position the item at position 1 will move to
0th position   */
266.                      displayform.delete(0);
267.                      /* This line will give the decremented value of
displayform.size()   */
268.                      noofobjects = displayform.size();
269.
270.              }
271.              /* This will set the current display to List containing the
itemcode and stock   */
272.              displaylist.setCurrent(items);
273.          }
```

```
274.          /* The code in this if condition is executed when an ok command on
the displayform
275.          is generated(i.e when an user press the Ok button)  */
276.          if(c == okcommand && !(htable.isEmpty()))
277.          {
278.               /* The urlvalue String contains a url pointing to JSP which
will update the database */
279.               String urlvalue =
"http://localhost:8080/examples/jsp/sql_order_mon.jsp?value=";
280.               /* The Code in this for loop is executed until there are no
Objects in the HashTable  */
281.               for (Enumeration e = htable.keys(); e.hasMoreElements();)
282.               {
283.                    Object hkey = e.nextElement();
284.                    /* The three int values indexitem,quan and rate are
arguments to be passed to  the
285.                    JSP application  */
286.                    int indexitem = vitem.indexOf((String)hkey);
287.                    int quan = Integer.parseInt((String)htable.get(hkey));
288.                    int rate =
Integer.parseInt((String)vrate.elementAt(indexitem));
289.                    /* The values indexitem,quan and rate are added to
this string which are arguments to
290.                    the JSP and these arguments will be updated in the
database
291.                    The First argument is the itemID(Item Code)
292.                    The Second argument is the Quantity of the Item to be
ordered
293.                    The third argument is the total amount of order of one
item(quan*rate)   */
294.                    urlvalue = urlvalue.concat((String)hkey + "*" +
(String)htable.get(hkey) + "*" +(quan*rate)+"*");
295.               }
296.               try
297.               {
298.                    /* Connecting to the given url  */
299.                    connection = (HttpConnection)Connector.open(urlvalue);
300.                    /* An inputstream is opened to read from that
connection  */
301.                    InputStream ins = connection.openInputStream();
302.               }
303.               catch(IOException ex)
304.               {
305.                    System.out.println("IOException occured");
306.               }
307.               /* Destroy App Called  */
308.               this.destroyApp(true);
309.               /* This will notify the application manager that the midlet is
destroyed  */
310.               this.notifyDestroyed();
311.          }
312.          /* This if Condition is executed to display the user an error message
*/
313.          if(c == okcommand && htable.isEmpty())
314.          {
```

```
315.                /* This Alert class is used to diaplay message to the user for
some seconds */
316.                Alert erroralert = new Alert("WHAT IS THIS","Please Don't mess
with me",null,AlertType.ERROR);
317.                /* This line will set the time for which the message will be
displayed to the user  */
318.                erroralert.setTimeout(5000);
319.                /* The alert screen is displayed  */
320.                displaylist.setCurrent(erroralert);
321.            }
322.        /* This if conditon is executed when the user presses Exit button  */
323.        if(c == exit)
324.        {
325.                /* Destroy App Called  */
326.                this.destroyApp(true);
327.                /* This will notify the application manager that the midlet is
destroyed  */
328.                this.notifyDestroyed();
329.            }
330.    }
331.
332.    /* This method is called when the application is paused*/
333.    public void pauseApp()
334.    {
335.        System.out.println("Pause applet called");
336.    }
337.
338.    /* This method is called when the application is terminated. This is the
ideal method to free
339.    resources */
340.    public void destroyApp(boolean b)
341.    {
342.        Vector vitem = null;
343.        Vector vquantity = null;
344.        Vector vrate = null;
345.        GetData gdata = null;
346.        Display displaylist = null;
347.        List items = null;
348.        entryform = null;
349.        displayform = null;
350.        itemselect = null;
351.        backcommand = null;
352.        totalcommand = null;
353.        okcommand = null;
354.        goback = null;
355.        enter = null;
356.        htable = null;
357.        connection = null;
358.        System.gc();
359.    }
360.  }
361.
362.  /* This is an inner class and this class opens a url and reads XML data
and on the fly, parses the data
363.  according to the conditions given. This class uses a java based XML
Parser. This parser is an event-based
```

```
364.   parser.This class calls a JSP which queries the database and generates XML
Data containing the Item Code
365.   available quantity and the rate of the item  */
366.   class GetData
367.   {
368.     /* This String object is url value to be connected to the HTTP Server*/
369.     String url = "http://localhost:8080/examples/jsp/sql_xml.jsp";
370.     /* HttpConnection Object */
371.     HttpConnection con = null;
372.     /* This InputStream Object is used to read data from the InputStream
opened on a URL */
373.     InputStream ins = null;
374.     /* ParserEvent isevent generated by the parser while parsing data */
375.     ParseEvent event;
376.     /* This class is an object of Abstract Xml parser  */
377.     AbstractXmlParser parser;
378.     /* Vector objects declared  */
379.     Vector itemcode,itemquantity,itemprice;
380.     /* Constructor of GetData Declared  */
381.     public GetData()
382.     {
383.
384.         try
385.         {
386.                 /* This makes an Http Connection, opens a stream to the
connection and passes this object
387.                 to the XmlParser class  */
388.                 con = (HttpConnection)Connector.open(url);
389.                 ins = con.openInputStream();
390.                 parser = new XmlParser(new InputStreamReader(ins));
391.         }
392.         catch(IOException ex)
393.         {
394.                 System.out.println("IOException occured");
395.         }
396.         /*Initialize the vector objects */
397.         itemcode = new Vector();
398.         itemquantity = new Vector();
399.         itemprice = new Vector();
400.     }
401.     /* This method parses the xml data and stores the data in the vectors
accordingly*/
402.     void parseData()
403.     {
404.         boolean founditem = false;
405.         boolean quantity = false;
406.         boolean price = false;
407.         do
408.         {
409.                 try
410.                 {
411.                         /* This reads the data from the stream and generates
parsing events  */
412.                         event = parser.read ();
413.                         /* This will check the start of the tag and the name
of the tag like <item_code>*/
```

```
414.                      if(event.getType()==Xml.START_TAG)
415.                      {
416.                              StartTag stag = (StartTag)event;
417.                              if(stag.getName().equals("item_code"))
418.                              {
419.                                      founditem = true;
420.                              }
421.                              if(stag.getName().equals("quantity"))
422.                              {
423.                                      quantity = true;
424.                              }
425.                              if(stag.getName().equals("unit_price"))
426.                              {
427.                                      price = true;
428.                              }
429.                      }
430.                              /* This will be true if there is
                                 some Text found like <item_code>156 */
431.                      if(event.getType()== Xml.TEXT)
432.                      {
433.                              TextEvent tevent = (TextEvent)event;
434.                              if(founditem)
435.                              {
436.                                      itemcode.addElement(tevent.getText());
437.                                      founditem = false;
438.                              }
439.                              if(quantity)
440.                              {
441.
442.                                  itemquantity.addElement(tevent.getText());
443.                                  quantity = false;
444.                              }
445.                              if(price)
446.                              {
447.                                      itemprice.addElement(tevent.getText());
448.                                      price = false;
449.                              }
450.                      }
451.              }
452.              catch(IOException ex)
453.              {
454.                      System.out.println("Exception occured");
455.              }
456.      }
457.      while (!(event instanceof EndDocument));
458. }
459.
460. /* This method will release the memory and free the resources */
461. void releaseMemory()
462. {
463.      con = null;
464.      ins = null;
465.      parser = null;
466.      itemcode = null;
467.      itemquantity = null;
468.      itemprice = null;
```

```
469.        }
470.
471.     /* The next three methods will return vector objects containing itemcode,
472.          item quantity and item price respectively  */
473.     Vector returnItem()
474.     {
475.          return itemcode;
476.     }
477.
478.     Vector returnStock()
479.     {
480.          return itemquantity;
481.     }
482.
483.     Vector returnPrice()
484.     {
485.          return itemprice;
486.     }
487.
}
```

Code explanation

♦ *Lines 1-30:* This includes the basic packages required by the different classes during the program. These statements import various GUI components such as `TextField`, `List`, and `StringItem`; Collection classes such as `Vector` and `HashTable`; HTTP Connection classes such as `HttpConnection` and `Connector`; classes for XML parsing; and classes for Communication such as `InputStream` and `InputStreamReader`.

♦ *Line 39:* This declares the class `OrderManager`.

♦ *Lines 42-78:* The declaration of objects. The objects declared are `Vector` objects for storing XML data; the `GetData` object, which is an inner class for the OrderManager class; objects for User Interface classes such as `List`, `Form`, and several `Command` objects.

♦ *Lines 81-95:* This represents the constructor for the class `OrderManager`. These lines initialize `List`, `HashTable`, and different `Command` objects. The commands are generated when the user presses any button on the device, and these commands are recognized using the `Command` objects.

♦ *Line 98:* The declaration of the `startApp()` method, which is called when the MIDlet starts.

♦ *Lines 101-116:* These lines initialize the `GetData` class. This class reads XML data from an `HttpConnection` and parses the XML data. The `parseData()` method of the `GetData` class parses the XML data and stores the required data in three different Vectors: the methods `returnItem()`, `returnStock()`, and `returnPrice()`, containing the item, the quantity, and the price of the item, respectively.

♦ *Lines 120-125:* The code is a `for` Loop to get the items and the quantity from the Vectors and append them to the list that will be displayed to the user.

♦ *Lines 127-147:* Displays the list and the two commands added to the list: the Exit command and the Total command. It also initializes two forms: the `entryform` with the `backcommand` added to it and the `displayform` with `goback` and `okcommand` added to it.

♦ *Line 154:* Declares the `commandAction` method, which performs the action when the user presses a button.

♦ *Lines 160-182:* An `if` condition that is executed when the user selects an item in the `List`. The String representation of the selected item is stored in a String object `str`. The object item code is extracted from that String. A `TextField` object is initialized. The `if` condition next to this will act as a `clear screen` method, which deletes the already existing objects from the form. The `TextField` is appended to the form and the form is displayed.

♦ *Lines 186-199:* An `if` condition that is executed when the user presses the Back button on the `entryform`. If there is a value entered in the `TextField`, the value is put in the `HashTable` with its item code and then the `List` is displayed.

♦ *Lines 203-250:* An `if` condition that is executed when the user presses the Total button. The `for` loop reads the values from the `HashTable`, converts the String into an integer, and calculates the amount of order per item. The `StringItem` object containing the item code and the amount of order for that item code is created. After the `for` loop, another `StringItem` object is created containing the total amount of order, and the form is displayed to the user.

♦ *Lines 253-273:* An `if` condition that is executed when the user presses the Back button on the display form. This `while` loop clears the screen, and `List` is displayed to the user.

♦ *Lines 276-311:* This `if` condition is executed when the user presses the OK button on the display form. This condition also checks whether the `HashTable` is empty, which indicates whether the user has ordered any item. This code updates the database with the order the user has given, and the `destroyApp()` method is called to destroy the MIDlet. The `notifyDestroyed` method will take the user back to the main menu.

♦ *Lines 313-321:* This `if` condition is executed when the user presses the OK button without giving the order. This will display an error message to the user.

♦ *Lines 323-329:* This `if` condition is executed when the user presses the Exit button. This will end the application.

♦ *Lines 333-336:* This is the declaration of the `pauseApp()` method.

♦ *Lines 340-359:* This is the declaration of the `destroyApp()` method. This method frees the memory, since it declares all the objects null. The `System.gc()` method is called, which will do the garbage collection.

♦ *Line 366:* This line bears the declaration of the inner class `GetData`.

♦ *Lines 369-379:* These lines of code declare objects.

♦ *Lines 381-400:* This is the `GetData()` constructor for the `GetData` class. This constructor makes an `HttpConnection` object and opens an `InputStream` to this connection object. This `InputStream` object is wrapped with the `InputStreamReader` class and passed as an argument to the constructor of the `XmlParser` class. This also initializes `Vector` objects.

♦ *Lines 402-458:* This code is for declaration of the `parseData()` method. This method reads from an `InputStream` and generates parsing events. On the basis of these events, one can recognize the starting and ending of a tag. For example, if the beginning of a tag is found, the `StartTag` event would be generated. The data parsed is stored accordingly in different Vectors.

♦ *Lines 461-469:* This method frees the memory.

♦ *Lines 473-486:* The methods in these lines return Vectors containing `itemcode`, `itemquantity`, and `itemprice`, respectively.

Listing 7-2: sql_xml.jsp

```
1.   <?xml version="1.0" ?>
2.   <jsp:root xmlns:jsp="http://java.sun.com/products/jsp/dtd/jsp_1_0.dtd">
3.   <main>
4.   <title>Branch Info</title>
5.
6.   <% Class.forName("sun.jdbc.odbc.JdbcOdbcDriver");%>
```

```
7.
8.   <% java.sql.Connection db =
java.sql.DriverManager.getConnection("jdbc:odbc:branch","dba","sql");   %>
9.
10.  <% java.sql.Statement st = db.createStatement(); %>
11.  <% java.sql.ResultSet rs;   %>
12.
13.  <% rs = st.executeQuery("select item_code, quantity, unit_price from
stock_mast; "); %>
14.  <% while (rs.next()) { %>
15.   <% String name = rs.getString("item_code");   %>
16.   <% int aId = rs.getInt("quantity"); %>
17.   <% int uPrice = rs.getInt("unit_price"); %>
18.
19.  <item_code><%= name %><quantity><%= aId %></quantity><unit_price><%= uPrice
%></unit_price></item_code>
20.
21.  <% }  %>
22.
23.  <% rs.close(); %>
24.
25.  </main>
26. </jsp:root>
```

Code explanation

♦ Line 6: Initialize and load the JDBC-ODBC driver.

♦ Line 8: To get the database connection. The JDBC url should contain a data source name (DSN), UserID, and the password for the ODBC data source.

♦ Line 10: To create statement object to execute the SQL Statement.

♦ Line 11: Declaring variable for storing the resultset of the statement.

♦ Line 13: Writing an SQL String, passing it to the DBMS and executing the statement. The SQL statement selects the item code, Quantity and unit price from the stock_mast table for displaying it.

♦ Line 14: While loop for checking the next record in the recordset.

♦ Line 15: Inserting the value of "item code" from the recordset rs in String variable name.

♦ Line 16: Inserting the value of "quantity" from the recordset rs in integer variable aId.

♦ Line 17: Inserting the value of "unit_price" from the recordset rs in integer variable uPrice.

♦ Line 19: Displaying the item code, quantity, unit price in the item code, quantity, unit price tags.

♦ Line 21: Closing the while loop

♦ Line 23: Closing the recordset rs.

Listing 7-3: sql_order_mon.jsp

```
1.   <% Class.forName("sun.jdbc.odbc.JdbcOdbcDriver");%>
2.   <% java.sql.Connection db =
java.sql.DriverManager.getConnection("jdbc:odbc:branch","dba","sql");   %>
3.
4.
5.   <% java.sql.Statement st1 = db.createStatement(); %>
6.   <% java.sql.Statement st2 = db.createStatement(); %>
```

```
7.   <% java.sql.Statement st3 = db.createStatement(); %>
8.
9.   <% java.sql.ResultSet rs;   %>
10.
11.  <% int oId = 0 ; %>
12.  <% String o_date = ""; %>
13.  <% String item_code = "" ; %>
14.
15   <% int item_qty = 0 ; %>
16.
17.  <% int item_rate = 0 ; %>
18.
19.  <% String parameters = ""; %>
20.
21.  <% int mon_date = 0; %>
22.  <% int day_date = 0; %>
23.  <% int year_date = 0; %>
24.
25.  <% java.util.Date now = new java.util.Date(); %>
26.
27.  <% day_date = now.getDate(); %>
28.  <% mon_date = 1 + now.getMonth(); %>
29.  <% year_date = 1900 + now.getYear(); %>
30.
31.  <% parameters = request.getParameter("value"); %>
32.
33.  <% rs = st1.executeQuery("select order_id from status; "); %>
34.  <% while (rs.next()) { %>
35.
36.    <%  oId = rs.getInt("order_id"); %>
37.    <order_id><%= oId %></order_id>
38.
39.    <order_date><%=now.getDate() %>/<%=now.getMonth() %>/<%=1900 +
now.getYear() %></order_date>
40.
41.  <% } %>
42.  <% rs.close(); %>
43.
44.  <% oId = oId + 1; %>
45.  <% st2.executeUpdate("update status set order_id =" + oId  ); %>
46.
47.
48.  <% java.util.StringTokenizer st = new java.util.StringTokenizer(parameters,
"*");
49.    while (st.hasMoreTokens())
50.       {
51.            item_code = st.nextToken();
52.     item_qty = Integer.parseInt(st.nextToken());
53.     item_rate = Integer.parseInt(st.nextToken());
54.     st3.executeUpdate("insert into \"order\" ( \"order_id\",\"order_date\",
\"item_code\", \"quantity\", \"rate\" ) values ( " + oId +        ","+
"YMD("+year_date+","+mon_date+","+day_date+")" +   ",'" + item_code + "'," +
item_qty + "," + item_rate + ");");
55.
56.       }
57.   %>
```

```
58.
59.   <% db.close(); %>
46)
```

Code explanation

- ♦ Line 1: Initializing and loading the JDBC-ODBC driver.
- ♦ Line 2: To get the database connection. The JDBC url should contain a data source name (DSN), UserID and the password for the ODBC data source.
- ♦ Lines 5-7: To create statement objects to execute the SQL Statements.
- ♦ Line 9: Declaring variable for storing the resultset of the statement.
- ♦ Lines 11-23: Declaring and intializing integer and string type variables.
- ♦ Line 25: Declaring and initializing the date type object now
- ♦ Line 27: Inserting the value of day in the variable day_date
- ♦ Line 28: Inserting the value of month in the variable mon_date
- ♦ Line 29: Inserting the value of year in the variable year_date
- ♦ Line 31: Inserting the parameter "value" int the string type variable parameters.
- ♦ Line 33: Writing an SQL String, passing it to the DBMS and executing the statement. The SQL statement enerates the next order no.from the status table which keeps the track of the current order no in process.
- ♦ Line 34: While loop for checking the next record in the recordset.
- ♦ Line 36: Inserting the value of "order_id" from the recordset in oId variable
- ♦ Line 37: Displaying the oId variable in the order_id tag.
- ♦ Line 39: Inserting the date object in the order_date tag and displaying the date in the date format (dd/mm/yyyy)
- ♦ Line 41: closing the while loop.
- ♦ Line 42: Closing the record set rs.
- ♦ Lines 44-45: Incrementing the value of order no and inserting the current order no in the status table.
- ♦ Line 48: Declaring the string tokenizer st
- ♦ Line 49: While loop for checking for more tokens in the string st.
- ♦ Line 51: Inserting the value of "item_code" from the String variable st by checking for more tokens.
- ♦ Line 52: Inserting the value of "quantity" from the String variable st by checking for more tokens.
- ♦ Line 53: Inserting the value of "unit_price" from the String variable st by checking for more tokens.
- ♦ Line 54: Writing an SQL String, passing it to the DBMS and executing the statement. The SQL statement inserts the order details (order_id, order_date, item_code, Quantity and rate) in the order table.
- ♦ Line 56: Closing the while loop
- ♦ Line 59: Closing the connection.

Summary

This chapter was a second full-blown application developed using MIDP for Mobile Phone. There are four more such applications to come in the following chapters. After going through this chapter, you should have a considerable command on MIDP APIs and on using J2ME wireless kit. We have another application based on MIDP in Chapter 10, and you can go to Chapter 10 directly if interested in developing a small portal for the Mobile Phone user. In Chapter 8 we will develop an application PersonalJava emulation environment which is CDC based. This is the only chapter on CDC.

Chapter 8

Project 3: MP3 Player for Pocket PC

In this chapter, we'll be looking at the development of an application for a CDC device, using the PersonalJava profile which operates on a Pocket PC. Personal Java devices offer a very feature-rich Java API, and many Java applications can easily be ported without difficulty. Because of the limited processing power on CDC devices, it is common to use them as network terminals for network access tasks. The exercise we'll be working through is a typical application that shows many of the techniques used on such devices.

We'll be looking at both the client and server sides of the application to demonstrate how the code differs and the areas of commonality. While most of this chapter will be taken up with code examples and explanations, we will also be examining some other topics, including working with a wireless Ethernet and what we would have to change in our application to move it to a CLDC device.

While the applications, a remote-control application for a MP3 player where in the device is used as remote control to play MP3 songs on the server, may not be typical of business software, it demonstrates the use of the various APIs for developing applications that involve audio streaming.

Working with the CDC Specification

The Connected Device Configuration specification is designed for devices capable of using networks and with graphical displays. The PersonalJava profile has been implemented for many operating systems and devices, including VxWorks (set-top boxes), EPOC (palm computers) and Pocket PC (more palm-top computers). Obviously, these different devices have very different requirements and specifications, something Java was originally intended to address and does. It is arguable that PersonalJava represents a much closer embodiment of what Java was originally intended to be: a lightweight, platform-independent, device-independent, development environment. At the time we're writing this book, PersonalJava is the only profile of the CDC available, so that's what we'll be working with here.

Also known as pJava, PersonalJava offers many advantages over its larger cousins, which are explored in depth elsewhere in this volume. We are really interested only in the Graphical User Interface and networking aspects, both of which are very similar to other Java editions. While the Swing API is absent in pJava, we still have the Abstract Windows Toolkit (AWT), which should prove more than sufficient for the kind of application we are planning to develop. On the networking side, RMI (Remote Method Invocation) is not yet available for pJava (though it is planned for a later release), so for the moment, we are restricted to using socket communications, and these operate considerably fast.

It is interesting to note that the Swing API is, of course, developed completely in Java and able to run on top of any Java Virtual Machine implementing the AWT. Therefore, it is possible to take all, or part, of the Swing API and install the classes onto a pJava compatible device, allowing applications to make use of Swing components. However, attempting to do this highlights the processing load Swing demands, as very few CDC devices are able to use Swing components without degradation in performance, reducing speed to the extent that it will affect usability in most cases.

Also missing from pJava are the Collections APIs, including `ArrayList` and `Stack`. While `Vector` can fulfill most of the roles Collections normally perform, it is more complex to use and can result in

longer source code. A full list of the pJava APIs is available from
`http://java.sun.com/products/personaljava/`.

Using Emulated Environments

Whenever we create applications for devices, we have to be aware that we cannot have all the functionality of a device in the emulator. While this should be true of all application development, as users may have different screen resolutions or color depth, it is particularly important when working on applications for completely different devices. Devices may have different input methods, screen layouts, and capabilities, and the Java developer must always be careful not to create device-specific code.

To aid development, we are provided with emulators, which attempt to show how the application will look when deployed on the device and run on our development platform. For our development, we will be using two emulation environments; one is provided by JavaSoft and emulates the pJava Virtual Machine, while the other actually emulates the Pocket PC operating system and gives us a much better impression of what our application is going to look like.

However, it is very important to test the final application on all the devices it is targeted to. This may not be practical for every pJava application, with over 35 different currently available devices and more coming. While testing on all of them would be ideal, it's not always possible for the small-scale developer, but it should be an ideal that is aimed for. For an application intended for wide-scale deployment, testing on every targeted operating system would be an acceptable minimum (EPOC, Pocket PC, VxWorks).

A good example of this is shown by the Pocket PC devices, which appear to offer a screen resolution of 240 x 320, but actually impose a taskbar of 8 pixels at the top of the screen, reducing the available space. A more serious problem on that same platform is the fact that, when inputting text, the virtual keyboard (or hand-writing area) covers the bottom 70 pixels! Many an application has proved unusable when text-input boxes have been placed too close to the bottom of the screen.

The PersonalJava Emulation Environment

The pJava Emulation Environment is available from
`http://www.javasoft.com/products/personaljava/pj-emulation.html`, and is available for Microsoft Windows and Sun Solaris only. It consists of only a runtime pJava Virtual Machine and associated class files. The pJava applications are compiled using the normal Java compiler (`javac`), and the class files are then executed using the pJava environment. When you choose to download the emulator, you will be asked what kind of interface you want to work with, and it's worth taking a moment to understand the options.

The AWT works by using local components, included as part of the operating system, and providing a wrapper for them in Java. For example, when you create a `Button` object in Java, the JVM asks the operating system for a `Button` object appropriate for that operating system and then allows the Java program to interact with the `Button` as though it were a proper Java object. This means that the same application running on an Apple Mac computer and a Microsoft Windows-based machine will look completely different, with Mac buttons being used on the Mac and Windows buttons being used on Windows. Giving a familiar interface is even more important with components like Menus, which may appear in different places in different operating systems (for example, at the top of the screen on a Mac). This also allows the Java application to make use of graphical components developed (most likely) in C and optimized to run extremely quickly on that operating system. The objects from the operating system used by the AWT are known as *peer objects* as they are peers of the Java objects, and this process is known as a *heavyweight* process because of the OS involvement. The Swing API used in J2SE is known as a *lightweight* process, as all Swing components are 100 percent Java objects, making them slow to use but much more flexible.

When working with pJava, we make use of local components for speed and platform-consistent appearance, and companies implementing pJava are encouraged to implement their own components specifically for Java application through a process called *Truffle*. With the pJava Emulation Environment, Sun provide two implementations — one using local components (Windows or Solaris) and the other using a Truffle set called *Touchable* developed for touch-sensitive screens. The Touchable interface was developed by Sun, who did massive amounts of research into what users needed in a touch-screen device and apparently decided that people like the color orange! It isn't a very pleasant interface, and there are no commercially available devices using it at the time of writing. For reference, the following shows the same application running using both interfaces, local and truffle.

This very simple GUI shown in Figures 8-1 and 8-2 consists of two `Button` objects, a `TextArea` and a `Label`, but it shows how Sun designed the components to be suitable for use with a finger. Note the button-controlled scrolling of the `TextArea`, which is provided by the Touchable component and not specified in the source code.

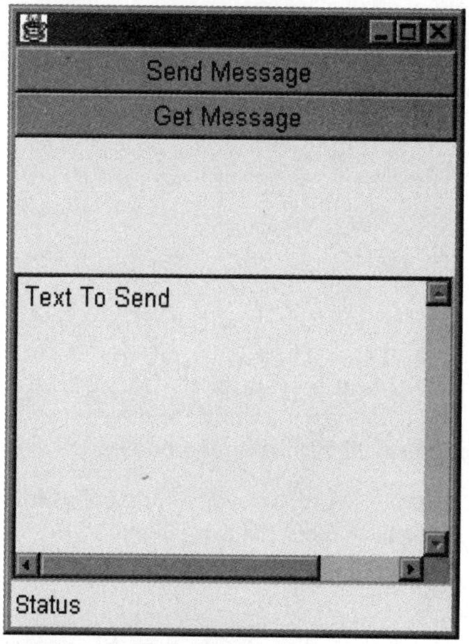

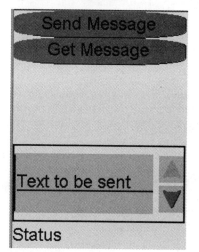

Figure 8-1: Normal Screen.

Figure 8-2: Touch Screen.

As we intend to deploy our application on a Pocket PC device, we will not be using Touchable, so we select a Windows interface for our pJava Emulation Environment.

Once it's downloaded and installed, we still need to configure our environment to be able to run applications in the pJava Virtual Machine. Strangely enough, the key thing we have to do is make sure our environment is not configured for Java development! CLASSPATH and JAVA_HOME are not used in pJava, so we need to make sure those aren't set in our shell by using the following commands;

```
set CLASSPATH=
set JAVA_HOME=
```

By leaving the values for these environment variables blank, we actually remove them from the memory to avoid using other Java libraries we might have installed. We can now run any Java application in our pJava Emulation Environment:

```
C:\pjee3.1\bin\pjava myJavaApplication
```

The preceding command assumes the Environment has been installed in the default directory (pjee3.1), which you will need to change if you have installed it anywhere else. You can also alter your path to allow you to run the Environment directly:

```
set PATH=%PATH%;c:\pjee3.1\bin
```

You will then be able to run your application just by specifying:

```
pjava myJavaApplication
```

Many applications will give errors when you try to run them using pJava. If any unsupported APIs are being used, such as Swing, the application will not run. Applications that don't make use of these APIs will work perfectly, and you may be surprised to see that they don't appear at all different from what they appear in Java 2 Standard Edition. Since the APIs not supported by pJava are normally the most recently developed ones, you will find that older Java applications should run perfectly without modification.

If you are developing under Microsoft Windows or Solaris, it's worth doing all your development using the pJava Emulation Environment, as it is easy to forget the limitations of the APIs available.

The Pocket PC emulation environment

Microsoft provides an emulator for the Pocket PC operating system as part of the freely available Pocket PC development kit, and this can be used for developing pJava applications. Unfortunately, it is not possible to download just the Pocket PC emulator; you have to download the C++ and Visual Basic development environments as well, making the whole download over 350 MB in size!

In addition, the emulator will run only under Windows 2000. There is no support for the emulator under Windows 98 or 95.

Once the emulator is installed, it produces a very accurate emulation of the interface you would expect to see on a Pocket PC device. Once the emulator is running, you will need to install the pJava environment, exactly as you would install it on a real device; see the "Installing the Application" section of this chapter for details.

Running applications on the Pocket PC emulator is a pretty good match with the real device, though you should be aware of ergonomic differences. Pocket PC devices interface with a pen rather than a mouse, and the user may have other applications installed that can change the appearance of the interface, so testing on the device itself is always a necessary step.

Working without emulation

While the emulators provide useful tools for working with pJava applications, they are not necessary. As pJava applications are compiled using the normal Java compiler, and the class files are identical, it's perfectly possible to develop an application without using an emulator at all. A pJava application is just a Java application that does not make use of particular APIs. As long as your application makes no use of unsupported APIs, you shouldn't have any problems.

As you gain experience working with pJava applications, the task of remembering not to use Swing and Collections should become second nature, and the lack of emulation will become less of a problem. Initially you should make frequent use of JavaCheck (see next section) to confirm that you haven't inadvertently used an unsupported API.

JavaCheck — *checks for pJava.*

JavaCheck is an application, written in Java, which analyses Java source code to confirm that it contains only API calls available in pJava. The intention is that it will, eventually, be able to analyze applications intended for different deployment platforms (such as CDC and the KVM), but for the moment, it supports checking only pJava compatibility.

While the pJava Emulation Environment will warn us if we try to use anything that isn't supported, it can be helpful to be able to run large amounts of code through a checking device, particularly if we are porting an existing application. It is also very useful if we don't have access to the pJava Emulation Environment (that is, if we are developing on a platform other than Microsoft Windows or Sun Solaris), where it provides the only method of checking our compatibility before deploying on the target device.

There are four possible states for an API. It can be Supported, Unsupported, Modified, or Optional. Supported APIs are obvious, and Unsupported is pretty clear, too. Modified APIs are slightly more complex, though the modifications are rarely as important as they might first appear. A good example of a Modified API is the `Frame` class, which, in pJava, can exist only once in each application.

Many classes are considered Optional, and this should be of concern to anyone developing applications for deployment on multiple platforms. However, at the time of writing, every pJava implementation implements every Optional class, making this much less of an issue. Future implementations may not have the Optional classes available, though this seems unlikely given the wide support already available.

JavaCheck can be downloaded from
`http://java.sun.com/products/personaljava/javacheck.html`. It is important to download not only the application itself, but also a specification file for the version of Java you wish to test against. As already mentioned in the first paragraph of this section, the only specification available is for pJava, but it still comes in a separate file and must be downloaded separately.

JavaCheck can be run in two different modes: from the command line or with a graphical user interface. Using the GUI is simple and effective. The GUI of JavaCheck can be invoked by executing the command:

```
java JavaCheckV
```

The V at the end of the name denotes that you are running the Visual version (with its GUI). We might also want to specify the CLASSPATH where the application can be found, which will depend on where we decided to install it. In my case, it's in a directory called `utils`, so I would run the application as follows:

```
java -cp /utils/JavaCheck/bin/JavaCheck.jar JavaCheckV
```

This will give us the following screen (Figure 8-3). Note the message at the top indicating that we have to load a specification file (see Figure 8-3); we select the specification file that we have already downloaded. Now we use the next Tab Classes as in Figure 8-4 to specify what files we want to check.

We'll be using the Server application that we'll be looking at in detail later. This application isn't actually intended to run on a pJava device (being the server), but it will serve to demonstrate how JavaCheck works.

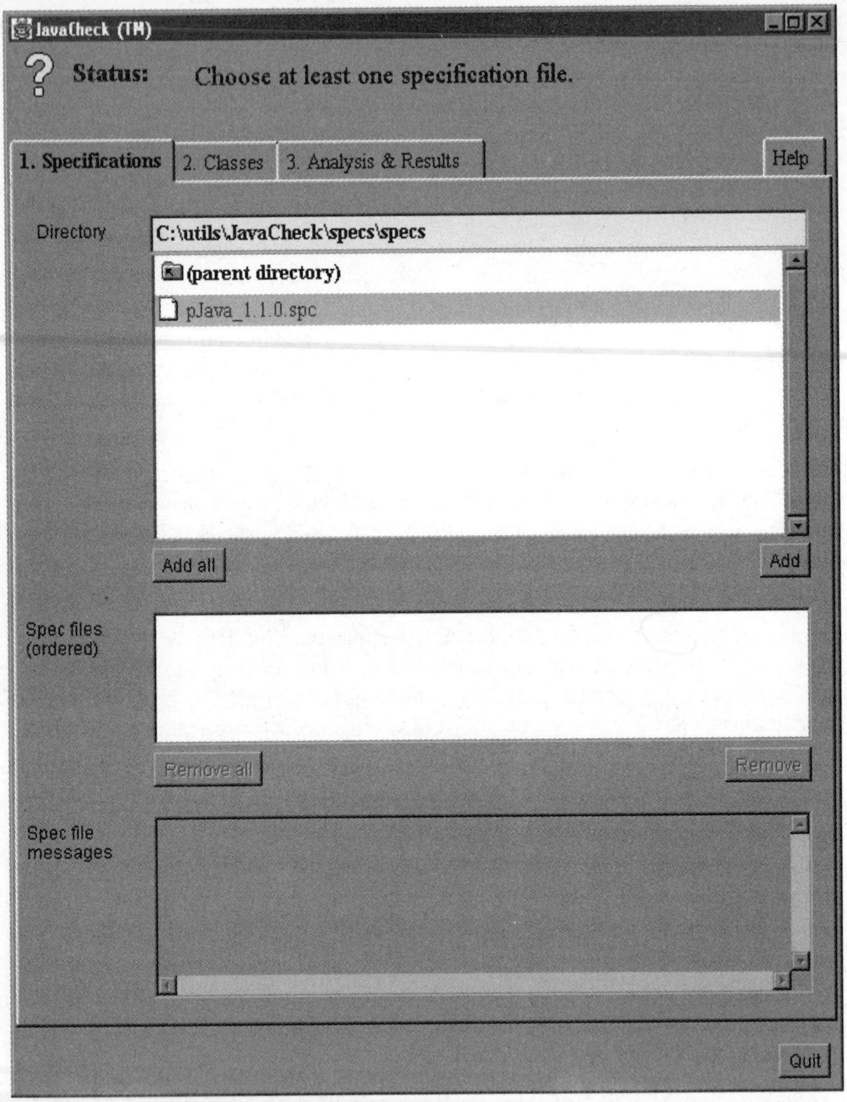

Figure 8-3: Java Check (Specification Compatibility).

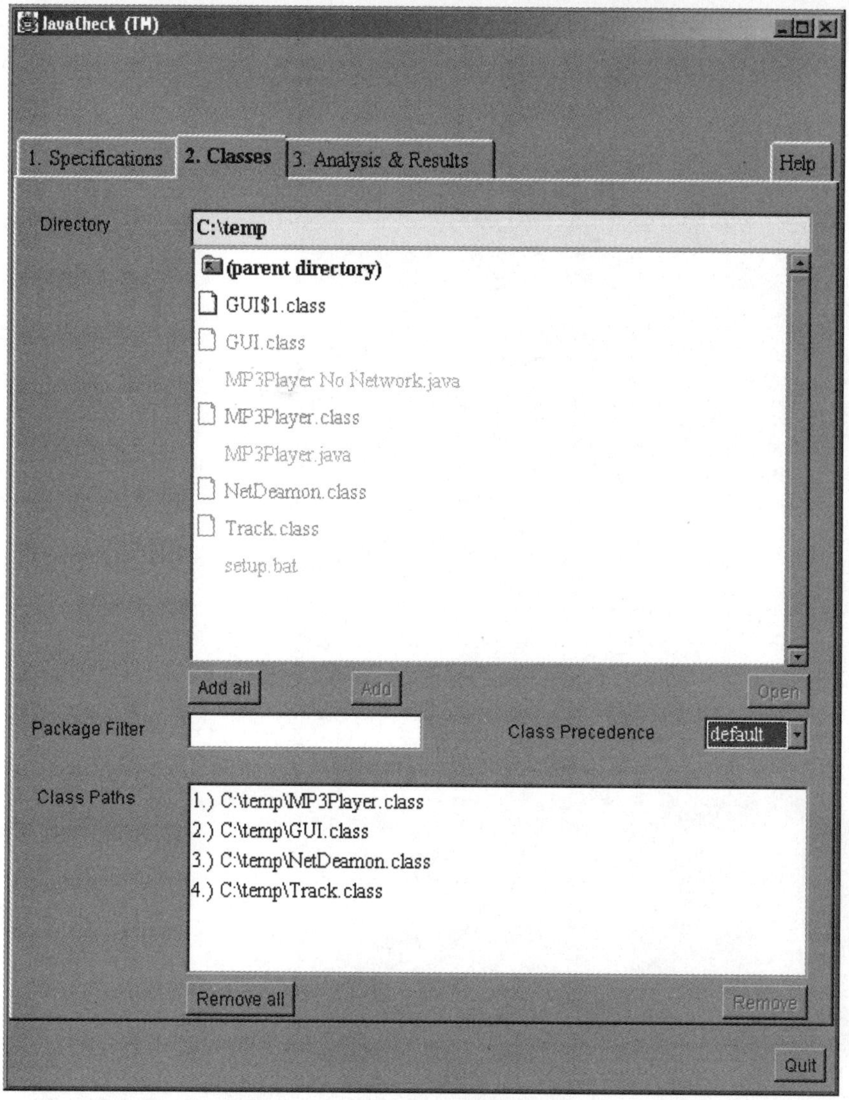

Figure 8-4: Java Check (Class to be Checked for Compatability).

Now that we've selected the files, we can start the analysis, which takes only a few seconds to produce the following result as shown in Figure 8-5.

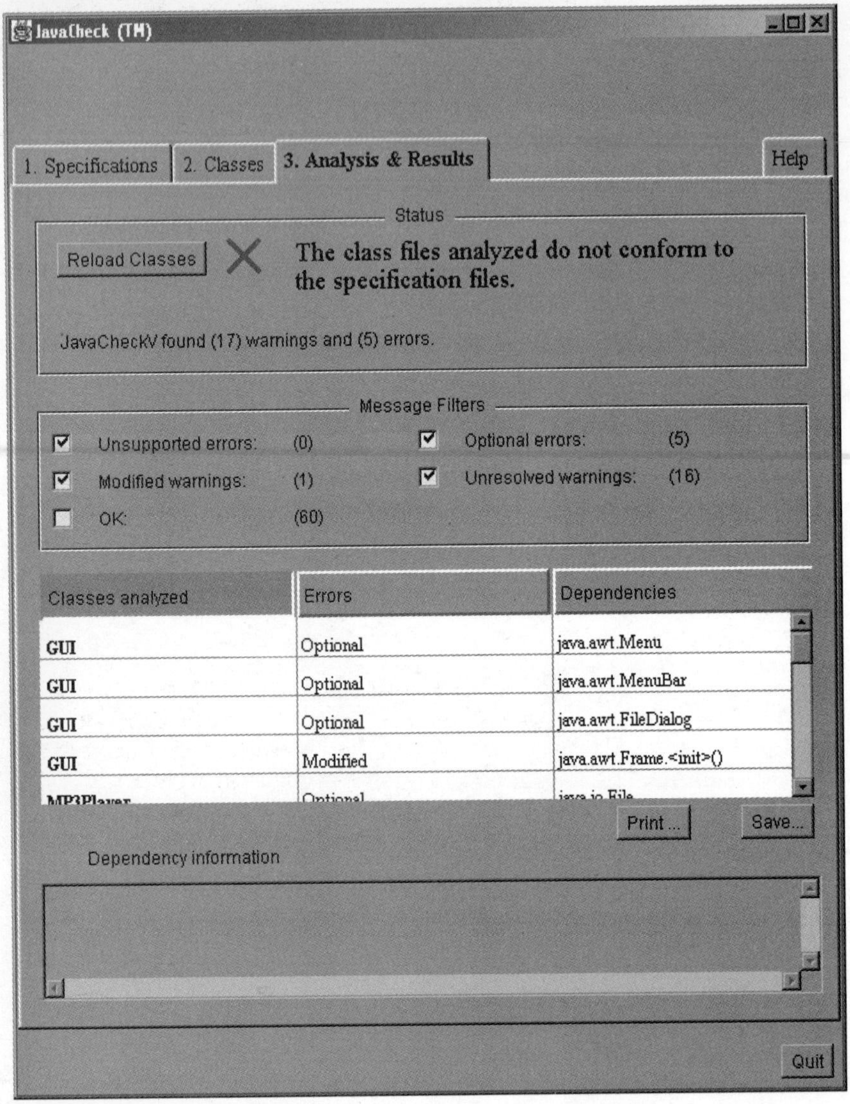

Figure 8-5: Java Check (Result).

It should come as no surprise that these classes do not conform to the pJava specification, as the application was not intended to be used on a CDC device, but this shows the kind of result you could expect. (Though this particular result would show that a lot of work is necessary to get these classes ported!) Selecting a particular class listed in the bottom window will show you some information about what the problem might be and what you might be able to do about it.

We can also invoke JavaCheck as a command-line application, though we have to specify everything on the same line:

```
C:\temp>java -cp /utils/JavaCheck/bin/JavaCheck.jar JavaCheck -v -i /utils/JavaC
heck/specs/specs/pJava_1.1.0.spc -classpath .
```

The parameter -v specifies that we want a Verbose response (with all the details), and -i specifies the specification file we want to use, while the -classpath points to where the files to be analyzed are located. The current directory is specified for the classpath, with the use of a ., so I'll run this command in the same place as my present working directory, and it will analyze all the class files in that directory.

This gives the same response as the graphical version but can be easier if you are going to be running it regularly as you develop your application. The output from the preceding example is very long (as my example used lots of unsupported classes), but we can look at the final summary output:

```
5 classes were loaded.
    JavaCheck:   82 dependencies were analyzed,
    JavaCheck:   0 dependencies were Unsupported,
    JavaCheck:   5 dependencies were Optionally implemented,
    JavaCheck:   1 dependency was Modified,
    JavaCheck:   16 dependencies were Unresolved,
    JavaCheck:   60 dependencies were OK.

    5 error(s), 17 warning(s) found.
The class files DO NOT CONFORM to the specified platform.
```

The only thing we really have to worry about are the Unsupported and Unresolved classes; in this case, there are no Unsupported classes, so if we wanted to port this to a pJava platform we would need to look at the Unresolved classes, that is, the classes which the Java Check was not able to resolve.

Introducing the project

Our application is a remote control for an MP3 player (though it will also play other audio formats), to which we are going to add a remote control. The remote control application will be written for a CDC device (a Pocket PC) using the pJava profile. While this may not be a typical business application, it does serve to demonstrate many of the techniques needed to work on hand-held devices, and its model of operation is very flexible and could easily be applied to many other applications. *JMF - needed ?*

The application itself is very simple, and makes use of the Java Media Framework (JMF) which can be downloaded from Sun at `http://www.javasoft.com/products/jmf`, where you will also find installation instructions. Discussing the application we are developing it takes a directory and draws up a list of files in that directory; it assumes that they are all audio files and starts playing first one while presenting the user with a basic user interface.. The remote control should be able to show the user a list of the tracks in the current directory, allowing the user to pause and resume playing, skip to the next and previous tracks, and skip to a particular track selected from the listing.

The networking will be done over TCP/IP, though it should be isolated to allow easy conversion to another networking system, such as IR or Bluetooth. All networking will be client driven, with the client making requests to the server.

This last aspect is very important for limited-function devices. It would be easy to design an application where the server expects the client to be available at all times, and while all CDC devices are capable of multi-tasking and can run background tasks, it is inadvisable to load a limited device with additional processing tasks.

How It Works

The first task is to define the protocol we are going to use for our communication. While there are many standard protocols available to choose from, we will be defining our own. Conforming to standards is often very useful, but any standard protocol will lead to gains in flexibility being offset by costs in efficiency. Depending on your application, you may wish to use HTTP or a similar protocol for the convenience of passing through firewalls, etc., though this will add considerably to the processing load imposed by the networking, which is something we want to keep to a minimum.

We will, therefore, be using the most basic protocol we can devise, both to keep network traffic to a minimum and keep the client-side processing requirement as small as possible.

As we have already stated that the client will initiate all communications, our server will be listening on a socket, waiting for clients to connect. First we must pick an appropriate socket to use; any number over 1,000 will do (numbers below 1,000 are reserved for standard defined protocols), so we'll select 1,710 as a reasonable, random, number.

Our client can perform certain tasks, which require interaction with the server, and we can list those tasks:

- ◆ Play next track
- ◆ Play previous track
- ◆ Play first track
- ◆ Play last track
- ◆ Get track listing
- ◆ Play track n (n = number of track from listing)
- ◆ Pause play
- ◆ Resume play

Each task will require a different message to be sent to the server from the client, and we can reduce these messages to a reasonable minimum to reduce network usage:

- ◆ Next
- ◆ Previous
- ◆ First
- ◆ Last
- ◆ Track listing
- ◆ Play n
- ◆ Pause
- ◆ Resume

It would be possible to further reduce the network bandwidth being used, ultimately by reducing each of the preceding to a single character, and while this would lead to very efficient bandwidth usage, it would be more complex to create and debug. It is always a good idea to keep your protocol commands to a human-readable form to aid development.

Since communication will be initiated by the client, it makes sense for the server to send the first message (when the client connects to it), so the client can be certain that the server is ready to receive a command. Therefore, we can decide that the server will respond with +OK to the initial connection. It is very common for server responses to start with a **+** or **−** preceding the message content, allowing the client to check the first character to see if the communication has been successful without having to look at the rest of the message.

So when the client initiates the connection and the server responds with +OK, the client then sends one of the preceding commands, and the server responds to say that the command has been carried out. It makes sense to combine that response with some useful information — in this case, the name of the currently playing track in the following format:

```
+OK Playing Track track name
```

This shall be the response to all commands, except `pause` and `track listing`, which will respond with **+**`paused` and a full listing of the currently loaded tracks, respectively. The track listing will be in the following format:

```
+Listing Follows
track name 1
track name 2
track name 3
.
```

Note that the listing is terminated with a single full stop alone on a line. This is a standard way of terminating a list of unknown length. (This list will be as long as the number of tracks loaded by the server.) This will cause a problem only if we ever have a track called `.`, which is not only unlikely, but as the track names are based on the file names, it is actually impossible on most personal computer systems.

We will also add a command, `status`, which simply responds with the currently playing track; this will enable the client to display the currently playing track on request.

We also have to decide on the case of the commands and responses. This is important, as it can cause hard-to-find problems later unless properly specified. In common with many modern protocols, we're going to define ours to be case-insensitive; any mix of case upper- and lowercase characters can be used. This will add some processing overhead but will prevent later problems.

Once we have defined our format, it's worth going through a dry run, working through typical client-server communications with a paper and pen to be certain we understand what's going to happen and to give us some examples to work from when we are testing the application. We will use a directory full of MP3 files and go through how the client and server communicate. See Table 8-1.

Table 8-1: Protocol Table

Client	Server
Open Connection	
	+OK
Track Listing	
	+Listing Follows
	EMF – You're Unbelievable
	Babylon Zoo – Spaceman
	Men Without Hats – Security
	Men Without Hats – On Tuesday
	Petula Clarck – Downtown
	.
Close Connection	
Open Connection	
	+OK
Status	
	+Playing Track EMF – You're Unbelievable

Close Connection	
Open Connection	
	+OK
Next	
	+Playing Track Babylon Zoo – Spaceman
Close Connection	
Open Connection	
	+OK
Previous	
	+Playing Track EMF – You're Unbelievable
Close Connection	
Open Connection	
	+OK
Last	
	+Playing Track Petula Clark – Downtown
Close Connection	
Open Connection	
	+OK
First	
	+Playing Track EMF – You're Unbelievable
Close Connection	
Open Connection	
	+OK
Play 3	
	+Playing Track Men Without Hats – Security
Close Connection	
Open Connection	
	+OK
Pause	

		+Paused
Close Connection		
Open Connection		
		+OK
Resume		
		+Playing Track Men Without Hats – Security
Close Connection		

This table shows us all the possible commands and the responses. We could go on to define the various error messages which could be returned and how we might cope with them, though we might want to start development to see the kind of problems that crop up. As this system simply allows a server to be controlled by a client through discrete transaction-based communications (one connection for each command), any error will be dealt with by shutting down the network connection and starting again.

Our server will not accept more than one command per connection, each transaction can perform only one action, and it's worth looking at why we have made this limitation and when it would be inappropriate. Our application is designed to give control of a function operating on a server to a client application and is strictly a "control" relationship. Having each command as a separate connection does add considerable overhead but makes for a much simpler client and server and makes error recovery easier. Because each transaction is independent, any individual transaction failure can be fixed just by repeating the transaction.

While this model of operation may not be suitable in every circumstance, some applications may have continuous communications between client and server and save resources by holding a connection open; in many situations, the simplicity and robustness outweigh the cost in resources. It is worth noting that this is the model on which HTTP operates and so do all Web-driven interfaces.

The next two figures display the flow of the application. Figure 8-6 displays the flow of server application and Figure 8-7 displays the flow of client application.

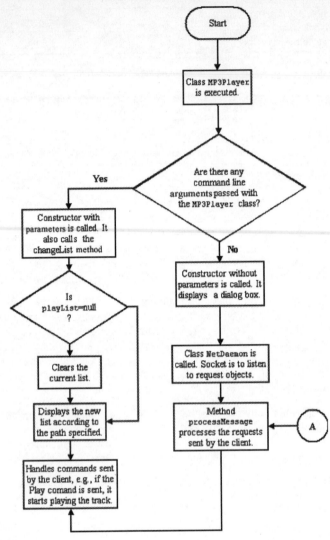

Figure 8-6: FlowChart Server.

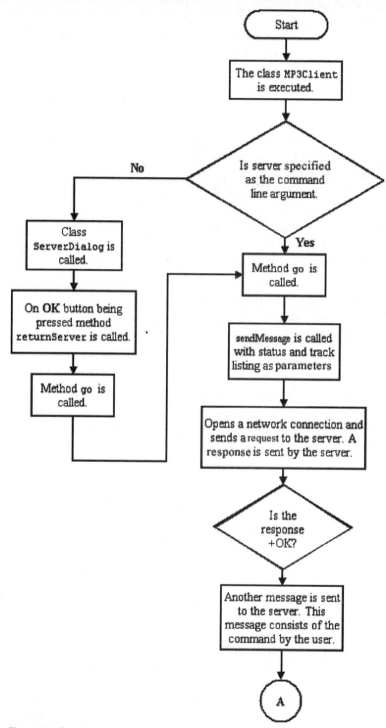

Figure 8-7: FlowChart Client.

How to Run

To run the server you have to type the following command on the command prompt.

```
java MP3Player
java MP3Player d:\mp3\
```

The server when started gives an output like Figure 8-8.

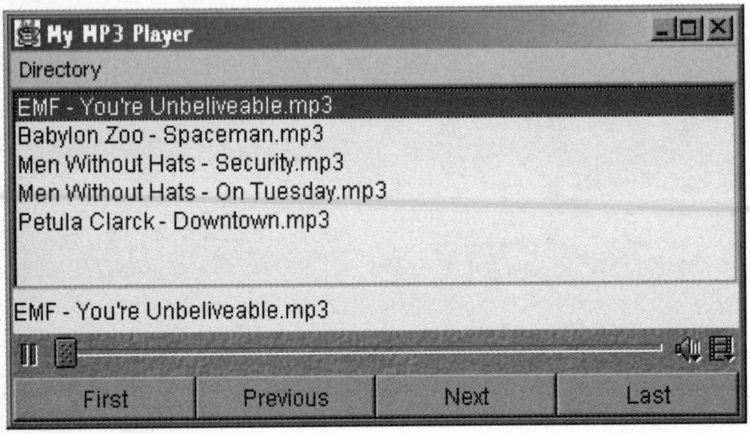

Figure 8-8: Server.

The actual process of installation the client will vary depending on the device being used. Since we are working with a Pocket PC device, we will be looking only at how to install the application onto that platform, which is very simple indeed. Other devices normally are similarly simple to use, but you will need to check the device documentation for details.

In order to be able to execute PersonalJava applications, the device first has to have a Java Virtual Machine installed. Most of these are available from Sun, though some companies provide their own implementation (for example, Symbian for the EPOC JVM). At the time of writing, the Pocket PC JVM is at final beta stage and is available only to users registered with the Sun Developer Connection, which requires (free) registration: the following URL should be used to register:

```
http://developer.java.sun.com/developer/earlyAccess/personaljava/
```

Once the beta is completed, the final version should be available from:

```
http://www.javasoft.com/products/personaljava
```

The file is provided in the form of a Pocket PC CAB file, which should be copied onto the device and executed. Follow the on-screen prompts to install the JVM.

Once the JVM is installed, it's just a matter of copying your class files onto the device and executing the file containing the main() method (MP3Client.class in our example).

This application MP3Client , when run, will produce something that looks like Figure 8-9 (though the exact appearance will, of course, depend on the device in which it is run).

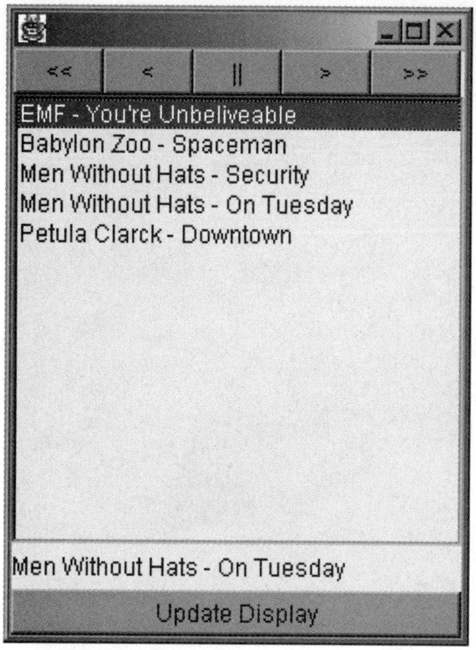

Make note of all PDA's in the lab.

Figure 8-9: Client.

Working With Wireless Networks

This application was designed to work on a Pocket PC device or a Compaq iPaq and to be used over a Wireless Ethernet network. Using wireless networks from Java is no different from any other TCP/IP network; the operating system (or, more accurately, the TCP/IP stack part of the operating system) takes responsibility for all error correction and routing issues. We just use sockets in the normal way as the operating system will take care of the actual communication done on the wireless network for the device.

It is possible to use technologies such as RMI and Java Enterprise Beans over Wireless Ethernet networks if you are working with devices that support that kind of technology (not CDC devices!).

Using Wireless Ethernet is a very effective and simple way to produce handheld applications linked to powerful servers, though it should be noted that battery life becomes a real problem. Wireless Ethernet consumes a great deal of power, and handheld devices can't be relied upon to provide long-term operation on such a network.

MP3Player.java

This class is part of Server for this application and caters to the request sent by the client. This class is the main class and is responsible for invoking the other three classes which are `NetDeamon`, `GUI` and `Track`.

Listing 8-1: MP3Player.java

```
// © 2001 Dreamtech Software India, Inc.
// All rights Reserved1.   import java.io.*;
2.   import java.net.*;
3.   import java.util.*;
4.   import java.awt.*;
5.   import java.awt.event.*;
6.   import javax.media.*;
7.
```

```
8.   public class MP3Player
9.   {
10.    ArrayList playList;
11.    GUI myGUI;
12.    NetDeamon myDeamon;
13.    Track currentlyPlaying;
14.    public static void main(String args[]) {
15.     MP3Player myPlayer;
16.     if (args.length != 0) {
17.         myPlayer = new MP3Player(args[0]);
18.     }
19.     else {
20.         myPlayer = new MP3Player();
21.     }
22.     myPlayer.playTrack(0);
23.    }
24.    public MP3Player(String path) {
25.     myGUI = new GUI(this);
26.     myDeamon = new NetDeamon(this);
27.     myDeamon.start();
28.     changeList(path);
29.    }
30.    public MP3Player() {
31.     myGUI = new GUI(this);
32.     myDeamon = new NetDeamon(this);
33.     myDeamon.start();
34.     myGUI.selectDir();
35.    }
36.    public void playTrack(int index) {
37.     currentlyPlaying.stop();
38.     currentlyPlaying = (Track)playList.get(index);
39.     myGUI.playingTrack(currentlyPlaying);
40.     currentlyPlaying.start();
41.    }
42.    public void trackFinished() {
43.     playNext();
44.    }
45.    public void playFirst() {
46.     playTrack(0);
47.    }
48.    public void playPrevious() {
49.     if (currentlyPlaying.getNumber() > 0) {
50.         playTrack(currentlyPlaying.getNumber() - 1);
51.     }
52.     else {
53.         playFirst();
54.     }
55.    }
56.    public void playNext() {
57.     if (currentlyPlaying.getNumber() < (playList.size()-1)) {
58.         playTrack(currentlyPlaying.getNumber() + 1);
59.     }
60.     else {
61.         playFirst();
62.     }
63.    }
```

```
64.    public void playLast() {
65.      playTrack(playList.size() - 1);
66.    }
67.    public void changeList(String path) {
68.      if (playList != null) {
69.          for (int i=0;i < playList.size(); i++) {
70.              currentlyPlaying = (Track)playList.get(i);
71.              currentlyPlaying.release();
72.          }
73.      }
74.      playList = new ArrayList();
75.      File folder = new File(path);
76.      String names[] = folder.list();
77.      for (int i=0;i < names.length;i++) {
78.          playList.add(new Track(this, folder + File.separator + names[i], i));
79.      }
80.      currentlyPlaying = (Track)playList.get(0);
81.      myGUI.layoutGUI(names);
82.      playTrack(0);
83.    }
84.    public Track getPlaying() {
85.      return currentlyPlaying;
86.    }
87.    public ArrayList getList() {
88.      return playList;
89.    }
90.  }
```

Code explanation

♦ Lines 1-6: These lines are the normal import statements you would expect to see in any Java network application. —

♦ Lines 8-13: These lines contains our class variables. `playList` stores all the Track objects we will be listening to and forms our play list. `myGUI` will be our graphical user interface, allowing the application to be used in standalone mode. `myDeamon` is our networking object, which will handle all the client commands. The `currentlyPlaying` variable holds the track that is currently being played. —

♦ Lines 14-23: Our main method is used to instantiate an instance of `MP3Player`, so we don't have to work with a static object. We want the application to be able to take a directory specified on the command line — here in these lines we check to see if a directory has been specified and run the appropriate constructor. —

♦ Lines 24-29: In these lines the constructor is used if a directory has been specified on the command line and creates the graphical user interface, network interface, and a new play list using the `changeList()` method. Note that `NetDeamon` is a threaded class and needs to be started here. We pass a reference to the GUI and network interfaces to allow them to call methods of our instance of `MP3Player` when commands come in (from the GUI or network). —

♦ Lines 30-35: The second constructor in these lines is almost identical, but runs a method of the GUI object to allow the user to select a directory using a `FileDialog`. —

♦ Lines 36-41: In these lines the method allows the selection of a particular track from the play list, which will be started. Note that the `currentlyPlaying` track must be stopped first, as the Java Media Framework is multithreaded and will happily play two tracks simultaneously, which makes for interesting effects, but not relaxing listening! We also have to tell the GUI that the track has been changed so it can update its display. If we wanted to have server-initiated contact to update the network client, too, we would put the code here, but it would depend on the client always being active, which we want to avoid. — ✓

♦ Lines 42-44: The method in these lines is called whenever a track finishes and simply plays the next track in the list. — ✓ *hmm, nice.*

♦ Lines 45-66: The GUI or NetDeamon classes call these four methods when commands are received to carry out these actions. This should happen in response to user input. — ✓

♦ Lines 67-83: This method in these lines is used whenever a new directory is selected; note that it first checks if playList has been initiated, as it wasn't the first time, and then releases each Track object held in the list. This is done to make sure that resources are properly released, as the Java Media Framework demands. We then create a new ArrayList and load it with files matching the names available in the directory passed as a parameter. We also make the GUI lay itself out again, to update the displayed list, and start playing the first track. As before, if we wanted to have server-initiated network contact to update the client, it would go here, but that would rely on the client being always available.

♦ Lines 84-90: The last two methods declared in these lines are used to get the currently playing Track object and complete the play list. The GUI and networking objects use these to update the display. — ✓

NetDeamon.java — *careful with this - bluetooth capabilities?*

This class is part of Server for this application. This extends thread and is used for receiving client connection and sending response to the client.

Listing 8-2: NetDeamon.java

// © 2001 Dreamtech Software India, Inc.
// All rights Reserved

```
1.    import java.io.*;
2.    import java.net.*;
3.    import java.util.*;
4.    import java.awt.*;
5.    import java.awt.event.*;
6.    import javax.media.*;
7.
8.    public class NetDeamon extends Thread {
9.      PrintWriter out = null;
10.     String s;
11.     MP3Player parent;
12.     public NetDeamon(MP3Player mp3)
13.     {
14.       parent = mp3;
15.     }
16.     public void run()
17.     {
18.       try
19.       {
20.           ServerSocket server = new ServerSocket(1710);
21.           Socket sock;
22.           while (true)
23.           {
24.               sock = server.accept();
25.               out = new PrintWriter(sock.getOutputStream());
26.               BufferedReader in = new BufferedReader (new InputStreamReader
(sock.getInputStream ()),1);
```

```
27.                   out.println("+OK");
28.                   out.flush();
29.                   processMessage(in.readLine().toUpperCase());
30.                   out.flush();
31.                   in.close();
32.                   out.close();
33.                   sock.close();
34.            }
35.      }
36.      catch (IOException e)
37.      {
38.              System.out.println("Networking Error");
39.      }
40.    }
41.    public void processMessage(String message)
42.    {
43.      if (message.startsWith("NEXT"))
44.      {
45.              parent.playNext();
46.              sendPlaying();
47.      }
48.      else if (message.startsWith("PREVIOUS"))
49.      {
50.              parent.playPrevious();
51.              sendPlaying();
52.      }
53.      else if (message.startsWith("FIRST"))
54.      {
55.              parent.playFirst();
56.              sendPlaying();
57.      }
58.      else if (message.startsWith("LAST"))
59.      {
60.              parent.playLast();
61.              sendPlaying();
62.      }
63.      else if (message.startsWith("STATUS"))
64.      {
65.              sendPlaying();
66.      }
67.      else if (message.startsWith("PAUSE"))
68.      {
69.              parent.getPlaying().pause();
70.              out.println("+Paused");
71.      }
72.      else if (message.startsWith("RESUME"))
73.      {
74.              parent.getPlaying().start();
75.      sendPlaying();
76.      }
77.      else if (message.startsWith("TRACK LISTING"))
78.      {
79.              ArrayList tracks = parent.getList();
80.              out.println("+Listing Follows");
81.              for (int i=0;i < tracks.size();i++)
82.              {
```

```
83.                     sendName((Track)tracks.get(i));
84.             }
85.         out.println(".");
86.     }
87.     else if (message.startsWith("PLAY"))
88.     {
89.         parent.playTrack(new Integer(message.substring(5)).intValue());
90.         sendPlaying();
91.     }
92.     else
93.     {
94.         out.println("-Unrecogonised Command : " + message);
95.     }
96.     }
97.     private void sendPlaying()
98.     {
99.     String s = parent.getPlaying().getName();
100.        out.println("+Playing " + s.substring(0,s.lastIndexOf(".")));
101.     }
102.     private void sendName(Track t)
103.     {
104.        String s = t.getName();
105.        out.println(s.substring(0,s.lastIndexOf(".")));
106.     }
107.     }
```

Code explanation

- Lines 1-6: These lines are the normal import statements you would expect to see in any Java network application.

- Lines 8-11: This class declared is used to handle the networking aspects of the client, receiving client connections, and responding to the commands issued by the client.

- Lines 12-15: In these lines a reference to the MP3Player object that instantiates this class is kept to allow us to call methods of that object when we receive appropriate commands. This reference is stored in the class variable parent.

- Lines 16-40: This is our main loop of the networking daemon; it enters an infinite loop and waits for an incoming connection. Contact is responded to with +OK, and the incoming message is then sent to the processMessage() method in uppercase to maintain our requirement for case-insensitivity. Since all communications consist of a single command and response, we shut down the network connection. Note the use of the flush() method after every network communication; this is very important, as otherwise communications can be lost when the connection is closed. Missing out the flush() method not only causes problems, but the problems are very hard to locate.

- Lines 41-96: Here in these lines we just have an if block that looks to find out what the incoming command is and carries out the appropriate action. Most of the commands are very simple, with only the "TRACK LISTING" command being complex, and that just requests an ArrayList of all the tracks from the parent object and outputs their names to the client. Almost all the commands respond with the name of the currently playing track, so we have a separate method just for that function:

- Lines 97-101: The method in these lines is used to send the currently playing track, with "+Playing" at the start, as specified in our protocol.

♦ Lines 102-107: This last method is just used to send the name of the track when a full play list is requested. Note that we send the track name only up to the last " . ", which is designed to cut off the .mp3 normally found at the end of media filenames. This code will cause problems if the filenames don't have a similar extension.

GUI.java

This class is part of Server for this application. This class creates and displays the Graphical User Interface for the application. It allows the user the same interaction as the client object but locally to the server. It would be possible to create this application without any interface at all, relying on the client to issue all the commands and specifying the directory on the command line when the server is run. However, having a local GUI makes testing a great deal easier and makes the application more useful. The ActionListener interface is used to catch menu events, allowing the user to change the directory to be used.

Listing 8-3: GUI.java

// © 2001 Dreamtech Software India, Inc.
// All rights Reserved

```
1.   import java.io.*;
2.   import java.net.*;
3.   import java.util.*;
4.   import java.awt.*;
5.   import java.awt.event.*;
6.   import javax.media.*;
7.
8.   public class GUI implements MouseListener, ActionListener
9.   {
10.     Frame f;
11.     java.awt.List nameList;
12.     Panel extras;
13.     Panel buttons;
14.     Button first,previous,next,last;
15.     Label playing;
16.     MP3Player parent;
17.
18.     public GUI(MP3Player MP3)
19.     {
20.       parent = MP3;
21.       f = new Frame("My MP3 Player");
22.       nameList = new java.awt.List();
23.       first = new Button("First");
24.       previous = new Button("Previous");
25.       next = new Button("Next");
26.       last = new Button("Last");
27.       first.addMouseListener(this);
28.       previous.addMouseListener(this);
29.       next.addMouseListener(this);
30.       last.addMouseListener(this);
31.       buttons = new Panel(new GridLayout(1,4));
32.       buttons.add(first);
33.       buttons.add(previous);
34.       buttons.add(next);
35.       buttons.add(last);
36.       MenuBar myMenuBar = new MenuBar();
37.       Menu myMenu = new Menu("Directory");
```

```
38.      MenuItem m1 = new MenuItem("Change Directory");
39.      m1.addActionListener(this);
40.      myMenu.add(m1);
41.      MenuItem m2 = new MenuItem("Exit");
42.      m2.addActionListener(this);
43.      myMenu.add(m2);
44.      myMenuBar.add(myMenu);
45.      f.setMenuBar(myMenuBar);
46.      f.setLayout(new BorderLayout());
47.      f.setSize(400,200);
48.      nameList.addMouseListener(this);
49.      f.addWindowListener(new WindowAdapter()
50.      {
51.           public void windowClosing (WindowEvent e) {
52.                 System.exit(0);
53.           }
54.      });
55.   }
56.
57.   public void layoutGUI(String[] names)
58.   {
59.    f.removeAll();
60.    nameList.removeAll();
61.    playing = new Label(names[0]);
62.    for (int i=0;i < names.length;i++)
63.    {
64.         nameList.add(names[i]);
65.    }
66.    extras = new Panel(new GridLayout(3,1));
67.    extras.add(playing);
68.    extras.add(new Label(""));
69.    extras.add(buttons);
70.    f.add(nameList, BorderLayout.CENTER);
71.    f.add(extras, BorderLayout.SOUTH);
72.    f.validate();
73.    f.setVisible(true);
74.   }
75.   public void playingTrack(Track t)
76.   {
77.    nameList.select(t.getNumber());
78.    playing.setText(t.getName());
79.    extras.removeAll();
80.    extras.add(playing);
81.    extras.add(t.getVisualComponent());
82.    extras.add(buttons);
83.    f.validate();
84.   }
85.   public void mouseClicked(MouseEvent e)
86.   {
87.    if (e.getComponent() == nameList)
88.    {
89.         parent.playTrack(nameList.getSelectedIndex());
90.    }
91.    else if (e.getComponent() == first)
92.    {
93.         parent.playFirst();
```

```
94.      }
95.      else if (e.getComponent() == previous)
96.      {
97.           parent.playPrevious();
98.      }
99.      else if (e.getComponent() == next)
100.          {
101.                  parent.playNext();
102.          }
103.          else if (e.getComponent() == last)
104.          {
105.                  parent.playLast();
106.          }
107.     }
108.     public void mouseEntered(MouseEvent e) {}
109.     public void mouseExited(MouseEvent e) {}
110.     public void mousePressed(MouseEvent e) {}
111.     public void mouseReleased(MouseEvent e) {}
112.
113.     public void actionPerformed(ActionEvent e)
114.     {
115.          String caption = e.getActionCommand();
116.          if(caption.equals("Change Directory"))
117.          {
118.                  selectDir();
119.          }
120.          else
121.          {
122.                  System.exit(0);
123.          }
124.     }
125.     public void selectDir()
126.     {
127.          FileDialog finder = new FileDialog(f, "Select A File In The
Directory");
128.          finder.setVisible(true);
129.          String newPath = finder.getDirectory();
130.          if (finder.getFile() != null)
131.          {
132.                  newPath = newPath.substring(0, newPath.length()-1);
133.                  parent.changeList(newPath);
134.          }
135.     }
136. }
```

Code explanation

♦ Lines 1-6: These lines are the normal import statements you would expect to see in any Java network application.

♦ Lines 8-16: These lines contain our class variables and should be familiar to any Java programmer. We aren't using Swing components for this application; the interface isn't complex enough to make it worth using. These are all AWT classes. Note the last variable, `parent`, which is used to maintain a reference to the `MP3Player` object, which instantiates this object. It means that we can call methods of that object when the user presses buttons, etc.

♦ Lines 18-55: The constructor in these lines is fairly typical of Graphical User Interface objects and shouldn't present any surprises. An anonymous adapter is used to close the application if the user tries to close the Window in an operating system-dependent fashion (that is, pressing Alt+F4 on a Microsoft Windows system).

◆ Line 57-74: The method in the preceding lines is used to lay out the GUI when a new list is being used; it takes a `String` array of the names of tracks.

◆ Lines 75-84: There are many ways for the track to be changed, either through user interaction, network commands, or just reaching the end of the current track. This updates the `List` to highlight the currently playing track. The GUI also has a `Label` showing the currently playing track, called `playing`, and this is updated to show the name of the current track.

◆ Lines 85-107: This code lines catches the mouse clicks on the buttons and play list and runs the appropriate methods of the `MP3Player` object passed into the constructor (called `parent`). If the play list was selected, the selected track number is passed to the `playTrack()` method of the `parent` object.

◆ Lines 108-111: The methods in these lines are needed for the `MouseListener` interface.

◆ Lines 113-124: The method in these lines is called when the user selects an item from the menu on the frame. As the menu has only two entries, the options are limited to changing the current directory or exiting the program.

◆ Lines 125-136: The last method allows the user to select a different directory to be used for the building of the file list. Note that the user is required to select a file within the directory chosen, as the `FileDialog` won't allow the selection of a directory itself. The actual file selected is ignored, but the directory containing it is then used to rebuild the play list and start playing the first track.

Track.java

media framework

This class is used to represent the actual files themselves and handles all the JMF functions. The JMF is not complex, at least for this level of functionality, and even if you're not familiar with this, you should have no problem following the example. The `ControllerListener` interface is used in the JMF to allow an object to respond to media events, as we shall see.

Listing 8-4: Track.java

```
1.   import java.io.*;
2.   import java.net.*;
3.   import java.util.*;
4.   import java.awt.*;
5.   import java.awt.event.*;
6.   import javax.media.*;
7.
8.   public class Track implements ControllerListener
9.   {
10.    File details;
11.    Player p;
12.    MP3Player parent;
13.    int number;
14.
15.    public Track(MP3Player mp, String fname, int n)
16.    {
17.      number = n;
18.      parent = mp;
19.      try
20.      {
21.          details = new File(fname);
```

```
22.              URL u = new URL("file:///" + fname);
23.              p = Manager.createPlayer(u);
24.              p.realize();
25.              p.prefetch();
26.              p.addControllerListener(this);
27.         }
28.         catch (MalformedURLException e)
29.         {
30.              System.out.println("URL Not Formed Properly");
31.         }
32.         catch (NoPlayerException e)
33.         {
34.              System.out.println("Unsupported Format");
35.         }
36.         catch (IOException e)
37.         {
38.              System.out.println("File not loaded or unavailable");
39.         }
40.     }
41.
42.     public int getNumber()
43.     {
44.       return number;
45.     }
46.     public String getName()
47.     {
48.       return details.getName();
49.     }
50.     public Component getVisualComponent()
51.     {
52.       return p.getControlPanelComponent();
53.     }
54.     public synchronized void controllerUpdate(ControllerEvent e)
55.     {
56.       if (e instanceof EndOfMediaEvent)
57.       {
58.            parent.trackFinished();
59.       }
60.       else if (e instanceof PrefetchCompleteEvent)
61.       {}
62.       else if (e instanceof RealizeCompleteEvent)
63.       {}
64.       else if (e instanceof StartEvent)
65.       {}
66.       else if (e instanceof DurationUpdateEvent)
67.       {}
68.       else if (e instanceof TransitionEvent)
69.       {}
70.       else if (e instanceof MediaTimeSetEvent)
71.       {}
72.       else if (e instanceof ControllerClosedEvent)
73.       {} else
74.       {
75.            System.out.println("Other Media Event");
76.            System.out.println(e.toString());
77.       }
```

```
78.    }
79.    public void start()
80.    {
81.      p.start();
82.    }
83.    public void pause()
84.    {
85.      p.stop();
86.    }
87.    public void stop()
88.    {
89.      p.stop();
90.      p.setMediaTime(new Time(0));
91.    }
92.    public void release()
93.    {
94.      p.stop();
95.      p.deallocate();
96.      p.close();
97.    }
98.    protected void finalize() throws Throwable
99.    {
100.          p.stop();
101.          p.deallocate();
102.          p.close();
103.     }
104.  }
```

Code explanation

♦ Lines 1-6: These lines are the normal import statements you would expect to see in any Java network application.

♦ Lines 8-13: These lines contains our class variables; we keep track of the file as well as creating a Player object (from the JMF) and a reference to the MP3Player object that instantiates this class. We also keep track of our position in the play list, so we know what track comes next!

♦ Lines 15-40: The constructor these lines creates all the class variables, including the Player object we'll be using to control the audio media. Note that the Player is created from the static Manager class, as specified in the JMF. We also use the realize() and prefetch() methods of Player, which causes the JMF to allocate resources to the Player object and gives us a very fast response when we start playing the audio. If we left out these two lines, the application would still work but would have a delay when we started playing every track.

♦ Lines 42-49: These two accessor methods declared in these lines just return details of the audio file being played.

♦ Lines 50-53: This method in these lines returns the control panel for the Player object. For audio files, this consists of a sliding bar and pause button.

♦ Lines 54-78: The method is required by the ControllerListener interface; it receives events relating to the audio file. Note that we actually ignore most events, becoming interested only when the track is finished and we want to move on to the next track.

♦ Lines 79-91: The methods in these lines pass on commands to the Player object. Note that the last method resets the position within the file to the start; without that, the object would remember where it was in the file and return to that position when play was requested next time.

- ◆ Lines 92-97: This method releases all the resources used in the Player, and closes it. Player objects have access to resources such as the sound card and must be properly released in this fashion.

- ◆ Lines 98-104: This finalize() method declared in these lines should be triggered by the garbage collector when the object is cleaned from memory. It also releases all the resources used by the Player and is put in as a confirmation that the resources have been released. In theory, this makes the previous release() method redundant, but as documented in the Java programming language, there is no guaranteeing when the finalize() method will be run, and it is best to release resources as quickly as possible.

MP3Client.java

This class is a part of client application a will run on the device. This class interacts with the server the communication between the client and the server is socket based. This class provides the GUI for the client running on the Device.

Listing 8-5: MP3Client.java

// © 2001 Dreamtech Software India, Inc.
// All rights Reserved

```
1.   import java.io.*;
2.   import java.net.*;
3.   import java.util.*;
4.   import java.awt.*;
5.   import java.awt.event.*;
6.
7.   public class MP3Client implements MouseListener
8.   {
9.     Frame f = new Frame();;
10.    Button first, previous, next, last, pause,update;
11.    Label status = new Label();;
12.    List tracks;
13.    String server;
14.
15.    public static void main(String args[])
16.    {
17.      MP3Client myClient = new MP3Client(args);
18.    }
19.
20.    MP3Client(String[] args)
21.    {
22.      if (args.length != 0)
23.      {
24.          go(args[0]);
25.      }
26.      else
27.      {
28.          ServerDialog getServer = new ServerDialog(f,this);
29.      }
30.    }
31.
32.    public void returnServer(String s)
33.    {
34.      go(s);
35.    }
```

```
36.
37.    public void go(String s)
38.    {
39.     server = s;
40.     first = new Button("<<");
41.     previous = new Button("<");
42.     next = new Button(">");
43.     last = new Button(">>");
44.     pause = new Button("||");
45.     update = new Button("Update Display");
46.     first.addMouseListener(this);
47.     previous.addMouseListener(this);
48.     next.addMouseListener(this);
49.     last.addMouseListener(this);
50.     pause.addMouseListener(this);
51.     update.addMouseListener(this);
52.     Panel controls = new Panel(new GridLayout(1,5));
53.     controls.add(first);
54.     controls.add(previous);
55.     controls.add(pause);
56.     controls.add(next);
57.     controls.add(last);
58.     Panel display = new Panel(new GridLayout(2,1));
59.     display.add(status);
60.     display.add(update);
61.     tracks = new java.awt.List();
62.     tracks.addMouseListener(this);
63.     f.setLayout(new BorderLayout());
64.     f.add(display, BorderLayout.SOUTH);
65.     f.add(tracks, BorderLayout.CENTER);
66.     f.add(controls, BorderLayout.NORTH);
67.     f.pack();
68.     f.setSize(240,320);
69.     f.setVisible(true);
70.     sendMessage("status");
71.     sendMessage("track listing");
72.     f.addWindowListener(new WindowAdapter()
73.     {
74.         public void windowClosing (WindowEvent e)
75.         {
76.                 System.exit(0);
77.         }
78.     });
79.    }
80.
81.    public void sendMessage(String message)
82.    {
83.     PrintWriter out = null;
84.     BufferedReader in;
85.     try
86.     {
87.         Socket sock = new Socket (server, 1710);
88.         in = new BufferedReader (new InputStreamReader(sock.getInputStream
()),1);
89.         String s = in.readLine().toUpperCase();
90.         if (s.startsWith("+OK"))
```

```
91.                {
92.                        out = new PrintWriter(sock.getOutputStream());
93.                        out.println(message);
94.                        out.flush();
95.                }
96.            else
97.                {
98.                        System.out.println("Error :" + s);
99.                }
100.                s = in.readLine();
101.                if (s.toUpperCase().startsWith("+PLAYING"))
102.                {
103.                        status.setText(s.substring(9));
104.                }
105.                else if (s.toUpperCase().startsWith("+PAUSED"))
106.                {
107.                        status.setText("Paused");
108.                }
109.                else if (s.toUpperCase().startsWith("+LISTING FOLLOWS"))
110.                {
111.                        tracks.removeAll();
112.                        s = in.readLine();
113.                        while (!s.startsWith("."))
114.                        {
115.                                tracks.add(s);
116.                                s = in.readLine();
117.                        }
118.                }
119.                else
120.                {
121.                        status.setText("Error :" + s);
122.                }
123.                out.close();
124.                in.close();
125.                sock.close();
126.            }
127.        catch (UnknownHostException e)
128.            {
129.                    status.setText("Unknown Server");
130.            }
131.        catch (IOException e)
132.            {
133.                    status.setText("Input/Output Error");
134.            }
135.    }
136.
137.    public void mouseClicked(MouseEvent e)
138.    {
139.        if (e.getComponent() == pause)
140.            {
141.                    if (((Button)e.getComponent()).getLabel().equals("||"))
142.                    {
143.                            sendMessage("pause");
144.                            ((Button)e.getComponent()).setLabel(">");
145.                    }
146.                    else
```

```
147.                    {
148.                           sendMessage("resume");
149.                           ((Button)e.getComponent()).setLabel("||");
150.                    }
151.             }
152.         else if (e.getComponent() == first)
153.             {
154.                    sendMessage("first");
155.             }
156.         else if (e.getComponent() == previous)
157.             {
158.                    sendMessage("previous");
159.             }
160.         else if (e.getComponent() == next)
161.             {
162.                    sendMessage("next");
163.             }
164.         else if (e.getComponent() == last)
165.             {
166.                    sendMessage("last");
167.             }
168.         else if (e.getComponent() == update)
169.             {
170.                    sendMessage("status");
171.                    sendMessage("track listing");
172.             }
173.         else if (e.getComponent() == tracks)
174.             {
175.                    sendMessage("play " + tracks.getSelectedIndex());
176.             }
177.     }
178.     public void mouseEntered(MouseEvent e) {}
179.     public void mouseExited(MouseEvent e) {}
180.     public void mousePressed(MouseEvent e) {}
181.     public void mouseReleased(MouseEvent e) {}
182. }
```

Code explanation

♦ Lines 1-5: The import statements are very typical for any Java application intended to have a graphical interface and provide networking capability.

♦ Line 7-13: Here we define our class variables, including our graphical objects and a String that we will use to hold the name of our server (its IP address).

♦ Lines 15-18: Our main method in the preceding lines instantiates an instance of the MP3Client class .

♦ Lines 20-30: The constructor in these lines checks to see if a server has been defined on the command line or if the user should be presented with a dialog box asking the user to specify a server. While specifying on the command line may be preferable, it should be noted that not every device or operating system has a command line available to the user. Pocket PC devices, for example, do not offer the user any kind of command line, and while parameters for Java applications can be specified through the use of platform specific settings, it's much easier to just ask the user where the server is.

♦ Lines 32-35: The getServer object (an instance of the ServerDialog class) calls the returnServer method defined in these lines when the user gets connected to a server.

◆ Lines 37-79: The code in these lines is fairly typical for setting up a Graphical User Interface. Note that the frame size is set to 240 x 300 pixels, which is the resolution of a Pocket PC device, but which may not be appropriate for other PersonalJava-compatible devices, such as set-top boxes. Again, an anonymous adapter is used to notice if the user quits the application in a platform specific manner (the only way to actually quit this application).

◆ Lines 81-100: This method in these lines is used to send messages to the server, the parameter message being the message to be sent. The method opens a network connection to the server and expects a +OK response. (Anything else generates an error.) The message is then sent and the response analyzed to see what action should be taken by the client (normally, updating the display to reflect the user action).

◆ Lines 101-125: Note that, in these lines, the received text is converted to uppercase to ensure that the protocol-specified case-independence is honored. The only complex response is when a full listing has been requested, such as when the List object tracks has to be updated to show the new list.

◆ Lines 126-135: Note that in these lines our catch blocks do not output to System.out; this is because System.out may not be visible on CDC devices. It is very important that applications designed for such devices have a method of displaying error conditions to the user without relying on standard output (stdout). In this case, we are using the status Label, which normally shows the currently playing track.

◆ Lines 137-177: The sendMessage() method is certainly the most important in the application, as it handles all the networking for this application. Any additional functionality will be routed through this method, and any problems are most likely to show themselves here. This method is called when the user clicks any of the Graphical User Interface components and performs the appropriate action (sending the right message to the server). It should be noted that the pause button becomes a "play" button once it's been pressed (and vice-versa). It should also be clear that if the client pauses playback, which is then restarted using the GUI on the server, the client will be unable to pause play, as when the pause button is pressed, it will send a "resume" message (being unaware that play has already recommenced). In such circumstances, the user will have to press the pause button twice to achieve the required effect.

◆ Lines 178-182: These final, methods are required by the MouseListener interface.

ServerDialog.java

This class is a part of client application a will run on the device. This class provides a Dialog box to the user for entering the server details.

Listing 8-6: ServerDialog.java

// © 2001 Dreamtech Software India, Inc.
// All rights Reserved

```
1.    import java.io.*;
2.    import java.net.*;
3.    import java.util.*;
4.    import java.awt.*;
5.    import java.awt.event.*;
6.
7.    class ServerDialog extends Dialog implements MouseListener
8.    {
9.     MP3Client parent;
10.     TextField t;
11.
12.     ServerDialog(Frame f, MP3Client mp3)
13.      {
```

```
14.     super(f, true);
15.     parent = mp3;
16.     add(new Label("Enter Server Name"), BorderLayout.CENTER);
17.     t = new TextField();
18.     add(t, BorderLayout.SOUTH);
19.     Button ok = new Button("OK");
20.     ok.addMouseListener(this);
21.     add(ok, BorderLayout.EAST);
22.     setSize(240,80);
23.     validate();
24.     setVisible(true);
25.   }
26.   public void mouseClicked(MouseEvent e)
27.   {
28.    parent.returnServer(t.getText());
29.    setVisible(false);
30.   }
31.   public void mouseEntered(MouseEvent e) {}
32.   public void mouseExited(MouseEvent e) {}
33.   public void mousePressed(MouseEvent e) {}
34.   public void mouseReleased(MouseEvent e) {}
35.  }
```

Code explanation

- Lines 1-5: The import statements are very typical for any Java application intended to have a graphical interface and provide networking capability.

- Line 7-10: This class simply presents a dialog box to the user to enter the name, or IP address, of the server to connect to.

- Lines 12-25: The user interface for this dialog box is very simple, consisting of only a `Button`, a `Label`, and a `TextArea`.

- Lines 26-30: When the OK button is pressed, the dialog box calls the `returnServer()` method of the object that instantiated this dialog box and makes itself invisible. Note that no attempt is made to establish if the server exists or is a valid server, though this functionality could be added without significant work.

- Lines 31-35: These methods in the preceding lines are required by the `MouseListener` interface.

Summary

This application shows a typical use of a PersonalJava compatible device being used to provide a mobile user interface to a server-managed operation. It is this capability to take applications with you that has made mobile devices so popular, and by using applications of standard socket communications, the application should be able to operate worldwide without difficulty.

While it is possible to generate much more complex client-side applications, it is important to consider the limitations of the device. If large amounts of processing are being done on the client, something is wrong, and the application design should be looked at to see if more work couldn't be shifted to the server to reduce the load on the client.

Mobile devices should be considered to be extensions of the desktop; while laptop devices provide much of the functionality of their desk-top equivalents, handheld devices never will, and it's important to remember that. By allowing users to take their interfaces with them, you can provide all the functionality of a desktop application without the processor load associated with it.

Chapter 9

Project 4: Peer-to-Peer Search Application

One of the most significant features of the Internet is that it enables the user to share files with another user anywhere in the world without requiring an intermediary, that is, without requiring an intermediate server. In the Client Server model, one system acts as a server and caters to the request sent, and the other server acts as a client and sends requests to the server for services. There is one server and many clients connected to the server requesting for services and the server acts as an intermediary if the clients want to communicate with each other. In case of a Peer-to-Peer model, however, there is no intermediary and the clients can communicate directly with each other. You not only can download files from sites having a presence on the Net, but also get connected with any casual user of the Net and download files from his computer. You can also make your files available to any other user. Thus the environment is informal and conducive to candid communication. Napster was one example of this mode known as the Peer-to-Peer (P2P) model. Another is Gnutella. The fact that they make sharing of all files possible may not appeal to those concerned about their intellectual property rights. But leaving aside the legal aspects, it cannot be denied that P2P is a new paradigm.

P2P applications are available for conventional computing environments. This means you can run such applications on your desktop system. But the Internet has gone much beyond PCs and servers. There are devices such as PDAs or cell phones that support the Internet. Can P2P applications work on these devices? We lent ourselves to this problem and worked out a simple solution that really works.

We present in this chapter an application that uses J2ME CLDC to provide Peer-to-Peer (P2P) file sharing. This application was originally developed using the Java 2 Standard Edition for the book *Peer-to-Peer Application Development* released in the *Cracking the Code series*. The Peer-to-Peer application in the book was developed using two programming languages: Java and C#. Both the versions are compatible with each other to the extent that you can use the Java Listener with the C# client and the C# Listener with the Java client. The application we are developing in this chapter is also compatible with both the Java and the C# Listener. However, the J2ME version does not offer exactly the same functionality. For instance, it does not allow you to download files. This is understandable, since a device such as a mobile phone cannot be expected or required to store downloaded files. Using this application, you can connect to any user and view the shared files, but you cannot download them. For that, you have to use the PC. The idea is that you will at least be able to find out where the required files are located even while on the move.

User Interface

When you start the application, the starting screen shows just two buttons: Start and Exit. Press the Start button and the next screen shows a scrollable list of users currently connected to the same server using this application. Being connected means that they have logged on to the Net with this application. Files can be searched in two ways: One is the server-level search, and the other is the user-level search. *Server-level search* is useful when the user knows what files he wants — or at least some characters in the name of that file so that he can then use wildcards for conducting the search. For example, if he knows that the name of the song he wants has the word *rock* in it, he can use this information as the search criterion and use wildcards (such as *) for searching for it. The other option is to conduct a *user-level search*. This will be useful if the user knows on whose system the required files are located.

The next screen is displayed when the user press Start button. The screen has two buttons at the top, labeled Refresh and Search. Pressing Refresh will update the users list. If the user wants to search some files, he has to press the Search button. There are two more buttons at the bottom, labeled Browse and Exit. If the user decides to see what files are available from a particular user, he can enter his choice in a `TextField` in the form of a user number. Then he has to press the Browse button. If the user presses the Exit button, the application will close.

This will take him to the screen showing the listing of shared folders and files on the root directory of that user's system. If necessary, he may select a folder and again press the Browse button. This can go on till he finds the files of his choice of his choice. At any stage during this process, he can press the Search button after entering the directory number in the `TextField`. This will give him a chance to enter his search criterion with any wildcard to locate the required files.

If the user does not have an idea of where the files are, he may directly press the Search button without pressing the Browse button. Upon this, he gets to see a screen with two `TextFields`, one each for entering the search criteria for the file name and for the user name. After entering these, the Search button has to be pressed. The user will be shown the files found in the search. The search can be cancelled by pressing the Cancel button.

How It Works

This application consists of five class files — namely, `peer_application`, `userlist_screen`, `serversearch`, `searchfiles`, and `showfiles`. In addition, it uses an external XML parser available in `org.kxml.parser` package. The application is started by executing the first class file — that is, `peer_application`. This class performs the following tasks:

- Importing the packages required, including those for handling and parsing XML (`org.kxml.*`, `org.kxml.io.*`, `org.kxml.parser`).
- Declaring variables for the XML parser, parse event, IP address, user list, and the text to be displayed in `ScrollTextBox`.
- Using the `Graphics` class to clear the screen and display the text welcoming the user, through `clearScreen` and `drawString` methods, respectively.
- Putting Start and Exit buttons on the screen by using the `paint` method.
- Defining event handling for the buttons via the `penDown` method. If the Start button is pressed, the current spotlet is unregistered and the method `startReading` is called. The Callbacks generated by the XML parser in the method `parseData()` are stored in three variables — namely, `ip_address`, `users_connected`, and `text_for_display`.
- Calling a method named `startReading`, which is responsible for sending a request to the server for the list of users connected at any time.
- Instantiating and calling the class `userlist_screen`, which displays the list of users. It takes its parameters as the three variables previously mentioned.
- Closing the application in case the user does not want to go further and presses the Exit button.
- Defining the method `startReading`. This method instantiates the preceding three variables and opens an `InputStream` on the ASP file named `userlist.asp`. It also shows an error if an `IOException` occurs.
- Defining the method `parseData`. It uses the XML parser previously mentioned and finds the `userinfo` tag with the help of a `do...while` loop and an `if` block. The attributes of this tag are obtained by using the `getValue` method and are then added to their appropriate positions. The vector `ip_address` is then returned to the calling class.

♦ The `parseData` method was available in the parser — it had only to be overridden. But we also need to return two more variables. For this reason, two more methods are defined. One is to return the `text_for_display` variable, and the other is to return the `users_connected` variable.

The class `userlist_screen` is called to display the list of users connected at a particular time as shown in Figure 9-1. It performs the following tasks:

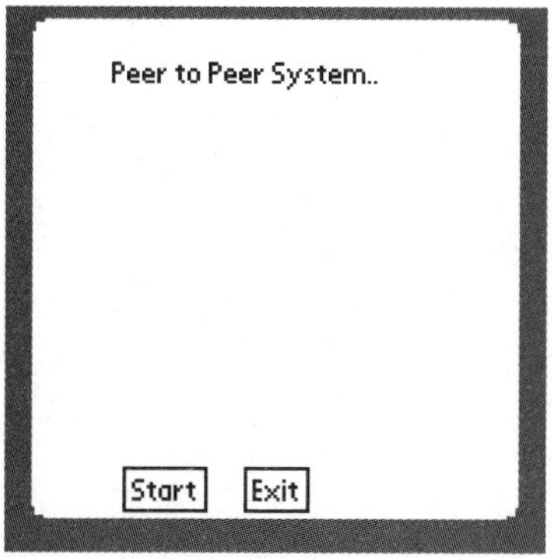

Figure 9-1: Initial Screen.

♦ Declaring variables for buttons, `ScrollTextBox`, `TextField`, `StreamConnection`, XML parser and parse event, `String` variables `folder_data`, `file_data`, vectors for the previously mentioned variables, and two more variables (`folder_vector` and `record_of_users`).

♦ Defining the constructor of the class to take `text`, `ip_address`, `users_connected`, `viewfile_flag`, and `record_of_users` as the parameters. The parameters are then initialized by the variables earlier defined. Using the `Graphics` class to display the user interface elements.

♦ Defining event handling via the `keyDown` and `penDown` methods. The former handles the input if the `TextField` is in use, and the latter handles the event of buttons being pressed. If necessary, control is transferred to a relevent class. For details of this method, you can refer to the line-by-line explanation after listing userlist_screen.java.

♦ Defining the method `appropriatelength`, which is called to make the application compatible with C# listeners. It is required because the C# listener cannot read more than 1,024 bytes at a time. This method takes an array called `file_bytes` and an integer called `file_size` as parameters and returns a byte array.

The class `showfiles` is called when a user is selected whose files/folders he wants to view and has pressed the Browse button as shown in Figure 9-2. It performs the following tasks:

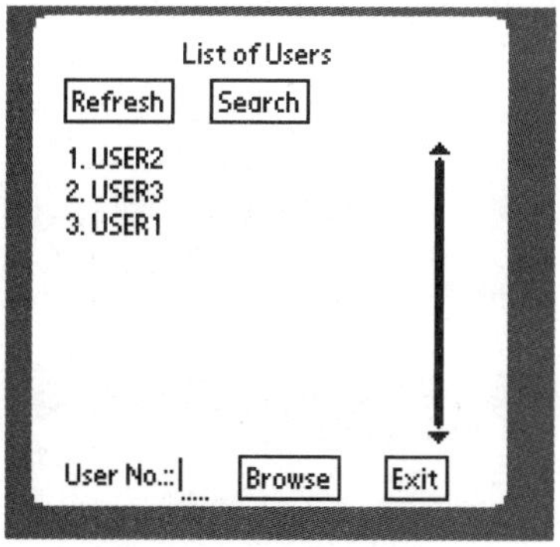

Figure 9-2: Users Connected.

♦ Creating the user interface for the screen showing shared files and folders as shown in Figure 9-3.

- Providing the user interface for the buttons, `TextField`, and the `ScrollTextBox`.
- Creating an object of the class `peer_application` and calling the method `startReading` to send a request to the server.
- Defining a method `browseDirectory` that is called when the Browse button is pressed. It shows the shared files in that directory.

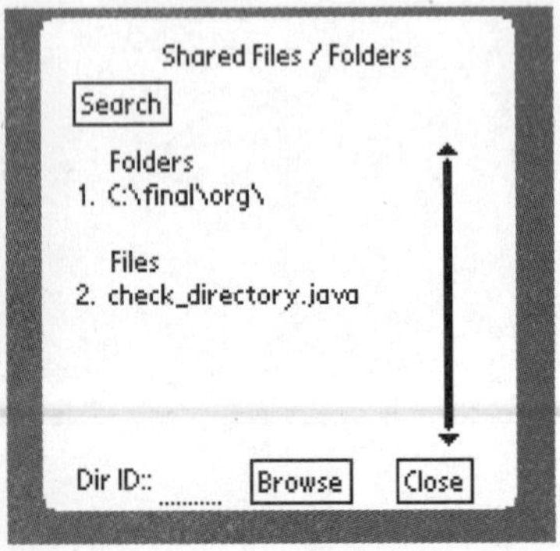

Figure 9-3: User's Shared Files and Folders.

The class `serversearch` is called when the user wants to search on all users as shown in Figure 9-4. It takes care of the following tasks:

Figure 9-4: Search for File.

- Declaring variables, buttons, `TextField`, `DataInputStream`, `Vector`, `ip_address`, and `users_connected`.
- Displaying the user-interface elements by using the `Graphics` class.
- Defining event handling through the `keyDown` method. It serves the purpose of shifting focus when the Tab key is pressed.
- Defining event handling through the `penDown` method. This method handles the events generated by pressing the buttons. If the Search button is pressed, the results satisfying the search criterion are displayed as shown in Figure 9-5. For details of this method, refer to the line-by-line explanation after Listing 9-5, serversearch.java.
- Defining the method `parseData` that holds the callbacks generated when XML parsing is done.

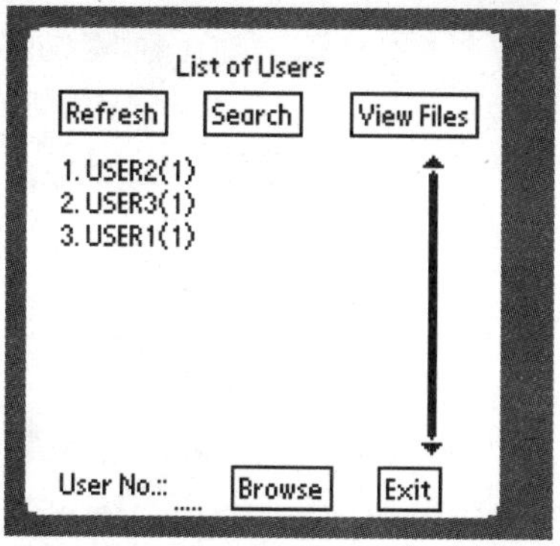

Figure 9-5: Search result.

The class `searchfiles` is called when the user has browsed to another user and wants to conduct a search as shown in Figure 9-6. It performs the following tasks:

Figure 9-6: Search a File in a Particular User.

♦ Declaring buttons, `TextField`, Strings (`parent_information`, `text_for_display`, `folder_data`, `file_data`, and `host_address`), XML parser and parse event, Vector `folder_vector`, `StreamConnection`, `InputStream`, and `OutputStream`.

♦ Defining the constructor to take `address` and `parent_information` as the parameters. The parameters are initialized with the variables already declared.

♦ Drawing the user-interface elements, including buttons and `TextField`.

♦ Defining event handling through `penDown` and `keyDown`. The former simply calls the latter if an option has the focus. The `penDown` method responds to events generated by pressing the button.

♦ The method `appropriatelength` is called to provide compatibility with C# listeners.

The basic flow of the program is shown in the flow chart (see Figures 9-7 and 9-8).

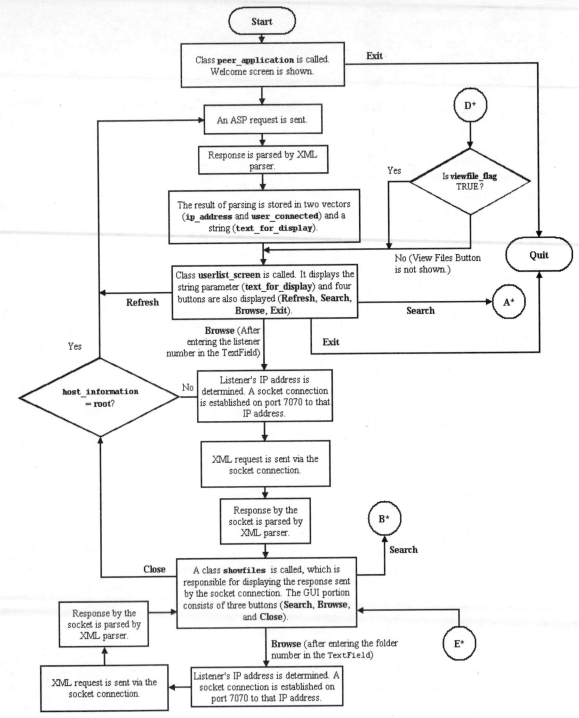

Figure 9-7: Flow Chart - I.

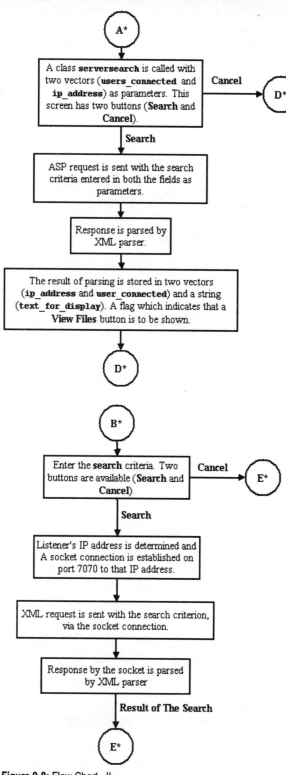

A*

A class **serversearch** is called with two vectors (**users_connected** and **ip_address**) as parameters. This screen has two buttons (**Search** and **Cancel**).

Cancel → D*

Search

ASP request is sent with the search criteria entered in both the fields as parameters.

Response is parsed by XML parser.

The result of parsing is stored in two vectors (**ip_address** and **user_connected**) and a string (**text_for_display**). A flag which indicates that a **View Files** button is to be shown.

D*

B*

Enter the **search** criteria. Two buttons are available (**Search** and **Cancel**)

Cancel → E*

Search

Listener's IP address is determined and A socket connection is established on port 7070 to that IP address.

XML request is sent with the search criterion, via the socket connection.

Response by the socket is parsed by XML parser

Result of The Search

E*

Figure 9-8: Flow Chart - II.

Source Code

Source code for `peer_application.java`, `java userlist_screen.java showfiles.serversearch.java`, `searchfiles.java` is given in Listings 9-1, 9-2, 9-3, 9-4, and 9-5, respectively.

Listing 9-1: peer_application.java

```
/**
 *    Importing the basic packages required by various classes during
 * the execution of the program.
 */
1.    import java.io.InputStream;
2.    import java.util.Hashtable;
3.    import java.util.Enumeration;
4.    import com.sun.kjava.*;
5.    import java.lang.*;
6.    import javax.microedition.io.*;
7.    import java.io.*;
8.    import java.util.*;


 /**
  *  The packages below are included because these packages are
  *  required by the XML classes.
  */


9.    import org.kxml.*;
10.   import org.kxml.io.*;
11.   import org.kxml.parser.*;
12.
 /**
  *  Declaration of a class peer_application. This is the first class
  *  of peer to peer aplication project which welcomes the user to the
  *  application and on pressing the Start button the user can go on to
  *  the actual task of the application.
  */
13.   public class peer_application extends Spotlet
14.   {
15.
 /**
  *    Declaring variables for the xmlparser and parse event(Where
  *    the call backs after the parsing will be stored.
  */
16.   AbstractXmlParser xmlparser;
17.   ParseEvent event;

 /**
  *    Declaring the variable for the DataInputStream (for reading
  *    the ASP, for Buttons (Start and Exit), for TextBox (message)etc.
  */
18.
19.   DataInputStream din;
20.   private Button start;
21.   private Button exit;
```

```
22.    private TextBox message;

/**
 *  Declaring three important variables ,IP_addresses of vector type
 *  to store the IP_addresses, a vector type variable users_connected
 *  which consists of  list of users connected and
 *  a String variable of the type text_for_display which consists of the
 *  text to be displayed on the ScrollTextBox.
 */
23.    Vector ip_addresses;
24.    Vector users_connected;
25.    String text_for_display;
26.    int counter = 1;

/**
 *  This is the main method which indicates the starting of the peer
 *  to peer application by calling the class peer_application.
 */
27.    public static void main(String args[])throws Exception
28.        {
29.      peer_application peer_to_peer = new peer_application();
30.    }
31.


// Constructor for the class peer_application.
32.    public peer_application()
33.    {
// To make the spotlet as the current spotlet..
34.      register(NO_EVENT_OPTIONS);
35.      Graphics graphics = Graphics.getGraphics();
36.
/**
 *  Initializing the variable of the graphics class and clearing
 *  the drawing region by calling the appropriate functions of
 *  the Graphics class namely (resetDrawRegion() and clearScreen()).
 */
37.      graphics.resetDrawRegion();
38.           graphics.clearScreen();
/**
 *  Displaying a string (Title) at a specified position by using
 *  the member function of the Graphics class
 */
39.      graphics.drawString("Peer to Peer System..",25,10);
40.
/**
 *  Initializing the button object Start, placing it on the screen
 *  at the appropriate position and then painting(drawing it).
 */
41.      start = new Button("Start",30,145);
42.      start.paint();
43.
/**
 *  Initializing the button object exit, placing it on the screen
 *  at the appropriate position and then painting(drawing it).
 */
44.      exit = new Button("Exit",70,145);
```

```
45.      exit.paint();
46.    }// End of constructor peer_application.
47.
 /**
  *   The code below pertains to event handling.
  */
48.    public void penDown(int x, int y)
49.    {
 /**
  *   If start button is pressed..then the current spotlet is unregistered
  *   and a method of the name startReading is called. This method is res-
  *   -ponsible for calling the ASP from the server. When the ASP is read
  *   an XMLParser is called which will parse the XML Data. A method
  *   parseData() is called  by the XML parser to
  *   generate callbacks from the XML parsing. These Callbacks are stored in
  *   three variables earlier declared (ip_addresses, users_connected and
  *   text_for_display).
  */
50.      if(start.pressed(x,y))
51.      {
 // To show a new class first unregister all the controls of the
 // existing class
52.           unregister();
 // Call to a method startReading which will request the server for all
 // the users connected at a particular time using the ASP.
53.           startReading();
 // The XMLParser will generate the Callbacks in the method parseData.
54.           ip_addresses = parseData();
55.
 /**
  *   A new Class userlist_screen is called which displays the users
  *   connected  at a particular instant of time, the class takes as its
  *   parameters a Text_for_display string variable (which contains the no.
  *   of users connected), a vector variable ip_addresses (which has the IP
  *   addresses of the all the users connected at a particular instant of
  *   time) and a vector variable containing the users_connected.
  */
56.           new userlist_screen(text_for_display, ip_addresses, users_connected,
false,null);
57.
58.      }
 /**
  *   If exit button is pressed then the application is closed and the
  *   control is returned to the OS.
  */
59.      else
60.      {
61.          System.exit(0);
62.      }
63.    } // End of event Handling method.
64.
65.    public void startReading()
66.    {
67.      try
68.      {
 // The three variables where the information is to be stored are
```

```
      // initialized.
69.          text_for_display = "";
70.          ip_addresses = new Vector();
71.          users_connected = new Vector();
72.

      // Using the Connector class of CLDC an InputStream is opened on
   // the ASP
73.          din = Connector.openDataInputStream("testhttp://www.s-
cop.com/userlist.asp");
74.

   // The InputStream opened on the URL is passed on to the XmlParser.
75.          xmlparser = new XmlParser(new InputStreamReader(din));
76.      }
77.      catch(IOException e)
78.      {
79.      System.out.println("Exception Occured while reading the XML from asp or
while passing it to the XML parser");
80.      }
81.   } // End of the method Startreading()..
82.

   // Function parseData (it will hold the callbacks generated by the
   // XMLParsing.
83.   Vector parseData()
84.   {
   // Move in infinite loop till the XML document ends..
85.      do
86.      {
87.       try
88.        {
89.        event = xmlparser.read ();
90.

91.          if(event.getType()==Xml.START_TAG)
92.          {
   // The StartTag is identified.
93.              StartTag stag = (StartTag)event;
94.

95.              String name = stag.getName();
96.

   // If the Tag encountered is userinfo then the Attributes of the
   // tag are taken using the function getValue() and are added at
   // their appropriate positions.
97.              if (name.equals("userinfo"))
98.              {
99.

100.                  text_for_display = text_for_display +counter + ". "
+stag.getValue("username")+"\n";
101.                  ip_addresses.addElement((Object)stag.getValue("ip"));
102.
users_connected.addElement((Object)stag.getValue("username"));
103.                  counter++;
104.                  }
105.

106.              }
107.

108.          }
109.       catch(IOException ex)
```

```
110.          {
111.               System.out.println("Exception occured");
112.            }
113.      }
114.        while (!(event instanceof EndDocument)); // end of document
115.
116.    System.out.println("**** END OF DOCUMENT ****");

117.    // The vector Ip_address is returned to the calling program.

118.    return (ip_addresses);
119.      }
120.
   // A function  to return the TextforDisplay to the calling program
121.    String returnTextForDisplay()
122.    {
123.       return (text_for_display);
124.    }
125.
   // A function  to return the vector usersConnected to the calling program
126.    Vector returnUsersConnected()
127.    {
128.       return (users_connected);
129.    }
130.
} // End of class
```

Code explanation

♦ Lines 1-8: Details the basic packages used by various classes in the project, such as `java.util.*` for vectors and enumerations and `java.io.*` for input and output, etc.

♦ Lines 9-11: Details the inclusion of the packages required by the various classes in the XML parser.

♦ Line 13: Declaration of a class `peer_application`. This is the first class of the Peer-to-Peer application project, which welcomes the user to the application, and on pressing the Start button, the user can go on to the actual task of the application.

♦ Lines 16-17: Declaring variables for the XML parser and `parseEvent` (where the Callbacks after the parsing will be stored).

♦ Lines 19-22: Declaring the variable for the `DataInputStream` for reading the ASP, for buttons (Start and Exit), for `TextBox` (message), etc.

♦ Lines 23-26: Declaring three important variables, `ip_addresses` of vector type to store the `ip_addresses`; the vector-type variable `users_connected`, which, as the name suggests, contains the list of users connected; and a String variable of the type `text_for_display`, which contains the text to be displayed on the `ScrollTextBox`.

♦ Lines 27-30: This is the main method that indicates the starting of the Peer-to-Peer application by calling the class `peer_application`.

♦ Lines 34-38: The code between these lines pertains to making the spotlet the current spotlet, initializing the variable of the `Graphics` class, and clearing the drawing region by calling the appropriate functions of the `Graphics` class — namely, `resetDrawRegion()` and `clearScreen()`.

♦ Line 39: Displaying a string (`Title`) at a specified position by using the member function of the `Graphics` class.

♦ Lines 41-46: Initializing the `Button` objects `start` and `exit`, placing them on the screen at the appropriate position and then painting (drawing) them.

♦ Lines 50-58: If the Start button is pressed, the current spotlet is unregistered and the method `startReading` is called. This method is responsible for calling the ASP from the server. When the ASP is read, an `XMLParser` is called, which will parse the XML data. A method, `parseData()`, is called by the XML parser to generate callbacks from the XML parsing. These Callbacks are stored in three variables declared earlier (`ip_addresses`, `users_connected`, and `text_for_display`).

♦ Lines 59-62: The code is used when the user presses the Exit button. When this button is pressed, the application is closed, and the control is returned to the operating system (OS).

♦ Lines 65-81: The code pertains to the method `startReading`. In this method, a request to the server is made using an ASP to get a list of users currently connected. This request is made using the class `Connector` of the CLDC'c `javax.microedition.io` package. The server returns an XML file. The XML stream is then directly passed on to the parser, which parses the XML file.

♦ Lines 83-119: The code between these lines pertains to an important function, `parseData`. This is the function in which the XML parser sends the Callbacks. The callbacks are identified accordingly by using the functions (whether the element obtained is the start tag or end tag, etc.).

  • 97: If the tag encountered is `userinfo`, the attributes of the tag are taken using the function `getValue()` and are added at their appropriate positions.

  • 118: In the end, a vector (`ip_addresses`) is returned, which consists of the IP addresses of all the users currently connected.

♦ Lines 121-124: The user-defined function `returnTextForDisplay` is declared, which, as the name signifies, returns the `text_for_display` (text displayed in the `ScrollTextBox`) to the calling program.

♦ Lines 126-129: The user-defined function `returnUsersConnected` is declared, which, as the name signifies, returns the users connected to the server at a particular instant of time.

Listing 9-2: userlist_screen.java

// © 2001 Dreamtech Software India, Inc.
// All rights Reserved

```
/**
 *    Importing the basic packages required by various classes during
 * the execution of the program.
 */
1.   import com.sun.kjava.*;
2.   import java.lang.*;
3.   import javax.microedition.io.*;
4.   import java.io.*;
5.   import java.util.*;
 /**
  *   The packages below are included because these packages are
  * required by the XML classes.
  */
6.   import org.kxml.*;
7.   import org.kxml.io.*;
8.   import org.kxml.parser.*;
9.
 //  Declaration of a class userlist_screen..

10.  public class userlist_screen extends Spotlet
11.  {
```

```
     // Declaring button variables.

12.   private Button refresh;
13.   private Button search;
14.   private Button viewfiles;
15.   private Button browse_user;
16.   private Button exit;
    // Declaring ScrollTextBox and textField variables.
17.   private ScrollTextBox userlist;
18.      private TextField option;

19.   Vector ip_address;
    // Declaring StreamConnection variable used for Sockets..
20.    StreamConnection socket = null;
    // Declaring InputStreams and OutputStreams used by the socket
    // connections.
21.   InputStream socket_inputstream;
22.      OutputStream socket_outputstream;
   /**
    *  Declaraing variables for the xmlparser and parse event(Where
    *  the callbacks after the parsing will be stored.
    */
23.   AbstractXmlParser xmlparser;
24.   ParseEvent event;
   /**
    *  Declaring variables for storing the parameters passed on to
    *  the class.
    */
25.   Vector folder_vector;
26.   Vector users_connected;
27.   String text_for_display;
   /**
    *  Declaring variables to folder_data where the folder information
    *  is stored, similarly the variable file_data where the file
    *  information is stored.
    */
28.   String folder_data;
29.   String file_data;
30.   int counter;
31.   String address;
32.   String user_data;
33.   Vector record_of_users;
34.
    // Constructor of the class userlist_screen is called..
35.   userlist_screen(String text, Vector ip_addresses,Vector users_connected,
boolean viewfile_flag ,Vector record_of_users)
36.   {
    // The current graphics is obtained...
37.     Graphics graphics = Graphics.getGraphics();
   /**
    *  Initializing the variable of the graphics class and clearing
    *  the drawing region by calling the appropriate functions of
    *  the Graphics class namely (resetDrawRegion() and clearScreen()).
    */
38.       graphics.resetDrawRegion();
```

```
39.            graphics.clearScreen();
40.
 /**
  *  Displaying a string (Title) at a specified position by using
  *  the member function of the Graphics class
  */
41.      graphics.drawString("List of Users",50,5);
42.


  // The parameters are initialized by the variables earlier defined

43.      ip_address = ip_addresses;
44.      user_data = text;
45.      this.users_connected = users_connected;
46.      this.record_of_users = record_of_users;

 // To make the spotlet as the current spotlet..

47.         register(NO_EVENT_OPTIONS);

 /**
  *  Initializing the button object "Refresh", placing it on the screen
  *  at the appropriate position and then painting(drawing it).
  */

48.      refresh = new Button("Refresh",10,20);
49.      refresh.paint();

 /**
  *  Initializing the button object "Search", placing it on the screen
  *  at the appropriate position and then painting it.
  */

50.      search = new Button("Search",60,20);
51.      search.paint();

 /**
  *  Initializing the button object "ViewFiles", placing it on the screen
  *  at the appropriate position, the painting of the "ViewFiles" button
  *  will be decided by checking the view_file flag. If the flag is true
  *  then the button will be painted on the screen else not.
  */

52.      viewfiles = new Button("View Files",110,20);
53.      if (viewfile_flag)
54.      {
55.       viewfiles.paint();
56.      }

 /**
  *  Initializing the ScrollTextBox object userlist, placing it on
  *  the screen at the appropriate position and then painting(drawing it).
  */

57.      userlist = new ScrollTextBox(text,10,40,130,100);
58.      userlist.paint();
```

```
/**
 *  Initializing the TextFiled object option, placing it on the screen
 *  at the appropriate position ,painting(drawing it) and making the
 *  caret blink by setting the TextField as the current field.
 */
59.     option = new TextField("User No.:",10,145,50,10);
60.     option.paint();
61.     option.setUpperCase(true);
62.         option.setFocus();
 /**
  *  Initializing the button object Browse_user, placing it on
  *  the screen at the appropriate position and then painting(drawing it).
  */
63.     browse_user = new Button("Browse",70,145);
64.     browse_user.paint();
 /**
  *  Initializing the button objectExit, placing it on the screen
  *  at the appropriate position and then painting(drawing it).
  */
65.     exit = new Button("Exit",120,145);
66.     exit.paint();
67.
68.    } // end of the constructor userlist_screen

 // Event Handling function. (KeyDown)..

69.     public void keyDown(int x)
70.         {
 // Handle the input if the TextField is in focus.
71.             if(option.hasFocus())
72.                 {
73.                     option.handleKeyDown(x);
74.                 }
75.         }    // End KeyDowm
76.
77.
    // Event Handling function. (penDown)..

78.     public void penDown(int x, int y)
79.         {
 // If refresh Button is pressed..
80.         if(refresh.pressed(x,y))
81.             {
 // Remove the focus from the TextField and kill the TextField
 // blinking caret.
82.                 option.loseFocus();
83.                 option.killCaret();
 // To show a new class first unregister all the controls of the
    // existing class
84.                 unregister();
 // Create an object of the class peer_application and call the
 // function startReading() to send a request to the server
85.                 peer_application refresh_application = new peer_application();
86.                 refresh_application.startReading();
```

```
        // Then call the parser function, it will return a vector.
87.               Vector ip_addresses =  refresh_application.parseData();
88.   String text_for_display = refresh_application.returnTextForDisplay();
89.
90.   Vector users_connected = refresh_application.returnUsersConnected();
91.
     // Call the class userlist_screen with the parameters obtained in the
     // previous lines..
92.
93.               new
userlist_screen(text_for_display,ip_addresses,users_connected,false,null);
94.
95.          }


     // If search(Server Search) Button is pressed


96.        if(search.pressed(x,y))
97.               {
98.
     // Remove the focus from the TextField and kill the TextField
     // blinking caret.
99.               option.loseFocus();
100.               option.killCaret();
     // To show a new class first unregister all the controls of the
     // existing class
101.               unregister();
     // Call the class serversearch with the parameters.
102.               new serversearch(user_data,ip_address,users_connected);
103.
104.          }
     // If ViewFiles is pressed..
105.
106.        if(viewfiles.pressed(x,y))
107.          {
108.
     // The option entered by the user in the TextField is obtained.
109.               String user_number = option.getText();
110.               try
111.               {

     //Converting it to an integer value.

112.                    int userID = Integer.parseInt(user_number);
113.                         try
114.                         {
     // The variables are assigned ..
115.                              String textDisplay = "";
116.                              String folderText="";
117.                              String fileText="";
118.
     // From the vector ip_address the address is obtained of the
     // user whose serial number is entered.
119.                         address = (String)ip_address.elementAt(userID-1);
120.
     // From vector record_of_users, an enumeration is
     // initialized.
```

```
121.                             Enumeration enum =
record_of_users.elements();
  // A while loop is used which matches the ip_address with the
  // enumeration
122.                             while (enum.hasMoreElements())
123.                             {
124.                                 if
(((String)enum.nextElement()).equals(address))
125.                                 {
126.                                     String temp =
(String)enum.nextElement();
127.
  // If a match is found then the flag for file / folder is
  // checked and accordingly the Files/ folders are placed in
  // their respective positions.
128.                                     if
(((String)enum.nextElement()).equals("1"))
129.                                     {
130.                                         fileText =
fileText+temp+"\n";
131.
132.                                     }
133.                                     else
134.                                     {
135.                                         folderText =
folderText+temp+"\n";
136.                                     }
137.                                 }
138.
139.                             }
140.
  // A string variable is used to display the text in the ScrollTextBox
141.    textDisplay = "        Folders     \n"+folderText+"\n"+"        Files
\n"+fileText;
142.
  // Remove the focus from the TextField and kill the TextField
  // blinking caret.

143.                             option.loseFocus();
144.                             option.killCaret();
  // To show a new class first unregister all the controls of the
  // existing class.
145.                             unregister();
146.
  // Call to the class show files...
147.                             new showfiles(textDisplay,null, null,
"ROOT",true);
148.
149.
150.                     }
151.                 catch(Exception e)
152.                 {
153.
154.                 }
155.             }
156.         catch(Exception e)
```

```
157.                              {
158.
159.                          }
160.
161.
162.             }
163.
    // If Browse button is pressed...
164.             if(browse_user.pressed(x,y))
165.                 {
    // Two boolean flags are initialized..
166.                 boolean connection_flag = false;
167.                 boolean ip_flag   = false;
168.
169.                 folder_vector = new Vector();
170.                 text_for_display = "";
171.                 folder_data = "";
172.                 file_data = "";
173.                 counter = 1;
    // Option entered by the user is taken
174.                 String user_number = option.getText();
175.
176.                 try
177.                     {
178. // Converted to integer..
179.                     int userID = Integer.parseInt(user_number);
180.                     try
181.                         {
    // The IP_address of the user selected is taken out
    // from the vector.
182.                         address = (String)ip_address.elementAt(userID-
1);
183.                         try
184.                             {
    // A Socket connection is made on a port with the Listener
185.                             socket =
186.
(StreamConnection)Connector.open("socket://"+address+":7070",
187.
Connector.READ_WRITE,true);
188.
189.
    // If the socket is null then the connection is not established..
190.                             if (socket != null)
191.                                 {
192.                                 System.out.println("Connection is established
to localhost on port 7070...");
193.                                 }
194.
195.   //   Opening the Input and Output Streams to the Socket.
196.
197.                             socket_inputstream = socket.openInputStream();
198.                             socket_outputstream = socket.openOutputStream();
199.                             }
200.                         catch(IOException ae)
201.                             {
```

```
202.                            System.out.println("Couldn't open socket:");
203.                    }
```
// An XMLReuest to be sent to the Listener is formed..
```
204.                    String xmlRequest = "<?xml version='1.0' encoding='utf-
8'?><p2p_lng>         <request type=\"SHOWFILES\"> </request></p2p_lng>";
205.
```
// It is converted to byte array
```
206.                        byte [] byteXmlRequest = xmlRequest.getBytes();
```

// The length of the byte array is taken out.

```
207.                    int byteXmlRequest_length = byteXmlRequest.length;
208.
```
```
/**
 * A function appropriate length is called which will make
 * this request equal to 1024 bytes in length. This is done in
 * order to make compatibility with the C# listeners.
 */
```

```
209.                    byteXmlRequest =
appropriatelength(byteXmlRequest,byteXmlRequest_length);
210.
```
// The xmlrequest is sent via socket connection to the Listener
// machine..
```
211.                    socket_outputstream.write(byteXmlRequest);
```
// The stream of response by the server is then passed on to
// the xmlparser for parsing..
```
212.                    xmlparser = new XmlParser(new
InputStreamReader(socket_inputstream));
213.
```
// Function used for parsing is called...
```
214.                    parseData();
215.
```
//And the ip_flag is made true..
```
216.                    ip_flag = true;
217.                }
218.                catch (Exception e)
219.                {
220.                            System.out.println(e);
```
// If any exception occurs then the ip_flag is made false..
```
221.                        ip_flag = false;
222.                        option.setText("");
223.                }
224.
225.
226.                    connection_flag = true;
227.            }
228.            catch (Exception e)
229.            {
230.                    connection_flag = false;
231.                    option.setText("");
232.            }
233.
```
// If ip_flag as well as as the connection_flag are true then
```
234.            if (connection_flag && ip_flag)
235.                {
```

```
         // Remove the focus from the TextField and kill the TextField
         // blinking caret
236.                         option.loseFocus();
237.                         option.killCaret();
         // To show a new class first unregister all the controls of the
         // existing class.
238.                         unregister();
         /// Class showfiles is called with the parameters..
239.                         new showfiles(text_for_display,folder_vector,
address, "ROOT",false);
240.                 }
241.
242.         }
243.
244.
   /**
    *  If Exit button is pressed then the application is closed and the
    * control is returned to the OS.
    */
245.          if(exit.pressed(x,y))
246.             {
247.                 System.exit(0);
248.             }
249.
     // Event handling for the ScrollTextBox.
250.          if (userlist.contains(x,y))
251.                 userlist.handlePenMove(x,y);
252.
253.         }
254.
     // Event handling for the ScrollTextBox.
255.     public void penMove(int x, int y)
256.        {
257.             if (userlist.contains(x,y))
258.                 userlist.handlePenMove(x,y);
259.        }
260.
   // Function parseData (it will hold the callbacks generated by the
   // XMLParsing.
261.         void parseData()
262.          {
   // Move in loop till the XML document ends..
263.         do
264.            {
265.             try
266.              {
267.                     event = xmlparser.read ();
268.                     if(event.getType()==Xml.START_TAG)
269.                        {
   // The Start Tag is identified
270.                             StartTag stag = (StartTag)event;
271.                             String name = stag.getName();
272.
   /**
    * If the Tag encountered is fileinfo then the attributes of the
    * tag are taken using the function getValue() and are added at
```

```
      * their appropriate positions.
      */
273.                              if (name.equals("fileinfo"))
274.                              {
275.
276.      String filename = stag.getValue("filename");
277.

         // A check is made for the filename and folders and
      // they are stored in seperate String variables.

278.                  if (!(filename.charAt(filename.length()-1)   == '\\'))
279.                  {
280.                  filename = filename.substring(filename.lastIndexOf('\\')+1);
281.                  file_data = file_data+filename+"\n";
282.
283.                  }
284.                  else
285.                  {
286.                  folder_data = folder_data + counter +".   "+filename+"\n";

      // The folders are also stored in a vector variable of the
      // name folder_vector.

287.                  folder_vector.addElement((Object)filename);
288.                  counter++;
289.                  }
290.
291.
292.                          }
293.
294.                  }
295.
296.
297.          }
298.          catch(IOException ex)
299.          {
300.                  System.out.println("Exception occured");
301.          }
302.       }
303.       while (!(event instanceof EndDocument));
304.
305.       System.out.println("**** END OF DOCUMENT ****");
      // end of document
      // Socket Connection and Input and OutputStreams are
      // closed...
306.       try
307.       {
308.       socket.close();
309.       socket_inputstream.close();
310.       socket_outputstream.close();
311.       }
312.       catch(IOException e)
313.       {
314.                  System.out.println("user list"+ e);
315.
316.       }
```

```
        // Numbering is done on the file name stored in the String
        // variable by the name file_data.
317.          file_data = counter+".  "+file_data;
318.          counter++;
319.          StringBuffer file_data_buffer = new StringBuffer();
320.
321.          for (int i = 0;i<file_data.length()-1 ;i++ )
322.          {
323.                  if (file_data.charAt(i) == '\n')
324.                  {
325.                          file_data_buffer =
file_data_buffer.append(file_data.charAt(i));
326.                          file_data_buffer = file_data_buffer.append(counter+".
");
327.                          counter++;
328.                  }
329.                  else
330.                  {
331.                          file_data_buffer =
file_data_buffer.append(file_data.charAt(i));
332.                  }
333.
334.          }
335.          file_data = file_data_buffer.toString();
336.
    //  the Final text to be displayed is stored in the
    //  variable textFor Display...
337.          text_for_display = "         Folders       \n"+folder_data+"\n"+"
Files \n"+file_data;
338.
339.      }
340.
    // This function is called to make the program compatible with
    // the C# Listeners.
341.          public byte [] appropriatelength(byte[] file_bytes, int file_size)
342.          {
343.                  int count = 0;
344.                  byte b[] = new byte[1024];
345.                  int remaining = 1024-file_size;
346.
347.                  for (int i = 0;i<file_bytes.length ;i++ )
348.                  {
349.                          b[i] = file_bytes[i];
350.                  }
351.
352.                  char a[] = new char[remaining];
353.
    // Length is known therefore 1024-length bytes are
    // filled with empty string...
354.                  for (int i = 0;i<remaining ;i++ )
355.                  {
356.                  a[i] = 13;
357.                  }
358.
359.                  String tempw = new String(a);
360.                  byte d[] = tempw.getBytes();
```

```
361.
362.                        for (int i=file_size;i<1024 ;i++ )
363.                        {
364.                        b[i] = d[(i-file_size)];
365.                        }
366.
367.                        return (b);
368.         }                    // End Appropriate length.....
369. } // End class userlist_screen....
```

Code explanation

- Lines 1-5: Details the inclusion of the basic packages used by various classes in the project, such as java.util.* for vectors and enumerations and java.io.* for input and output.

- Lines 6-8: Details the inclusion of the packages required by the various classes in the XML parser.

- Line 10: Declares a class userlist_screen. This class displays to the user a list of the various listeners connected to the server at a particular instant of time. Along with this information, it also provides the user certain buttons for various uses, such as the Browse button, which the user presses after keying in a particular serial number. On pressing this button, the user is shown a screen that consists of all the files/folders shared by a particular listener. A Search button is also provided that the user can use to search for a file or a range of files for a single user or a range of users connected at a particular instant of time, etc.

- Lines 12-18: Declares the Button, ScrollTextBox, and the TextField variables, which are used as the GUI of this screen.

- Lines 20-22: A StreamConnection-type variable (socket) is also declared, which is used to create a socket connection with the listener. Apart from this, an inputstream and an outputstream variables are also declared, which are used for communication between the socket on the user's machine and the socket on the listener's machine.

- Lines 23-24: Declares variables for the XML parser and parse event (where the callbacks after the parsing will be stored).

- Lines 25-27: Declares variables for storing the parameters passed on to the class.

- Lines 28-33: Declares variable folder_data, where the folder information is stored, and the variable file_data, where the file information is stored.

- Lines 37-39: Pertains to making the spotlet the current spotlet and initializing the variable of the Graphics class and clearing the drawing region by calling the appropriate functions of the Graphics class — namely, resetDrawRegion() and clearScreen().

- Line 41: Displays a string (Title) at a specified position by using the member function of the Graphics class.

- Lines 43-46: Pertains to the assigning of the variables defined earlier in Lines 20-27 with the parameters passed on to the class.

- Line 47: Pertains to making the spotlet the current spotlet. The system keys can cancel the spotlet at any time.

- Lines 48-66: Pertains to initializing the Button objects Refresh, Search, Exit, and Browse, placing them on the screen at the appropriate positions and then painting (drawing) them. The button object ViewFiles is also initialized. However, the button is painted only when the flag view_file is true.

- Lines 80-95: Pertains to the action taken when the user presses the Refresh button.

  - 82-84: The caret on the TextField is killed, and the spotlet is unregistered, thereby making way for the next spotlet.

- 85-86: Pertains to the creation of an object of the class `peer_application` and calls the function `startReading()` to send a request to the server.

- 93: A class (`userlist_screen`) is called with the parameters `text_for_display` (text displayed in the `ScrollTextBox`), `ip_addresses` (IP addresses of the users connected at a particular instant of time), `users_connected` (names of the users connected at a particular instant of time), `false` (indicating that the View Files button is not to be shown), and record of users (name and IP addresses of the users connected at a particular instant of time).

- Lines 96-104: The code pertains to the action taken when the user presses the Search button.

  - 99-101: The caret on the `TextField` is killed, and the spotlet is unregistered, thereby making way for the next spotlet.

  - 102: A class of the name `serversearch` is called, which will implement the server-level search with parameters as two vectors and a String variable. The vectors have the data: the names of users and the IP addresses of the users.

- Lines 106-162: The code pertains to the action taken when the user, after entering a certain user number, presses the `ViewFiles` button.

  - 109-112: The user number entered by the user is taken from the `TextField` variable and is converted to an integer. If anything goes wrong, the exception is caught and the user input is made null.

  - 119: From the vector `ip_address`, the address is obtained from the user whose serial number is entered.

  - 121: From another vector, `record_of_users`, an enumeration is initialized.

  - 122-139: A `while` loop is started, which matches the contents of enumeration with the `ip_address` variable obtained earlier. If a match occurs, the next element of the enumeration is checked for the String value, and if the String value is `1`, the matched record is appended in the `file_text` variable; otherwise, it is appended in the `folder_text` variable.

  - 141: A String variable `text_for_display` is assigned with the values of `folder_text` and `file_text`.

  - 143-145: The caret on the `TextField` is killed, and the spotlet is unregistered, thereby making way for the next spotlet.

  - 147: A class `showfiles` is called with the parameters `text_for_display`.

- Lines 164-242: The code pertains to the action taken when the user, after entering a certain user number in the `TextField`, presses the Browse button.

  - 166-167: Various flags are initialized to check the occurrence of any exception.

  - 174-179: The user number entered by the user is taken from the `TextField` variable and is converted to an integer. If anything goes wrong, the exception is caught and the user input is made null.

  - 182: From the vector `ip_address`, the IP address of the user whose serial number is entered is obtained.

  - 185-198: A socket connection is made on port 7070 with the user whose IP address is obtained on Line 182. If the socket connection fails, a message pops up. Input and output streams on that socket are also obtained.

  - 204-207: An XML request, which is to be sent to the listener's machine, is formed using a String variable, `xmlRequest`. The XML request is converted to a `byte array` and its length is determined.

  - 209: A function of `appropriate_length` is called, which will make this request equal to 1,024 bytes in length; this is done in order to create compatibility with the C# listeners.

- 211-212: The modified XML request is then sent to the listener, and since the mode of communication between the listener and the client is XML, the response sent by the listener is passed directly on to the XML parser.

- 214: A function `parseData` is called, which is used for parsing the XML response sent by the listener to the client machine, making the `connection_flag` true.

- 234-240: If both the `connection_flag` and the `ip_flag` are true, the caret on the `TextField` is killed and the spotlet is unregistered, thereby making way for the next spotlet. A class `showfiles` is called, which contains the parameters constructed during the parsing.

♦ Lines 245-248: The code is used when the user presses the Exit button. When this button is pressed, the application is closed, and the control is returned to the OS.

♦ Lines 261-339: The code pertains to an important function `parseData`. This is the function in which the XML parser sends the Callbacks. The callbacks are identified accordingly, using the functions (whether the element obtained is the start tag or end tag, etc.).

- 276: If the tag encountered is `fileinfo`, the attributes of the tag are taken using the function `getValue()` and are added at their appropriate positions.

- 278-286: A check is made here to see whether the filename generated is a folder or a file. If a file is found, it is appended on to the `file_data`; otherwise, it is appended onto the `folder_data`.

- 287: The `folder_data` is also added to a vector for later use.

- 306-316: When the parsing is complete, the socket connection and the socket streams (both input and output streams) are closed.

- 317-337: The code pertains to adding the numbers to the file names generated. A variable `text_for_display` is assigned the values of the `folder_data` and the `file_data`.

♦ Lines 341-368: A function `appropriatelength` is declared. This function is responsible for making the request sent to the listener machine equal to 1,024 bytes in length. This is done by first creating the character array out of the byte array and then filling char 13 (\0) till the length 1,024 is attained and the character array is converted back to byte array.

Listing 9-3: showfiles.java

// © 2001 Dreamtech Software India, Inc.
// All rights Reserved

```
/**
 *   Importing the basic packages required by various classes during
 * the execution of the program.
 */
1.  import com.sun.kjava.*;
2.  import java.lang.*;
3.  import javax.microedition.io.*;
4.  import java.io.*;
5.  import java.util.*;
 /**
  *   The packages below are included because they are
  * required by the XML classes.
  */
6.  import org.kxml.*;
7.  import org.kxml.io.*;
8.  import org.kxml.parser.*;
9.
 //  Declaration of a class showfiles

10.  public class showfiles extends Spotlet
```

```
11.   {

  //   Declaring button variables.

12.    private Button browse_directory;
13.    private Button search;
14.    private Button close;
  // Declaring ScrollTextBox and textField variables.
15.    private ScrollTextBox filelist;
16.       private TextField option;
17.


18.    Vector information_vector;
19.    String parent_information;
20.    String text_for_display;
  /**
   *   Declaring variables to folder_data where the folder information
     *   is stored, similarly the variable file_data where the file
     *   information is stored.
     */
21.    String folder_data;
22.    String file_data;
23.
24.    int counter;
25.
26.    String host_address;
  //  Declaring StreamConnection variable used for Sockets..
27.    StreamConnection socket = null;
  //  Declaring InputStreams and OutputStreams used by the socket
  //  connections.
28.   InputStream socket_inputstream;
29.    OutputStream socket_outputstream;

30.    Vector folder_vector;
  /**
   *   Declaraing variables for the xmlparser and parse event(Where
     *   the call backs after the parsing will be stored.
     */
31.    AbstractXmlParser xmlparser;
32.    ParseEvent event;
33.  // Constructor for the class showfiles..
34.    showfiles(String text_for_display, Vector folder_vector, String address,
String parent_information,boolean viewfiles_flag)
35.    {
  // initializing the parameters with the varaiables declared
  // earlier.
36.         host_address = address;
37.         information_vector = folder_vector;
38.         this.parent_information = parent_information;
  // The current graphics is obtained...
39.     Graphics graphics = Graphics.getGraphics();
  /**
   *  Initializing the variable of the graphics class and clearing
   * the drawing region by calling the appropriate functions of
   * the Graphics class namely (resetDrawRegion() and clearScreen()).
   */
```

```
40.          graphics.resetDrawRegion();
41.            graphics.clearScreen();
42.
 /**
   *  Displaying a string (Title) at a specified position by using
      * the member function of the Graphics class
      */
43.          graphics.drawString("Shared Files / Folders",40,5);
44.
 // To make the spotlet as the current spotlet..
45.          register(NO_EVENT_OPTIONS);
46.
 // Initializing the button object "search",placing it on the screen.
47.    search = new Button("Search",10,20);
48.

 /**
   *  Initializing the ScrollTextBox object filelist, placing it on
    * the screen at the appropriate position and then painting(drawing it).
      */
49.    filelist = new ScrollTextBox(text_for_display,10,40,130,100);
50.    filelist.paint();
 // Initializing the TextField object "option", placing it on the screen
51.    option = new TextField("Dir ID:",10,145,50,10);
52.
 // Initializing the button object "Browse_directory", placing it
 // on the screen.
53.    browse_directory = new Button("Browse",70,145);
54.
 /**
   *  Initializing the button object Close, placing it on the screen
    * at the appropriate position and then painting(drawing it).
    */
55.    close = new Button("Close",120,145);
56.    close.paint();
 // If the viewfiles_flag is false then paint the buttons initialized
 // earlier else not.
57.
58.            if(!viewfiles_flag)
59.    {
60.    search.paint();
61.    browse_directory.paint();
62.    option.paint();
63.    option.setUpperCase(true);
64.        option.setFocus();
65.    }
66.
67.    }// End Constructor..
68.
 // Event Handling function. (KeyDown).
69.      public void keyDown(int x)
70.          {
 // Handle the input if the TextField is in focus.
71.            if(option.hasFocus())
72.                {
73.                    option.handleKeyDown(x);
```

```
74.                    }
75.              }   // End KeyDowm
76.
   // Event Handling function. (penDown)..

77.       public void penDown(int x, int y)
78.          {
   // If search(Client Search) Button is pressed
79.          if(search.pressed(x,y))
80.                 {
   // Remove the focus from the TextField and kill the TextField
   // blinking caret.
81.                    option.loseFocus();
82.                    option.killCaret();
   // To show a new class, first unregister all the controls of the
   //  existing class
83.                    unregister();
   // Call the class serverfiles with the parameters.
84.                    new searchfiles(host_address,parent_information);
85.          }
86.
87.
   // If Browse button is pressed then call the
   // method browse_directory() with parameter 1.
88.          if(browse_directory.pressed(x,y))
89.              {
90.
91.                    browseDirectory(1);
92.          }
93.
94.
   // If close button is pressed.
95.          if(close.pressed(x,y))
96.                 {
   // If the parent_information is root then..
97.                 if (parent_information.equals("ROOT"))
98.                    {
   // Remove the focus from the TextField and kill the TextField
   // blinking caret.
99.                    option.loseFocus();
100.                      option.killCaret();
   // To show a new class, first unregister all the controls of the
    // existing class
101.                       unregister();
   // Create an object of the class peer_application and call the
   // function startReading() to send a request to the server
102.                       peer_application refresh_application = new
peer_application();
103.                       refresh_application.startReading();
   // Then call the parser function, it will return a vector.
104.                       Vector ip_addresses =  refresh_application.parseData();
105.                  String text_for_display =
refresh_application.returnTextForDisplay();
106.                  Vector users_connected =
refresh_application.returnUsersConnected();
107.
```

```
          // Call the class userlist_screen with the parameters obtained in the
          // previous lines..
108.                    new
userlist_screen(text_for_display,ip_addresses,users_connected, false,null);
109.                    }    // End If...
          // Else if parent_information is not root then call the method
          // browseDirectory() with parameter 0.
110.                    else
111.                    {
112.                        browseDirectory(0);
113.                    }
114.
115.                }
          // Event handling for the ScrollTextBox.
116.
117.                if (filelist.contains(x,y))
118.                        filelist.handlePenMove(x,y);
119.        }         // End penDown
120.
          // Event handling for the ScrollTextBox.
121.       public void penMove(int x, int y)
122.       {
123.           if (filelist.contains(x,y))
124.                   filelist.handlePenMove(x,y);
125.       }
126.
          // method browseDirectory()
127.    void browseDirectory(int state)
128.    {
129.        if (state == 1)
130.        {
          // Two boolean flags are initialized..
131.                boolean connection_flag = false;
132.                boolean directory_flag  = false;
133.                String directory_name = "";
134.
135.                folder_vector = new Vector();
136.
137.                text_for_display = "";
138.                folder_data = "";
139.                file_data = "";
140.                counter = 1;
          // Option entered by the user is taken
141.                String directory_number = option.getText();
142.
143.                try
144.                    {
          // Converted to integer..
145.                    int directoryID = Integer.parseInt(directory_number);
146.                    try
147.                        {
          // The ip_address of the user selected is taken out
          // from the vector.
148.                        directory_name =
(String)information_vector.elementAt(directoryID-1);
149.
```

```
150.                    try
151.                    {
      // A Socket connection is made on a port with the Listener
152.                    socket =
(StreamConnection)Connector.open("socket://"+host_address+":7070",Connector.READ_
WRITE,true);
153.
      // If the socket is null then the connection is not established.
154.                    if (socket != null)
155.                    {
156.                    System.out.println("Connection is established to
localhost on port 7070...");
157.                    }
158.
159.    ///  Opening the Input and Output Streams to the Sockets....

160.
161.                    socket_inputstream = socket.openInputStream();
162.                    socket_outputstream = socket.openOutputStream();
163.                    }
164.                    catch(IOException ae)
165.                    {
166.                     System.out.println("Couldn't open socket:");
167.                    }
      // An XMLRequest which is to be sent to the Listener is formed..
168.        String xmlRequest = "<?xml version='1.0' encoding='utf-8'?>
<p2p_lng><request type=\"SEARCH\"><scope type=\""+directory_name+"*.*\"
mask=''></scope></request></p2p_lng>";
169.
      // It is converted to byte array
170.        byte [] byteXmlRequest = xmlRequest.getBytes();
      // The length of the byte array is taken out.

171.        int byteXmlRequest_length = byteXmlRequest.length;
 /**
  * A function appropriate length is called which will make
  *this request equal to 1024 bytes in length. This is done in
  *order to make compatibility with the C# listeners.
  */
172.        byteXmlRequest =
appropriatelength(byteXmlRequest,byteXmlRequest_length);
173.
      // The xmlrequest is sent via socket connection to the Listener
      // machine..
174.        try
175.        {
176.        socket_outputstream.write(byteXmlRequest);
      // The stream of response by the server is then passed on to
      // the xmlparser for parsing..
177.        xmlparser = new XmlParser(new
InputStreamReader(socket_inputstream));
178.        }
179.        catch(IOException e)
180.        {
181.        System.out.println(e);
182.            }
```

```
        // Function used for parsing is called...
183.     parseData();
184.
185.     directory_flag = true;
186.   }
187.   catch (Exception e)
188.   {
189.     System.out.println(e);
190.     directory_flag = false;
191.     option.setText("");
192.   }
193.
194.   connection_flag = true;
195.   }
196.   catch (Exception e)
197.   {
198.     connection_flag = false;
199.     option.setText("");
200.   }
201.
      // If dircetory_flag as well as  the connection_flag are true then
202.       if (connection_flag && directory_flag)
203.       {
      // Remove the focus from the TextField and kill the TextField
      // blinking caret
204.     option.loseFocus();
205.     option.killCaret();
      // To show a new class, first unregister all the controls of the
      // existing class.
206.     unregister();
      /// Class showfiles is called with the parameters..
207.     new showfiles(text_for_display,folder_vector,host_address,
directory_name,false);
208.       }
209.     }  // End If....
210.     else
211.   {
212.         folder_vector = new Vector();
213.         text_for_display = "";
214.         folder_data = "";
215.         file_data = "";
216.         counter = 1;
217.             try
218.                 {
      // A Socket connection is made on a port with the Listener
219.                 socket =
(StreamConnection)Connector.open("socket://"+host_address+":7070",Connector.READ_
WRITE,true);
220.
      // If the socket is null then the connection is not established..
221.                 if (socket != null)
222.                 {
223.         System.out.println("Connection is established to localhost on port
7070...");
224.                 }
225.
```

```
226.
227.            ///   Opening the Input and Output Streams...

228.                  socket_inputstream = socket.openInputStream();
229.                  socket_outputstream = socket.openOutputStream();
230.            }
231.         catch(IOException ae)
232.         {
233.         System.out.println("Couldn't open socket:");
234.         }
   // An XMLRequest which is to be sent to the Listener is formed..
235.
236.         String xmlRequest = "<?xml version='1.0' encoding='utf-8'?><p2p_lng>
   <request type=\"SHOWFILES\">      </request></p2p_lng>";
237.
   // It is converted to byte array

238.         byte [] byteXmlRequest = xmlRequest.getBytes();

   // The length of the byte array is taken out.

239.         int byteXmlRequest_length = byteXmlRequest.length;

 /**
  * A function appropriate length is called which will make
  * this request equal to 1024 bytes in length. This is done in
  * order to make compatibility with the C# listeners.
  */

240.         byteXmlRequest =
appropriatelength(byteXmlRequest,byteXmlRequest_length);
241.
242.
243.         try
244.         {
   // The xmlrequest is sent via socket connection to the Listener
   // machine..
245.                  socket_outputstream.write(byteXmlRequest);

   // The stream of response by the server is then passed on to
   // the xmlparser for parsing..

246.            xmlparser = new XmlParser(new
InputStreamReader(socket_inputstream));
247.
248.         }
249.         catch(IOException e)
250.         {
251.         }
252.
   // Function used for parsing is called...
253.         parseData();
254.
   // Remove the focus from the TextField and kill the TextField
   // blinking caret
255.         option.loseFocus();
```

```
256.          option.killCaret();
   // To show a new class, first unregister all the controls of the
   // existing class.
257.          unregister();
   /// Class showfiles is called with the parameters..
258.          new showfiles(text_for_display,folder_vector,host_address,
"ROOT",false);
259.
260.          }                    // End Else
261.       }
262.
263.
   // Function parseData (it will hold the callbacks generated by the
   // XMLParsing.
264.    void parseData()
265.          {
   // Move in loop till the XML document ends..
266.          do
267.           {
268.            try
269.             {
270.                    event = xmlparser.read ();
271.                    if(event.getType()==Xml.START_TAG)
272.                     {
273.                        StartTag stag = (StartTag)event;
   // The Start Tag is identified
274.                        String name = stag.getName();
   /**
    * If the Tag encountered is fileinfo then the Attributes of the
    * tag are taken using the function getValue() and are added at
    * their appropriate positions.
    */
275.                            if (name.equals("fileinfo"))
276.                             {
277.
278.              String filename = stag.getValue("filename");
279.
280.
   // A check is made for the filename and folders and
   // they are stored in seperate String variables.

281.              if (!(filename.charAt(filename.length()-1)  == '\\'))
282.              {
283.              filename = filename.substring(filename.lastIndexOf('\\')+1);
284.              file_data = file_data+filename+"\n";
285.              }
286.              else
287.              {
288.
289.              folder_data = folder_data + counter +".  "+filename+"\n";
   // The folders are also stored in a vector variable of the
   // name folder_vector.
290.              folder_vector.addElement((Object)filename);
291.              counter++;
292.              }
293.           }
```

```
294.          }
295.      }
296.    catch(IOException ex)
297.    {
298.                System.out.println("Exception occured");
299.    }
300.  }
301.  while (!(event instanceof EndDocument));
302.
303.  System.out.println("**** END OF DOCUMENT ****");
   // end of document
   // Socket Connection and Input and OutputStreams are
   // closed...
304.  try
305.  {
306.  socket.close();
307.  socket_inputstream.close();
308.  socket_outputstream.close();
309.  }
310.      catch(IOException e)
311.      {
312.                System.out.println(e);
313.
314.      }
   // Numbering is done on the file name stored in the String
   // variable by the name file_data.
315.      if (!file_data.equals(""))
316.      {
317.        file_data = counter+".  "+file_data;
318.        counter++;
319.      }
320.      StringBuffer file_data_buffer = new StringBuffer();
321.
322.      for (int i = 0;i<file_data.length()-1 ;i++ )
323.      {
324.              if (file_data.charAt(i) == '\n')
325.              {
326.                    file_data_buffer =
file_data_buffer.append(file_data.charAt(i));
327.                    file_data_buffer = file_data_buffer.append(counter+".
");
328.                    counter++;
329.              }
330.            else
331.            {
332.                    file_data_buffer =
file_data_buffer.append(file_data.charAt(i));
333.            }
334.
335.      }
336.      file_data = file_data_buffer.toString();
337.
   // the Final text to be displayed in the
   // variable textFor Display...
338.      text_for_display = "      Folders    \n"+folder_data+"\n"+"
Files     \n"+file_data;
```

```
339.    }
340.
     // This function is called to make the program compatible with
     // the C# Listeners.
341.        public byte [] appropriatelength(byte[] file_bytes, int file_size)
342.        {
343.                    int count = 0;
344.                    byte b[] = new byte[1024];
345.                    int remaining = 1024-file_size;
346.
347.                    for (int i = 0;i<file_bytes.length ;i++ )
348.                    {
349.                        b[i] = file_bytes[i];
350.                    }
351.
352.                    char a[] = new char[remaining];
353.
354.                    for (int i = 0;i<remaining ;i++ )
355.                    {
356.                    a[i] = 13;
357.                    }
358.
359.                    String tempw = new String(a);
360.                    byte d[] = tempw.getBytes();
361.
362.                    for (int i=file_size;i<1024 ;i++ )
363.                    {
364.                    b[i] = d[(i-file_size)];
365.                    }
366.
367.                    return (b);
368.        }                   // End Appropriate length.....
369.    }// End showfiles...
```

Code explanation

♦ Lines 1-5: Includes the basic packages used by various classes in the project, such as java.util.* for vectors and enumerations and java.io.* for input and output.

♦ Lines 6-8: Includes the packages required by the various classes in the XML parser.

♦ Line 10: Declares a class showfiles. This class displays the list of the various files/folders shared by a particular listener, which the user decides to browse at a particular instant of time. It also provides certain buttons for various uses, such as the Browse button, which the user presses after keying in a particular serial number of the directory. On pressing this button, the user is shown a screen that consists of all the files/folders that are included in that particular directory. A Search button is also provided, which the user can use to search for a file or a range of files in the files shown.

♦ Lines 12-17: Declares the Button, ScrollTextBox, and TextField variables, which are used as the GUI of this screen.

♦ Lines 18-20: Declares variables for storing the parameters passed on to the class.

♦ Lines 21-22: Declares variables to folder_data, where the folder information is stored, and the variable file_data, where the file information is stored.

♦ Lines 27-29: A StreamConnection-type variable (socket) is also declared, which is used to create a socket connection with the listener. Apart from this, inputstream and outputstream variables are also declared, which are used for communication between the socket on the user's machine and the socket on the listener's machine.

◆ Lines 31-32: Declares variables for the XML parser and parse event (where the callbacks after the parsing will be stored).

◆ Lines 36-38: Assigns the variables defined from Lines 10-32 with the parameters passed on to the class.

◆ Lines 39-41: Makes the spotlet the current spotlet and initializes the variable of the Graphics class and clears the drawing region by calling the appropriate functions of the Graphics class — namely, resetDrawRegion() and clearScreen().

◆ Line 43: Displays a String (Title) at a specified position by using the member function of the Graphics class.

◆ Line 45: Makes the spotlet the current spotlet. The system keys can cancel the spotlet at any time.

◆ Lines 47-56: Initializes various GUI component buttons (Search, Close, Browse), ScrollTextBox variable filelist, TextField variable option, etc. The ScrollTextBox and the Close Button are painted on the screen.

◆ Lines 58-65: If the view_file flag is true, the Buttons Search and Browse are painted on the screen, the TextField option is painted on the screen, and the caret is displayed along with it.

◆ Lines 79-85: The action taken when the user presses the Search button.

  • 81-83: The caret on the TextField is killed, and the spotlet is unregistered, thereby making way for the next spotlet.

  • 84: A class searchfiles is called, which implements the client-level search.

◆ Lines 88-92: The code pertains to the action taken when the user presses the Browse button. Then a method browseDirectory with a parameter 1 is passed.

◆ Lines 95-115: The code pertains to the action taken when the user presses the Close button.

  • 97: A check is made whether the parent_information variable contains a value ROOT.

  • 99-101: The caret on the TextField is killed, and the spotlet is unregistered, thereby making way for the next spotlet.

  • 102-103: Creation of an object of the class peer_application and the calling of the function startReading() to send a request to the server.

  • 108: A class (userlist_screen) is called with the parameters text_for_display (text displayed in the ScrollTextBox), ip_addresses (IP addresses of the users connected at a particular instant of time), users_connected (name of the users connected at a particular instant of time), false (indicating that the View Files button is not to be shown), and record of users (name and IP addresses of the users connected at a particular instant of time).

  • 110-113: If the value contained in the variable parent_information is not ROOT, a method browseDirectory is called with a parameter 0.

◆ Lines 127-261: Pertains to an important method, browseDirectory.

  • 129: If the parameter passed is 1, the following code is executed.

  • 131-132: Various flags are initialized to check the occurrence of any exception.

  • 141-145: The user number entered by the user is taken from the TextField variable and is converted to an integer. If something is wrong, the exception is caught and the user input is made null.

  • 148: From the vector ip_address, the IP address of the user whose serial number is entered is obtained.

- 150-167: A socket connection is made on a port 7070 with the user whose IP address is obtained on the previous line. If the socket connection fails due to some error or network problem, a message pops up. Input and output streams on that socket are also obtained.

- 168-171: An XML request to be sent to the listener's machine is formed using a String variable, xmlRequest. The XML request is converted to a byte array and its length is determined.

- 172: A function appropriatelength is called, which will make this request equal to 1,024 bytes in length; this is done in order to create compatibility with the C# listeners.

- 174-182: The modified XML request is then sent to the listener, and since the mode of communication between the listener and the client is XML, the response sent by the listener is passed directly on to the XML parser.

- 183: A function parseData is called, which is used for parsing the XML response sent by the listener to the client machine, making the connection_flag true.

- 202-208: If both the connection_flag and the directory_flag are true, the caret on the TextField is killed and the spotlet is unregistered, thereby making way for the next spotlet. A class showfiles is called, which contains the parameters constructed during the parsing activity.

- 210: If the method browseDirectory is passed with a parameter 0, the following code is executed.

- 219-229: A socket connection is made on a port 7070 with the user whose IP address is in the variable host_address. If the socket connection fails due to some reason, a message pops up. Input and output streams on that socket are also obtained.

- 236-239: An XML request to be sent to the listener's machine is formed using a String variable, xmlRequest. The XML request is converted to a byte array and its length is determined.

- 240: A function appropriatelength is called, which will make this request equal to 1,024 bytes in length. This is done in order to create compatibility with the C# listeners.

- 245-246: The modified XML request is then sent to the listener, and since the mode of communication between the listener and the client is XML, the response sent by the listener is passed directly on to the XML parser.

- 253: A function, parseData, is called, which is used for parsing the XML response sent by the listener to the client machine, making the connection_flag true.

- 255-257: The caret on the TextField is killed and the spotlet is unregistered, thereby making way for the next spotlet. A class showfiles is called, which contains the parameters constructed during the parsing activity.

- Lines 264-339: The code between these lines pertains to an important function, parseData. This is the function in which the XML parser sends the Callbacks. The callbacks are identified accordingly, using the functions (whether the element obtained is the start tag or end tag, etc.).

  - 274: If the tag encountered is fileinfo, the attributes of the tag are taken using the function getValue() and are added at the appropriate positions.

  - 281-289: A check is made here to see whether the filename generated is a folder or a file. If a file is found, it is appended onto the file_data; otherwise, it is appended onto the folder_data.

  - 290: The folder_data is also added to a vector for later use.

  - 304-314: When the parsing is complete, the socket connection and the socket streams — both input and output — are closed.

  - 315-338: The code between these lines pertains to adding the numbers to the filenames generated. A variable text_for_display is assigned the values of the folder_data and the file_data.

♦ Lines 341-368: A function `appropriatelength` is declared; this is responsible for making the request sent to the listener machine equal to 1,024 bytes in length. This done by first creating the character array out of the byte array and then filling char 13 (\0) till the length 1,024 is attained and the character array is converted back to byte array.

Listing 9-4: serversearch.java

// © 2001 Dreamtech Software India, Inc.
// All rights Reserved

```
/**
 *   The packages below are included because these packages are
 *   required by the XML classes.
 */
1.   import com.sun.kjava.*;
2.   import org.kxml.*;
3.   import org.kxml.parser.*;
/**
 *   Importing the basic packages required by various classes during
 *   the execution of the program.
 */
4.   import java.lang.*;
5.   import javax.microedition.io.*;
6.   import javax.microedition.io.Connector;
7.   import java.io.*;
8.   import java.util.*;
9.
 //  Declaration of a class serversearch used for server level
 // searching.
10.  public class serversearch extends Spotlet
11.  {
12.      Vector record_of_users;
 /**
 *   Declaraing variables for the xmlparser and parse event(Where
 *   the callbacks after the parsing will be stored.
 */
13.      AbstractXmlParser xmlparser;
14.      ParseEvent event;
15.
16.      DataInputStream din;
17.          String tt= "";
 // Declaring and initializing the buttons..
18.      private Button search = new Button("Search", 25,120);
19.          private Button cancel = new Button("Cancel", 65,120);
 // Declaring and initializing the TextField..
20.          private TextField t_file_name_search = new TextField("File Names ",
 10, 35,130,10);
 // Declaring and initializing the TextField..
21.          private TextField t_computer_name_search = new TextField("On Computer/s
 ", 10, 70,130,10);
22.
 // The current graphics is obtained...
23.          Graphics gr = Graphics.getGraphics();
24.      Vector ip_address;
25.      Vector users_connected;
26.
27.
```

```
    // serversearch constructor
28.    public serversearch(String user_data, Vector ip_address, Vector
users_connected)
29.          {
30.
/**
 * Initializing the variable of the graphics class and clearing
 * the drawing region by calling the appropriate functions of
 * the Graphics class namely (resetDrawRegion() and clearScreen()).
 */
31.      gr.resetDrawRegion();
32.          gr.clearScreen();
// To make the spotlet as the current spotlet..
33.      register(NO_EVENT_OPTIONS);
34.
/**
 * Displaying a string (Title) at a specified position by using
 * the member function of the Graphics class
 */
35.          gr.drawString("Server Level Search",35,10);
// Painting the textfield on the screen and making it the current
// textfield.
36.          t_file_name_search.paint();
37.          t_file_name_search.setFocus();
// Painting the textfield on the screen
38.          t_computer_name_search.paint();
// Painting the buttons on the screen
39.          search.paint();
40.          cancel.paint();
41.
// initializing the parameters with the variables declared
// earlier.
42.      this.ip_address = ip_address;
43.      this.users_connected =users_connected;
44.          }      // end constructor
45.
46.
// Event Handling function. (KeyDown)..
47.          public void keyDown( int x)
48.          {
    // If TAB button is pressed then the focus shifts from one
    // textfield to the other..
49.              if(t_file_name_search.hasFocus())
50.              {
51.                t_file_name_search.handleKeyDown(x);
52.              String tt = t_file_name_search.getText();
53.              if (x == 9)
54.              {
55.                  t_file_name_search.loseFocus();
56.                  t_computer_name_search.setFocus();
57.              }
58.              }
59.
60.              else if(t_computer_name_search.hasFocus())
61.              {
62.                t_computer_name_search.handleKeyDown(x);
```

```
63.                        if (x == 9)
64.               {
65.                    t_computer_name_search.loseFocus();
66.                    t_file_name_search.setFocus();
67.
68.                 }
69.
70.              }
71.          }
72.
73.
74.
  // Event Handling function. (penDown)..
75.          public void penDown( int x, int y)
76.            {
77.
78.  // if search button is pressed...
79.                  if(search.pressed(x,y))
80.                  {
81.
82.                    record_of_users = new Vector();
83.
84.                    boolean b_file = false;
85.                    boolean b_computer = false;
86.                    int pointfind = 0;
87.                    String file_name = t_file_name_search.getText();
  // Various checks to ensure that no field is left empty..
88.                    if(file_name.equals(""))
89.                    {
90.                    file_name = "*";
91.                    b_file = true;
92.                    }
93.                    else
94.                    {
95.                    pointfind = file_name.indexOf(".");
96.                    if( pointfind > 0)
97.                    {
98.                    b_file = true;
99.                    }
100.                       }
101.                    String computer_name =
t_computer_name_search.getText();
102.                    if(computer_name.equals(""))
103.                    {
104.                    computer_name = "*";
105.                    b_computer = true;
106.                    }
107.                    else
108.                    {
109.                    if( pointfind > 0)
110.                    {
111.                    b_computer = true;
112.                    }
113.                    }
114.
115.
```

```
116.                     if (b_computer == true && b_file == true)
117.                     {
118.                     }
119.                     else
120.                     {
121.                         String text_for_display = "";
122.                         int number = 1;
123.
124.                         try
125.                         {
    // Using the Connector class of CLDC an InputStream is opened on
    // the ASP
126.                         din =
Connector.openDataInputStream("testhttp://www.s-cop.com/search.asp?us=" +
computer_name + "&fs=" + file_name);
127. // The stream of response by the server is then passed on to
    // the xmlparser for parsing..

128.                         xmlparser = new XmlParser(new
InputStreamReader(din));
129.                         }
130.                         catch(IOException e)
131.                         {
132.                             System.out.println("Server Search Exception:
"+e);
133.
134.                         }
    // Function used for parsing is called...
135.                         parseData();
136.
137.
    // An enumeration is generated from the vector users_connected..
138.                         Enumeration enumeration =
users_connected.elements();
    // A loop is executed till enumeration has no more elements
139.                         while (enumeration.hasMoreElements())
140.                         {
141.                             int increment = 0;
142.                             Object temp = enumeration.nextElement();
143.
144.                             Enumeration enum =
record_of_users.elements();
145.                         while (enum.hasMoreElements())
146.                         {
147.                             Object temp1 = enum.nextElement();
148.
    // If match is found, then count is increased by 1.
149.                             if (temp1.equals(temp))
150.                             {
151.                                 increment++;
152.                             }
153.                         }
154.
    // The count is shown with the text_for_display.
155.                             text_for_display = text_for_display+number+".
"+(String)temp+"("+increment+")"+"\n";
```

```
156.                                    increment = 0;
157.                                    number++;
158.                                }
159.
   // the caret on the textField is killed.
160.                                t_file_name_search.loseFocus();
161.                                t_file_name_search.killCaret();
162.
   // the caret on the textField is killed.
163.                                t_computer_name_search.loseFocus();
164.                                t_computer_name_search.killCaret();
165.
   // The Spotlet is unregistered..
166.                                unregister();
167.
 // Call to the userlist_screen is made with appropriate parameters
168.                                new userlist_screen(text_for_display,
ip_address,users_connected,true, record_of_users);
169.
170.                                }
171.
172.                        }
 // If Cancel button is pressed..
173.                    else if(cancel.pressed(x,y))
174.                        {
 // textfield caret's are killed..
175.                        t_file_name_search.loseFocus();
176.                        t_file_name_search.killCaret();
177.
178.                        t_computer_name_search.loseFocus();
179.                        t_computer_name_search.killCaret();
180.
   // Spotlet is unregistered.
181.                        unregister();
 // Create an object of the class peer_application and call the
 // function startReading() to send a request to the server
182.                        peer_application refresh_application = new
peer_application();
183.                        refresh_application.startReading();
   // Then call the parser function, it will return a vector.
184.                        Vector ip_addresses =  refresh_application.parseData();
185.                        String text_for_display =
refresh_application.returnTextForDisplay();
186.
187.
188.                        Vector uers_connected =
refresh_application.returnUsersConnected();
189.  // class userlist_screen is called with appropriate parameters..
190.                        new
userlist_screen(text_for_display,ip_addresses,users_connected,  false,null);
191.
192.
193.
194.                    }
195.            }
196.
```

```
     // Function parseData (it will hold the callbacks generated by the
     // XMLParsing.
197.    void parseData()
198.        {
199.            do
     // Move in loop till the XML document ends..
200.            {
201.              try
202.                {
203.                        event = xmlparser.read ();
204.
205.                        if(event.getType()==Xml.START_TAG)
206.                        {
207.                                StartTag stag = (StartTag)event;
208.
209.                                String name = stag.getName();
     // The Start Tag is identified
210.
  /**
   * If the Tag encountered is result then the Attributes of the
   * tag are taken using the function getValue() and are added to
   * their appropriate position.
   */
211.                                if (name.equals("result"))
212.                                {
213.
214.                                String folder_identity = "";
215.
216.                                String ip = stag.getValue("ip").trim();
217.                                String username =
stag.getValue("username").trim();
218.                                String filename = stag.getValue("filename");
219.
220.
     // For files and folders appropriate flags are attached..
221.                                if (!(filename.length() == 0))
222.                                {
223.                                        filename.trim();
224.                                }
225.
226.            if (!(filename.length() == 0))
227.                {
228.
229.
230.                if (!(filename.charAt(filename.length()-1)   == '\\'))
231.                {
232.                folder_identity = "1";
233.                }
234.                else
235.                {
236.                folder_identity = "0";
237.                }
238.
239.
     // The username , ip address, the file /foldername and the
     // file /folder flag are added to the vector.
```

```
240.            record_of_users.addElement((Object)username);
241.            record_of_users.addElement((Object)ip);
242.            record_of_users.addElement((Object)filename);
243.            record_of_users.addElement((Object)folder_identity);
244.                     }
245.                 }
246.           }
247.
248.         }
249.       catch(IOException ex)
250.       {
251.                 System.out.println("Exception occured");
252.       }
253.    }
254.    while (!(event instanceof EndDocument));
255.         System.out.println("**** END OF DOCUMENT ****");
   // End of parsing...
256.    }
257.    }      // End of serversearch...
```

Code explanation

♦ Lines 1-3: Details the inclusion of the packages required by the various classes in the XML parser.

♦ Lines 4-8: Details the inclusion of the basic packages used by various classes in the project, such as java.util.* for vectors and enumerations and java.io.* for input and output , etc.

♦ Line 10: The class serversearch is declared. This class is responsible for implementing the server-level search, wherein the browser can search for a particular file or a class of files on a particular computer or a set of computers. When the search is over, a list of users connected at a particular instant of time is displayed, along with the number of files (displayed in brackets) that satisfy a particular search criterion.

♦ Lines 13-14: Declares variables for the XML parser and parse event (where the callbacks after the parsing will be stored).

♦ Lines 18-21: Declares the various GUI components used in the class. These GUI components include two Buttons with the labels Search and Cancel and two TextFields.

♦ Lines 24-25: Two vector variables, users_connected and ip_addresses, are declared. These variables keep a record of the IP addresses of the users connected, along with the names of the users connected at a particular instant of time.

♦ Lines 31-32: Initializes the variable of the Graphics class and clears the drawing region by calling the appropriate functions of the Graphics class — namely, resetDrawRegion() and clearScreen().

♦ Line 33: Pertains to making the spotlet the current spotlet; however, the system keys can cancel the spotlet at any time.

♦ Line 35: Displaying a String (Title) at a specified position by using the member function of the Graphics class.

♦ Lines 36-40: Pertains to the painting of the various GUI components such as the two TextField's and the two buttons on the screen.

♦ Lines 42-43: Pertains to initializing the parameters with the variables declared earlier.

♦ Lines 47-71: The code is executed when the user presses a key. If the Tab key is pressed from a normal QWERTY keyboard, the current text field's caret is made to disappear and the caret is made to appear in the other TextField.

♦ Lines 79-172: The code is executed when the user, after entering some search criteria in the two text fields, presses the Search button.

- 88-121: Various checks are made in these lines. These checks ensure that no field is left empty, and if one is empty, the variable of the empty field is assigned a *. However, if both the fields are empty, a flag (boolean variable) is assigned a value false so that further execution of the code is stopped.

- 126: After the checking is over, using the Connector class of the CLDC's javax.microedition.io package, an HTTP request is made to the server. The request also passes the search criteria as parameters to the server.

- 128: Since the response from the server is an XML response, the stream used for the response is directly passed to the XML parser.

- 135: A function, parseData, is called. This function is responsible for generating the parsed data from the XML and storing the data in an appropriate format in a vector.

- 138-153: An enumeration is generated from the Vector (users_connected), and a loop is executed till the total number of elements in the Vector are extracted. At this stage, another enumeration of the parsed data collected is also generated, and an inner loop is moved through, thereby matching the contents of the earlier enumeration with each element of the current enumeration. If a match occurs, a counter that starts at each loop is incremented by one. At the end of the loop, the counter is appended to an item in the list of the users connected.

- 160-166: The caret on the TextField is killed, and the spotlet is unregistered, thereby making way for the next spotlet.

- 168: A class (userlist_screen) is called with the parameters text_for_display (text displayed in the ScrollTextBox), ip_addresses (IP addresses of the users connected at a particular instant of time), users_connected (names of the users connected at a particular instant of time), true (indicating that the View Files button is to be shown), and record of users (name and IP addresses of the users connected at a particular instant of time).

♦ Lines 173-194: The code pertains to the action taken when the user presses the Cancel button.

- 175-181: The caret on the TextField is killed, and the spotlet is unregistered, thereby making way for the next spotlet.

- 182-188: The code here pertains to the creation of an object of the class peer_application and calls the function startReading() to send a request to the server.

- 190: A class (userlist_screen) is called with the parameters text_for_display (text displayed in the ScrollTextBox), ip_addresses (IP addresses of the users connected at a particular instant of time), users_connected (names of the users connected at a particular instant of time), false (indicating that the View Files button is not to be shown), and record of users (names and IP addresses of the users connected at a particular instant of time).

♦ Lines 197-256: The code pertains to an important function, parseData. This is the function in which the XML parser sends the Callbacks. The callbacks are identified accordingly, using the functions (whether the element obtained is the start tag or end tag, etc.).

- 211: If the Tag encountered is result, the attributes of the tag are taken using the function getValue() and are added at their appropriate positions.

- 221-237: A check is made here to see whether the filename generated is a folder or a file. If a file is found, a flag folder_identity is set to 0, and if a folder is found, the folder_identity is set to 1.

- 240-243: All this data generated by the parser is then added to a vector of the name record_of_users.

Listing 9-5: searchfiles.java

```
/**
 *    Importing the basic packages required by various classes during
 * the execution of the program.
 */
1.   import com.sun.kjava.*;
2.   import java.lang.*;
3.   import javax.microedition.io.*;
4.   import java.io.*;
5.   import java.util.*;

 /**
  *  The packages below are included because these packages are
  *  required by the XML classes.
  */
6.   import org.kxml.*;
7.   import org.kxml.io.*;
8.   import org.kxml.parser.*;
9.
 //  Declaration of a class searchfiles used for client level
 // searching.
10.  public class searchfiles extends Spotlet
11.  {
 //  Declaring button variables.
12.    private Button search;
13.    private Button cancel;

 // Declaring textField variables.
14.      private TextField option;
15.
16.    String parent_information;
17.    String text_for_display;
 /**
  *   Declaring variables to folder_data where the folder information
  *    is stored similarly the variable file_data where the file
  *    information is stored.
  */
18.    String folder_data;
19.    String file_data;
20.
21.    int counter;
22.
 // Storing the parent address..
23.    String host_address;
 //  Declaring StreamConnection variable used for Sockets..
24.    StreamConnection socket = null;
 //  Declaring InputStreams and OutputStreams used by the socket
 //  connections.
25.    InputStream socket_inputstream;
26.      OutputStream socket_outputstream;
27.    Vector folder_vector;
 /**
  *   Declaring variables for the xmlparser and parse event(Where
```

```
    *    the callbacks after the parsing will be stored.
    */
28.    AbstractXmlParser xmlparser;
29.    ParseEvent event;
30.
 // searchfiles constructor
31.    searchfiles(String address, String parent_information)
32.    {
 // initializing the parameters with the variables declared
 // earlier.
33.         host_address = address;
34.         this.parent_information = parent_information;
35.
 // The current graphics is obtained...
36.         Graphics graphics = Graphics.getGraphics();
 /**
   *  Initializing the variable of the graphics class and clearing
   * the drawing region by calling the appropriate functions of
   * the Graphics class namely (resetDrawRegion() and clearScreen()).
   */
37.         graphics.resetDrawRegion();
38.          graphics.clearScreen();
39.
 /**
   *  Displaying a string (Title) at a specified position by using
     *  the member function of the Graphics class
     */
40.         graphics.drawString("Search for Files / Folders",30,15);

 // To make the spotlet as the current spotlet..

41.         register(NO_EVENT_OPTIONS);
42.
 /**
   *  Initializing the button object "Search", placing it on the screen
   *  at the appropriate position and then painting(drawing it).
   */
43.         search = new Button("Search",25,95);
44.         search.paint();
45.
 /**
   *  Initializing the button object "Cancel", placing it on the screen
   * at the appropriate position and then painting(drawing it).
   */
46.         cancel = new Button("Cancel",65,95);
47.         cancel.paint();
48.
 /**
   *  Initializing the TextFiled object option, placing it on the screen
   *  at the appropriate position ,painting(drawing it) and making the
   *  caret blink by setting the TextField as the current field.
   */
49.         option = new TextField("Search Criteria:",10,45,140,15);
50.         option.paint();
51.         option.setUpperCase(true);
52.         option.setFocus();
```

```
53.     }// End Constructor..
54.
  // Event Handling function. (KeyDown)..
55.     public void keyDown(int x)
56.         {
  // Handle the input if the TextField is in focus.
57.             if(option.hasFocus())
58.                 {
59.                     option.handleKeyDown(x);
60.                 }
61.         }
62.
  // Event Handling function. (penDown)..
63.     public void penDown(int x, int y)
64.         {
  // If search button is pressed..
65.         if(search.pressed(x,y))
66.             {
67.                 folder_vector = new Vector();
  // The variables are assigned ..
68.             text_for_display = "";
69.             folder_data = "";
70.             file_data = "";
71.             counter = 1;
72.                 try
73.                     {
  // A Socket connection is made on a port with the Listener(host address)
74.                     socket =
(StreamConnection)Connector.open("socket://"+host_address+":7070",Connector.READ_
WRITE,true);
75.
  // If the socket is null then the connection is not established.
76.                     if (socket != null)
77.                         {
78.                         System.out.println("Connection is established to
localhost on port 7070...");
79.                         }
80.
81.
82.                         ///  Opening the Input and Output Streams...

83.
84.                         socket_inputstream = socket.openInputStream();
85.                         socket_outputstream = socket.openOutputStream();
86.                     }
87.                 catch(IOException ae)
88.                     {
89.                     System.out.println("Couldn't open socket:");
90.                     }
91.
  // An XMLRequest which is to be sent to the Listener is formed..
92.                     String xmlRequest = "<?xml version='1.0'
encoding='utf-8'?> <p2p_lng><request type=\"SEARCH\"><scope
type=\""+parent_information+option.getText()+"\"
mask=''></scope></request></p2p_lng>";
93.
```

```
       // It is converted to byte array
94.  byte [] byteXmlRequest = xmlRequest.getBytes();
       // The length of the byte array is taken out.
95.     int byteXmlRequest_length = byteXmlRequest.length;
96.
 /**
  * A function appropriate length is called which will make
  * this request equal to 1024 bytes in length this is done in
  * order to make compatibility with the C# listeners.
  */
97.  .             byteXmlRequest =
appropriatelength(byteXmlRequest,byteXmlRequest_length);
98.
99.             try
100.                {
       // The xmlrequest is sent via socket connection to the Listener
       // machine..
101.                     socket_outputstream.write(byteXmlRequest);
       // The stream of response by the server is then passed on to
       // the xmlparser for parsing..

102.                     xmlparser = new XmlParser(new
InputStreamReader(socket_inputstream));
103.                   }
104.             catch(IOException e)
105.                {
106.                }
107.
    // Function used for parsing is called...
108.                 parseData();
109.    // Remove the focus from the TextField and kill the TextField
       // blinking caret
110.                 option.loseFocus();
111.                 option.killCaret();
       // To show a new class first unregister all the controls of the
       // existing class.
112.                 unregister();
       /// Class showfiles is called with the parameters..
113.                 new
showfiles(text_for_display,folder_vector,host_address,  "LOST",false);
114.           }
       // If cancel is pressed...
115.           if(cancel.pressed(x,y))
116.               {
117.                   folder_vector = new Vector();
118.                   text_for_display = "";
119.                   folder_data = "";
120.                   file_data = "";
121.                   counter = 1;
122.                   try
123.                      {
       // A Socket connection is made on a port with the Listener
124.                   socket =
(StreamConnection)Connector.open("socket://"+host_address+":7070",Connector.READ_
WRITE,true);
125.
```

```
          // If the socket is null then the connection is not established.
126.                              if (socket != null)
127.                              {
128.                              System.out.println("Connection is established
to localhost on port 7070...");
129.                              }
130.
131.                              ///
132.                              ///  Opening the Input and Output Streams...

133.
134.
135.                              socket_inputstream = socket.openInputStream();
136.                              socket_outputstream = socket.openOutputStream();
137.                         }
138.                    catch(IOException ae)
139.                    {
140.                    System.out.println("Couldn't open socket:");
141.                    }
142.
          // An XMLReuest which is to be sent ot the Listener is formed..
143.                              String xmlRequest = "<?xml version='1.0'
encoding='utf-8'?> <p2p_lng><request type=\"SEARCH\"><scope
type=\""+parent_information+"*.*\" mask=''></scope></request></p2p_lng>";
       // It is converted to byte array

144.
145.                         byte [] byteXmlRequest = xmlRequest.getBytes();
       // The length of the byte array is taken out.
146.                         int byteXmlRequest_length = byteXmlRequest.length;
147.
 /**
   * A function appropriate length is called which will make
   * this request equal to 1024 bytes in length, this is done in
   * order to make compatibility with the C# listeners.
   */
148.    .          byteXmlRequest =
appropriatelength(byteXmlRequest,byteXmlRequest_length);
149.
150.
151.                    try
152.                    {
       // The xmlrequest is sent via socket connection to the Listener
       // machine..
153.                         socket_outputstream.write(byteXmlRequest);
       // The stream of response by the server is then passed on to
       // the xmlparser for parsing..

154.
155.                         xmlparser = new XmlParser(new
InputStreamReader(socket_inputstream));
156.                    }
157.                    catch(IOException e)
158.                    {
159.                    }
160.
```

```
      // Function used for parsing is called...
161.                   parseData();
162.
   // Remove the focus from the TextField and kill the TextField
   // blinking caret
163.                   option.loseFocus();
164.                   option.killCaret();
   // To show a new class, first unregister all the controls of the
   // existing class.
165.                   unregister();
   /// Class showfiles is called with the parameters.
166.    new showfiles(text_for_display,folder_vector,host_address,  "ROOT",false);

167.
168.           }
169.        }
170.
   // Function parseData (it will hold the callbacks generated by the
   // XMLParsing).
171.        void parseData()
172.          {
   // Move in loop till the XML document ends..
173.           do
174.            {
175.             try
176.              {
177.                   event = xmlparser.read ();
178.                   if(event.getType()==Xml.START_TAG)
179.                    {
180.                         StartTag stag = (StartTag)event;
   // The Start Tag is identified
181.                         String name = stag.getName();
   /**
    * If the Tag encountered is fileinfo, then the Attributes of the
    * tag are taken using the function getValue() and are added to
    * their appropriate position.
    */

182.                         if (name.equals("fileinfo"))
183.                          {
184.
185.    String filename = stag.getValue("filename");
186.
   // A check is made for the filename and folders and
   // they are stored in separate String varaiables.
187.
188.             if (!(filename.charAt(filename.length()-1)   == '\\'))
189.             {
190.             filename = filename.substring(filename.lastIndexOf('\\')+1);
191.             file_data = file_data+filename+"\n";
192.             }
193.             else
194.             {
195.
196.             folder_data = folder_data + counter +".  "+filename+"\n";
   // The folders are also stored in a vector variable of the
```

```
       // name folder_vector.
197.             folder_vector.addElement((Object)filename);
198.             counter++;
199.             }
200.
201.                     }
202.
203.                     }
204.
205.
206.         }
207.         catch(IOException ex)
208.         {
209.                 System.out.println("Exception occured");
210.         }
211.     }
212.     while (!(event instanceof EndDocument));
213.
214.     System.out.println("**** END OF DOCUMENT ****");
       // end of document
       // Socket Connection and Input and OutputStreams are
       // closed...
215.     try
216.     {
217.     socket.close();
218.     socket_inputstream.close();
219.     socket_outputstream.close();
220.     }
221.     catch(IOException e)
222.     {
223.             System.out.println(e);
224.
225.         }
   // Numbering is done on the file name stored in the String
   // variable by the name file_data.
226.     if (!file_data.equals(""))
227.     {
228.      file_data = counter+".  "+file_data;
229.      counter++;
230.     }
231.      StringBuffer file_data_buffer = new StringBuffer();
232.
233.     for (int i = 0;i<file_data.length()-1 ;i++ )
234.     {
235.             if (file_data.charAt(i) == '\n')
236.             {
237.                 file_data_buffer =
file_data_buffer.append(file_data.charAt(i));
238.                 file_data_buffer = file_data_buffer.append(counter+".
");
239.                 counter++;
240.             }
241.         else
242.             {
243.                 file_data_buffer =
file_data_buffer.append(file_data.charAt(i));
```

```
244.                    }
245.
246.              }
247.           file_data = file_data_buffer.toString();
     //  the Final text to be displayed is stored in the
     //  variable text for display..
248.
249.           text_for_display = "        Folders     \n"+folder_data+"\n"+"
Files       \n"+file_data;
250.
251.     }
252. // This function is called to make the program compatible with
     // the C# Listeners.
253.           public byte [] appropriatelength(byte[] file_bytes, int file_size)
254.            {
255.                    int count = 0;
256.                    byte b[] = new byte[1024];
257.                    int remaining = 1024-file_size;
258.
259.                    for (int i = 0;i<file_bytes.length ;i++ )
260.                    {
261.                        b[i] = file_bytes[i];
262.                    }
263.
264.                    char a[] = new char[remaining];
265.
266.                    for (int i = 0;i<remaining ;i++ )
267.                    {
268.                    a[i] = 13;
269.                    }
270.
271.                    String tempw = new String(a);
272.                    byte d[] = tempw.getBytes();
273.
274.                    for (int i=file_size;i<1024 ;i++ )
275.                    {
276.                    b[i] = d[(i-file_size)];
277.                    }
278.
279.                    return (b);
280.            }              // End Appropriate length.....
281.
282. }      // End of the class searchfiles...
```

Code explanation

♦ Lines 1-5: Details the inclusion of the basic packages used by various classes in the project, such as java.util.* for vectors and enumerations and java.io.* for input and output.

♦ Lines 6-8: Details the inclusion of the packages required by the various classes in the XML parser.

♦ Line 10: The code here pertains to the declaration of the class searchfiles. This class helps the user perform the client-level search that is searching the present contents of the spotlet for a filename or a subset of filenames.

♦ Lines 12-14: Declares the Button and TextField variables, which are used as the GUI of this screen.

♦ Lines 18-19: Declares variables for `folder_data`, where the folder information is stored, and also the variable `file_data`, where the file information is stored.

♦ Lines 24-26: A `StreamConnection`-type variable (`socket`) is declared, which is used to create a socket connection with the listener. Apart from this, `inputstream` and `outputstream` variables are also declared and are used for communication between the socket on the user's machine and the socket on the listener's machine.

♦ Lines 28-29: Declares variables for the XML parser and parse event (where the callbacks after the parsing will be stored).

♦ Lines 33-34: Assigns the variables defined from Lines 10-29 with the parameters passed on to the class.

♦ Lines 36-38: Makes the spotlet the current spotlet, initializing the variable of the graphics class and clearing the drawing region by calling the appropriate functions of the Graphics class — namely, `resetDrawRegion()` and `clearScreen()`.

♦ Line 40: Displays a String (`Title`) at a specified position by using the `member` function of the `Graphics` class.

♦ Lines 43-47: Initializes the button objects Search and Cancel, placing them on the screen at the appropriate position, and then painting (drawing) them.

♦ Lines 49-52: Initializes the `TextField` object `option`, placing it on the screen at the appropriate position, painting (drawing) it, and making the caret blink by setting the `TextField` as the current field.

♦ Lines 65-114: The action taken when the user, after entering certain data (search criteria) in the `TextField`, presses the Search button.

  • 72-85: A socket connection is made on a port 7070 with the user whose IP address is in the variable `host_address`. If the socket connection fails for some reason, a message pops up. Input and output streams on that socket are also obtained.

  • 92-95: An XML request to be sent to the listener's machine is formed using a String variable `xmlRequest`. The XML request is converted to a byte array and its length is determined.

  • 97: A function `appropriatelength` is called, which will make this request equal to 1,024 bytes in length. This is done in order to create compatibility with the C# listeners.

  • 99-106: The modified XML request is then sent to the listener, and since the mode of communication between the listener and the client is XML, the response sent by the listener is passed directly on to the XML parser.

  • 108: A function, `parseData`, is called, which is used for parsing the XML response sent by the listener to the client machine.

  • 110-113: The caret on the `TextField` is killed and the spotlet is unregistered, thereby making way for the next spotlet. A class `showfiles` is called, which contains the parameters constructed during the parsing activity.

♦ Lines 115-168: The action taken when the user presses the Cancel button.

  • 122-141: A socket connection is made on port 7070 with the user whose IP address is in the variable `host_address`. If the socket connection fails, a message pops up. Input and output streams on that socket are also obtained.

  • 143-146: An XML request, which is to be sent to the listener's machine, is formed using a String variable `xmlRequest`. The XML request is converted to a byte array and its length is determined.

  • 148: A function, `appropriatelength`, is called, which will make this request equal to 1,024 bytes in length. This is done in order to create compatibility with the C# listeners.

- 151-159: The modified XML request is then sent to the listener, and since the mode of communication between the listener and the client is XML, the response sent by the listener is passed directly on to the XML parser.

- 161: A function, `parseData`, is called, which is used for parsing the XML response sent by the listener to the client machine.

- 163-166: The caret on the `TextField` is killed and the spotlet is unregistered, thereby making way for the next spotlet. A class `showfiles` is called, which contains the parameters constructed during the parsing.

- ◆ Lines 171-251: The code pertains to an important function, `parseData`. This is the function in which the XML parser sends the Callbacks. The callbacks are identified accordingly, using the functions (whether the element obtained is the start tag or end tag, etc.).

- 181: If the tag encountered is `fileinfo`, the attributes of the tag are taken using the function `getValue()` and are added to the appropriate positions.

- 188-196: A check is made here to see whether the filename generated is a folder or a file. If a file is found, it is appended onto the `file_data`; otherwise, it is appended onto the `folder_data`.

- 197: The `folder_data` is also added to a vector for later use.

- 215-225: When the parsing is complete, the socket connection and the socket streams — both input and output — are closed.

- 226-249: Adds the numbers to the filenames generated. A variable `text_for_display` is assigned the values of the `folder_data` and the `file_data`.

- Lines 253-280: A function, `appropriatelength`, is declared. This is responsible for making the request sent to the listener machine equal to 1,024 bytes in length. This is done by first creating the character array out of the byte array and then filling char 13 (`\0`) till the length 1,024 is attained and the character array is converted back to byte array.

Summary

This chapter describes the fourth full-blown application we have developed using J2ME in this book. This application is developed for Palm devices. The application is Peer search and is a Peer-to-Peer based application. Although a brief summary of the Peer-to-Peer application is given in this chapter, we recommend you go through the book *Peer-to-Peer Application Development* for better understanding of the concept. Chapter 10 is on developing a small portal for mobile phones using MIDP.

Chapter 10

Project 5: Mobile Web Services

Many things that once required a trip to the market or elsewhere you can now do on the Internet. You can purchase books, groceries, and even vegetables on the Net. An ocean of information is also within your reach if you can access the Net. You can contact people without making an international call and avail yourself of many other services. Such services have been available for several years, but until recently, actually using them required considerable effort.

The next phase was to integrate already available services and add new ones to reduce the user's involvement in installing different software on a machine to a minimum. In the resulting network of services, various components would interact automatically to deliver to you exactly what you need. This goal was the idea behind Microsoft's .NET, as well as Sun Microsystems' SunOne initiatives. These initiatives aim to provide services not only on desktop systems that connect to the Internet, but on mobile devices as well.

The last few years also saw an explosion of mobile and/or wireless devices. The same services that you find on larger systems — or at least any that the device can deliver —are now becoming available on small, mobile, wireless devices. The application that we discuss in this chapter is a portal which is made available for small devices.

We name our application *Mobile Web Services*. It offers the user three services — namely, Weather, Movies, and News. As part of the Weather service, the user gets information about the weather in certain cities. The Movies service enables the user to discover what films are running at which movie hall and also to book a ticket for any film. The News service makes available the headlines and detailed news to the user on a mobile phone. We created the application by using MIDP so that you can run it from a mobile phone or a two-way pager. Because MIDP is now available for Palm, too, you can port the same application to a Palm device with very little effort.

User Interface

The initial screen of the application is the application launch screen shown in Figure 10-1, and the next screen shows the user a list of the available services. These are, as mentioned in the preceding section, Weather, Movies, and News as shown in Figure 10-2. The user highlights the service he/she wants to avail and presses the Select button. To quit the application, he/she can press the EXIT button.

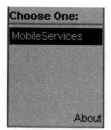

Figure 10-1: Application Launch Screen.

Figure 10-2: List of Services.

If the user selects the Weather service, he/she will see a screen listing names of cities as shown in Figure 10-3. There will be two buttons, labeled OK and Cancel. After the user scrolls to a particular city and presses the OK button, the weather details, such the temperature, sunrise, sunset, moonrise, moonset, etc., for that city are shown as in Figure 10-4. Pressing the Cancel button will take the user back to the initial screen.

Figure 10-3: List of cities for Weather Details.   **Figure 10-4:** Weather Report.

If the service selected is Movies, the user will see a list of cinema halls as shown in Figure 10-5. The screen will display a button labeled Back to return to the previous screen. On selecting a theater, the user is shown the name of the film running at that hall as in Figure 10-6. Every screen from here on will have a Back button. The user then can select the movies he/she wants to see. The dates on which that movie will play are shown in Figure 10-7, and the user can select a date.

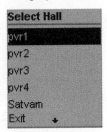

Figure 10-5: List of Theaters.   **Figure 10-6:** List of Movie running.

Figure 10-7: Date of Show.

The user is now presented with details about the movie, such as the show time, ticket rate, and so on, as in Figure 10-8. The screen will have two buttons, Back and Book. On pressing Book, he/she is prompted to enter his/her name as in Figure 10-9. Two buttons are available in Figure 10-9, Back and OK. Pressing Back will return the user to the previous screen, that is, Figure 10-8.

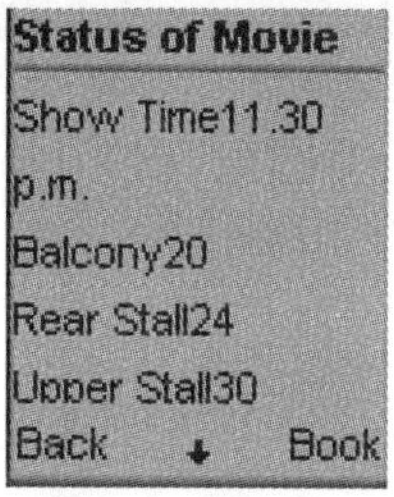

Status of Movie

Show Time11.30
p.m.
Balcony20
Rear Stall24
Upper Stall30
Back   ↓   Book

Figure 10-8: Movie Availability Status.

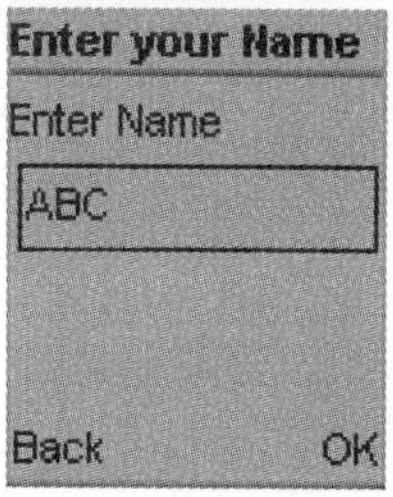

Enter your Name

Enter Name

ABC

Back   OK

Figure 10-9: Enter Detail Screen - Name.

If the user presses OK, he/she is prompted to enter his/her e-mail ID as in Figure 10-10. Again, there are two buttons, Back and OK. The user now has to select the category, such as balcony, box, etc as shown in Figure 10-11. The last thing to enter is the number of tickets required as shown in Figure 10-12. As soon as the Book button is pressed, the tickets are booked.

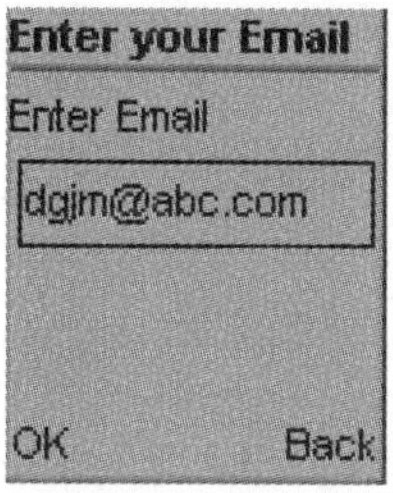

Enter your Email

Enter Email

dgjm@abc.com

OK   Back

Figure 10-10: Enter Detail Screen - Email.

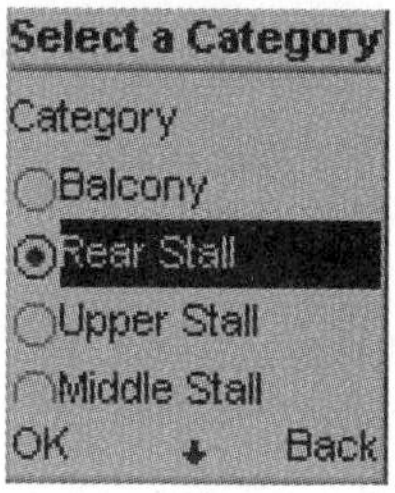

Select a Category

Category
◯Balcony
◉Rear Stall
◯Upper Stall
◯Middle Stall
OK   ↓   Back

Figure 10-11: Enter Detail Screen - Category.

Enter the Tickets

Enter Ticket

2

BOOK   Back

Figure 10-12: Enter Detail Screen – No. of Tickets.

If the user selects the News service, he/she will see the subjects on which news is available, such as the economy, politics, etc shown in Figure 10-13. This screen will have the buttons OK and Cancel. The user may scroll to a subject and press the OK button for the highlights on that subject as in Figure 10-14.

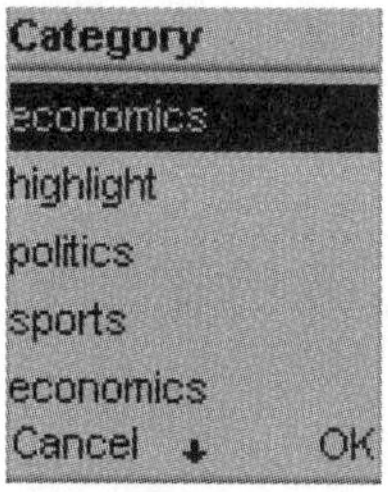

Category

economics
highlight
politics
sports
economics
Cancel   ↓   OK

Figure 10-13: News Category.

News of politics

Parliament
China not a factor
in Indo-US ties:
Jaswant
Back   ↑   View

Figure 10-14: News Headlines.

Two buttons, labeled Back and View, are present to let the user either go back to the list of subjects or to read the news in some detail as in Figure 10-15, respectively. On the screen showing the news in detail are two buttons, Previous and Start. Previous takes the user to the previous screen and Start to the initial screen.

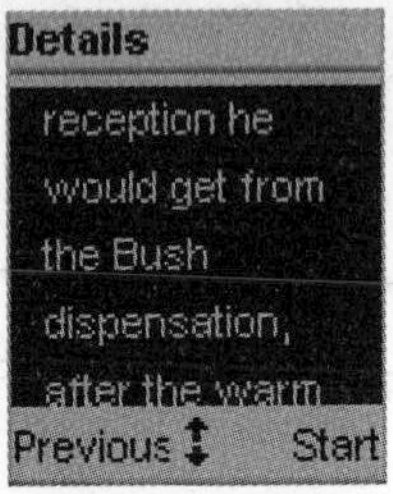

Figure 10-15: Detail news.

How to Run

To run this application, you should have the J2ME Wireless Toolkit installed, as we explained in Chapter 4. The steps involved for running the application would be:

1. Start KToolbar of the J2ME Wireless Toolkit from the Start menu.
2. Begin a new project by clicking New Project.
3. Enter a name for the project — say, MobileServices.
4. Enter the name of the main MIDlet class, which is also named Main.
5. Click Create Project.
6. Copy the source code for the project in the `C:\J2MEWTK\apps\MobileServices` directory.
7. Now come back to the KToolbar and click the Build button.

Once the project is successfully compiled and preverified, click the Run button.

How It Works

Before getting into the details of the application, let's first examine the Database for this application. We have used SQLServer on the backend. Lets examine the Table structure of the Database. The table shown in Figure 10-16 is a Weather table which stores the weather details.

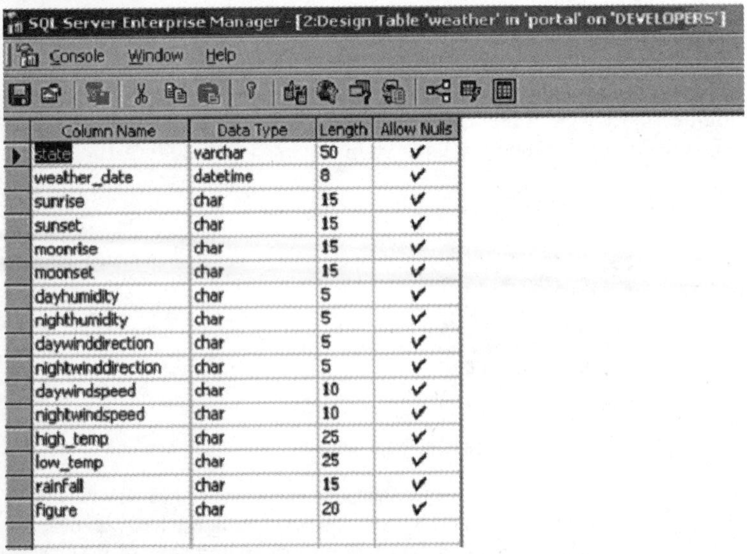

Column Name	Data Type	Length	Allow Nulls
state	varchar	50	✔
weather_date	datetime	8	✔
sunrise	char	15	✔
sunset	char	15	✔
moonrise	char	15	✔
moonset	char	15	✔
dayhumidity	char	5	✔
nighthumidity	char	5	✔
daywinddirection	char	5	✔
nightwinddirection	char	5	✔
daywindspeed	char	10	✔
nightwindspeed	char	10	✔
high_temp	char	25	✔
low_temp	char	25	✔
rainfall	char	15	✔
figure	char	20	✔

Figure 10-16: Weather Table.

The table shown in Figure 10-17 is a theater table and stores information related to theaters like the name of the theater, its id, and the address. This table is used for the Movies service. There are three more tables used for Movies service and these are the movie table shown in Figure 10-18, status table shown in Figure 10-19, and user table shown in Figure 10-20. The movie table stores information related to the movie like the movie name and ID. The status table stores information related to the status of the movie like the number of tickets available on the basis of category like balcony, upper_stall etc. The user table shown in Figure 10-20 stores information about the user booking the tickets.

SQL Server Enterprise Manager - [2:Design Table 'hall' in 'portal' on 'DEVELOPERS']

Console   Window   Help

Column Name	Data Type	Length	Allow Nulls
hall_id	numeric	9	
hall_name	varchar	50	✓
address	varchar	100	✓

Figure 10-17: Theater Table.

SQL Server Enterprise Manager - [2:Design Table 'movie' in 'portal' on 'DEVELOPERS']

Console   Window   Help

Column Name	Data Type	Length	Allow Nulls
movie_id	numeric	9	
movie_name	varchar	100	✓

Figure 10-18: Movie Table.

SQL Server Enterprise Manager - [2:Design Table 'status' in 'portal' on 'DEVELOPERS']

Console   Window   Help

Column Name	Data Type	Length	Allow Nulls
hall_id	numeric	9	
movie_id	numeric	9	
showtime	char	10	
balcony	numeric	9	✓
rear_stall	numeric	9	✓
upper_stall	numeric	9	✓
middle_stall	numeric	9	✓
movie_date	char	25	✓

Figure 10-19: Status Table.

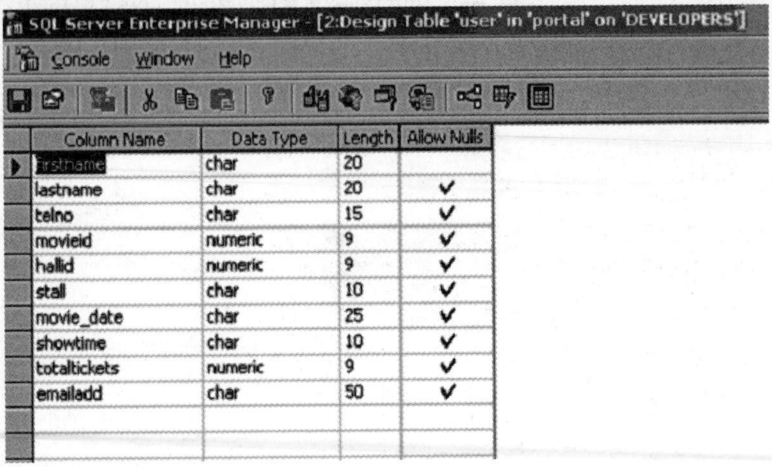

Figure 10-20: User Table.

The table shown in Figure 10-21 is a news table which stores the news details. The table contains information regarding the news subjects there, headlines, heading ID, and the news description i.e., the detail news.

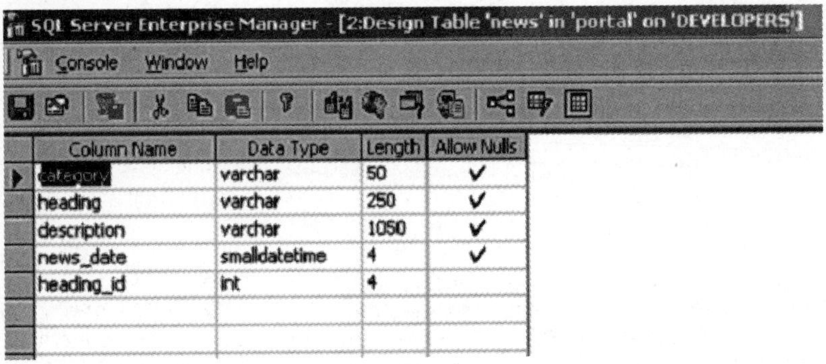

Figure 10-21: News Table.

The application is started when the class `MainClass` is executed. This class displays the list of the services available. The three services, as we have seen, are *Weather*, *Movies*, and *News*. If the user decides to quit and presses the Exit button, the `destroyApp` method is called for the MIDlet `MainClass`, and the application closes.

If, instead, the user decides to further explore and selects the Weather service, another class, `Weather`, is called. This class, in turn, calls the class `DataParser`, which parses the XML and throws the result. The data thrown is entered into the device database (`RecordStore`). Now, if the user presses the Cancel button, the MIDlet `Weather` is destroyed. At this stage, the user is shown a list of cities for which the weather report is available. If the user selects a city and presses the OK button, data is read from the device's database and displayed to the user. There are two buttons, labeled Back and Cancel. Pressing Cancel results in the MIDlet `Weather` being destroyed as before. Pressing Back takes the user to the previous screen.

The second service is Movies. If the user selects this service, a class `MoviesList` is called. This class, in turn, calls the `parseDataMovies` method of the `DataParser`. As a result, the list of movie halls is displayed. The event handling defined in the `MoviesList` class ensures that the appropriate screen is shown to the user, as described in the preceding section.

If the user selects the News service, a class `News` is called. This class displays the list of subjects on which news is available. Pressing the Cancel button takes the user to the initial screen of the application showing the list of services. On the user's pressing OK, headlines are displayed about the selected subject. There are two buttons, labeled Back and View. Pressing View presents to the user detailed news concerning that headline. On this last screen, the Start button is available, which can take the user to the initial screen of the News service. All this is achieved by defining event handling for the class `News`. Throughout the running of this application, SQL Server runs in the background and Throws the results in XML format.

The `MainClass` just serves the purpose of defining the methods required for managing the application life cycle. The list of services is displayed and, depending on the item selected, other MIDlets are called. Event handling consists of mainly checking the item selected by the user. One thing to be noted in this class is that an object, `displaymenu`, of the `Display` class, is being passed to any other MIDlet being called from here. This is required because, otherwise, there wouldn't be a way of showing the GUI of the next class (for example, `Weather`). Similarly, when the class that has once been called is destroyed — say, by pressing the Exit button — the `getDisplayObject` method of this class is called to get the display back. Here, too, the `display` object is being passed as a parameter. Without passing this object between the classes of the application, we would be left with the existing screen whenever any class is destroyed after following the first class or another class is called.

The main purpose of the class `DataParser`, as its name suggests, is to parse XML received from the server. It uses the package `org.kxml.*` for this purpose. It makes a connection to the specified URL that refers to an XML file — for example,
`http://192.192.168.100/midlet/template/midlet_news.xml`. The class uses `Vectors`, `Hashtables`, and the device's database to store parsed data. It contains methods for different functions such as reading the data, adding records to data, etc. The method `sourceurl` is called in every MIDlet except `MainClass`. It accepts a string representing the URL, establishes the connection, opens a stream to read from the URL, and creates a `parser` object. It then passes this `stream` object to the constructor of the XML parser.

This class has a method, `read_record`, that reads the data from an XML file in accordance with the selected city and creates a new record in the device's database for each city. It also performs other tasks related to managing this database. The method `read_record` internally calls a `record_add` method, which adds a record into the database and returns an integer value (`record ID`). These record IDs are stored in a `Hashtable`. Another method, `returnstate`, returns a `Hashtable` containing the names of the cities and the corresponding record IDs. There is one more method, `deleterecord`, which deletes records from the device database. This method is called when the `Weather` MIDlet is closed, to free the resources.

The method `parseDataMovies` is called by the class `MoviesList`. An integer argument is passed to this method, which serves as a condition for parsing. If the value of this argument is 1, it will get the list of movie theaters and will store the hall names and hall IDs in a `Vector`. If the argument is 2, the details relating to the hall will be stored in a `Vector`. The second case will apply when the user selects a particular hall.

The method `read_category` reads the list of subjects, or *categories*, from an XML file (`midlet_news.xml`) when the News MIDet is started. Another method, `read_news`, reads the headlines from the XML file when a particular subject is selected. The class `DataParser` has one more method, called `returnDetails`, for use in the News class. This method reads the detailed news when a particular news headlines is selected.

In the class `Weather`, the values associated with fields of the weather table are read from the server (where they are retrieved from a database into an XML file, whose URL is passed) by calling the read_record method of the DataParser class. The names of the cities are stored in Hashtable; the weather fields such as Date, Sunrise, Sunset, etc., are stored in a Vector; and the values associated with these fields are stored in the device's database (using the RecordStore class). The DataParser class is used to parse the XML received from SQL Server, which has the capability to receive a query and to send back the result in XML format. The XML generated by SQL Server in case of Weather Service is shown in Figure 10-22.

```xml
<?xml version="1.0" encoding="UTF-8" ?>
- <ROOT xmlns:sql="urn:schemas-microsoft-com:xml-sql">
  - <weather>
      <city>NewYork</city>
      <weather_date>2001-05-14T00:00:00</weather_date>
      <sunrise>06:39:00</sunrise>
      <sunset>18:54:00</sunset>
      <moonrise>07:35:00</moonrise>
      <moonset>20:09:00</moonset>
      <dayhumidity>35</dayhumidity>
      <nighthumidity>24</nighthumidity>
      <daywinddirection>west</daywinddirection>
      <nightwinddirection>west</nightwinddirection>
      <daywindspeed>8 Knots</daywindspeed>
      <nightwindspeed>6 Knots</nightwindspeed>
      <high_temp>39</high_temp>
      <low_temp>24</low_temp>
      <rainfall>Nil</rainfall>
      <figure>clearday</figure>
    </weather>
  - <weather>
      <city>Sydney</city>
      <weather_date>2001-05-14T00:00:00</weather_date>
      <sunrise>06:30:00</sunrise>
      <sunset>18:50:00</sunset>
      <moonrise>07:30:00</moonrise>
      <moonset>20:00:00</moonset>
      <dayhumidity>40</dayhumidity>
      <nighthumidity>25</nighthumidity>
      <daywinddirection>north</daywinddirection>
      <nightwinddirection>north</nightwinddirection>
      <daywindspeed>5 Knots</daywindspeed>
```

Figure 10-22: Weather.xml.

The Movies service of this application is handled by the class MoviesList. When this class is started by selecting the Movies service, the URL of an XML file, midlet_movies.xml (shown in Figure 10-23) is passed as a parameter to the method sourceurl, which is called by a DataParser object. This class has a method, getAllData, that is passed a String and an integer counter as parameters. The value of the counter variable is used for checking the conditions in the if blocks, just as in the method parseDataMovies. If the value is 1, a new List object is created, and the URL of an XML file, midlet_status.xml (shown in Figure 10-24) is passed to the method sourceurl, which is called by the DataParser object parsemoviedata. Then this object calls the parseMovieData method with a parameter value of 2.

```xml
<?xml version="1.0" encoding="UTF-8" ?>
- <ROOT xmlns:sql="urn:schemas-microsoft-com:xml-sql">
  - <hall>
      <hall_id>1</hall_id>
      <hall_name>pvr1</hall_name>
      <address>New Delhi, Saket, in PVR complext I floor</address>
    </hall>
  - <hall>
      <hall_id>2</hall_id>
      <hall_name>pvr2</hall_name>
      <address>New Delhi, Saket, in PVR complext II floor</address>
    </hall>
  - <hall>
      <hall_id>3</hall_id>
      <hall_name>pvr3</hall_name>
      <address>New Delhi, Saket, in PVR complext III floor</address>
    </hall>
  - <hall>
      <hall_id>4</hall_id>
      <hall_name>pvr4</hall_name>
      <address>New Delhi, Saket, in PVR complext II floor</address>
    </hall>
  - <hall>
      <hall_id>5</hall_id>
      <hall_name>Satyam</hall_name>
      <address>Delhi, West Patel Nagar</address>
    </hall>
  - <hall>
      <hall_id>6</hall_id>
      <hall_name>Priya</hall_name>
      <address>Delhi, Vasant Kunj, In priya Comlex</address>
    </hall>
  - <hall>
```

Figure 10-23: `midlet_movies.xml`.

If the value of the counter variable is 2, the dates on which a particular movie will be screened are displayed. And if the value is 3, details of the show, such as the time of the show and ticket rates for different categories, are displayed. Event handling, defined in the method `commandAction` of the `CommandListener` class, takes care of the rest of the things, depending on the command generated when the user makes the choices.

```
<?xml version="1.0" encoding="UTF-8" ?>
- <ROOT xmlns:sql="urn:schemas-microsoft-com:xml-sql">
  - <hall>
    <hall_name>pvr2</hall_name>
    - <movie>
        <movie_name>Proof of Life(Drama)</movie_name>
        <movie_id>2</movie_id>
      - <status>
          <movie_date>22 May</movie_date>
          <showtime>11.30 a.m.</showtime>
          <balcony>0</balcony>
          <rear_stall>18</rear_stall>
          <upper_stall>13</upper_stall>
          <middle_stall>20</middle_stall>
        </status>
      - <status>
          <movie_date>22 May</movie_date>
          <showtime>2.00 p.m.</showtime>
          <balcony>15</balcony>
          <rear_stall>12</rear_stall>
          <upper_stall>20</upper_stall>
          <middle_stall>22</middle_stall>
        </status>
      </movie>
    - <movie>
        <movie_name>Speed2(thriller)</movie_name>
        <movie_id>4</movie_id>
      - <status>
          <movie_date>20 May</movie_date>
          <showtime>12.00 p.m.</showtime>
          <balcony>3</balcony>
          <rear_stall>21</rear_stall>
```

Figure 10-24: `midlet_status.xml`.

The News service of this application is handled by the class News. When this class is started by selecting the News service, the URL of an XML file, `midlet_news.xml` (shown in Figure 10-25), is passed as a parameter to the method `sourceurl`, which is called by a DataParser object. The XML file is parsed and values stored in a Vector object vnews. The values in vnews object is News category which is displayed to the user. When the user selects a category the `sourceurl` method is passed the URL of an XML file, `midlet_news_det.xml` (shown in Figure 10-26) as argument. The XML file is parsed and the Headlines of News are displayed to the user. When the user selects a Headline again the `sourceurl` method is passed the URL of an XML file, `midlet_news_description.xml`   (shown in Figure 10-27) as argument. The XML file is parsed and the detail news is displayed to the user.

```xml
<?xml version="1.0" encoding="UTF-8" ?>
- <ROOT xmlns:sql="urn:schemas-microsoft-com:xml-sql">
  - <news>
      <category>economics</category>
    </news>
  - <news>
      <category>highlights</category>
    </news>
  - <news>
      <category>politics</category>
    </news>
  - <news>
      <category>sports</category>
    </news>
  </ROOT>
```

Figure 10-25: midlet_news.xml.

```xml
<?xml version="1.0" encoding="UTF-8" ?>
- <ROOT xmlns:sql="urn:schemas-microsoft-com:xml-sql">
  - <news>
      <category>economics</category>
      <news_date>2001-05-14T00:00:00</news_date>
      <heading>Centre becomes more pro-active in Enron case</heading>
      <heading_id>20</heading_id>
    </news>
  - <news>
      <category>economics</category>
      <news_date>2001-05-14T00:00:00</news_date>
      <heading>Godbole panel moots financial revamp of DPC</heading>
      <heading_id>21</heading_id>
    </news>
  - <news>
      <category>economics</category>
      <news_date>2001-05-14T00:00:00</news_date>
      <heading>Zee yet to come clean on Rs 220-cr investment</heading>
      <heading_id>22</heading_id>
    </news>
  - <news>
      <category>economics</category>
      <news_date>2001-05-14T00:00:00</news_date>
      <heading>Bank's exposure to brokers should be diversified</heading>
      <heading_id>23</heading_id>
    </news>
  - <news>
      <category>economics</category>
      <news_date>2001-05-14T00:00:00</news_date>
      <heading>Brokers face tough time as trading comes to halt</heading>
      <heading_id>24</heading_id>
```

Figure 10-26: midlet_news_det.xml.

```
<?xml version="1.0" encoding="UTF-8" ?>
- <ROOT xmlns:sql="urn:schemas-microsoft-com:xml-sql">
  - <news>
      <heading>Crowe, Roberts bag Oscars</heading>
      <description>LOS ANGELES: Russell Crowe and Julia Roberts took the top acting Oscars and
          Asian martial arts spectacle "Crouching Tiger, Hidden Dragon" was voted best foreign film
          at the Academy Awards here Sunday. Crowe was honoured for his role as a general turned
          slave turned fighter in "Gladiator," earning the film its fourth</description>
  </news>
  </ROOT>
```

Figure 10-27: `midlet_news_description.xml`.

Let's examine the working of the complete application. The flow charts in Figures 10-28, 10-29, 10-30, 10-31 and 10-32 explain the complete flow of the application.

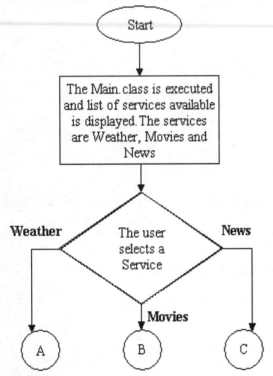

Figure 10-28: Flow Chart - I.

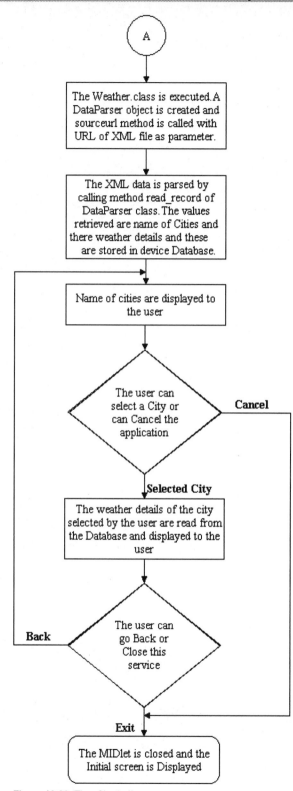

Figure 10-29: Flow Chart - II.

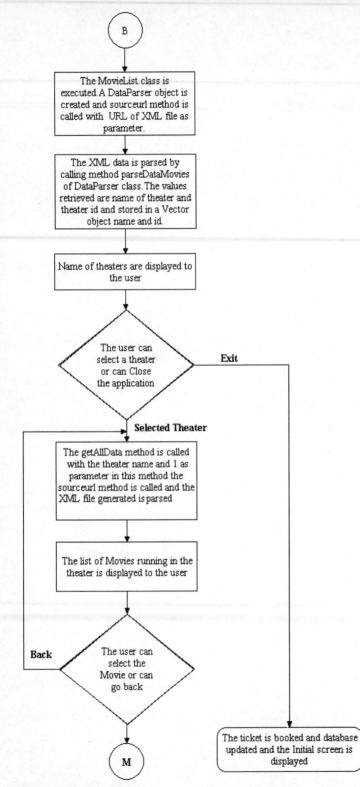

Figure 10-30: Flow Chart - III.

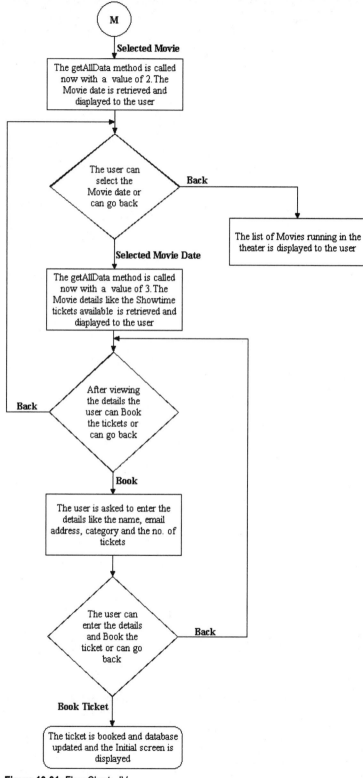

Figure 10-31: Flow Chart - IV.

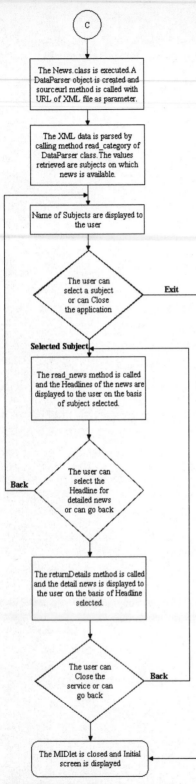

Figure 10-32: Flow Chart - V.

MainClass.java

This class launches the Mobile services. This is main class and calls the other three MIDlets of this application. The list of services is displayed to the user and on selecting a service, this class passes control to another MIDlet (Listing 10-1).

Listing 10-1: MainClass.java

```
1.   import javax.microedition.midlet.MIDlet;
2.
3.   import javax.microedition.lcdui.List;
4.   import javax.microedition.lcdui.Display;
5.   import javax.microedition.lcdui.CommandListener;
6.   import javax.microedition.lcdui.Command;
7.   import javax.microedition.lcdui.Displayable;
8.   /* This class is the first class to be invoked.This class internally calls
three different MIDlets
9.   depending on the item selected
10.  */
11.  public class MainClass extends MIDlet implements CommandListener
12.  {
13.    /*    This list object will contain the Services */
14.    private List menu = null;
15.    /*    Display object declared */
16.    private Display displaymenu = null;
17.    /*    MovieList object declared. The movielist class is a MIDlet which will
make the user book movie
18.      tickets */
19.    MoviesList bookmovie = null;
20.    /*    News object declared. The News class is a MIDlet which will make the
user read news   */
21.    News readnews = null;
22.    /*    Weather object declared. This class is also a MIDlet which will give
the user weather
23.      details based on the city selected */
24.    Weather seeweather = null;
25.    /* Command object declared   */
26.    Command exit;
27.    /* MainClass constructor declared */
28.    public MainClass()
29.    {
30.      /* This will get the display object */
31.      displaymenu = Display.getDisplay(this);
32.      /* Exit command initialized */
33.      exit = new Command("EXIT",Command.EXIT,1);
34.    }
35.    /* The startApp method declared */
36.    public void startApp()
37.    {
38.      /* Initializing List */
39.      menu = new List("Menu",List.IMPLICIT);
40.      /* This will add three items in the list which are the services provided
*/
```

```
41.      menu.append("Weather",null);
42.      menu.append("Movies",null);
43.      menu.append("News",null);
44.      /* This will register the list for events handling */
45.      menu.setCommandListener(this);
46.      /* The list will be displayed to the user */
47.      displaymenu.setCurrent(menu);
48.      /* Exit command added to the list */
49.      menu.addCommand(exit);
50.    }
51.    /* The pauseApp() method declared */
52.    public void pauseApp()
53.    {
54.      System.out.println("pause app called");
55.    }
56.    /* The destroyApp() method declared */
57.    public void destroyApp(boolean b)
58.    {
59.      menu = null;
60.      displaymenu = null;
61.      bookmovie = null;
62.      readnews = null;
63.      seeweather = null;
64.    }
65.    /* This method handles user events */
66.    public void commandAction(Command c, Displayable d)
67.    {
68.      /* This if condition is true if any item in the list is selected */
69.      if(c == List.SELECT_COMMAND)
70.      {
71.          /* This String will contain the string representation of the item
selected */
72.          String menuselect = menu.getString(menu.getSelectedIndex());
73.          /* The if condition is executed if the user selects "Weather". The
weather MIDlet is
74.              initialized and its startApp() method is called
75.          */
76.          if(menuselect.equals("Weather"))
77.          {
78.              /* Weather MIDlet initialized, two arguments passed to the
constructor Display object
79.                  and the object of MainClass */
80.              seeweather = new Weather(displaymenu,this);
81.              /* startApp() method called */
82.              seeweather.startApp();
83.          }
84.          /* This if condition is executed if the user selects "Movies". The
MovieList MIDlet is
85.              initialized and its startApp() method is called
86.          */
87.          if(menuselect.equals("Movies"))
88.          {
89.              /* MovieList MIDlet initialized, two arguments passed to the
constructor Display object
90.                  and the object of MainClass */
91.              bookmovie = new MoviesList(displaymenu,this);
```

```
92.                    /* startApp() method called */
93.                    bookmovie.startApp();
94.
95.          }
96.          /* This if condition is executed if the user selects "News". The
MovieList MIDlet is
97.                    initialized and its startApp() method is called
98.          */
99.          if(menuselect.equals("News"))
100.               {
101.                    /* News MIDlet initialized two arguments passed to the
constructor Display object
102.                    and the object of MainClass */
103.                    readnews = new News(displaymenu,this);
104.                    /* startApp() method called */
105.                    readnews.startApp();
106.               }
107.          }
108.          /* This if condition is true if the user presses the button
indicating "EXIT" */
109.          if(c == exit)
110.          {
111.                    /* destroyApp() method called */
112.                    destroyApp(true);
113.                    notifyDestroyed();
114.          }
115.     }
116.     /* This method is to get the Display object back */
117.     public void getDisplayObject(Display dis)
118.     {
119.          displaymenu = dis;
120.          displaymenu.setCurrent(menu);
121.     }
122. }
```

Code explanation

+ Lines 1-7: Import statements, which import the required classes to run this application.

+ Line 11: Declaring MainClass. This class is a MIDlet, and this is the main class. This class calls the other three MIDlets in this application.

+ Lines 14-26: The lines of code here declare different objects.

+ Lines 28-34: Constructor declaration. The code in the constructor gets the Display object and initializes a command. This command is an exit command.

+ Lines 36-50: The startApp() method is declared. This will initialize a List, which will display to the user the services provided. The user can see the weather details, book movie tickets, or read news. It will also register the list for event handling and adds a command to the list.

+ Lines 52-55: The pauseApp() method is declared.

+ Lines 57-64: The destroyApp() method is declared. All the objects declared are set to null. This will help in freeing resources.

+ Line 66: The commandAction() method is declared. This method is called whenever a user event is generated on the GUI components.

+ Lines 69-107: This if condition is true if the user selects an item in the list. The list contains three items: Weather, Movies, and News.

- 76-83: The `if` condition here is true if the user selects `Weather` in the list. The weather MIDlet is initiated, and its `startApp()` method is called. Two arguments are passed to the MIDlet. The first one is the `Display` object, and the other one is the object of `MainClass` ('this' class). The `Display` object will be used to display the GUI components of `Weather` class, and the `MainClass` object will get the `Display` object back.

- 87-94: This `if` condition is true if the user selects `Movies` in the list. The `MoviesList` MIDlet is initiated, and its `startApp()` method is called. The same two objects are passed to this MIDlet.

- 98-106: If the user selects `News`, this `if` condition is executed. The `News` MIDlet is initiated, and its `startApp()` method is called. The same two objects are passed to this MIDlet.

♦ Lines 109-114: The code in this `if` condition is executed when the user presses the Exit button . This will destroy the MIDlet and close the application.

♦ Lines 117-121: This is the method that will get the `Display` object back to this class. The other MIDlets will call this method, and the `Display` object will be passed as a parameter. This method will again display the list to the user.

DataParser.java

This class is used for handling Http requests and reading and parsing XML data. This class caters to the request of the three MIDlets used in this application (Listing 10-2).

Listing 10-2: DataParser.java

```
1.   import java.io.InputStream;
2.   import java.io.IOException;
3.   import java.io.InputStreamReader;
4.
5.   import org.kxml.*;
6.   import org.kxml.parser.XmlParser;
7.   import org.kxml.parser.*;
8.
9.   import java.util.Vector;
10.  import java.util.Hashtable;
11.
12.  import javax.microedition.io.HttpConnection;
13.  import javax.microedition.io.Connector;
14.
15.  import java.lang.String;
16.  import javax.microedition.rms.*;
17.  public class DataParser
18.  {
19.    /* HttpConnection Object */
20.    HttpConnection con = null;
21.    /* This InputStream Object is used to read data from the InputStream
opened on a URL */
22.    InputStream ins = null;
23.    /* ParserEvent is event generated by the parser while parsing data */
24.    ParseEvent event;
25.    /* This class is an object of Abstract Xml parser  */
26.    AbstractXmlParser parser;
27.    /* Vector objects declared  */
28.    Vector hall_id,hall_name,halldata,vnews;
```

```
29.    /* Hashtable objects declared */
30.    Hashtable htable;
31.    /* RecordStore object declared. This object is used to store data in the
database */
32.    RecordStore recordStore = null;
33.
34.    /* Constructor of GetData Declared  */
35.    public DataParser()
36.    {
37.     hall_id = new Vector();
38.     hall_name = new Vector();
39.     halldata = new Vector();
40.     vnews = new Vector();
41.     htable = new Hashtable();
42.     htable = new Hashtable();
43.    }
44.    /* This method is used to establish an http connection, open a stream with
the connection and
45.    create a parser object and pass this stream to the parser  */
46.    public void sourceurl(String url)
47.    {
48.     try
49.     {
50.         /* This will create an HTPP connection object */
51.         con = (HttpConnection)Connector.open(url);
52.         /* This will open an InputStream to the connection */
53.         ins = con.openInputStream();
54.         /* This is initializing  a parser object  */
55.         parser = new XmlParser(new InputStreamReader(ins));
56.     }
57.     catch(IOException ex)
58.     {
59.         System.out.println("IOException occured");
60.     }
61.    }
62.
63.    void read_category()
64.    {
65.     boolean foundnews = false;
66.     do
67.     {
68.         try
69.         {
70.
71.                 event = parser.read ();
72.                 if(event.getType()==Xml.START_TAG)
73.                 {
74.
75.                     /* get the tag value*/
76.                     StartTag stag = (StartTag)event;
77.
78.                     /* If tag value is equal to category, then enter  this
if condition */
79.                     if(stag.getName().equals("category"))
80.                     {
81.                         /* foundnews variable true */
```

```
82.                                foundnews = true;
83.                        }
84.                }
85.                if(event.getType()== Xml.TEXT)
86.                {
87.
88.                        TextEvent tevent = (TextEvent)event;
89.                        if(foundnews)
90.                        {
91.                                vnews.addElement(tevent.getText());
92.                                foundnews = false;
93.                        }
94.                }
95.        }
96.        catch(IOException ex)
97.        {
98.                System.out.println("Exception occured");
99.        }
100.        }
101.        while (!(event instanceof EndDocument));
102.    }
103.
104.    void read_record()
105.    {
106.        int k, id;
107.        String state = "", data = "";
108.        boolean founditem = false, foundstate = false;
109.    try
110.    {
111.        /*  Opens RecordStore for insertion of records */
112.        recordStore = RecordStore.openRecordStore("addresses", true);
113.        }
114.    catch(RecordStoreException rse)
115.    {
116.        rse.printStackTrace();
117.    }
118.        do
119.        {
120.                try
121.                {
122.                        /* Events generated by the parser while parsing XML
file */
123.                        event = parser.read ();
124.
125.                        /* Type of event generated while parsing XML File */
126.                        if(event.getType()==Xml.START_TAG)
127.                        {
128.                                StartTag stag = (StartTag)event;
129.                                if(stag.getName().equals("weather"))
130.                                {
131.                                        founditem = true;
132.                                }
133.                                if(stag.getName().equals("state"))
134.                                {
135.                                        foundstate = true;
136.                                }
```

```
137.                        }
138.                        if(event.getType()== Xml.TEXT)
139.                        {
140.                                TextEvent tevent = (TextEvent)event;
141.                                if(foundstate)
142.                                {
143.                                        state =  tevent.getText();
144.                                        data = data+"?"+state;
145.                                        foundstate = false;
146.                                }
147.                                else
148.                                {
149.                                        data = data+"?"+ tevent.getText();
150.                                }
151.                        }
152.
153.                        if(event.getType()==Xml.END_TAG)
154.                        {
155.                                EndTag etag = (EndTag)event;
156.                                if(etag.getName().equals("weather"))
157.                                {
158.                                        data = data+"?";
159.                                        founditem = false;
160.                                        /* Calling the method for insertion of
record into the database */
161.                                        id = record_add(data);
162.                                        /* insertion of record into the
hashtable */
163.                                        htable.put((Object)state,
Integer.toString(id));
164.                                        data = "";
165.                                }
166.                        }
167.                }
168.                catch(IOException ex)
169.                {
170.                        System.out.println("Exception occured");
171.                }
172.        }
173.        while (!(event instanceof EndDocument));
174.        try
175.        {
176.                /*  Closes  RecordStore after insertion of records */
177.                recordStore.closeRecordStore();
178.        }
179.        catch(RecordStoreException rse)
180.        {
181.                rse.printStackTrace();
182.        }
183.
184.    }
185.    /* Function for record addtion...*/
186.    int record_add(String data)
187.    {
188.        int i = 0;
189.        try
```

```
190.              {
191.                      byte b[] = data.getBytes();
192.                      i = recordStore.addRecord(b,0, b.length);
193.              }
194.          catch (RecordStoreException rse)
195.          {
196.              rse.printStackTrace();
197.          }
198.          return i ;
199.      }
200.
201.      /* Method for deletion of records from the Recordstore   */
202.      void deleterecords()
203.      {
204.          try
205.          {
206.                  recordStore.deleteRecordStore("addresses");
207.          }
208.          catch (RecordStoreException rse)
209.          {
210.              rse.printStackTrace();
211.          }
212.
213.      }
214.      void read_news()
215.      {
216.          int k, id;
217.          String news = "", data = "", head_id = "", head = "";
218.          boolean foundnews = false, foundhead = false, foundhead_id = false;
219.          do
220.          {
221.                  try
222.                  {
223.                      event = parser.read ();
224.                      if(event.getType()==Xml.START_TAG)
225.                      {
226.                              StartTag stag = (StartTag)event;
227.                              if(stag.getName().equals("news"))
228.                              {
229.                                  foundnews = true;
230.                              }
231.                              if(stag.getName().equals("heading"))
232.                              {
233.                                  foundhead = true;
234.
235.                              }
236.                              if(stag.getName().equals("heading_id"))
237.                              {
238.                                  foundhead_id = true;
239.                              }
240.                      }
241.                      if(event.getType()== Xml.TEXT)
242.                      {
243.                              TextEvent tevent = (TextEvent)event;
244.                              if(foundhead_id)
245.                              {
```

```
246.                                          head_id  =  tevent.getText();
247.                                          foundhead_id = false;
248.                                     }
249.                                if(foundhead)
250.                                {
251.                                          head  =  tevent.getText();
252.                                          foundhead = false;
253.                                }
254.                          }
255.                     if(event.getType()==Xml.END_TAG)
256.                     {
257.                                EndTag etag = (EndTag)event;
258.                                if(etag.getName().equals("news"))
259.                                {
260.
261.                                          foundnews = false;
262.                                          htable.put((String)head,
(Object)head_id);
263.                                          head = "";
264.                                }
265.                          }
266.                }
267.             catch(IOException ex)
268.             {
269.                     System.out.println("Exception occured");
270.             }
271.        }
272.        while (!(event instanceof EndDocument));
273.   }
274.   String returnDetails()
275.   {
276.        int k, id;
277.        String news = "", data = "", description = "";
278.        boolean found_description = false;
279.        do
280.        {
281.                try
282.                {
283.                     event = parser.read ();
284.                     if(event.getType()==Xml.START_TAG)
285.                     {
286.                                StartTag stag = (StartTag)event;
287.                                if(stag.getName().equals("description"))
288.                                {
289.                                          found_description = true;
290.                                }
291.                     }
292.                     if(event.getType()== Xml.TEXT)
293.                     {
294.                                TextEvent tevent = (TextEvent)event;
295.                                if(found_description)
296.                                {
297.                                          description  =  tevent.getText();
298.                                          found_description = false;
299.                                }
300.                     }
```

```
301.                    }
302.                catch(IOException ex)
303.                {
304.                        System.out.println("Exception occured");
305.                }
306.        }
307.        while (!(event instanceof EndDocument));
308.        return description ;
309.    }
310.    /* This method is called by the MovieList class. This method parses data
related to movies */
311.    void parseDataMovies(int i)
312.    {
313.        boolean foundhallid = false;
314.        boolean hall = false;
315.        boolean moviename = false;
316.        boolean moviestatus = false;
317.        boolean moviedate = false;
318.        boolean showtime = false;
319.        boolean balcony = false;
320.        boolean rear = false;
321.        boolean upper = false;
322.        boolean middle = false;
323.        /* This if condition is true when this method is called first time.
ie when data related
324.        to hallname and hallid is to be read */
325.        if(i == 1)
326.        {
327.            do
328.            {
329.                try
330.                {
331.
332.                    /* This will read the data form the stream and
generate parsing events  */
333.                    event = parser.read ();
334.                    if(event.getType()==Xml.START_TAG)
335.                    {
336.                        StartTag stag = (StartTag)event;
337.                        if(stag.getName().equals("hall_id"))
338.                        {
339.                            foundhallid = true;
340.                        }
341.                        if(stag.getName().equals("hall_name"))
342.                        {
343.                            hall = true;
344.                        }
345.
346.                    }
347.                    /* This will be true if there is some text
found */
348.                    if(event.getType()== Xml.TEXT)
349.                    {
350.                        TextEvent tevent = (TextEvent)event;
351.                        if(foundhallid)
352.                        {
```

```
353.
 hall_id.addElement(tevent.getText());
354.                                         foundhallid = false;
355.                                 }
356.                                 if(hall)
357.                                 {
358.
 hall_name.addElement(tevent.getText());
359.                                         hall = false;
360.                                 }
361.                         }
362.                     }
363.                 catch(IOException ex)
364.                     {
365.                         System.out.println("Exception occured");
366.                     }
367.                 }
368.             while (!(event instanceof EndDocument));
369.         }
370.         /* This if condition is true when this method is called second time.
ie when data related
371.         to a particular hall is read */
372.         if(i == 2)
373.         {
374.             do
375.             {
376.                 try
377.                 {
378.
379.                     /* This will read the data from the stream and
generate parsing events */
380.                         event = parser.read ();
381.                         if(event.getType()==Xml.START_TAG)
382.                         {
383.                             StartTag stag = (StartTag)event;
384.                             if(stag.getName().equals("movie_name"))
385.                             {
386.                                 moviename = true;
387.                                 halldata.addElement("ms");
388.                             }
389.                             if(stag.getName().equals("status"))
390.                             {
391.                                 moviestatus = true;
392.                                 halldata.addElement("st");
393.
394.                             }
395.                             if(stag.getName().equals("movie_date"))
396.                             {
397.                                 moviedate = true;
398.                             }
399.                             if(stag.getName().equals("showtime"))
400.                             {
401.                                 showtime = true;
402.                             }
403.                             if(stag.getName().equals("balcony"))
404.                             {
```

```
405.                                        balcony = true;
406.                                    }
407.                                    if(stag.getName().equals("rear_stall"))
408.                                    {
409.                                        rear = true;
410.                                    }
411.                                    if(stag.getName().equals("upper_stall"))
412.                                    {
413.                                        upper = true;
414.                                    }
415.                                    if(stag.getName().equals("middle_stall"))
416.                                    {
417.                                        middle = true;
418.                                    }
419.                                }
420.
421.                        if(event.getType()== Xml.TEXT)
422.                        {
423.                                TextEvent tevent = (TextEvent)event;
424.                                if(moviename)
425.                                {
426.
 halldata.addElement(tevent.getText());
427.                                        moviename = false;
428.                                }
429.                                if(moviestatus)
430.                                {
431.
432.
 halldata.addElement(tevent.getText());
433.                                        moviestatus = false;
434.                                }
435.                                if(moviedate)
436.                                {
437.
 halldata.addElement(tevent.getText());
438.                                        moviedate = false;
439.                                }
440.                                if(showtime)
441.                                {
442.
 halldata.addElement(tevent.getText());
443.                                        showtime = false;
444.                                }
445.                                if(balcony)
446.                                {
447.
 halldata.addElement(tevent.getText());
448.                                        balcony = false;
449.                                }
450.                                if(rear)
451.                                {
452.
 halldata.addElement(tevent.getText());
453.                                        rear = false;
454.                                }
```

```
455.                                    if(upper)
456.                                    {
457.
 halldata.addElement(tevent.getText());
458.                                        upper = false;
459.                                    }
460.                                    if(middle)
461.                                    {
462.
 halldata.addElement(tevent.getText());
463.                                        middle = false;
464.                                    }
465.                                }
466.                            }
467.                        catch(IOException ex)
468.                            {
469.                                System.out.println("Exception occured");
470.                            }
471.                    }
472.                while (!(event instanceof EndDocument));
473.            }
474.    }
475.    /* This method will release the memory and free the resources */
476.    void releaseMemory()
477.    {
478.        con = null;
479.        ins = null;
480.        parser = null;
481.        hall_name = null;
482.        hall_id = null;
483.
484.    }
485.
486.    /* The next three methods will return vector objects containing hall_id,
487.       hall_name, halldata and inews respectively  */
488.    Vector hall_id()
489.    {
490.        return hall_id;
491.    }
492.
493.    Vector hall_name()
494.    {
495.        return hall_name;
496.    }
497.
498.    Vector halldata()
499.    {
500.        return halldata;
501.    }
502.
503.    Vector returnNews()
504.    {
505.        return vnews;
506.    }
507.    /* This method will return Hashtable object containing values*/
508.    Hashtable returnHash_id()
```

```
509.    {
510.        return htable;
511.    }
512.    /* This method will return Hashtable object containing values */
513.    Hashtable returnState()
514.    {
515.        return htable;
516.    }
517. }
```

Code explanation

♦ Lines 1-16: Import statements, which will import the required classes to run this application.

♦ Line 17: Declaring DataParserclass. This class is an important class, as it is used to make the HTTP connection and XML parsing.

♦ Lines 19-32: The lines of code here declare different objects.

♦ Lines 35-43: Constructor declaration. The code here initializes Vector and Hashtable objects.

♦ Lines 46-61: The sourceurl() method is declared. This method takes a String value as a parameter, which is the address of the HTTP server. This method makes an HTTP connection with the specified URL and opens a stream from that connection to read data. This also initializes an XmlParser object.

♦ Lines 63-102: The read_category() method is declared. This method is called by the News MIDlet, and this method gets the news category from the database.

• 71-84: This will read the XML data and generate parser events. The if condition is true if the START_TAG event is generated. The tag name is compared, and if the tag name is category, foundnews is set to true.

• 85-94: This if condition is true if text is found while parsing. This will Throw a TEXT event, get the text, and store it in the Vector.

♦ Lines 104-183: The read_record() method is declared. This method is called by the Weather MIDlet, and this method gets the state name and the weather details.

• 109-113: A RecordStore object is created to add data to the device's database.

• 123-137: This will read the XML data and generate parser events. The if condition is true if the START_TAG event is generated. The tag name is compared, and if the tag name is weather, founditem is set to true; if the tag name is state, foundstate is also set to true.

• 138-151: This if condition is true if text is found while parsing. This will throw a TEXT event, get the text, and store it in a String variable with delimiter ?.

• 153-166: This if condition is true if an END_TAG event is generated. This will add the data in the device's database and store the state name and the record id in the Hashtable.

• 173-182: On the event of ENDDocument, the recordStore will be closed.

♦ Lines 186-199: The record_add() method is declared. This method will add a record to the database. This method is called by the read_record() method.

♦ Lines 202-213: The deleterecord() method is declared. This method will delete the record from the database.

♦ Lines 214-273: The read_news() method is declared. This method is called by the News MIDlet. This will read text related to tags such as news, heading, and heading_id. The data read is stored in Hashtable.

♦ Lines 274-309: The returndetails() method is declared. This method is called by the News MIDlet. This will read the description of the news when the tag description is found and stores the text in a String.

♦ Lines 311-474: The `parseDataMovies()` method is declared. This method is called by the `MovieList` MIDlet. This has to deal with two URLs; therefore, an integer value is passed to this method. If the value is 1, it will read the hall Name and hall Id and store them in a `Vector`. If the value is 2, it will read the data related to the hall, such as show date and tickets available, and store them in another `Vector`.

♦ Lines 476-484: The `releaseMemory()` method is declared. This will free the memory.

♦ Lines 488-491: This method will return the `Vector` object containing `Hall_id`. This method is called by the `MovieList` MIDlet.

♦ Lines 493-496: This method will return the `Vector` object containing `Hall_name`. This method is called by the `MovieList` MIDlet.

♦ Lines 498-501: This method will return the `Vector` object containing `Hall_data`. This method is called by the `MovieList` MIDlet.

♦ Lines 503-506: This method will return the `Vector` object containing `news`. This method is called by the `News` MIDlet.

♦ Lines 508-511: This method will return the `Hashtable` object containing `news`. This method is called by the `News` MIDlet.

♦ Lines 513-516: This method will return the `Hashtable` object containing the `States` list. This method is called by the `Weather` MIDlet.

Weather.java

This class is used to provide the user with details on the weather. The class calls the DataParser class to send requests for weather details and get the response. This class first displays the names of the cities for which weather details are available and on selecting the city, the user is displayed the weather details of that city. Before this class is destroyed it passes the control to the Main class (Listing 10-3).

Listing 10-3: Weather.java

// © 2001 Dreamtech Software India, Inc.
// All rights Reserved

```
1.   /* Importing the basic packages required by various classes
2.    during execution of the program     */
3.   import java.util.Hashtable;
4.   import javax.microedition.midlet.*;
5.   import javax.microedition.lcdui.*;
6.   import javax.microedition.rms.*;
7.   import javax.microedition.io.*;
8.   import java.util.*;
9.   import java.io.*;
10.  import java.lang.*;
11.
12.
13.  /* Declaration of the class Weather. */
14.  public class Weather extends MIDlet implements CommandListener
15.  {
16.    /* Declare an object for GetData class */
17.    DataParser getd;
18.
19.    /* Declaring  variable for requesting that object to be displayed on the
device */
20.    private Display displaylist;
21.
```

```
22.    /* Declaring List type variables for storing and displaying list of cities
and details of weather  */
23.    private List states, details;
24.
25.    /* Declare and create vector type variables for storing list of cities and
 list of labels  */
26.    private Vector vstate = new Vector();
27.    private Vector vlist = new Vector();
28.
29.    /* Declaring variables for Command Buttons and initializing with null */
30.    private Command cancelcommand = null;
31.    private Command okcommand = null;
32.    private Command goback = null;
33.    private Command exit = null;
34.
35.    /*    Declaring Hashtable object and initializing it with null  */
36.    private Hashtable htable = null;
37.
38.    /* Creating  object of RecordStore type and initializing it with null */
39.    RecordStore recordstore = null;
40.
41.    /* Declaring object of Class MainClass */
42.    private MainClass lastscreen;
43.
44.    /* Declaring constructor of Class Weather */
45.    public Weather(Display displayweather, MainClass obj)
46.    {
47.     /* initializing Mainclass object lastscreen with the argument obj */
48.     lastscreen = obj;
49.
50.     /* Getting the current reference of any object which is present at run
time
51.        for displaying it on the cellpone screen */
52.     displaylist = displayweather;
53.
54.         /* Create an object of List type to store the list of Cities */
55.     states = new List("States",List.IMPLICIT);
56.
57.     /* Registering the List object states for event Handling */
58.     states.setCommandListener(this);
59.
60.     /* Creates an object for hashtable htable */
61.     htable = new Hashtable();
62.
63.     /* Creates an object for exit command defined as screen and give the
priority 2  */
64.      exit = new Command("Exit",Command.EXIT,2);
65.
66.     /* Creates an object for Back  command defined as Command and give the
priority 2 */
67.      goback = new Command("Back",Command.BACK,1);
68.
69.     /* Creates an object for OK command defined as screen and give the
priority 1 */
70.      okcommand = new Command("OK",Command.SCREEN,1);
71.
```

```
72.      /* Creates an object for Cancel command defined as Screen and give the
priority 2 */
73.      cancelcommand = new Command("Cancel",Command.SCREEN,2);
74.
75.      /* Inserts label into vector vlist */
76.      vlist.insertElementAt("State",0);
77.      vlist.insertElementAt("Date",1);
78.      vlist.insertElementAt("Sunrise",2);
79.      vlist.insertElementAt("Sunset",3);
80.      vlist.insertElementAt("Moonrise",4);
81.      vlist.insertElementAt("Moonset",5);
82.      vlist.insertElementAt("Day Humidity",6);
83.      vlist.insertElementAt("Night Humidity",7);
84.      vlist.insertElementAt("Day Wind Direction",8);
85.      vlist.insertElementAt("Night Wind Direction",9);
86.      vlist.insertElementAt("Day Wind Speed",10);
87.      vlist.insertElementAt("Night Wind Speed",11);
88.      vlist.insertElementAt("High Temp",12);
89.      vlist.insertElementAt("Low Temp",13);
90.      vlist.insertElementAt("Rain Fall",14);
91.      vlist.insertElementAt("Forecast",15);
92.      }
93.     /* Declaration of the method startApp */
94.     /* Application starts from this method */
95.     public void startApp()
96.     {
97.
98.     /* Store the path of xml file in url object as string */
99.     String url = new
String("http://192.192.168.100/midlet/template/midlet_weather.xml");
100.
101.        /* Creating an object for DataParser class */
102.        getd = new DataParser();
103.
104.        /* Calling the method sourceurl and sending the path of the xml file
*/
105.        getd.sourceurl(url);
106.
107.        /* Calling  the read_record method for parsing XML file and
108.         storing the records into the Database and Hashtable */
109.        getd.read_record();
110.
111.        /* Calling  the returnState method and returning the records in
hashtable */
112.        htable = getd.returnState();
113.
114.        /* Creates an object that implements the Enumeration interface
generating a series of elements
115.             and the loop will execute till no element is present in
Enumeration e object */
116.             for (Enumeration e = htable.keys(); e.hasMoreElements() ;)
117.             {
118.                 /* Adding values to List Object states, present in the
hashtable */
119.                 states.append( (String)e.nextElement() , null);
120.             }
```

```
121.         /* display List states on cellphone screen */
122.         displaylist.setCurrent(states);
123.
124.         /* To attach the ok command button with List states */
125.         states.addCommand(okcommand);
126.
127.         /* To attach the cancel command button with List states */
128.         states.addCommand(cancelcommand);
129.    }
130.
131.    /* Declaring method for eventhandling routines */
132.    public void commandAction(Command c, Displayable d)
133.    {
134.
135.        /* if condition is associated with ok command button when the user
clicks it   */
136.        if(c == okcommand)
137.        {
138.                String st = "";
139.                /* get the position which is selected by the user in the List
states   */
140.                int index  = states.getSelectedIndex();
141.
142.                /* Retrieving the hashtable value according to the index
number */
143.                String hash_id = (String)htable.get(states.getString(index));
144.
145.                /* Create an object details of List type to display the
Weather Details */
146.                details = new List("Weather of " +  states.getString(index)
, List.IMPLICIT) ;
147.
148.                /* Registering the List object details for event Handling */
149.                details.setCommandListener(this);
150.
151.                /* displays List details on cellphone screen */
152.                displaylist.setCurrent(details);
153.
154.                try
155.                {
156.                        /* Opens the Recordstore addresses for retrieving the
records */
157.                        recordstore = RecordStore.openRecordStore("addresses",
true);
158.
159.                        /* Retrieving the record from the recordstore and
storing it as String */
160.                        st = new
String(recordstore.getRecord(Integer.parseInt(hash_id)));
161.
162.                        /* Closes the Recordstore after retrieving the records
*/
163.                        recordstore.closeRecordStore();
164.
165.                }
166.                catch(RecordStoreException rse)
```

```
167.                    {
168.                            rse.printStackTrace();
169.                    }
170.
171.            /* Declaring integer variables  */
172.            int st_index = 0, end_index = 0, ctr = 0, pos ;
173.            /* Storing the string length retrieved from the database */
174.            int len = st.length();
175.
176.            /* Declaring String type variable for storing the substring */
177.            String sub_st = "";
178.
179.            /* Declaring the character type array, creating space for
array and
180.                defining the size equivalent to string length */
181.            char[] c_arr = new char[len];
182.
183.            /* Inserting String into character type array. */
184.            c_arr = st.toCharArray();
185.
186.            /* For Loop to retreive Weather record from the string and
display it
187.                on the cellphone screen */
188.            for (pos = 0; pos < len ; pos++)
189.            {
190.                if(c_arr[pos] == '?')
191.                {
192.                        st_index = end_index ;
193.                        end_index = pos ;
194.                        ctr = ctr + 1;
195.                        if (ctr > 1)
196.                        {
197.                                sub_st = st.substring(st_index +
1,end_index);
198.
 details.append((String)vlist.elementAt(ctr - 2) + " " + sub_st, null);
199.                        }
200.                }
201.            }
202.            /*  To attach the goback and exit command buttons with List
details */
203.            details.addCommand(goback);
204.            details.addCommand(exit);
205.        }
206.
207.        /* if condition is associated with exit command button when the user
clicks it */
208.        if(c == exit)
209.        {
210.            /* Destroys the weather application */
211.            destroyApp( true );
212.            /* Confirms application destroyed */
213.            notifyDestroyed();
214.
215.            /* The getDisplayObject method takes displayobject as
parameter and displays the first screen of the application  */
```

```
216.                    lastscreen.getDisplayObject(displaylist);
217.            }
218.            /* if condition is associated with cancel command button when the
user clicks  */
219.            if(c == cancelcommand)
220.            {
221.                    /* Destroys the weather application */
222.                    destroyApp(true);
223.                    /* Confirms application destroyed */
224.                    notifyDestroyed();
225.
226.                    /* The getDisplayObject method takes displayobject as
parameter and displays the first screen of the application  */
227.                    lastscreen.getDisplayObject(displaylist);
228.            }
229.            /* if condition is associated with goback command button when the
user clicks  */
230.            if(c == goback)
231.            {
232.                    /* displays List states on cellphone screen */
233.                    displaylist.setCurrent(states);
234.
235.                    /*  To attach the ok and cancel command buttons with List
states */
236.                    states.addCommand(okcommand);
237.                    states.addCommand(cancelcommand);
238.            }
239.    }
240.
241.    /* Method called when the application is destroyed     */
242.    public void destroyApp(boolean b)
243.    {
244.        /* Deletes the records from the database by calling the deleterecords
method   */
245.        getd.deleterecords();
246.    }
247.    /* This method is called when the midlet is paused */
248.    public void pauseApp()
249.    {}
250.  }
```

Code explanation

♦ Lines 3-10: The inclusion of the basic packages used by various classes in the project, such as Hashtable and Enumerations (java.util.*), for input and output (java.io.*), etc.

♦ Line 14: The code here pertains to the declaration of the class Weather. This class is called when the user selects Weather in the menu containing services.

♦ Line 17: Declaration of the object getd of the GetData class.

♦ Lines 20-42: Declaring variables of List type for storing and displaying a list of cities and details of the weather, the variable of Display type for requesting that object to be displayed on the device, and the variable of Vector type for storing the list of cities and the list of labels; the command buttons variables Cancel, OK, Back, and Exit, for moving to the next field, to the previous field, and exiting from the Weather screen; the variable of Hashtable, for storing the list of cities available for weather details; and the Recordstore type for handling records in the database.

- ◆ Line 42: Declaring the object `lastscreen` of the class `MainClass`.

- ◆ Lines 45-75: Declaring the constructor of the class `Weather`, with arguments of `Display` and `Mainclass` types, and initializing the `Mainclass` object `lastscreen` with the argument `obj`. Creating an object of `List` type to store the list of cities; registering the `List` object `states` for event handling; creating an object for `Hashtable htable`; creating an object for Exit command, defined as `screen` and giving it the priority 2; creating the object for the Back command, defined as `Command` and giving it the priority 2; creating the object for the OK command, defined as `screen` and giving it the priority 1; creating the object for the Cancel command, defined as `screen` and giving it the priority 2.

- ◆ Lines 76-91: The code between these lines inserts labels into the `Vector` for displaying on the cell-phone screen.

- ◆ Lines 95-129: The code between these lines is for the declaration of the method `startApp`. The application starts from this method. In this method, the path of XML file is stored in the `url` object as a String, and an object of `DataParser` class is created. The method `sourceurl` of `DataParser` class is called, and the path of the XML file is sent as a String argument. A `for` loop is used for adding values to `List` object `states`, present in the `Hashtable`, and an object that implements the `Enumeration` interface generating a series of elements is created; the loop will execute till any element is present in the `Enumeration` object. OK and Cancel command buttons are attached with the `List` states.

- ◆ Lines 132-239: The code between these lines is for the declaration of the method `commandAction` for event-handling routines.

  - • 136-205: The code between these lines is for the `if` condition associated with the OK command button when the user clicks it. The position that is indicated by the user in the `List` states is selected, and the `hashtable` value is retrieved according to the index number. An object `details` of `List` type is created to display the weather details.

  - • 208-217: The code between these lines is for the `if` condition associated with the Exit command button when the user clicks it. The Weather application is destroyed and confirmed. The `getDisplayObject` method takes a `Display` object as parameter to display the first screen of the application.

  - • 219-228: The code between these lines is for the `if` condition associated with the Cancel command button when the user clicks it. The Weather application is destroyed, , and the `getDisplayObject` method takes a `Display` object as a parameter to display the first screen of the application.

  - • 230-238: The code between these lines is for the `if` condition associated with the Back command button when the user clicks it. The Weather application is destroyed, , and the `getDisplayObject` method takes a `Display` object as a parameter to display the first screen of the application.

- ◆ Lines 242-246: Thise code deletes the records from the database by calling the `deleterecords` method of the `DataParser` class.

News.java

This class as the name says facilitates the user to read news. The class calls the DataParser class to send requests for News and get the response. This class first displays the subjects for which news is available and on selecting the subject the user is displayed the headlines of the news. The user has to select a headline. Before this class is destroyed, it passes the control to the Main class (Listing 10-4).

Listing 10-4: News.java

```
1.   /* Importing the basic packages required by various classes
2.    during execution of the program      */
3.   import java.util.Hashtable;
4.   import javax.microedition.midlet.*;
5.   import javax.microedition.lcdui.*;
6.   import javax.microedition.io.*;
7.   import java.util.*;
8.   import java.io.*;
9.   import java.lang.*;
10.
11.  /* Declaration of the class News */
12.  public class News extends MIDlet implements CommandListener
13.  {
14.  /* Create an object of class Dataparser */
15.  DataParser getd;
16.
17.  /* Declaring  variable for requesting that object to be displayed on the
device */
18.  private Display displaylist;
19.
20.  /* Declaring List type variables for storing and displaying list of
categories ,
21.     news and news details  */
22.  private List category, news, details;
23.
24.  /* Declare and create vector type variable for storing news */
25.  private Vector vnews = new Vector();
26.
27.  /* Declaring variables for Command Buttons and initializing with null */
28.  private Command cancelcommand = null;
29.  private Command okcommand = null;
30.  private Command goback = null;
31.  private Command exitcommand = null;
32.  private Command previouscommand = null;
33.  private Command backcommand = null;
34.  private Command viewcommand = null;
35.  private Command startcommand = null;
36.
37.  /*    Declaring variables for Hashtable and initializing with null   */
38.  public Hashtable htable = null;
39.
40.  /* Declaring object of Class MainClass */
41.  private MainClass lastscreen;
42.
43.  /* Declaring constructor of Class News */
44.  public News(Display displaynews,MainClass obj)
45.  {
46.
47.    lastscreen = obj;
48.
49.     /* Get the current reference of any object which is present at run time
for displaying
50.        on the cellpone screen */
51.        displaylist = displaynews;
52.
53.     /* Create an object of List type to store the list of Categories */
```

```
54.      category = new List("Category",List.IMPLICIT);
55.
56.      /* Registering the List object category for event Handling */
57.      category.setCommandListener(this);
58.
59.      /* Creates an object for OK command button defined as SCREEN and given
the priority 1 */
60.      okcommand = new Command("OK",Command.SCREEN,1);
61.
62.      /* Creates an object for Cancel command button defined as SCREEN and
given the priority 2 */
63.      cancelcommand = new Command("Cancel",Command.SCREEN,2);
64.
65.      /* Creates an object for Back command button defined as BACK and given
the priority 1 */
66.      backcommand = new Command("Back",Command.BACK,1);
67.
68.      /* Creates an object for View command button defined as SCREEN and given
the priority 2 */
69.      viewcommand = new Command("View",Command.SCREEN,2);
70.
71.      /* Creates an object for Previous command button defined as BACK and
given the priority 1 */
72.      previouscommand = new Command("Previous",Command.BACK,1);
73.
74.      /* Creates an object for Start command button defined as SCREEN and given
the priority 2 */
75.      startcommand = new Command("Start",Command.SCREEN,2);
76.
77.    }
78.
79.    /* Declaration of the method startApp */
80.    /* Application Starts from this method */
81.    public void startApp()
82.    {
83.      /* Store the path of xml file in url object object as string */
84.      String url = new
String("http://192.192.168.100/midlet/template/midlet_news.xml");
85.
86.      /* Create an object for DataParser class */
87.      getd = new DataParser();
88.
89.      /* Calling the method sourceurl and sending the path of the xml file */
90.      getd.sourceurl(url);
91.
92.      /* Calling the read_category methods for parsing the XML file and
inserting
93.          the records in the vector news */
94.      getd.read_category();
95.
96.      /* Calling  the returnNews method and returning the records in vector
vnews */
97.      vnews = getd.returnNews();
98.
99.      /* Creates an object that implements the Enumeration interface generating
a series of elements */
```

```
100.         Enumeration e = vnews.elements();
101.
102.         /* The loop executes till no elements are present in Enumeration e
object */
103.         while (e.hasMoreElements())
104.         {
105.                 /*  append all vector values in List category */
106.                 category.append( (String)e.nextElement()  , null);
107.         }
108.
109.         /* Displays values of List category on cellphone screen */
110.         displaylist.setCurrent(category);
111.
112.         /* To attach the ok command button with List category */
113.         category.addCommand(okcommand);
114.
115.         /* To attach the cancel command button with List category */
116.         category.addCommand(cancelcommand);
117.     }
118.
119.    /* Declaring method for eventhandling routines */
120.    public void commandAction(Command c, Displayable d)
121.     {
122.         int index = 0 ;
123.
124.         /* if condition is associated with the Ok command button when the
user clicks it */
125.         if(c == okcommand)
126.         {
127.                 /* Creates an object for hashtable htable */
128.                 htable = new Hashtable();
129.
130.                 /* get the postion which is selected by the user in the List
category */
131.                 index  = category.getSelectedIndex();
132.
133.                 /* Retrieving the List value into String according to the
index number */
134.                 String st = category.getString(index);
135.
136.                 /* Storing the path of xml file in url object as string */
137.                 String url = new
String("http://192.192.168.100/midlet/template/midlet_news_det.xml?ctg="+st  );
138.
139.                 /* Calling the method sourceurl and sending the path of the
xml file */
140.                 getd.sourceurl(url);
141.
142.                 /* Calling  the read_record method for parsing XML file and
143.                    storing the records into the Hashtable */
144.                 getd.read_news();
145.
146.                 /* Calling the returnHash_id method and returning the records
in hashtable */
147.                 htable = getd.returnHash_id();
148.
```

```
149.                    /* Create an object news of List type to display the News of
the category selected */
150.                    news = new List("News of " + category.getString(index),
List.IMPLICIT) ;
151.
152.                    /* Registering the List object news for event Handling */
153.                    news.setCommandListener(this);
154.
155.                    /* Creates an object that implements the Enumeration interface
generating a series of elements
156.                        and the loop will execute till no element is present in
Enumeration e object */
157.                    for (Enumeration e = htable.keys(); e.hasMoreElements() ;)
158.                    {
159.                         /* appending  hashtable values in List object news */
160.                         news.append((String)e.nextElement(), null);
161.                    }
162.
163.                    /* displays List object news on cellphone screen */
164.                    displaylist.setCurrent(news);
165.
166.                    /* To attach the Back Command Button with List object news */
167.                    news.addCommand(backcommand);
168.
169.                    /* To attach the View Command Button with List object news */
170.                    news.addCommand(viewcommand);
171.
172.        }
173.
174.        /* if condition is associated with the Cancel command button when the
user clicks it */
175.        if(c == cancelcommand)
176.        {
177.                    destroyApp(true);
178.                    notifyDestroyed();
179.                    /* The getDisplayObject method takes displayobject as
parameter and displays the first
180.                        screen of the application  */
181.                    lastscreen.getDisplayObject(displaylist);
182.        }
183.
184.        /* if condition is associated with the Back command button when the
user clicks it */
185.        if(c == backcommand )
186.        {
187.
188.                    /* displays List object category on cellphone screen */
189.                    displaylist.setCurrent(category);
190.
191.                    /* To attach the OK Command Button with List object category
*/
192.                    category.addCommand(okcommand);
193.
194.                    /* To attach the Cancel Command Button with List object
category */
195.                    category.addCommand(cancelcommand);
```

```
196.          }
197.
198.          /* if condition is associated with the Start Command Button when the
user clicks it */
199.          if(c == startcommand )
200.          {
201.
202.              /* displays List object category on cellphone screen */
203.              displaylist.setCurrent(category);
204.
205.              /* To attach the OK Command Button with List object category
*/
206.              category.addCommand(okcommand);
207.
208.              /* To attach the Cancel Command Button with List object
category */
209.              category.addCommand(cancelcommand);
210.          }
211.
212.          /* if condition is associated with the View Command Button when the
user clicks it */
213.          if(c == viewcommand)
214.          {
215.              /* Create an object of List type to store the details of the
News */
216.              details = new List("Details",List.IMPLICIT);
217.
218.              /* declare a String object */
219.              String st = "";
220.
221.              /* get the postion (index number) which is selected by the
user in the List object news  */
222.              index   = news.getSelectedIndex();
223.
224.              /* Retrieving the List value according to the index number */
225.              st = news.getString(index);
226.
227.              /* Retrieving the hashtable value according to the index
number */
228.              String hash_id = (String)htable.get(news.getString(index));
229.
230.              /* Storing the path of xml file in String object url */
231.              String url = new
String("http://192.192.168.100/midlet/template/midlet_news_description.xml?headin
g_id="+hash_id);
232.
233.
234.              /* Calling the method sourceurl and sending the path of the
xml file */
235.              getd.sourceurl(url);
236.
237.              /* Calling  the returnDetails method for parsing XML file and
238.                  returning  the record into a String  */
239.              String st_details = getd.returnDetails();
240.
241.              /* Adding the String to List Object details */
```

```
242.                     details.append((String)st_details , null);
243.
244.                     /* Registering the List object details for event Handling */
245.                     details.setCommandListener(this);
246.
247.                     /* displays List Object details on cellphone screen */
248.                     displaylist.setCurrent(details);
249.
250.                     /*  To attach the Previous Command Button with List Object
details */
251.                     details.addCommand(previouscommand);
252.
253.                     /*  To attach the Start Command Button with List Object
details */
254.                     details.addCommand(startcommand);
255.
256.          }
257.
258.         /* if condition is associated with previous command button when the
user clicks it   */
259.          if(c == previouscommand)
260.          {
261.                  /* Registering the List object news for event Handling */
262.                  news.setCommandListener(this);
263.
264.                  /* displays List Object news on cellphone screen */
265.                  displaylist.setCurrent(news);
266.
267.                  /*  To attach the Back Command Button with List Object news */
268.                  news.addCommand(backcommand);
269.
270.                  /*  To attach the Add Command Button with List Object news */

271.                  news.addCommand(viewcommand);
272.          }
273.    }
274.
275.    public void destroyApp(boolean b)
276.    {}
277.    public void pauseApp()
278.    {}
279.  }
```

Code explanation

♦ Lines 3-9: The code between these lines pertains to the inclusion of the basic packages used by various classes in the project, such as Hashtable and Enumerations (java.util.*), for input and output (java.io.*), etc.

♦ Line 12: The code here pertains to declaration of the class News. This class is called when the user selects News in the menu containing services.

♦ Line 15: Declaration of the object getd of the DataParser class.

♦ Lines 18-38: Declaring variables of Display type for requesting that object to be displayed on the device; List type for storing and displaying list of categories, news and news details; and Vector type for storing the list of Headlines and list of labels; declaring variables for command buttons and initializing them with null; the command buttons variables Cancel, OK, Back, Exit, Previous,

Back, View, and Start, for moving to the next screen, to the previous screen, and exiting from the News screen; `Hashtable` variables for storing the list of categories, news, and news details available.

♦ Line 41: Declaring the object `lastscreen` of the class `MainClass`.

♦ Lines 44-77: Declaring the constructor of the class `News`, with arguments of `Display` and `Mainclass` types, and initializing the `Mainclass` object `lastscreen` with the argument `obj`. Creating an object of `List` type to store the list of categories; registering the `List` object categories for event handling; creating the object for the OK command, defined as `screen` and given the priority `1`; creating an object for the Cancel command, defined as `screen` and given the priority `2`; creating the object for the Back command, defined as `Back` and given the priority `1`; creating the object for the View command, defined as `screen` and given the priority `2`; creating the object for the Previous command, defined as `Back` and given the priority `1`; creating the object for the Start command, defined as `screen` and given the priority `2`.

♦ Lines 81-117: The code between these lines is for the declaration of the method `startApp`. The application starts from this method. In this method, the path of the XML file is stored in the `url` object as a String, and an object of `DataParser` class is created. The method `sourceurl` of the `DataParser` classs is called, and the path of the XML file is sent as a String argument. The `read_category` method is called for parsing the XML file and returning the records into the `Vector News`. A `for` loop is declared for adding values to the `List` object category, present in the `Vector`. An object that implements the `Enumeration` interface generating a series of elements is created, and the loop will execute till any element is present in the `Enumeration` object. Values of the `List` category are displayed on the cell-phone screen. OK and Cancel command buttons are attached with the `List` category.

♦ Lines 120-273: Declaration of the method `commandAction` for event-handling routines.

 • 125-172: The code between these lines is for the `if` condition associated with the OK command button when the user clicks it. An object for `Hashtable htable` is created. The position that is selected by the user in the `List` category is stored in the integer variable index, and the `List` value is retrieved into a String variable according to the index number. The path of the XML file is stored in the String variable `url`, and the method `sourceurl` is called and the path of the XML file sent as an argument. The `read_record` method is called for parsing the XML file and storing the records into the `Hashtable`. The `returnHash_id` method is called, and the records in `hashtable` are returned into the `hashtable` object `htable`. The object news of the `List` type is created to display the news of the category selected; the `List` object news is registered for event handling. A `for` loop is used for adding values to the `List` object news, present in the Hashtable. An object that implements the Enumeration interface generating a series of elements is created, and the loop will execute till any element is present in Enumeration object. Values of `List` news are displayed on the cell-phone screen. Back and View command buttons are attached with the `List` news.

 • 175-182: The code between these lines is for the `if` condition associated with the Cancel command button when the user clicks it. The News application is destroyed, d, and the `getDisplayObject` method takes the `Display` object as a parameter to display the first screen of the application.

 • 185-196: The code between these lines is for the `if` condition associated with the Back command button when the user clicks it. It displays the `List` object category on the cell-phone screen. The OK and Cancel command buttons are attached with the `List` object category.

 • 199-210: The code between these lines is for the `if` condition associated with the Start command button when the user clicks it. It displays the `List` object category on the cell-phone screen. The OK and Cancel command buttons are attached with the `List` object category.

 • 213-256: The code between these lines is for the `if` condition associated with the View command button when the user clicks it. It creates an object of `List` type to store the details of the news. A String type object is declared. The position (index number) that is selected by the user in the `List` object `news` is used to retrieve the Hashtable value.

The path of the XML file is stored in the String object `url`, and the method `sourceurl` is called and the path of the XML file sent as an argument. The `returnDetails` method is called for parsing the XML file and returning the record into a String, which is added to the `List` object `details`. The `List` object `details` is registered for event handling, and the `List` object `details` values are displayed on the cell-phone screen. Previous and Start command buttons are attached with the `List` object `details`.

- 259-272: The code between these lines is for the `if` condition associated with the Previous command button when the user clicks it. The `List` object `news` is registered for event handling, and the `List` object `news` is displayed on the cell-phone screen. Back and View command buttons are attached with the `List` object `news`.

MoviesList.java

This class facilitates the user to book tickets for a movie. The class calls DataParser class to send requests for movie details and get the response. This class first displays to the user the list of theaters. On selecting the theater, the movies shown at the theater are displayed. The user has to select the movie and the date on which the movie shown is displayed. Upon selecting the date, the user is shown the details of the movie like the show time, no of tickets available on the basis of category. The user after viewing the details can book the tickets and has to give details like name, emailId, number of tickets, and so on. Before this class is destroyed it passes the control to the Main class (Listing 10-5).

Listing 10-5: MoviesList.java

```
// © 2001 Dreamtech Software India, Inc.
// All rights Reserved
```

```
1.   import javax.microedition.midlet.MIDlet;
2.
3.   import javax.microedition.lcdui.List;
4.   import javax.microedition.lcdui.Display;
5.   import javax.microedition.lcdui.CommandListener;
6.   import javax.microedition.lcdui.Command;
7.   import javax.microedition.lcdui.Displayable;
8.   import javax.microedition.lcdui.Form;
9.   import javax.microedition.lcdui.StringItem;
10.  import javax.microedition.lcdui.TextField;
11.  import javax.microedition.lcdui.ChoiceGroup;
12.
13.  import java.util.Vector;
14.  import java.util.Enumeration;
15.  /* This MIDlet is called when the user selects Movies from the MainClass
List */
16.  public class  MoviesList extends MIDlet implements CommandListener
17.  {
18.    static int counter = 0;
19.    /* Declaration of different objects */
20.    String hallname,realhall,showdate,bookname,bookemail,booktime,bookcategory
21.         ,strshow,strbal,strrear,strupper,strmiddle;
22.    DataParser parsemoviedata;
23.    Vector name,id,details;
24.    int commandvalue = 0;
25.    private Display displaymovielist;
26.    private List halllist,listmovies,listdate;
```

```
27.     private Form
statusform,yourname,emailform,categoryform,/*timeform,*/ticketform;
28.     private StringItem sitem;
29.     private Command backtodate,backtomovie,backtohall,bookticket,backtostatus,
30.
 emailscreen,backtoname,categoryscreen,backtoemail,backtocat,ticketscreen,
31.          finalbook,exitcommand;
32.     private TextField entername,enteremail,enterticket;
33.     private ChoiceGroup categorybuttons;
34.     private MainClass lastscreen;
35.     /* Constructor of the Movielist class declared */
36.     MoviesList(Display disp,MainClass obj)
37.     {
38.      lastscreen = obj;
39.      displaymovielist = disp;
40.      exitcommand = new Command("Exit",Command.EXIT,1);
41.      halllist = new List("Select Hall",List.IMPLICIT);
42.      halllist.setCommandListener(this);
43.      halllist.addCommand(exitcommand);
44.
45.     }
46.     /* This is start of the application. This method is called when the
application is invoked */
47.     public void startApp()
48.     {
49.      parsemoviedata = new DataParser();
50.      /* This will make an Http connection and open an InputStream to read from
the connection */
51.
 parsemoviedata.sourceurl("http://192.192.168.100/midlet/template/midlet_movies.
xml");
52.      /* This will parse the XML data */
53.      parsemoviedata.parseDataMovies(1);
54.      /* values taken in a vector */
55.      name = parsemoviedata.hall_name();
56.      id = parsemoviedata.hall_id();
57.      /* This will create a list with the hall name to be displayed to the user
*/
58.      for(Enumeration enum = name.elements() ; enum.hasMoreElements() ;)
59.      {
60.          halllist.append((String)enum.nextElement(),null);
61.      }
62.        /* List displayed */
63.      displaymovielist.setCurrent(halllist);
64.      /* Command objects declared */
65.      backtodate = new Command("Back",Command.BACK,1);
66.      backtomovie = new Command("Back",Command.BACK,1);
67.      backtohall = new Command("Back",Command.BACK,1);
68.      bookticket = new Command("Book",Command.SCREEN,1);
69.      backtostatus = new Command("Back",Command.BACK,1);
70.      emailscreen = new Command("OK",Command.SCREEN,1);
71.      backtoname = new Command("Back",Command.SCREEN,1);
72.      categoryscreen = new Command("OK",Command.SCREEN,1);
73.      backtoemail = new Command("Back",Command.SCREEN,1);
74.      backtocat = new Command("Back",Command.SCREEN,1);
75.      ticketscreen = new Command("OK",Command.SCREEN,1);
```

```
76.        finalbook = new Command("BOOK",Command.SCREEN,1);
77.
78.    }
79.    /* destroyApp() method declared. This will free the resources */
80.    public void destroyApp(boolean b)
81.    {
82.     backtodate = null;
83.     backtomovie = null;
84.     backtohall = null;
85.     bookticket = null;
86.     backtostatus = null;
87.     emailscreen = null;
88.     backtoname = null;
89.     categoryscreen = null;
90.     backtoemail = null;
91.     backtocat = null;
92.     ticketscreen = null;
93.     finalbook = null;
94.     exitcommand = null;
95.    }
96.
97.    public void pauseApp()
98.    {}
99.    /* This method is used for event handling */
100.    public void commandAction(Command c, Displayable d)
101.    {
102.        /* this is true if an item is selected in the list */
103.        if(c == List.SELECT_COMMAND)
104.        {
105.            if(halllist.isShown())
106.            {
107.                realhall =
halllist.getString(halllist.getSelectedIndex());
108.                hallname =
halllist.getString(halllist.getSelectedIndex());
109.            }
110.            else if(listmovies.isShown())
111.                hallname =
listmovies.getString(listmovies.getSelectedIndex());
112.            else if(listdate.isShown())
113.                hallname =
listdate.getString(listdate.getSelectedIndex());
114.            counter++;
115.            getAllData(hallname,counter);
116.        }
117.        /* This will display the date list. On click of Back button */
118.        if(c == backtodate)
119.        {
120.            displaymovielist.setCurrent(listdate);
121.            counter = 2;
122.        }
123.        /* This will display the movie list, on click of Back button */
124.        if(c == backtomovie)
125.        {
126.            displaymovielist.setCurrent(listmovies);
127.            counter = 1;
```

```
128.                }
129.                /* This will display the hall list, on click of Back button */
130.           if(c==backtohall)
131.           {
132.                   displaymovielist.setCurrent(halllist);
133.                   counter = 0;
134.           }
135.           /* This will display a form asking the user to enter his name,. on
click of Book button */
136.           if(c==bookticket)
137.           {
138.                   yourname = new Form("Enter your Name");
139.                   yourname.setCommandListener(this);
140.                   yourname.addCommand(emailscreen);
141.                   yourname.addCommand(backtostatus);
142.                   entername = new TextField("Enter Name","",20,TextField.ANY);
143.                   yourname.append(entername);
144.                   displaymovielist.setCurrent(yourname);
145.           }
146.           /* This will display the status form, oOn click of Back button */
147.           if(c == backtostatus)
148.           {
149.                   displaymovielist.setCurrent(statusform);
150.           }
151.           /* This will display the form asking the user to enter his name, oOn
click of Back button */
152.           if(c == backtoname)
153.           {
154.                   displaymovielist.setCurrent(yourname);
155.           }
156.           /* This will display the form asking the user to enter his email, oOn
click of Back button */
157.           if(c == backtoemail)
158.           {
159.                   displaymovielist.setCurrent(emailform);
160.           }
161.           /* This will display the form for selecting a category like "balcony"
and "rear stall" etc
162.           , on click of Back button */
163.           if(c == backtocat)
164.           {
165.                   displaymovielist.setCurrent(categoryform);
166.           }
167.           /* This will ask the user to enter his email address,on click of OK
button */
168.           if(c == emailscreen)
169.           {
170.                   bookname = entername.getString();
171.                   emailform = new Form("Enter your Email");
172.                   emailform.setCommandListener(this);
173.                   enteremail = new TextField("Enter
Email","",30,TextField.EMAILADDR);
174.                   emailform.append(enteremail);
175.                   emailform.addCommand(backtoname);
176.                   emailform.addCommand(categoryscreen);
177.                   displaymovielist.setCurrent(emailform);
```

```
178.          }
179.          /* This will ask the user to select a category,on click of OK button
*/
180.          if(c == categoryscreen)
181.          {
182.                  bookemail = enteremail.getString();
183.                  categoryform = new Form("Select a Category");
184.                  categoryform.setCommandListener(this);
185.                  categorybuttons = new
ChoiceGroup("Category",ChoiceGroup.EXCLUSIVE);
186.                  categorybuttons.append("Balcony",null);
187.                  categorybuttons.append("Rear Stall",null);
188.                  categorybuttons.append("Upper Stall",null);
189.                  categorybuttons.append("Middle Stall",null);
190.                  categoryform.append(categorybuttons);
191.                  categoryform.addCommand(backtoemail);
192.                  categoryform.addCommand(ticketscreen);
193.                  displaymovielist.setCurrent(categoryform);
194.          }
195.          /* This will ask the user to enter the number of tickets to be
booked,on click of OK button */
196.          if(c == ticketscreen)
197.          {
198.                  bookcategory =
categorybuttons.getString(categorybuttons.getSelectedIndex());
199.                  ticketform = new Form("Enter the Tickets");
200.                  ticketform.setCommandListener(this);
201.                  enterticket = new TextField("Enter
Ticket","",6,TextField.NUMERIC);
202.                  ticketform.append(enterticket);
203.                  ticketform.addCommand(backtocat);
204.                  ticketform.addCommand(finalbook);
205.                  displaymovielist.setCurrent(ticketform);
206.          }
207.          /* This will book the tickets for the user, on click of  Book Button
*/
208.          if(c == finalbook)
209.          {
210.                  String url = "fname="+bookname +"&email="+ bookemail
+"&hallid="+Integer.parseInt((String)id.elementAt(name.indexOf(realhall)))+  "&"
+bookcategory+"="+ Integer.parseInt(enterticket.getString())+ "&showtime=" +
booktime +"&showdate="+showdate;
211.                  try
212.                      {
213.                      /* This will create an HTPP connection object */
214.                      HttpConnection con =
(HttpConnection)Connector.open(url);
215.                      /* This will open an InputStream to the connection */
216.                      InputStream ins = con.openInputStream();
217.                      ins.close();
218.                      }
219.                  catch(IOException ex)
220.                      {
221.                              System.out.println("IOException occured");
222.                      }
223.                  destroyApp(true);
```

```
224.                 notifyDestroyed();
225.                 lastscreen.getDisplayObject(displaymovielist);
226.         }
227.         /* This will delete the MIDlet and close the application */
228.         if(c == exitcommand)
229.         {
230.                 destroyApp(true);
231.                 notifyDestroyed();
232.                 lastscreen.getDisplayObject(displaymovielist);
233.         }
234.    }
235.    /* This method is very important method. This method is used to
manipulate more than one List */
236.    private void getAllData(String str,int counter)
237.    {
238.         /* this if condition is true if an item is selected from the hall
list */
239.         if(counter == 1)
240.         {
241.                 listmovies = new List("List of Movies",List.IMPLICIT);
242.                 listmovies.setCommandListener(this);
243.                 listmovies.addCommand(backtohall);
244.
 parsemoviedata.sourceurl("http://192.192.168.100/midlet/template/midlet_status.
xml?tname=" + str);
245.                 parsemoviedata.parseDataMovies(2);
246.                 details = parsemoviedata.halldata();
247.                 details.trimToSize();
248.                 for (Enumeration enum =
details.elements();enum.hasMoreElements();)
249.                 {
250.                         if(enum.nextElement().equals("ms"))
251.                         {
252.
 listmovies.append((String)enum.nextElement(),null);
253.                         }
254.                 }
255.                 displaymovielist.setCurrent(listmovies);
256.         }
257.         /* this if condition is true if an item is selected from the movies
list */
258.         if(counter == 2)
259.         {
260.                 listdate = new List("Show Date",List.IMPLICIT);
261.                 listdate.setCommandListener(this);
262.                 listdate.addCommand(backtomovie);
263.                 int indexofmovie = details.indexOf(str);
264.                 int indexofms = details.indexOf("ms",indexofmovie+2);
265.                 if(indexofms == -1)
266.                         indexofms = details.size();
267.                 while(indexofmovie < indexofms)
268.                 {
269.                         if((details.elementAt(indexofmovie)).equals("st"))
270.                         {
271.
 listdate.append((String)details.elementAt(indexofmovie+1),null);
```

```
272.                              }
273.                      indexofmovie++;
274.                  }
275.              displaymovielist.setCurrent(listdate);
276.
277.          }
278.      /* this if condition is true if user selects date from the date list
*/
279.      if(counter == 3)
280.          {
281.              showdate = str;
282.              statusform = new Form("Status of Movie");
283.              statusform.setCommandListener(this);
284.              statusform.addCommand(backtodate);
285.              statusform.addCommand(bookticket);
286.              int indexdate = details.lastIndexOf(str);
287.              int indexms = details.indexOf("ms",indexdate);
288.              int indexst = details.indexOf("st",indexdate);
289.              indexdate+=1;
290.              if(indexst == -1)
291.                      indexst = details.size();
292.              if(indexms == -1)
293.                      indexms = details.size();
294.              String sarray[] = {"Show Time","Balcony","Rear Stall","Upper
Stall","Middle Stall"};
295.              int i = 0;
296.              while((indexdate) < indexms)
297.                  {
298.                      if(i > 4)
299.                              break;
300.                      if(i==0)
301.                          {
302.                              booktime =
 (String)details.elementAt(indexdate);
303.                          }
304.                      sitem = new
StringItem(sarray[i],(String)details.elementAt(indexdate));
305.                      statusform.append(sitem);
306.                      indexdate++;
307.                      i++;
308.                  }
309.              displaymovielist.setCurrent(statusform);
310.          }
311.  }
312.  }
```

Code explanation

♦ *Lines 1-14:* These are `import` statements that will import the necessary classes for running this application.

♦ *Line 16:* Declaring `MoviesList` class. This class is a MIDlet and is used to book movie tickets. The user can also view the status of the movie.

♦ Lines 18-34: The code in these lines declare different objects.

♦ Lines 36-45: Constructor declaration. The constructor is passed two arguments: One is the `Display` object, and the other is the object of `MainClass`. This also initializes a list, which will display to the user the movie theaters available. A command object is also initialized, which is an Exit command, and will be added to the hall List.

♦ Lines 47-78: The startApp() method is declared. This method is called when the application starts.

- 49-56: Here the DataParser class is instantiated. The source url method of the DataParser method is called. This method is passed the URL to connect to. The parseDataMovies() method is called, which parses the XML data. The argument 1 passed to this method will get the theater list with its IDs. See the DataParser class. The hall_name method will return a Vector object containing the hall Names, and the hall_id() method will return a Vector object containing hall IDs.

- 58-61: The for loop here will read the hall names from the name Vector and append it to the list to be displayed to the user. Then the list is displayed to the user.

- 65-76: Different commands are initialized.

♦ Lines 80-95: The destroyApp() method is declared. All the objects declared are set to null. This will help in freeing resources.

♦ 97-98: The pauseApp() method is declared.

♦ Lines 100: The commandAction() method is declared. This method is called whenever a user event is generated on GUI components.

♦ Lines 103-116: This if condition is true if the user selects an item in the list. As there are three lists in this MIDlet, we have to recognize which list has generated the event. This is done by checking which list is shown by calling isShownmethod. Note that, at a particular time, only one condition out of three will be true.

- 105-109: This if condition is true if the halllist is shown. The value of the item selected is taken in a String.

- 110-111: This if condition is true if the listmovies is shown containing the names of movies. The value of the item selected is taken in a String.

- 112-113: This if condition is true if the listdate is shown containing the dates on which the movies will be screened. The value of the item selected is taken in a String.

- 114-115: This will increment the value of counter. The getAllData() method is called with the value selected by the user and the counter passed as a parameter to this method.

♦ Lines 118-122: The backtodate command is generated when the user presses the Back button on the Status screen. This will display to the user the screen with the date of the movies.

♦ Lines 124-128: The backtomovie command is generated when the user presses the Back button on the Date screen. This will display the screen containing the list of movies.

♦ Lines 130-134: The backtohall command is generated when the user presses the Back button on the Movies screen. This will display the screen containing the list of halls.

♦ Lines 136-145: The bookticket command is generated when the user presses the Book button on the Status screen. This will display a screen containing the form where the user has to enter his/her name.

♦ Lines 147-150: The backtostatus command is generated when the user presses the Back button on the Enter Your Name screen. This will display to the user the screen containing the status of movie.

♦ Lines 152-155: The backtoname command is generated when the user presses the Back button on the Enter Your E-mail screen. This will display to the user the screen asking the user to enter his/her name.

◆ Lines 157-160: The `backtoemail` command is generated when the user presses the Back button on the Select Category screen. This will display to the user the screen asking the user to enter his/her e-mail address.

◆ Lines 163-166: The `backtocat` command is generated when the user presses the Back button on the Enter the Tickets screen. This will display to the user the screen containing the categories, such as Balcony, Rear Stall, etc.

◆ Lines 168-178: The `emailscreen` command is generated when the user presses the OK button on the Enter Your Name screen. This will display to the user a screen containing the form where the user has to enter his/her e-mail address.

◆ Lines 180-194: The `categoryscreen` command is generated when the user presses the OK button on the Enter Your E-mail screen. This will display to the user a screen containing radio buttons with category names. The user has to select one of the categories.

◆ Lines 196-206: The `ticketscreen` command is generated when the user presses the OK button on the Category screen. This will display to the user a screen containing the form where the user has to enter the number of tickets to be booked.

◆ Lines 208-226: The `finalbook` command is generated when the user presses the Book button on the Enter the Tickets screen. This will establish an HTTP connection and update the database. This will also destroy the MIDlet and return the `Display` object to the `MainClass` by calling `getDisplayObject()`.

◆ Lines 228-233: The `exitcommand` command is generated when the user presses the Exit button on the Hall List screen. This will destroy the MIDlet and return the `Display` object to the `MainClass` by calling `getDisplayObject()`.

◆ Lines 236-311: The `getAllData` method is declared. This method is used to handle multiple lists, as this MIDlet has three lists to manipulate. This is a private method and can be used only by this class. A String and an integer value are passed as arguments to this method. The String is the item selected by the user from the list, and the integer is a counter value.

  • 239-256: Counter value 1 will make this `if` condition true. The counter value is set to 1 when the user makes a selection from the Hall List screen. A new list is created, which will be the list of movies running on the movie hall the user selected. In this case, another HTTP connection is made, and all the data related to this hall is read and stored in a `Vector`.

  • 258-277: Counter value 2 will make this `if` condition true. The counter value is set to 2 when the user makes a selection from the Movies List screen. Here also a new list is created, which will be the list of dates on which the movie is running. In this case, only the dates are taken from the `Vector` containing the data of the movie hall, based on the movie selected.

  • 279-310: Counter value 3 will make this `if` condition true. The counter value is set to 3 when the user makes a selection from the Date List screen. Here, a form is created, which will display to the user the status of the movie, such as the Timing, Tickets Available, etc. In this case, all the data except date is taken from the `Vector`.

Summary

This chapter was a full-blown application developed using MIDP for Mobile Phone. After reading this chapter, the reader can manipulate the application provided in this chapter to add create a complete portal and can add more services. In Chapter 11 we will develop an application using CLDC and Kjava APIs and it is the last chapter containing a project.

Chapter 11

Project 6: Target Practice Game

Game development has always been one of the most popular programming exercises. Whether a programming environment facilitates developing good games is one important criterion for judging the effectiveness of that environment. In fact, some programmers criticize MIDP because it isn't possible to create higher-end games using it. Whether this criterion for judging a programming environment is right or not, we have to remember that J2ME is still in its infancy, even while gauging it.

Anyway, we are going to demonstrate that you can make simple games even with CLDC, let alone MIDP. Of course, this can be done only by using the KJava package, since that is where we can get the user interface. The fact that KJava is a temporary arrangement doesn't really matter much, because in practice, CLDC will always be backed up with a user interface functionality — whether from a profile or the native operating system on the device.

The game we present in this chapter is a simple one. The purpose is to illustrate how some more classes of CLDC can be used for developing applications. One of these classes is the `Thread` class of the `java.lang` package. You may be familiar with some of the classes already, as we have used them in the CLDC case studies and other projects. Classes of the KJava package are used for the UI part. Learning how to use them may be useful for more than just testing the CLDC applications. The KJava package is likely to become a regular feature of some profile in a modified version. Even if it doesn't, the experience of providing UI with Java on constrained devices will be rewarding.

The project is a game of "shooting." A target moves, and the player has to shoot at it. He gets points for every successful hit. Not very exciting for a seasoned player used to playing games on his PC, but a newcomer to the J2ME platform can hopefully get some excitement from developing an application such as this with just CLDC.

User Interface

On starting the game, the user sees a screen as shown in Figure 11-1 with two sets of radio buttons (of the class `RadioButton`) and three buttons (of the class `Button`). He can make his choice of the level at which he wants to play the game (simple or difficult) and about the number of shots he can use for target practice by selecting one radio button each. With the three buttons, he can start playing (Play Now), read instructions (Instructions), or exit the game if he wants to discontinue playing. There aren't many instructions to read because this is a simple game.

On pressing the Play Now button, the starting screen is shown as in Figure 11-2. This screen shows the target and the "gun." There are two buttons (Start and Exit) to either begin shooting or to quit — there should always be an escape option available. Press the Start button, and the target begins to move. A third button simultaneously appears as in Figure 11-3. This button (Shoot) is for shooting. The player can quit the game at any time as desired. Otherwise, he shoots for the number of times he selected in the initial screen (Figure 11-1). Once he has availed all the chances to hit the target, another screen shows his score as in Figure 11-4. Two buttons (Play Again and Exit) on this screen allow him to either have another try or to quit the game.

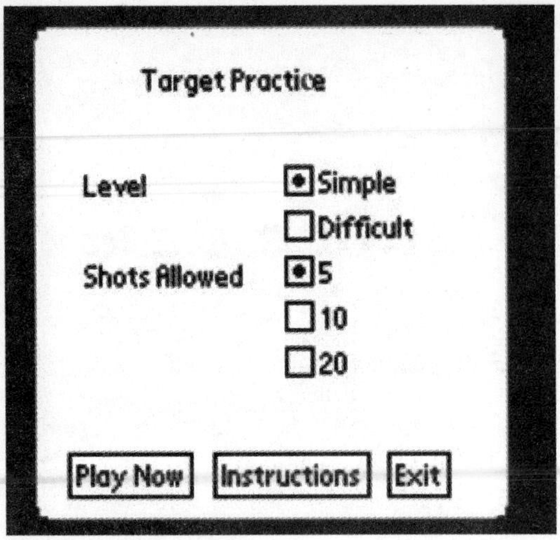

Figure 11-1: Initial Screen.

How It Works

You can run the application by using the batch file provided with the source code. Before clicking it, you will have to change the paths to match those on your machine, as usual. This will also take care of compilation and preverification. The class `TargetPractice` is the starting class of this application. When this class is executed, it shows the initial screen as described in the preceding section and shown in Figure 11-1. It is responsible for the following tasks:

- It provides the user interface for the initial class, which includes the `RadioButtons` for options and simple buttons.
- It stores the values for options in the variables `level_information` and `shot_information`.
- It provides the event handling for the radio buttons and the buttons. The `penDown` method is used for this.
- It calls the class `MainClass` for handling the game.

The main class of the application is called simply `MainClass`. The important tasks performed in this class are as follows:

- Creating the user interface for the screen before the game starts and also retaining it for the time when it is being played. This is done with the help of the classes provided in KJava API. These include `RadioButton` and `Button`. The String class of `java.lang` package is used for creating Strings. All objects are drawn and redrawn on the screen, as before, by using the `Graphics` class of KJava. This class is used in a way that is similar to the `Graphics` class of J2SE (`java.awt` package).

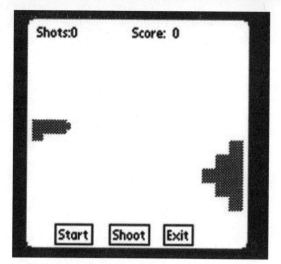

Figure 11-2: Target starts moving.

♦ A constructor that takes parameters for the level of game and the number of shots is defined. One of the tasks performed inside this constructor include registering the spotlet. Some variables, such as the `score`, are given their initial values. A `Thread` is declared, and its two possible times of sleep are given values. These "sleep times" determine the level of the game. Drawing operations on the user interface elements are performed inside the constructor.

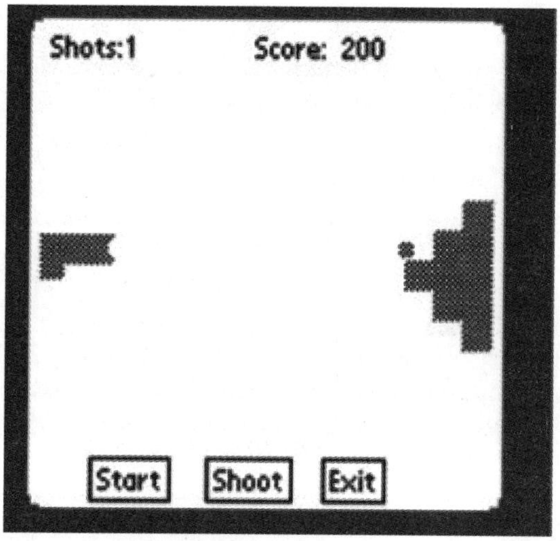

Figure 11-3: Gun is fired.

♦ A counter is used to keep track of the number of times the player has shot at the target. Its value is incremented after every shot by calling the `reload()` method. When the value of the counter becomes equal to the number of shots selected by the player in the beginning, the spotlet is unregistered, the screen is cleared, and the `Result` class is called with the `score` parameter.

♦ The thread is started in the method `run()`. If...else blocks are used to control the position of the target, as well as for drawing and redrawing it. The main thing is to make sure that, as the target goes out of the screen on one side, it is made to reappear from the other side for another shot.

♦ All the event handling for the game is defined in this class within the method `keyDown()`. It takes care of drawing and redrawing the barrrel and the bullet. The method is invoked when the user presses the Enter key on the keyboard or when he presses the Shoot button on the Palm device. The job of maintaining scores also belongs to this method.

Thanks for playing..

Your Score is 1800

Play Again   **Exit**

Figure 11-4: Final score.

Once the game is finished, the scores are shown by the class `Result`. It provides the UI and event handling for the result screen and calls the main class again if the player presses the Play Again button.

Program flow is described as follows and shown in Figure 11-5:

◆ The game is started by executing the class `TargetPractice`. It performs the tasks described previously and shows the initial screen. If Exit is pressed, the application will end.

◆ On the user's pressing the Play Now button, the class `MainClass` is called with the `level` and `shot` values as the parameters. This sets up the stage for the game and shows the next screen. The `exit` option is there, too.

◆ On the user's pressing the Start button, a thread is activated, which allows the target to move up and down. A new button, labeled Shoot, appears in addition to the Start and Exit buttons.

◆ On the user's pressing the Shoot button, the value of the Boolean variable `shoot` becomes true. As a result, the bullet and the target are shown moving by drawing and redrawing them in changing postions. This is done by using `if...else` blocks in the methods `run()` and `keyDown()`. Checks are applied to see that they reappear on the screen as they go out of it. The method `reload()` is called to repeat the process of firing the bullet and moving the target.

◆ When the value of the counter becomes equal to the maximum shots chosen, the class `MainClass` is unregistered, and the class `Result` is called.

◆ If the Play Again button is pressed, the class `TargetPractice` is called again so that the game can be played again.

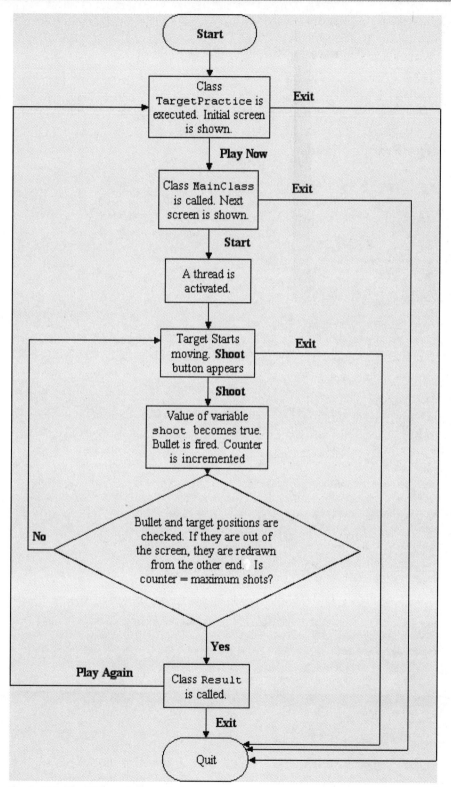

Figure 11-5: Flow Diagram for the project.

Source Code

Source code TargetPractice.java MainClass.java, and Result.java is given.

TargetPractice.java

This class acts as the first class of the program. It provides the user with various options (level and shots that the user can fire). Along with this, the class also provides a button to display the instructions to the user (Listing 11-1).

Listing 11-1: TargetPractice.java

```
/**
 *    Basic packages used by various classes used in the game.
 *
 */
1.  import com.sun.kjava.*;
2.  import java.lang.*;
3.  import javax.microedition.io.*;
4.  import java.io.*;
5.  import java.util.*;
6.
/**
 *   The code below pertains to declaring a class TargetPractice.
 *   This class acts as the first class of the program. It provides
 *  the user with various options (level and shots that the user
 *  can fire). Along with this, the class also provides a button to
 *  display the instructions to the user.
 */

7.  public class TargetPractice extends Spotlet
8.  {

/**
 *    Declaring button variables.
 *  For starting the game -- Play.
 *  Quit the game -- exit.
 *  Instructions for playing the game -- Instructions.
 */
9.     private Button play;
10.    private Button instr;
11.    private Button exit;

/**
 *  Declaring and initializing the variables for level and number
 *  of shots that user can fire.
 *  level    --      level_information
 *  shots    --      shot_information
 */
12.
13.    String level_information = "simple";
14.    int shot_information = 5;

/**
 *   Initializing a RadioGroup of the name level. All the RadioButtons
 *  pertaining to level will be placed in this RadioGroup.
 *   This way only one of the buttons can be checked at a time.
```

```
    * The RadioButton with the label "Simple" is given the variable name
    * "simple" and similarly the RadioButton with the label Difficult is
    * given the variable name as "difficult".
    */

15.      private RadioGroup level = new RadioGroup(2);
16.      private RadioButton simple = null;
17.      private RadioButton difficult = null;

 /**
   *  Similarly, initializing a RadioGroup of the name "shots".
   * All the RadioButtons pertaining to shots will be placed in
   * this RadioGroup. This way only one of the buttons can be checked
   * at a time.The RadioButton with the label "5" is given the
   * variable name "five", the RadioButton with the label "10" is
   * given the variable name as "ten" and similarly the RadioButton
   * with the label "20" is given the variable name as "twenty".

   */

18.
19.      private RadioGroup shots = new RadioGroup(3);
20.      private RadioButton five = null;
21.      private RadioButton ten = null;
22.      private RadioButton twenty = null;
23.
  // Declaring a variable of the class Graphics. This class is
  // responsible for showing all the graphics (labels etc.) on
  //   the screen.
24.    Graphics graphics;
25.
26.    public TargetPractice()      // Constructor TargetPractice
27.     {
28.
  // To make the spotlet as the current spotlet...
29.     register(NO_EVENT_OPTIONS);
30.
 /**
   *  Initializing the variable of the graphics class and clearing
   * the drawing region by calling the appropriate functions of
   * the Graphics class, namely resetDrawRegion() and clearScreen().
   */
31.     graphics = Graphics.getGraphics();
32.     graphics.resetDrawRegion();
33.     graphics.clearScreen();
34.
 /**
   *  Displaying a string (Title) at a specified position by using
   * the member function of the Graphics class.
   */

35.     graphics.drawString("Target Practice",35,10);
36.
 /**
   *  Initializing the button object 'play', placing it on the screen
   * at the appropriate position and then painting (drawing it).
```

```
     */
37.     play = new Button("Play Now",10,140);
38.     play.paint();
39.
 /**
  *  Initializing the button object instr, placing it on the screen
  * at the appropriate position and then painting (drawing it).
  */

40.     instr = new Button("Instructions",60,140);
41.     instr.paint();
42.
43.
 /**
  *  Initializing the button object exit, placing it on the screen
  * at the appropriate position and then painting(drawing it).
  */

44.    exit = new Button("Exit",120,140);
45.    exit.paint();
46.
47.
 /**

  *  Displaying a string "Level" at a specified position on the screen.
  * This acts as the label of group of radio buttons.
  */
48.     graphics.drawString("Level",15,45);
49.
50.
 /**
  *  Initializing the RadioButton object simple, placing it
  * on the screen at the appropriate position and then drawing it.
  */

51.     simple = new RadioButton(85,45,"Simple");
 // Initially this button is to be kept selected. Therefore, a function
 // setState is called, which is passed a parameter 'true', which will
 //care of this.
52.     simple.setState(true);
53.     simple.paint();
54.
 /**
  *  Initializing the RadioButton object 'difficult', placing it
  * on the screen at the appropriate position and then drawing it.
  */

55.     difficult = new RadioButton(85,60,"Difficult");
56.     difficult.paint();
57.
 /**
  *  Adding the RadioButtons to the RadioButton group, thereby ensuring
  * that only one of the buttons will be selected at a particular instant
  * of time.
  */
58.     level.add(simple);
```

```
59.    level.add(difficult);
60.
61.
 /**
  * Displaying a string "Shots Allowed" at a specified position
  *on the screen. It acts as the Label of a group of radion buttons.
  */

62.    graphics.drawString("Shots Allowed",15,75);
63.
 /**
  * Initializing the RadioButton object 'five', placing it
  *on the screen at the appropriate position and then drawing it.
  */

64.    five = new RadioButton(85,75,"5");

 // Initially this button is to be kept selected. Therefore, a function
 // setState is called which is passed a parameter true which will
 // do the same.

65.    five.setState(true);
66.    five.paint();
67.
 /**
  * Initializing the RadioButton object 'five', placing it
  *on the screen at the appropriate position and then drawing it.
  */
68.    ten = new RadioButton(85,90,"10");

69.    ten.paint();
70.
 /**
  * Initializing the RadioButton object 'five', placing it
  *on the screen at the appropriate position and then drawing it.
  */

71.    twenty = new RadioButton(85,105,"20");
72.    twenty.paint();
73.
 /**
  * Adding the RadioButtons to the RadioButton group, thereby ensuring
  *that only one of the buttons will be selected at a particular instant
  *of time.
  */

74.    shots.add(five);
75.    shots.add(ten);
76.    shots.add(twenty);
77.
78.    }// End of the constructor TargetPractice.
79.
 /**
  * The code below pertains to event handling.
  */
```

```
80.      public void penDown(int x, int y)
81.      {
/**
 *  If the Play button is pressed, the information stored in the
 * two variables of the name 'level_information' and 'shot_informat-
 * ion' is taken and passed as a parameter to a user defined class
 *  of the name MainClass. It is this class which manages the
 * entire game.
 */
82.      if(play.pressed(x,y))
83.      {
84.          new MainClass(level_information,shot_information);
85.
86.      }
/**
 *  If Exit button is pressed, the game is closed and the
 * control is returned to the OS.
 */
87.      else if (exit.pressed(x,y))
88.      {
89.          System.exit(0);
90.      }
/**
 *  If the Instructions button is pressed, a class of the name
 * HelpDisplay is called. This is responsible for displaying the
 * instructions to the user.
 */
91.      else if (instr.pressed(x,y))
92.      {
// To show a new class, first unregister all the controls of the
// existing class.
93.          unregister();
94. // Clear the screen and reset the draw region.
95.          graphics.resetDrawRegion();
96.          graphics.clearScreen();

97. // Place the help text in the String variable helpText
98. String helpText = "Instruction for the program \n\n\n
       Choose the level and no. of shots and then press the Start
       button to  start the game.";
99. // Call to the class HelpDisplay to display the help text.
99. (new HelpDisplay(helpText,"TargetPractice",
       NO_EVENT_OPTIONS)).register(NO_EVENT_OPTIONS);
101.          }
/**
 *  If a radio button is pressed, the appropriate variable connected to
 * that radio button is assigned that value. For example, if radio-
 * button of the label Simple is selected, then then the variable
 * label_information is given the value simple.
 */
102.          else if (simple.pressed(x,y))
103.          {
104.              level_information = "simple";
105.              simple.handlePenDown(x,y);
106.          }
107.          else if (difficult.pressed(x,y))
```

```
108.            {
109.                   level_information = "difficult";
110.                   difficult.handlePenDown(x,y);
111.            }
112.            else if (five.pressed(x,y))
113.            {
114.                   shot_information = 5;
115.                   five.handlePenDown(x,y);
116.            }
117.            else if (ten.pressed(x,y))
118.            {
119.                   shot_information = 10;
120.                   ten.handlePenDown(x,y);
121.            }
122.            else if (twenty.pressed(x,y))
123.            {
124.                   shot_information = 20;
125.                   twenty.handlePenDown(x,y);
126.            }
127.     }    // End of the event handling function..
128.  // The main method which is the entry point of this application.

129.    public static void main(String args[])
130.    {
131.         new TargetPractice();
132.    }
133.  // End of the class TargetPractice.
134. }
```

Code explanation

♦ Lines 1-5: The code here pertains to the inclusion/importing of the various packages required by the various classes during the program. These include packages such as com.sun.kjava, which are used by the classes that help in creating the GUI, and the Graphics class, which is responsible for the creation of rectangles for the target, circles for the bullets, etc.

♦ Line 7: This is for declaring the class TargetPractice. This class acts as the first class of the program. It provides the user with various options (level and shots that the user can fire). It also provides a button to display the instructions to the user.

♦ Lines 9-11: Objects of the class Button are declared. These buttons are used for various purposes — for example, Play (for starting the game), Exit (for quitting the game), and Instructions (for instructions on how to play the game).

♦ Lines 13-14: Used for declaring and initializing the two variables level_information and shot_information. These two variables store the information about the level of the game (difficult or simple) and the number of shots that can be fired (5, 10, or 20).

♦ Lines 15-22: For the declaration of various radio buttons and radio groups. The radio groups are declared to ensure that only one radio button can be selected at a time. There are two radio groups declared: level and shots. The radio buttons declared are Simple, Difficult, 5, 10, and 20.

♦ Line 29: The spotlet is made the current spotlet here. The system keys can cancel the spotlet at any time.

♦ Lines 31-33: These codes are for getting the Graphics object of the spotlet, resetting the drawing region, and clearing the spotlet screen.

♦ Line 35: Drawing and positioning a String at a specified position on the spotlet. This String acts as the title/heading of the game.

- Lines 37-45: These statements represent initializing the Button objects declared earlier (play, exit, and instr), placing them at an appropriate position and then drawing them on the screen.

- Lines 51-56: These lines serve to initialize the RadioButton objects and paint the RadioButton objects at an appropriate position on the screen. These radio buttons have the labels Simple and Difficult. In line 52, the state of the radio button with the label Simple is made true, which implies that, when the game is run, the radio button with the label Simple is selected by default.

- Lines 58-59: These correspond to adding the two radio buttons initialized and drawn earlier into the radio group level, thereby ensuring that the user can select only one from the two radio buttons.

- Lines 64-72: The code here initializes the RadioButton objects and paints the RadioButton objects at an appropriate position on the screen. These radio buttons have the labels 5, 10, and 20. In line 65, the state of the radio button with the label 5 is made true, which implies that, when the game is run, the radio button with the label 5 is selected by default.

- Lines 74-76: These are for adding the three radio buttons initialized and drawn earlier into a radio group shots, thereby ensuring that the user can select only one among the three radio buttons.

- Lines 82-86: When the user presses the button Play, this code block is activated. When the button is pressed, the class MainClass which has two parameters, level and shots, is called. The information stored in these two parameters is the level of play and the number of shots that the user can hit.

- Lines 87-90: The exit event is coded in these lines. When the Exit button is pressed, the game is closed, and the control is returned to the OS.

- Lines 91-101: This is the code for the Instructions button. When the button is pressed, the current spotlet is made passive by calling the unregister method of the spotlet. The screen is redrawn, and then the class HelpDisplay is called with the textual information about the game.

- Lines 102-111: The events of the user's pressing of any of the radio buttons labeled Simple or Difficult are encoded here. The if statements identify the button and then assign the appropriate label to the String variable of the name level declared earlier.

- Lines 112-125: These lines represent the corresponding events when the user presses any of the radio buttons labeled 5, 10, or 20. The if statements identify the button and then assign the appropriate label to the String variable of the name shots declared earlier.

- Lines 129-132: These lines encode the main program, which calls the class TargetPractice.

MainClass.java

As the name suggests, this is the main class of the project that is responsible for starting the game. This class implements a Runnable interface as well, which is used to include the thread capability in the class. The functionality this class provides is the movement of the gun, movement of bullet, and displaying the score to the user (Listing 11-2).

Listing 11-2: MainClass.java

```
/**
 *     Basic packages used by various classes used in the Game.
 *
 */
1.   import com.sun.kjava.*;
2.   import java.lang.*;
3.   import javax.microedition.io.*;
4.   import java.io.*;
5.   import java.util.*;
6.
/**
```

```
      *   The code below pertains to declaring the class MainClass.java
      * As the name suggests this is the main class of the project that is
      * responsible for starting the game. This class implements a Runnable
      * interface as well, which is used to include the thread capability
      * in the class.
      */
7.  public class MainClass extends Spotlet implements Runnable
8.  {
9.

  /**
      *   Declaring button variables.
      * For starting the game -- start.
      * Firing the pistol -- shootnow.
      * Quit the game -- exit.
      */

10.    Button exit,start,shoot_now;

  // Declaring a variable of the class Graphics this class is
  // responsible for showing all the graphics (lables etc.) on
  //  the screen.

11.    Graphics graphics;

  /**
      *   The code pertains to the declaration of the three of this class. These
  three variables are all
      * of integer type. Their use is as follows:
      * initial_position  -- initial position of the target bar.
      * initial_position_bullet -- as the name suggests, this variable
      *                            describes the initial position of the
      *                            bullet.
      * initial_position_barrel -- Initial position of the gun.
      */

12.    int initial_position = 0;
13.    int *initial_position_bullet = 0;
14.    int initial_barrel_position = 0;

  //  Another important variable is declared. This variable is of
  // boolean type and of the name shoot. When this variable is
  // true, the gun is fired, else the gun remains loaded and ready
  // to fire.

15.    boolean shoot = false;

  //  Declaring a thread

16.    Thread t;
17.    String level;

  /**
      * Declaring the variables for number of shots, sleeptime(delay)
      * score, counter (used as number of shots), cont (continue the
      * game).
      */
```

```
18.   int shots;
19.   int sleeptime  = 35;
20.   int score = 0;
21.   int counter = 0;

22.   boolean cont = true;
23.
 /**
  *  Constructor of the MainClass. It takes two parameters, a string
  * parameter which denotes the level and an integer parameter
  * which indicates the number of shots.
  */
24.   public MainClass(String level, int shots)
25.   {
26.
 // To make the spotlet the current spotlet...

27.     register(NO_EVENT_OPTIONS);

 // Make the initial score value 0.

28.     score = 0;

 /**
  *  Initializing a variable of the graphics class and clearing
  * the drawing region by calling the appropriate functions of
  * the Graphics class namely resetDrawRegion() and clearScreen().
  */

29.     graphics = Graphics.getGraphics();
30.        graphics.resetDrawRegion();
31.          graphics.clearScreen();
32.
 /**
  *  Initializing the variables 'level' and 'shots' with the parameters.
  *
  */
33.     this.level = level;
34.     this.shots = shots;
35.
 /**
  *   Adjusting the delay (sleeptime) according to the level. If the
  * level is simple, the dealy is more. Otherwise it is less.
  */
36.     if (level.equals("simple"))
37.     {
38.         sleeptime = 35;
39.     }
40.     else
41.     {
42.         sleeptime = 15;
43.     }
44.
45.
 //  Initializing the initial position of the bullet.
```

```
46.     initial_position_bullet = 25;
47.
   /**
    * Drawing two labels of the name 'shots' and 'score' on the screen
    * to monitor and display the shots fired and the score      *     .
    */

48.     graphics.drawString("Shots: ",5,2);
49.     graphics.drawString("Score: ",75,2);

50.
51.     graphics.drawString(""+counter,30,2);
52.     graphics.drawString(""+score,105,2);
53.
54.
   // Initial position of the Gun.

55.     initial_barrel_position = 70;

   // Drawing the gun. using the Graphics class method drawRectangle().

56.     graphics.drawRectangle(2,70,25,10,Graphics.GRAY,0);      // Barral
57.     graphics.drawRectangle(2,80,8,5,Graphics.GRAY,0);        // Butt
58.
   // Drawing the Bullet

59.     graphics.drawRectangle(initial_position_bullet,72,5,5,Graphics.GRAY,2);

60.
   // Drawing the Target for target practice at an initial position

61.     initial_position = 45;
62.     graphics.drawRectangle(127,initial_position+20,10,10,Graphics.GRAY,0);

63.     graphics.drawRectangle(137,initial_position+10,10,30,Graphics.GRAY,0);

64.
65.     graphics.drawRectangle(147,initial_position,10,50,Graphics.GRAY,0);

66.
   /**
    * Initializing the button object called 'Exit'; placing it on the screen
    * at the appropriate position and then painting(drawing it).
    */

67.     exit = new Button("Exit",100,145);

   /**
    * Initializing the button object called 'Start', placing it on the screen
    * at the appropriate position and then painting (drawing it).
    */

68.     start = new Button("Start",20,145);

   /**
```

```
      *  Initializing the button object 'Shootnow', placing it on the    screen at
   the appropriate position. The 'Shoot' button
      * however will be painted when the user presses the start button
      * to start the game.
      */

69.    shoot_now = new Button("Shoot",60,145);
70.
71.    exit.paint();
72.    start.paint();
73.
74.    }// End of the constructor MainClass
75.
   /**
      *  The code below pertains to event handling.
      */

76.    public void penDown(int x, int y)
77.    {
   /**
      *  If Exit button is pressed then the game is closed and the
      * control is returned to the OS.
      */
78.    if (exit.pressed(x,y))
79.    {
80.        System.exit(0);
81.    }
   /**
      *  If the start button is pressed then the boolean variable
      * shoot is assigned a value false, i.e. the gun is loaded.The 'Shoot_
      * ' button is painted on the screen. A thread object of the
      * name 't' is initialized and its start method is called. This threadis
   responsible for handling the game.
      */
82.    else if (start.pressed(x,y))
83.    {
84.        shoot = false;
85.        shoot_now.paint();
86.        t = new Thread(this);
87.        t.start();
88.    }
   /**
      *  If Shoot button is pressed, then the boolean variable 'shoot' is
      * assigned a value true indicating that the gun is fired.
      */
89.    else if (shoot_now.pressed(x,y))
90.    {
91.        shoot = true;
92.    }
93.
94.    }// End of event handling function.
95.
   /**
      *  When the start method of a thread is called, it calls the
      * run method. Thus, in this case, when the start method is
      * called at line 87 this run method is called.
```

```
     */
96.    public void run()
97.    {
98.
 /**
  *  Loop infinitely till the boolean variable cont (continue)
  *  is true.
  */
99.      while(cont)
100.         {
 /**
  *  Erase the target from its current position. This is done by
  * using the drawRectangle method of the Graphics class and using
  * the erase macro in place of the 4th parameter.
  */
101. graphics.drawRectangle(127,initial_position+20,10,
       10,Graphics.ERASE,0);
102. graphics.drawRectangle(137,initial_position+10,10,
       30,Graphics.ERASE,0);
103. graphics.drawRectangle(147,initial_position,10,50,Graphics.ERASE,0);
104.
 /**
  * Now the initial position is decremented by 2, giving an
  * appearance that the target is moving. The target is redrawn.
  */
105.         initial_position = initial_position-2;
106.
107. graphics.drawRectangle(127,initial_position+20,10,10,
       Graphics.GRAY,0);
108. graphics.drawRectangle(137,initial_position+10,10,
       30,Graphics.GRAY,0);
109. graphics.drawRectangle(147,initial_position,10,50,Graphics.GRAY,0);
110.
 /**
  *  A check is also applied to check if the target has gone out
  * of the screen. If it has, then the initial position is made such
  * that it appears to be coming out from the other end.
  */
111.         if (initial_position  <= -50)
112.         {
113.                 initial_position = 160;
114.         }
 /**
  *  If the boolean variable shoot is true, indicating that the
  * user has pressed the shoot button then the bullet is erased
  * and then after adjusting the position, is redrawn again in a
  * similar manner as that of the target.
  */
115.         if (shoot)
116.         {
117. graphics.drawRectangle(initial_position_bullet,
       initial_barrel_position+2,5,5,Graphics.ERASE,2);
118. initial_position_bullet = initial_position_bullet + 2;
118. graphics.drawRectangle(initial_position_bullet,
       initial_barrel_position+2,5,5,Graphics.GRAY,2);
```

```
120.
 /**
  *  When the bullet is shot, certain checks are applied to see
  * whether the bullet has hit the target or not or has gone
  * past the target.
  * If the bullet has hit some target then accordingly the points
  * are added to the score and the boolean variable shoot is
  * assigned a value false, indicating that the gun is to be reloaded.
  */
121.          if (initial_position_bullet >=123)
122.          {
123. if ((initial_barrel_position >= initial_position+20)
     &&(initial_barrel_position <= initial_position+30))
124.          {
125.                 score = score + 800;
126.                 shoot = false;
127.             reload();
128.          }
129.          else if (initial_position_bullet >=133)
130.          {
131. if ((initial_barrel_position >= initial_position+10)
     &&(initial_barrel_position <= initial_position+40))
132.            {
133.                 score = score + 400;
134.                 shoot = false;
135.             reload();
136.            }
137.            else if (initial_position_bullet >=143)

138.            {
139. if ((initial_barrel_position >= initial_position)&&
     (initial_barrel_position <= initial_position+50))
140.            {
141.                 score = score + 200;
142.                 shoot = false;
143.             reload();
144.            }
 /**
  *  Else if the bullet has not been able to hit the target and
  *  gone past all together, then also the gun is to reloaded for
  *  the next attack.
  */
145.            else
146.            {
147.              shoot = false;
148.                 reload();
149.            }
150.
151.            } // End if's
152.          }    // End if's
153.        }      // End if's
154.
155.
156.        }
157.
 /**
```

```
        *  The thread is made to sleep for a number of milliseconds as
        *  decided by the level variable.
        */
158.        try
159.        {
160.         Thread.sleep(sleeptime);
161.        }
162.
163.        catch(InterruptedException e)
164.        {
165.                System.out.println("Interruption in thread sleeping");
166.  }
167.
168.        }        // End of the infinite while loop.
169.
170.    }    // End of the method run...
171.
  /**
   *   This method keyDown handles all the events generated when
   *   the user presses any key or taps on the screen.
   */
172.    public void keyDown(int keyCode)
173.    {
  /**
   *  If the key pressed by the user is Enter key on the normal
   *  "QWERTY" keyboard, then make the boolean variable shoot
   *  = true, indicating that the gun should be fired.
   */
174.        if (keyCode == 13)
175.        {
176.                shoot = true;
177.        }
  /**
   *  if the key pressed is the up key on the emulator then gun is
   *  to be moved up therefore the same strategy of erasing first
   *  and then redrawing is employed.
   */
178.        if (keyCode == 11)
179.        {
180.
181. graphics.drawRectangle(2,initial_barrel_position,25,10,Graphics.ERASE,0);
182.
183.
184. graphics.drawRectangle(2,initial_barrel_position+10,8,5,Graphics.ERASE,0);
185.
186.
187.graphics.drawRectangle(initial_position_bullet,initial_barrel_position+2,5,5,
Graphics.ERASE,2);
188.
189.
  /**
   *  A check is introduced so that the gun may not move out from
   *  display screen.
   */
190.            if (initial_barrel_position <= 15)
```

```
191.                    {
192.                        initial_barrel_position = 15;
193.                    }
194.                    else
195.                    {
196.                        initial_barrel_position = initial_barrel_position - 2;
197.                    }
198.                                // Barrel
199. graphics.drawRectangle(2,initial_barrel_position,
     25,10,Graphics.GRAY,0);
200.                            // Butt
201.
202. graphics.drawRectangle(2,initial_barrel_position+10,
     8,5,Graphics.GRAY,0);
203.
204.                //Bullet
205. graphics.drawRectangle(initial_position_bullet,
     initial_barrel_position+2,5,5,Graphics.GRAY,2);
206.          }
207.
208.
  /**
   *  Similarly, if the key pressed is the down key on the emulator
   *  then the gun is to be moved down. Therefore, the same strategy
   *  of erasing first and then redrawing is employed.
   */
209.          else if (keyCode == 12)
210.          {
211.
212. graphics.drawRectangle(2,initial_barrel_position,
     25,10,Graphics.ERASE,0);
213.
214.
215. graphics.drawRectangle(2,initial_barrel_position+10,
     8,5,Graphics.ERASE,0);
216.
217.
218. graphics.drawRectangle(initial_position_bullet,
     initial_barrel_position+2,5,5,Graphics.ERASE,2);
219.
  /**
   *  A check is introduced so that the gun may not move out from
   *  display screen.
   */
220.
221.              if (initial_barrel_position >= 128)
222.              {
223.                  initial_barrel_position = 128;
224.              }
225.              else
226.              {
227.                  initial_barrel_position = initial_barrel_position + 2;
228.              }
229.
230. graphics.drawRectangle(2,initial_barrel_position,
     25,10,Graphics.GRAY,0);
```

```
231.
232.
233. graphics.drawRectangle(2,initial_barrel_position+10,
       8,5,Graphics.GRAY,0);
234.
235.
236. graphics.drawRectangle(initial_position_bullet,
       initial_barrel_position+2,5,5,Graphics.GRAY,2);
237.         }
238.     }     // End of keyDown routine.
239.
  /**
   *   The method reload caters to some important tasks.
   * 1. Increasing the counter(number of shots fired) by the player.
   * 2. Displaying the counter (number of shots fired) and current
   *      score on the user's screen.
   * 3. Checking if the counter is equal to the maximum number of
   * shots fired, then moving on to the results screen.
   */

240.    void reload()
241.    {
242.         counter++;
243.
244.         graphics.drawString("         ",30,2);
245.         graphics.drawString(""+counter,30,2);
246.
247.         graphics.drawString("         ",105,2);
248.         graphics.drawString(""+score,105,2);
249.
250.
  /**
   *  If the counter is equal to the maximum number of shots that
   *  can be fired, then unregister the current spotlet, clear the
   *  graphics region and call a new class Result (which is
   *  responsible for displaying the results) with the score parameter
   *  as the total score of the user.
   */
251.         if (counter  == shots)
252.         {
253.                 unregister();
254.                 graphics.resetDrawRegion();
255.                 graphics.clearScreen();
256.                 cont = false;
257.                 new Result(score);
258.         }
259.
260. graphics.drawRectangle(initial_position_bullet,
       initial_barrel_position+2,5,5,Graphics.ERASE,2);
261.
262.    initial_position_bullet = 25;
263. graphics.drawRectangle(initial_position_bullet,
       initial_barrel_position+2,5,5,Graphics.ERASE,2);
264.    }     // End of the method reload...
265.
```

```
266.  }// End of the class MainClass...
```

Code explanation

♦ Lines 1-5: These statements correspond to the inclusion/importing of the various packages required by the various classes during the tenure of this program. These include packages such as com.sun.kjava, and the Graphics class, which is responsible for the creation of rectangles for the target, circles for the bullets, etc.

♦ Line 7: The class MainClass is declared here. This class, as the name suggests, is the main class of the game program responsible for game play and scoring. This class implements a Runnable interface as well, which is used to include the Thread capability in the class.

♦ Line 10: This code is for declaring objects of the class button. These buttons are Play (for starting the game), Shoot (for firing the shots), and Exit (for quitting the game).

♦ Lines 12-14: The three most important variables of this class are declared here. These three variables are all of the integer type. Their use is as follows:

  • initial_position: Describes initial position of the target bar.

  • initial_position_bullet: Describes the initial position of the bullet.

  • initial_position_barrel: Describes the initial position of the gun.

♦ Line 15: Declaration of the variable shoot. This variable is of the Boolean type. When this variable is true, the gun is fired; otherwise, the gun remains loaded and ready to fire.

♦ Lines 18-22: These statements declare the variables for the number of shots, sleeptime (delay), score, counter (used as number of shots), and cont (continue the game).

♦ Line 27: The spotlet is made the current spotlet by this code. However, the system keys can cancel the spotlet at any time.

♦ Lines 29-31: The process of getting the Graphics object of the spotlet, resetting the drawing region, and clearing the spotlet screen are encoded here.

♦ Lines 34-35: Initializing the variables level and shots with their parameters.

♦ Lines 36-43: Using the if – else statements, the level variable is checked and, accordingly, the sleep time (delay) is adjusted. The sleep time is less for Difficult and more for Simple.

♦ Lines 48-52: Shots and score are displayed on the screen

♦ Lines 55-57: The gun is drawn at an initial position specified.

♦ Line 59: The bullet is also drawn at an initial position specified.

♦ Lines 61-65: The target is drawn. It consists of three rectangles, one on top of the other.

♦ Lines 67-72: Initializing the button objects declared earlier (play, shoot, and exit); placing them on the screen at an appropriate position and then drawing on the screen are achieved by these. Only the Shoot button is not drawn, as it will be drawn only when the user presses the Start button.

♦ Lines 78-80: Used for activating the Exit button. When the Button is pressed, the game is closed, and the control is returned to the OS.

♦ Lines 82-88: The code between these lines corresponds to the user pressing the Start button. When the Start button is pressed, the Boolean flag shoot is made false, indicating that the gun is loaded. The Shoot button is painted on the screen, and a new thread is generated to take care of the target's moving.

♦ Lines 89-92: The code between these lines is executed when the user presses the Shoot button. When this is done, the Boolean flag shoot is made true, indicating that the gun is fired.

♦ Lines 96 –170: When the new thread is created in the code between lines 82-88, the control is transferred to this method.

♦ Line 99: An infinite loop is generated, which is run till the shots are over or the user decides to end the game.

♦ Lines 101-109: To erase the target from its current position. This is done by using the `drawRectangle` method of the `Graphics` class and using the erase macro in place of the fourth parameter. Then the initial position variable is adjusted (decremented by 2), and then, again, the target is redrawn.

♦ Lines 111-114: A check is also made to ensure that the target reaches a specified position and then appears to come again from the other end, thereby giving an illusion of a rotating target.

♦ Lines 115-120: If the `shoot` flag is true — that is, the Shoot button is pressed — the bullet is also erased from the current position, the new position is adjusted, and the bullet is again drawn.

♦ Lines 121-144: The testing of the bullet's position with respect to the target is accomplished here. If the bullet has hit the target, the specified position is identified, and accordingly, the appropriate score is given to the user. The Boolean flag `shoot` is made false, indicating that the gun is to be reloaded. A `reload` method is called, which will do the job of reloading the gun.

♦ Lines 178-208: This code is executed when the user presses the up-arrow key, indicating that the gun should go up from its current position. When the up-arrow key is pressed, its key code is identified; the gun at its current position is erased, the position is recalculated (decremented by 2), and the gun is redrawn. A check is also made, which will ensure that the gun will not altogether leave the display.

♦ Lines 209-237: The code block is executed when the user presses the down-arrow key, indicating that the gun should go down from its current position. When the down-arrow key is pressed, its key code is identified; the gun at its current position is erased, the position is recalculated (incremented by 2), and the gun is again redrawn. A check is also made to ensure that the gun will not altogether leave the display.

♦ Lines 240-266: A `reload` method is declared here. This method first checks the total number of shots fired. If the total number of shots fired becomes equal to the `shots` variable, the `result` class is called by providing a parameter that is the total score of the user. If some shots are still left, the gun is reloaded — that is, the bullet is redrawn at the initial position.

Result.java

As the name suggests, this class is responsible for displaying the result of the game to the user and also for providing the user with a choice of repeat play by giving a button with the label "Play Again" (Listing 11-3).

Listing 11-3: Result.java

```
/**
 *    Basic packages used by various classes used in the Game.
 *
 */
1.   import com.sun.kjava.*;
2.   import java.lang.*;
3.   import javax.microedition.io.*;
4.   import java.io.*;
5.   import java.util.*;
6.
/**
 *   The code below pertains to declaring a class Result.java. As
 * the name suggests, this class is responsible for displaying the
 * result of the game to the user and also for providing the
 * user with a choice of repeat play by giving a button with the
 * label "Play Again".
```

```
    */
7.   public class Result extends Spotlet
8.   {
 /**
  *   Declaring button variables.
  * For restarting the game - Play Again.
  * Quit the game -- Exit.
  */

9.    private Button playagain;
10.    private Button exit;

 // Declaring a variable of the class Graphics. This class is
 // responsible for showing all the graphics (lables etc.) on
 //  the screen.

11.    Graphics graphics;
12.
 // Constructor of the class. This takes as its argument an int
 // (the score), scored by the user in the game.

13.    public Result(int score)
14.    {
15.
 // To make the spotlet the current spotlet..
16.      register(NO_EVENT_OPTIONS);
17.
 /**
  *  Initializing the variable of the graphics class and clearing
  * the drawing region by calling the appropriate functions of
  * the Graphics class, namely resetDrawRegion() and clearScreen().
  */
18.      graphics = Graphics.getGraphics();
19.      graphics.resetDrawRegion();
20.      graphics.clearScreen();
21.
 /**
  *   Drawing the label at the specified position on the screen
  * and placing the score alongside the label.
  */
22.      graphics.drawString("Thanks for playing..",25,25);
23.      graphics.drawString("Your Score is ",25,45);
24.      graphics.drawString(""+score,85,45);
25.
 /**
  *  Initializing the button object 'playagain', placing it on
  * the screen at the appropriate position and then drawing it.
  */
26.      playagain = new Button("Play Again",15,140);

27.      playagain.paint();
28.
 /**
  *  Initializing the button object exit, placing it on the screen
  * at the appropriate position and then painting(drawing it).
  */
```

```
29.      exit = new Button("Exit",85,140);
30.      exit.paint();
31.
32.    }// end of the constructor Result.
33.
 /**
  *  The code below pertains to event handling.
  */
34.    public void penDown(int x, int y)
35.      {
 /**
  *  If playagain button is pressed, then the main class of the
  * project of the name TagetPractice is called again.
  */
36.        if(playagain.pressed(x,y))
37.        {
38.            new TargetPractice();
39.        }
 /**
  *  If Exit button is pressed, the game is closed and the control
  * is returned to the OS.
  */
40.        else if (exit.pressed(x,y))
41.        {
42.            System.exit(0);
43.        }
44.
45.    }    // End of event handling routine...
46.
47.  } // End of the class Result.java
```

Code explanation

♦ Lines 1-5: Inclusion/importing of the various packages required by the various classes during the program are being accomplished here. These include packages such as – com.sun.kjava, which is used by the classes that help in creating the GUI, and the Graphics class, which is responsible for the creation of rectangles for the target, circles for the bullets, etc.

♦ Line 7: The code here pertains to declaring the class result. This class, as the name suggests, is responsible for displaying the results of the game to the user, along with providing the option to the user to play the game again.

♦ Lines 9-10: Declaring objects of the class button. These buttons are used for Play Again (restarting the game) and Exit (quitting the game).

♦ Line 16: The spotlet is made the current spotlet. However, the system keys can cancel the spotlet at any time.

♦ Lines 18-20: These are for getting the Graphics object of the spotlet, resetting the drawing region and clearing the spotlet screen.

♦ Lines 22-24: Used to display a message and the the user's score while playing the game.

♦ Lines 26-30: Initializing the button objects declared earlier (playagain and exit); placing them on the screen at appropriate positions and then drawing them on the screen are encoded.

♦ Lines 36-38: The action involved when the user presses the Play Again button. The user is shown the main/starting screen of the game program by calling the constructor of the class TargetPractice.

- ◆ Lines 40-43: The code between these lines is used when the user presses the Exit button. When the button is pressed, the game is closed, and the control is returned to the OS.

Summary

This chapter was a Final full-blown application developed using CLDC and Kjava APIs for PDAs. This chapter follows on from Chapter 6. You can develop your own game or even modify this game as required. In Chapter 12 we will discuss a very important aspect of converting an existing J2SE application to J2ME. This chapter is a must read as it will provide guidelines for the conversions of applications.

Chapter 12

Converting J2SE Applications to J2ME

Whenever a new version of a technology is in the market, older versions face the risk of becoming obsolete as everyone prefers the applications to cover the newer version. This is why all new versions have to consider the question of backward compatibility. This is less of a problem when the newer technology simply adds to the functionality of a previous one. Addition of functionality is related to the availability of more hardware resources. But when we are faced with a new technology such as J2ME, the situation is different. In this case, the hardware resources available are few, sometimes drastically so. For example, the resources on a pager and those on a PC are just not comparable. This means that, if we want to use existing Java applications intended for the PCs on a pager, we are faced with a much bigger problem than just the question of compatibility.

Our task in this chapter is to find out whether converting applications is possible, and if it is, how existing Java applications can be used for devices that run J2ME. The differences between J2ME and J2SE can be really vast — so much so that they may turn out to be unbridgeable. The real extent of these differences depends on what part of J2ME is being considered. There is a very wide gap between CLDC (and the profiles made for it) and J2SE. On the other hand, when it comes to CDC and the Foundation Profile, the differences are marginal. This situation will further change when more profiles become available and the devices with which we are concerned get equipped with better hardware. PersonalJava technology, which is going to be merged in J2ME in the form of Personal Profile, has more or less the functionality of JDK1.1.

Issues Involved in Conversion

Before proceeding to find ways to convert (if possible) J2SE applications to J2ME, we have to consider the issues involved. These issues include hardware and the functionality provided by various APIs, which are part of the J2SE and J2ME platforms. Another aspect that is equally important is the variety of devices for which conversion can be done.

Differences in Java language support and virtual machines

J2SE applications are, of course, based on full Java language support. This is not true for CLDC-MIDP applications. CLDC has rather restricted Java language support in the following respects:

- CLDC does not have floating-point support. This means that you cannot declare a variable as a `float`.

- Finalization is not available in CLDC. This is because there is no `finalize` method in the `Object` class of the `java.lang` package.

- CLDC has more or less equivalent support for exception handling when compared to J2SE, but there is only a limited number of error-handling classes. This is meant to reduce the overheads, keeping in mind the memory limitations of small devices.

Some other limitations pertain to the differences in the virtual machines. CLDC uses KVM, and CDC uses CVM, both of which are optimized versions of the conventional JVM, the former being more so. Some of the differences between the virtual machines of conventional JVM and KVM are as follows:

- CLDC does not have a Java Native Interface.
- User-defined class loaders are not supported in CLDC.
- Multithreading is allowed in CLDC but not thread-grouping or daemon threads.
- Weak references are not allowed in CLDC.

Differences in the hardware

As we have seen in Chapter 2, the hardware differences between different devices can be due to the following factors:

- **Processing speed:** It is not unusual today for a desktop system to have processing speed in the range of 1 GHz, whereas a small device may have to do with just 20 MHz. In fact, it may be even lower than this for pagers. With set-top boxes, the processing power may be comparable to lower-end PCs.

- **Memory and storage restrictions:** Today, PCs have RAMs in the range of 64-128 MB or higher. In contrast to this, PDAs have RAMs anywhere between 4 to 16 MB. Higher-end PDAs have more RAM, but the gap between PCs and small devices will remain considerable. Similar is the case with secondary storage. Small devices such as mobile phones or PDAs have just enough RAM so as not to cause concern, but what is more important is that they have no secondary storage, while desktop systems may have hard disks with 20 GB or more capacity.

- **Input and output:** Few small or limited connected devices can afford to have input devices that are essential parts of a PC, such as the mouse and the keyboard. Mobile phones have to do with a numeric keyboard and a few extra buttons. Text is also entered through the same numeric keyboard, which involves pressing the same button more than once to enter one letter. PDAs use handwriting recognition, which is not a very effective technology, at least at present. The display available on such devices is inferior in terms of both area and resolution. The resolution may improve (and is, in fact, improving), but the area will have to be limited in view of the very nature of these devices.

- **Networking:** Connection speeds on various devices may often necessitate changes in application development approach. Speeds of both wired and wireless connections may have to be considered. For example, a PDA will connect to other devices through wireless connection, but when it needs to be synchronized, it has to be connected via a "cradle" to the desktop system, which is not wireless.

- **Other constraints:** Applications developed for mobile devices may have to be designed to tackle some other constraints, such as the unreliability of connection, localization of information, etc.

Problems due to device variety

The problems involved in the conversion of applications are not restricted to the deficiencies of processing power, memory, input/output, etc. The vast variety of devices adds to it. There are many categories of devices — cell phones, screen phones, smart phones, PDAs, set-top boxes, pagers, handheld PCs, embedded devices, and many others. Even in a particular category of devices, there may be numerous models available on the market. And each day brings more of these models. One model of cell phone may differ from another in all the aspects that we considered in the preceding section. This means that, when we try to port a J2SE application to J2ME, we cannot be certain about which model that our application will target, even if we have decided that it will run on only one kind of device — say, a PDA.

Differences in the application models

The Java 2 Standard Edition platform supports various kinds of applications, such as standalone applications, applets, servlets, etc. None of these are applicable to CLDC-MIDP, which uses a new model called a MIDlet, although it is similar in some respects to applets. CDC-Foundation Profile supports applets. Other profiles may introduce new models in future. This will seriously affect our conversion efforts.

Differences in APIs

Due to the preceding differences between devices, it is quite natural that the APIs required will also be different. This is true not just for J2SE and J2ME, but also for CLDC and CDC. APIs being different means that one platform may have certain APIs that another platform may not have. Let us consider some examples:

♦ The combination of CLDC and MIDP, which are parts of J2ME, has only three of the packages in common with the J2SE core API: `java.io`, `java.lang`, and `java.util`.

♦ In case of CDC plus Foundation Profile, there are far fewer differences, because the Foundation Profile is based mainly on the J2SE 1.3 API. Moreover, the C Virtual Machine on which CDC and Foundation Profile run has full Java language support. There is, however, one difference: This combination has no GUI available — not even the AWT API. This is because CDC, being a configuration, is not supposed to have GUI, and the Foundation Profile is also meant to be just what its name suggests — the foundation on which other profiles can be added.

♦ Even though the Foundation Profile is based on the J2SE 1.3 API, it doesn't have many packages that are now commonly employed while writing applications using J2SE. Those it does have include, among others, the Swing packages.

But it also means that those APIs that are common are not identical. For example, while comparing J2SE and J2ME, we observe the following differences:

♦ Package `java.io` is present in both J2SE and J2ME, but there are only two interfaces available in MIDP — namely, `DataInput` and `DataOutput`. On the other hand, J2SE has as many as ten interfaces, including `Externalizable` and `Serializable`.

♦ The same is the case with the other classes of the same package. There are no buffered input/output streams available in MIDP, nor are there any of the various filter stream classes such as `FilterReader` and `FilterWriter`.

♦ Package `java.math` is present in both CDC plus Foundation Profile and J2SE, but the former does not have the `BigDecimal` class, which is used to represent immutable, signed numbers with arbitrary precision. These numbers allow the developer to completely control how his numbers will be rounded.

Another difference is even more significant for us. This relates to the completely new APIs added with a platform (or configuration/profile). The varying needs of devices targeted by the platforms dictate that, at least in some cases, new APIs have to be introduced. This is because the existing model on which the present APIs are based is not applicable in the case of these devices. Here are a few examples:

♦ CLDC API introduces a new Generic Connection Framework in the package `javax.microedition.io`. This framework is necessitated by the fact that different devices have different levels of support for networking, in addition to other hardware limitations. This means that support for all kinds of connections cannot be added in a configuration meant for pagers and PDAs. For this reason, a single `connector` class with a hierarchy of interfaces is used to represent all kinds of connections. Actual implementation for any protocol is not provided in CLDC. For every protocol, there has to be at least one class. These classes are to be made available in profiles. For example, the MIDP has an `HttpConnection` class in the `javax.microedition.io` package. This class provides the support for HTTP connections. It is also present in the Foundation Profile for use in certain cases, although there is a complete `java.net` package available in this profile.

♦ Since the CLDC-MIDP combination does not have the AWT API, a different model had to be provided so that the developers could add some form of user interface. For this reason, a package named `javax.microedition.lcdui` has been added. This API is based on the Screen model. In other words, every user interface element is either a kind of screen (in that it extends the `Screen` class) or it is added to a screen — directly or as part of a `Form`.

♦ Devices such as mobile phones have no secondary storage. Data cannot be stored in the form of files in many devices. But some form of persistence is required for any effective application development. This need is fulfilled by the `javax.microedition.rms` package in the MIDP. This is done with a class called `RecordStore`.

What Conversion Entails

Now we come to the actual task of porting existing applications to the J2ME platform. Before proceeding further, it is necessary to point out that, in many (perhaps the majority of) cases, conversion may not be possible at all. We have to remember that the small devices we are concerned with are limited-function, specific-purpose devices. Therefore, not all kinds of applications can be run on all devices. In fact, a particular device is often meant to run only a certain kind of application — there is no reason to port other applications to that device.

Another thing to be clarified is that, as of now, there is no automatic tool available to carry out the conversion. Some tools may become available in future, but you should not expect them to be too effective. The only effective way available in the near future will be to manually convert applications to view the steps involved in conversion refer to Figure 12-1. Let us now look at some of the strategies involved.

Modifying the application design, if necessary

The first thing to decide is whether we need to overhaul or to at least modify the basic design of the application. This may not be necessary in all the cases. By design, we mean the following aspects (these aspects are discussed in detail in the upcoming section "Analyzing the design"):

♦ Data design

♦ Architecture design

♦ Interface design

♦ Component level design

Reducing the GUI

One of the rules to be followed while designing new applications, as well as converting applications to J2ME, is that the GUI should be reduced to the minimum. This means that it should be limited to the output capabilities of the device and the GUI features available on the native operating system. Using the features of the native OS results in performance gain.

If we want to convert an application to CLDC-MIDP, we will have to replace AWT and Swing with LCDUI. This will not just affect things such as `Frames` and `Graphics2D`, but will also involve modifying the event-handling part. There is no separate package like `java.awt.event` for event handling in MIDP.

As mentioned before, there is no user interface in CDC-Foundation Profile. But PersonalJava, which is poised to become the Personal Profile, does support AWT. Therefore, when you port an application to PersonalJava/Personal Profile, you can retain the AWT part of your GUI. But this is not the case with the Swing packages. Theoretically, CDC-Foundation Profile allows the use of external, 100-percent Java libraries. Hence, you can install the Swing packages on the device and use them, but that will consume all the processing power. What is more, these packages are not part of the regular configurations and profiles (so far), and using them will mean that the user has to install them first in order to run the application.

Removing unnecessary or impossible functionality

Applications developed for J2SE may have features that are not required on a small device. You can remove these features and functionality. In fact, you will have to do so to reduce the resources required by the application. For example, an e-mail application made for a PC usually comes with such features as entering rich text (RTF) and adding stationery images. You can also send attachments with the mail. These features may not be required by an equivalent application made for a cell phone. Perhaps it would be more precise to say that these features are difficult to implement on a cell phone, even though it is possible.

Optimizing the use of resources

When trying to convert an application, we will have to carefully consider all features that consume resources. We can then decide whether to keep them (if they are essential and will not overstretch the device capabilities), to remove them (if they are not essential and/or will affect performance adversely), or to modify them so that the load they put on the resources is within acceptable limits.

Using JavaCheck

Wouldn't it be wonderful if we had some tool to automatically find out which classes and methods are not supported by the platform or configuration/profile to which we want to port the application? There is, indeed, a way to do this. As we saw in Chapter 8, there is tool called JavaCheck that can check whether the classes and methods you use in your application are available on the platform to which you are shifting your application. But the trouble is that it requires a specification in the form of an SGML-compliant, encoded text file, and presently, the only specification available in this form is for PersonalJava. In other words, you cannot use it for other platforms or configurations/profiles. Still, we have to be aware of its existence, because other specifications may become available. To find out how to run it and check dependencies, refer to Chapter 8 section "JavaCheck."

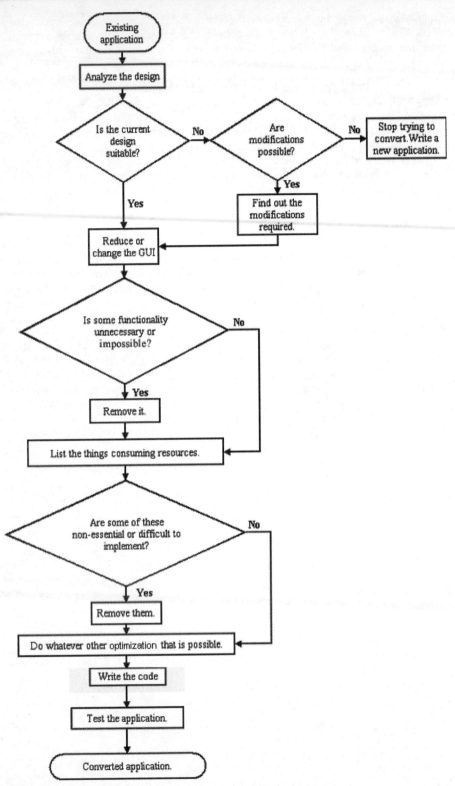

Figure 12-1: Conversion Flow.

An Example of Conversion

The process described previously is better explained through an example. The application we are going to convert was originally made in J2SE. It is a peer-to-peer application, somewhat like the famous Napster or Gnutella software. You can use it to share any of the files on your system with anyone, anywhere, who's connected to the Net at that moment. There is no need to remain permanently connected like a Web server. You just have to log on and see the list of other users connected to the Net. If they have any files that they want to share, you can download them. Similarly, you can make available your files to them. A search facility is, of course, provided. For more details about the J2SE version of this application, you may refer to the book *Peer To Peer Application Development – Cracking the Code Series*, by Hungry Minds Publishing, Inc. Here we will detail the process through which this conversion passed. This process roughly follows the flow chart shown in Figure 12-1.

Analyzing the design

The first step in the conversion process is to analyze the design. This means we have to consider the following aspects:

- **Data design:** There are no database files needed in this application, since its purpose is just to search for files or upload your own files. Whatever data transacts between the client and the server is in the form of XML, which is platform independent. Therefore, we may very well use the same data carrier in our J2ME application.

- **Architecture design:** In this aspect, too, we don't have to make any substantial changes.

- **Interface design:** As part of interface design, we have to consider the relations between parts of the application and between the application and the user. In the first respect, the requests are being sent and the responses are being received in XML and are being parsed by a parser. The only difference is that the parser is of a different kind. The parser in the J2SE application is IBM's Xerces. We cannot use it here because of memory constraints. So for the J2ME version of our application, we choose the kXML parser (in the `org.kxml` package). Its memory requirements are within the range of 10-20K.

For example, in the J2SE version, we may import the XML parser with these statements:

```
import org.xml.sax.*;
import org.apache.xerces.parsers.SAXParser;
```

In the J2ME version, we will have to use the following statements instead:

```
import org.kxml.*;
import org.kxml.io.*;
import org.kxml.parser.*;
```

When we use the parser in the J2SE application, we use the following code:

```
try
{
XMLReader parser = new SAXParser();  // Generate an object of the
                                      // XMLParser class...

// Generate an Object of the MyContentHandler Class it is in this class that
// the xml parser generates the call backs...

MyContentHandler contHandler = new MyContentHandler();

   parser.setContentHandler(contHandler);
   parser.parse(uri);
   // call the parse function of the XMLParser class with the
```

```
                            // file information as the parameter...

     values = contHandler.values_attributes();
// Returns a Vector that contains the parsed results.
```

In the J2ME application, the code to use the parser is as follows:

```
// Call to a method startReading which will request the server for all
// the users connected at a particular time using the ASP.
   startReading();
// The XMLParser will generate the Callbacks in the method parseData.
   ip_addresses = parseData();
// Returns a Vector that contains the parsed results.
```

It is when we come to the user interface that we have to make major changes. We will take these up in a later step.

♦ **Component level design:** This part involves analyzing the application at the code-block level. This will require modifications, since the two platforms are different in terms of APIs, Java language support, virtual machine, etc. The devices on which we want to run the converted application have different memory and storage capabilities, processing power, etc. This will necessitate changes at the component level also.

Now we come to the question of whether the design of the J2SE application is suitable for conversion. As we discussed previously, the differences are not so much so as to make the design unsuitable for conversion. Thus the answer to this question is yes, and so we can consider the next question.

The modifications are definitely possible. We are not going to use another language, just an optimized version of the J2SE platform. Moreover, in several areas, there are no differences at all. So we need not drop the idea of conversion and can go ahead.

Reducing the GUI

We have used tables extensively in the J2SE version. We were able to show the list of files/folders, their sizes, and their extensions. Since there is no JTable class in the J2ME version, Swing packages are not present. As an alternative, we decide to use a simple ScrollTextBox, available in Kjava. In this Textbox, we display the list of files and folders. We do not display their sizes or extensions. These latter modifications are due to the fact that the Palm (or similar) devices for which our converted application is meant will have a limited display area.

The J2SE application uses the JTable class as follows:

```
   default_table = new AbstractTableModel()
   {
        // These methods always need to be implemented.
        public int getColumnCount() { return names.length; }
    public int getRowCount() { return data.length;}
        public Object getValueAt(int row, int col) {return data[row][col];}

    // The default implementations of these methods in
        // AbstractTableModel would work, but we can refine them.
        public String getColumnName(int column) {return names[column];}
        public Class getColumnClass(int col) {return
                                        getValueAt(0,col).getClass();}
        public boolean isCellEditable(int row, int col) {return (col==4);}
        public void setValueAt(Object aValue, int row, int column) {
                data[row][column] = aValue;
    fireTableCellUpdated(row, column);
            }
```

```
        };

    // Positioning and Initializing the GUI Component (Table)...

    client_listing = new JTable(default_table);
```

We are using `ScrollTextBox` in the J2ME version, the code for which is:

```
    userlist = new ScrollTextBox(text,10,40,130,100);
    userlist.paint();
```

Another factor is that, normally, there is no QWERTY keyboard on the Palm devices. These devices, as we know, use a stylus (or pen) to enter text, using some handwriting-recognition software. So we have to substitute the text-entry parts (such as entering the user number) with something equivalent. For example, we use the `penDown` method of the `spotlet` class for event handling. Since there is no mouse on these devices, we also have to use the pen to simulate mouse clicks.

In the J2SE version, the event handling code is as follows:

```
public void actionPerformed(ActionEvent ae)
  {
   if (ae.getSource() == file_open )// When Open Button is pressed...
   {
     // Create a socket connection to the desired user and browse the shared
files / folders on his / her machine.
   }

}
```

Equivalent code in the J2ME version is:

```
  public void penDown(int x, int y)
   {
      if(browse_user.pressed(x,y))   // When the Browse Button is pressed.
      {
       // Create a socket connection to the desired user and browse the shared
files / folders on his / her machine.
      }
    }
```

Is some functionality unnecessary or impossible?

Almost all the functionality of the J2SE application can be ported to the J2ME application. The only major difference is that Palm devices have no hard disks to store the downloaded files. So the functionality involving downloading files to the client is not possible. It isn't essential either, because the user can note down where the files are available and can download them from the PC subsequently. Even if the device had some storage disk, downloading would have been difficult on a wireless connection. The same holds true for uploading the files as well. So we decide to remove this functionality from the J2ME version.

For downloading files in the J2SE version, we use the following code:

```
// Beginning of download class...
public class download_file extends Jframe {
...
...
// Identify the item to download...
    row = file_listing.getSelectedRow();
// Get the selection of the user...
```

```
        InetAddress inet = InetAddress.getByName(ip_address);
        file_socket = new Socket(inet,7070);// Establish a socket connection
                                    with the Listener on the port 7070
     // Get the output as well as the input Streams on that socket...
...
...
// if the selection is a folder then pop up  a message for denial of download.
...
...

// else form an XML request consisting of the file to be downloaded
...
...
     writer.requestFString("DOWNLOAD",information[row][0]); // requestFString...
...
...
// Popping up a file Dialog, get the location where the file is to be stored.
        // File Dialog to place the file.
...
...
     str1 = file_final.getPath();// Get the path where the file is being saved..
...
...

     BufferedOutputStream out_file = new BufferedOutputStream(new
FileOutputStream(str1)); // Create an outputstream to that path...
...
...
   while ((y = br_socket.read(f,0,32))>0) // Read the socket and write on to the
file...
...
...

     // Monitoring the progress of the progress monitor
...
...

     // Close the Streams and the Socket Connections.
...
...
   }    // End Class Download_file...
```

This code is no longer needed, since we would not be adding the functionality to download or upload files.

Another point is that we cannot have the ServerSocket class in J2ME. This presents no problem, since we cannot upload files anyway. The same listener (ServerSocket class) made in J2SE will be used at the server. There will be no listener on the Palm device. More information is available in the book *Peer To Peer Application Development – Cracking the Code series*, by Hungry Minds Publishing, Inc.

Listing the items consuming resources

The first entity that consumes resources is the XML parser. We have already decided to replace it and use another parser that can work without hassles on the target device. The second item liable to consume resources is the JTable, which again is to be substituted. Then we cannot afford to allow browsing of more than one user at the same time in our J2ME application. In the J2SE version, you can open more than one window (one for each user) and do downloading and uploading with all of them separately. In contrast, in the J2ME version, you will be able to browse only a single user, and if you want to browse another user, you will have to close the connection with the first user and then open a connection with the other. This will involve sending and receiving new requests and responses and parsing them. No other optimizations are possible anymore. So we can now proceed to write the code.

Testing the application

The converted application was tested, and minor bugs were removed. The source code of the final application is given in Chapter 9.

Summary

After doing all the programming, one would be interested to learn whether the already developed Java applications using Java Standard Edition can be converted to Java 2 Micro Edition with minimum efforts. This chapter discusses this aspect and provides guidelines on converting the application. We have discussed how we converted an existing Java 2 Standard Edition application to Java 2 Micro Edition; this will be of great help to the reader.

Appendix A

About the CD-ROM

This appendix provides you information on the contents of the CD-ROM that accompanies this book. For the latest and greatest information, please refer to the ReadMe file located at the root of the CD.

System Requirements

Make sure that your computer meets the minimum system requirements listed in this section. If your computer does not conform to these requirements, you may have a problem using the contents of the CD. Your system must be equipped with the following:

- **Microsoft Windows** 9*x* or Windows 2000
- **A CD-ROM drive** — double-speed (2x) or faster

What's on the CD

The CD-ROM contains source-code examples, applications, and an electronic version of the book. The following sections summarize the contents of the CD-ROM, arranged by category.

Source code

The source code of the projects discussed in this book is given in the Source Code folder. The Source Code folder contains different sub-folders containing the Source code of the case studies and the projects. The following list describes the folders in the Source Code folder:

- **CLDC CaseStudies:** This folder contains the Case Studies of the CLDC and Kjava APIs (Chapter 3).
- **MIDP CaseStudies:** This folder contains the Case Studies of the MIDP APIs (Chapter 4).
- **XML Parsing CaseStudy:** This folder contains the Case Studies of XML parsing using kXML parser (Chapter 5).
- **Online Testing Engine:** This folder contains the Source code for our first project, Online Testing Engine (Chapter 6).This project is built using CLDC and Kjava.
- **Online Ordering Systems:** This folder contains the Source code for our second project, Online Ordering Systems (Chapter 7). This project is built using MIDP.
- **MP3 Player:** This folder contains the Source code for our third project, MP3 Player for Pocket PC (Chapter 8). This project is built using PersonalJava.
- **P2P search Application:** This folder contains the Source code for our fourth project, Peer-to-Peer Search Application (Chapter 9). This project is built using CLDC and Kjava.
- **Mobile Services:** This folder contains the Source code for our fifth project, Mobile Web Services (Chapter 10). This project is built using MIDP.
- **Target Game:** This folder contains the Source code for our sixth project, Target Practice Game (Chapter 11).This project is built using CLDC and Kjava.

Applications

The following applications are on the CD-ROM:

♦ **Java 2 Software Development Kit Standard Edition version 1.3 for Windows:** Java 2 SDK 1.3 or later is a kit to develop a standard Java application. The compilation of the programs made for J2ME has been done using this kit, so you need to have JDK to compile your programs for J2ME.This kit can be downloaded from `http://java.sun.com/j2se/1.3`.

♦ **Forte for Java, release 2.0 Community Edition for All Platforms:** The Forte for Java release 2.0 software is an integrated development environment used for devloping Java applications. It is an IDE provided by Sun Microsystems. For more information, visit `http://www.sun.com/forte/ffj/`.

♦ **Java 2 Platform, Micro Edition, Wireless Toolkit 1.01 (J2ME):** This kit is released by Sun to develop MIDP applications. The development is very easy for the programmers since this kit has a GUI base. This comes with a cell phone emulator from Sun and Motorola and a two-way pager emulator from RIM and can also be integrated with the Palm OS 3.5, provided that you have the emulator on your system.This kit can be downloaded from `http://java.sun.com/products/j2mewtoolkit`

♦ **kXML APIs:** These are XML parsing APIs and come in a Zip file. We have used the minimum version of this parser.This parser is available at `http://kxml.enhydra.org/`.

♦ **Tomcat:** Tomcat is the Web server extension used to execute server-side Java components such as servlets and JSP. We have used JSP in our Online Ordering Systems project (Chapter 7).This can be downloaded from `http://jakarta.apache.org/tomcat`.

E-Book

Those readers who desire an electronic copy of the contents in the book can find one on the CD-ROM that accompanies this book. This CD-ROM contains the PDF files of all the chapters, as well as the appendix, in the book. These files can be viewed through the Acrobat Reader 5.0 software, which has been incorporated on the CD-ROM.

Troubleshooting

If you encounter difficulty installing or using the CD-ROM programs, try the following schedule:

♦ **Turn off any antivirus software that you may have running:** Installers sometimes mimic virus activity and can make your computer incorrectly believe that it is being infected by a virus. (Be sure to turn the antivirus software back on later.)

♦ **Close all running programs:** The more programs you are running, the less memory is available to other programs. Installers also typically update files and programs; if you keep other programs running, installation may not work correctly.

If you still have trouble with the CD, please call the Hungry Minds Customer Service phone number: (800) 762-2974. Outside the United States, call (317) 572-3994. You can also contact Hungry Minds Customer Service by e-mail at `techsupdum@hungryminds.com`. Please note that Hungry Minds will provide technical support only for installation and other general quality-control items; for technical support on the applications themselves, consult the program's vendor or author.

Index

Hungry Minds, Inc.
End-User License Agreement

READ THIS. You should carefully read these terms and conditions before opening the software packet(s) included with this book ("Book"). This is a license agreement ("Agreement") between you and Hungry Minds, Inc. ("HMI"). By opening the accompanying software packet(s), you acknowledge that you have read and accept the following terms and conditions. If you do not agree and do not want to be bound by such terms and conditions, promptly return the Book and the unopened software packet(s) to the place you obtained them for a full refund.

1. **License Grant.** HMI grants to you (either an individual or entity) a nonexclusive license to use one copy of the enclosed software program(s) (collectively, the "Software") solely for your own personal and non-commercial purposes on a single computer (whether a standard computer or a workstation component of a multi-user network). The Software is in use on a computer when it is loaded into temporary memory (RAM) or installed into permanent memory (hard disk, CD-ROM, or other storage device). HMI reserves all rights not expressly granted herein.

2. **Ownership.** HMI is the owner of all right, title, and interest, including copyright, in and to the compilation of the Software recorded on the disk(s) or CD-ROM ("Software Media"). Copyright to the individual programs recorded on the Software Media is owned by the author or other authorized copyright owner of each program. Ownership of the Software and all proprietary rights relating thereto remain with HMI and its licensers.

3. **Restrictions on Use and Transfer.**

   (a) You may only (i) make one copy of the Software for backup or archival purposes, or (ii) transfer the Software to a single hard disk, provided that you keep the original for backup or archival purposes. You may not (i) rent or lease the Software, (ii) copy or reproduce the Software through a LAN or other network system or through any computer subscriber system or bulletin-board system, or (iii) modify, adapt, or create derivative works based on the Software.

   (b) You may not reverse engineer, decompile, or disassemble the Software. You may transfer the Software and user documentation on a permanent basis, provided that the transferee agrees to accept the terms and conditions of this Agreement and you retain no copies. If the Software is an update or has been updated, any transfer must include the most recent update and all prior versions.

4. **Restrictions on Use of Individual Programs.** You must follow the individual requirements and restrictions detailed for each individual program in the What's on the CD-ROM appendix of this Book. These limitations are also contained in the individual license agreements recorded on the Software Media. These limitations may include a requirement that after using the program for a specified period of time, the user must pay a registration fee or discontinue use. By opening the Software packet(s), you will be agreeing to abide by the licenses and restrictions for these individual programs that are detailed in the What's on the CD-ROM appendix and on the Software Media. None of the material on this Software Media or listed in this Book may ever be redistributed, in original or modified form, for commercial purposes.

5. **Limited Warranty.**

   (a) HMI warrants that the Software and Software Media are free from defects in materials and workmanship under normal use for a period of sixty (60) days from the date of purchase of this Book. If HMI receives notification within the warranty period of defects in materials or workmanship, HMI will replace the defective Software Media.

(b) **HMI AND THE AUTHOR OF THE BOOK DISCLAIM ALL OTHER WARRANTIES, EXPRESS OR IMPLIED, INCLUDING WITHOUT LIMITATION IMPLIED WARRANTIES OF MERCHANTABILITY AND FITNESS FOR A PARTICULAR PURPOSE, WITH RESPECT TO THE SOFTWARE, THE PROGRAMS, THE SOURCE CODE CONTAINED THEREIN, AND/OR THE TECHNIQUES DESCRIBED IN THIS BOOK. HMI DOES NOT WARRANT THAT THE FUNCTIONS CONTAINED IN THE SOFTWARE WILL MEET YOUR REQUIREMENTS OR THAT THE OPERATION OF THE SOFTWARE WILL BE ERROR FREE.**

(c) This limited warranty gives you specific legal rights, and you may have other rights that vary from jurisdiction to jurisdiction.

6. **Remedies.**

(a) HMI's entire liability and your exclusive remedy for defects in materials and workmanship shall be limited to replacement of the Software Media, which may be returned to HMI with a copy of your receipt at the following address: Software Media Fulfillment Department, Attn.: *Wireless Programming with J2ME™: Cracking the Code*, Hungry Minds, Inc., 10475 Crosspoint Blvd., Indianapolis, IN 46256, or call 1-800-762-2974. Please allow four to six weeks for delivery. This Limited Warranty is void if failure of the Software Media has resulted from accident, abuse, or misapplication. Any replacement Software Media will be warranted for the remainder of the original warranty period or thirty (30) days, whichever is longer.

(b) In no event shall HMI or the author be liable for any damages whatsoever (including without limitation damages for loss of business profits, business interruption, loss of business information, or any other pecuniary loss) arising from the use of or inability to use the Book or the Software, even if HMI has been advised of the possibility of such damages.

(c) Because some jurisdictions do not allow the exclusion or limitation of liability for consequential or incidental damages, the above limitation or exclusion may not apply to you.

7. **U.S. Government Restricted Rights.** Use, duplication, or disclosure of the Software for or on behalf of the United States of America, its agencies and/or instrumentalities (the "U.S. Government") is subject to restrictions as stated in paragraph (c)(1)(ii) of the Rights in Technical Data and Computer Software clause of DFARS 252.227-7013, or subparagraphs (c) (1) and (2) of the Commercial Computer Software - Restricted Rights clause at FAR 52.227-19, and in similar clauses in the NASA FAR supplement, as applicable.

8. **General.** This Agreement constitutes the entire understanding of the parties and revokes and supersedes all prior agreements, oral or written, between them and may not be modified or amended except in a writing signed by both parties hereto that specifically refers to this Agreement. This Agreement shall take precedence over any other documents that may be in conflict herewith. If any one or more provisions contained in this Agreement are held by any court or tribunal to be invalid, illegal, or otherwise unenforceable, each and every other provision shall remain in full force and effect.

Sun Microsystems, Inc.
Binary Code License Agreement

READ THE TERMS OF THIS AGREEMENT AND ANY PROVIDED SUPPLEMENTAL LICENSE TERMS (COLLECTIVELY "AGREEMENT") CAREFULLY BEFORE OPENING THE SOFTWARE MEDIA PACKAGE. BY OPENING THE SOFTWARE MEDIA PACKAGE, YOU AGREE TO THE TERMS OF THIS AGREEMENT. IF YOU ARE ACCESSING THE SOFTWARE ELECTRONICALLY, INDICATE YOUR ACCEPTANCE OF THESE TERMS BY SELECTING THE "ACCEPT" BUTTON AT THE END OF THIS AGREEMENT. IF YOU DO NOT AGREE TO ALL THESE TERMS, PROMPTLY RETURN THE UNUSED SOFTWARE TO YOUR PLACE OF PURCHASE FOR A REFUND OR, IF THE SOFTWARE IS ACCESSED ELECTRONICALLY, SELECT THE "DECLINE" BUTTON AT THE END OF THIS AGREEMENT.

1. LICENSE TO USE. Sun grants you a non-exclusive and non-transferable license for the internal use only of the accompanying software and documentation and any error corrections provided by Sun (collectively "Software"), by the number of users and the class of computer hardware for which the corresponding fee has been paid.

2. RESTRICTIONS. Software is confidential and copyrighted. Title to Software and all associated intellectual property rights is retained by Sun and/or its licensors. Except as specifically authorized in any Supplemental License Terms, you may not make copies of Software, other than a single copy of Software for archival purposes. Unless enforcement is prohibited by applicable law, you may not modify, decompile, or reverse engineer Software. You acknowledge that Software is not designed, licensed or intended for use in the design, construction, operation or maintenance of any nuclear facility. Sun disclaims any express or implied warranty of fitness for such uses. No right, title or interest in or to any trademark, service mark, logo or trade name of Sun or its licensors is granted under this Agreement.

3. LIMITED WARRANTY. Sun warrants to you that for a period of ninety (90) days from the date of purchase, as evidenced by a copy of the receipt, the media on which Software is furnished (if any) will be free of defects in materials and workmanship under normal use. Except for the foregoing, Software is provided "AS IS". Your exclusive remedy and Sun's entire liability under this limited warranty will be at Sun's option to replace Software media or refund the fee paid for Software.

4. DISCLAIMER OF WARRANTY. UNLESS SPECIFIED IN THIS AGREEMENT, ALL EXPRESS OR IMPLIED CONDITIONS, REPRESENTATIONS AND WARRANTIES, INCLUDING ANY IMPLIED WARRANTY OF MERCHANTABILITY, FITNESS FOR A PARTICULAR PURPOSE OR NON-INFRINGEMENT ARE DISCLAIMED, EXCEPT TO THE EXTENT THAT THESE DISCLAIMERS ARE HELD TO BE LEGALLY INVALID.

5. LIMITATION OF LIABILITY. TO THE EXTENT NOT PROHIBITED BY LAW, IN NO EVENT WILL SUN OR ITS LICENSORS BE LIABLE FOR ANY LOST REVENUE, PROFIT OR DATA, OR FOR SPECIAL, INDIRECT, CONSEQUENTIAL, INCIDENTAL OR PUNITIVE DAMAGES, HOWEVER CAUSED REGARDLESS OF THE THEORY OF LIABILITY, ARISING OUT OF OR RELATED TO THE USE OF OR INABILITY TO USE SOFTWARE, EVEN IF SUN HAS BEEN ADVISED OF THE POSSIBILITY OF SUCH DAMAGES. In no event will Sun's liability to you, whether in contract, tort (including negligence), or otherwise, exceed the amount paid by you for Software under this Agreement. The foregoing limitations will apply even if the above stated warranty fails of its essential purpose.

6. Termination. This Agreement is effective until terminated. You may terminate this Agreement at any time by destroying all copies of Software. This Agreement will terminate immediately without notice from Sun if you fail to comply with any provision of this Agreement. Upon Termination, you must destroy all copies of Software.

7. Export Regulations. All Software and technical data delivered under this Agreement are subject to US export control laws and may be subject to export or import regulations in other countries. You agree to comply strictly with all such laws and regulations and acknowledge that you have the responsibility to obtain such licenses to export, re-export, or import as may be required after delivery to you.

8. **U.S. Government Restricted Rights.** If Software is being acquired by or on behalf of the U.S. Government or by a U.S. Government prime contractor or subcontractor (at any tier), then the Government's rights in Software and accompanying documentation will be only as set forth in this Agreement; this is in accordance with 48 CFR 227.7201 through 227.7202-4 (for Department of Defense (DOD) acquisitions) and with 48 CFR 2.101 and 12.212 (for non-DOD acquisitions).

9. **Governing Law.** Any action related to this Agreement will be governed by California law and controlling U.S. federal law. No choice of law rules of any jurisdiction will apply.

10. **Severability.** If any provision of this Agreement is held to be unenforceable, this Agreement will remain in effect with the provision omitted, unless omission would frustrate the intent of the parties, in which case this Agreement will immediately terminate.

11. **Integration.** This Agreement is the entire agreement between you and Sun relating to its subject matter. It supersedes all prior or contemporaneous oral or written communications, proposals, representations and warranties and prevails over any conflicting or additional terms of any quote, order, acknowledgment, or other communication between the parties relating to its subject matter during the term of this Agreement. No modification of this Agreement will be binding, unless in writing and signed by an authorized representative of each party.

Java(TM) 2 Software Development Kit (J2SDK), Standard Edition, Version 1.3 SUPPLEMENTAL LICENSE TERMS

These supplemental license terms ("Supplemental Terms") add to or modify the terms of the Binary Code License Agreement (collectively, the "Agreement"). Capitalized terms not defined in these Supplemental Terms shall have the same meanings ascribed to them in the Agreement. These Supplemental Terms shall supersede any inconsistent or conflicting terms in the Agreement, or in any license contained within the Software.

1. **Software Internal Use and Development License Grant.** Subject to the terms and conditions of this Agreement, including, but not limited to Section 4 (Java(TM) Technology Restrictions) of these Supplemental Terms, Sun grants you a non-exclusive, non-transferable, limited license to reproduce internally and use internally the binary form of the Software complete and unmodified for the sole purpose of designing, developing and testing your Java applets and applications intended to run on the Java platform ("Programs").

2. **License to Distribute Software.** Subject to the terms and conditions of this Agreement, including, but not limited to Section 4 (Java (TM) Technology Restrictions) of these Supplemental Terms, Sun grants you a non-exclusive, non-transferable, limited license to reproduce and distribute the Software in binary code form only, provided that (i) you distribute the Software complete and unmodified and only bundled as part of, and for the sole purpose of running, your Programs, (ii) the Programs add significant and primary functionality to the Software, (iii) you do not distribute additional software intended to replace any component(s) of the Software, (iv) you do not remove or alter any proprietary legends or notices contained in the Software, (v) you only distribute the Software subject to a license agreement that protects Sun's interests consistent with the terms contained in this Agreement, and (vi) you agree to defend and indemnify Sun and its licensors from and against any damages, costs, liabilities, settlement amounts and/or expenses (including attorneys' fees) incurred in connection with any claim, lawsuit or action by any third party that arises or results from the use or distribution of any and all Programs and/or Software.

3. **License to Distribute Redistributables.** Subject to the terms and conditions of this Agreement, including but not limited to Section 4 (Java Technology Restrictions) of these Supplemental Terms, Sun grants you a non-exclusive, non-transferable, limited license to reproduce and distribute the binary form of those files specifically identified as redistributable in the Software "README" file ("Redistributables") provided that: (i) you distribute the Redistributables complete and unmodified (unless otherwise specified in the applicable README file), and only bundled as part of Programs, (ii) you do not distribute additional software intended to supersede any component(s) of the Redistributables, (iii) you do not remove or alter any proprietary legends or notices contained in or on the Redistributables, (iv) you only distribute the Redistributables pursuant to a license agreement that protects Sun's interests consistent with the terms contained in the Agreement, and (v) you agree to defend and indemnify Sun and its licensors from and against any damages, costs, liabilities, settlement amounts and/or expenses (including attorneys' fees) incurred in connection

with any claim, lawsuit or action by any third party that arises or results from the use or distribution of any and all Programs and/or Software.

4. Java Technology Restrictions. You may not modify the Java Platform Interface ("JPI", identified as classes contained within the "java" package or any subpackages of the "java" package), by creating additional classes within the JPI or otherwise causing the addition to or modification of the classes in the JPI. In the event that you create an additional class and associated API(s) which (i) extends the functionality of the Java platform, and (ii) is exposed to third party software developers for the purpose of developing additional software which invokes such additional API, you must promptly publish broadly an accurate specification for such API for free use by all developers. You may not create, or authorize your licensees to create, additional classes, interfaces, or subpackages that are in any way identified as "java", "javax", "sun" or similar convention as specified by Sun in any naming convention designation.

5. Trademarks and Logos. You acknowledge and agree as between you and Sun that Sun owns the SUN, SOLARIS, JAVA, JINI, FORTE, STAROFFICE, STARPORTAL and iPLANET trademarks and all SUN, SOLARIS, JAVA, JINI, FORTE, STAROFFICE, STARPORTAL and iPLANET-related trademarks, service marks, logos and other brand designations ("Sun Marks"), and you agree to comply with the Sun Trademark and Logo Usage Requirements currently located at http://www.sun.com/policies/trademarks. Any use you make of the Sun Marks inures to Sun's benefit.

6. Source Code. Software may contain source code that is provided solely for reference purposes pursuant to the terms of this Agreement. Source code may not be redistributed unless expressly provided for in this Agreement.

7. Termination for Infringement. Either party may terminate this Agreement immediately should any Software become, or in either party's opinion be likely to become, the subject of a claim of infringement of any intellectual property right.

For inquiries please contact: Sun Microsystems, Inc. 901 San Antonio Road, Palo Alto, California 94303

License Agreement: Forte for Java, release 2.0 Community Edition for All Platforms

To obtain Forte for Java, release 2.0, Community Edition for All Platforms, you must agree to the software license below.

Sun Microsystems Inc., Binary Code License Agreement

READ THE TERMS OF THIS AGREEMENT AND ANY PROVIDED SUPPLEMENTAL LICENSE TERMS (COLLECTIVELY "AGREEMENT") CAREFULLY BEFORE OPENING THE SOFTWARE MEDIA PACKAGE. BY OPENING THE SOFTWARE MEDIA PACKAGE, YOU AGREE TO THE TERMS OF THIS AGREEMENT. IF YOU ARE ACCESSING THE SOFTWARE ELECTRONICALLY, INDICATE YOUR ACCEPTANCE OF THESE TERMS BY SELECTING THE "ACCEPT" BUTTON AT THE END OF THIS AGREEMENT. IF YOU DO NOT AGREE TO ALL THESE TERMS, PROMPTLY RETURN THE UNUSED SOFTWARE TO YOUR PLACE OF PURCHASE FOR A REFUND OR, IF THE SOFTWARE IS ACCESSED ELECTRONICALLY, SELECT THE "DECLINE" BUTTON AT THE END OF THIS AGREEMENT.

1. LICENSE TO USE. Sun grants you a non-exclusive and non-transferable license for the internal use only of the accompanying software and documentation and any error corrections provided by Sun (collectively "Software"), by the number of users and the class of computer hardware for which the corresponding fee has been paid.

2. RESTRICTIONS. Software is confidential and copyrighted. Title to Software and all associated intellectual property rights is retained by Sun and/or its licensors. Except as specifically authorized in any Supplemental License Terms, you may not make copies of Software, other than a single copy of Software for archival purposes. Unless enforcement is prohibited by applicable law, you may not modify, decompile, or reverse engineer Software. You acknowledge that Software is not designed, licensed or intended for use in the design, construction, operation or maintenance of any nuclear facility. Sun disclaims any express or implied warranty of fitness for such uses. No right, title or interest in or to any trademark, service mark, logo or trade name of Sun or its licensors is granted under this Agreement.

3. LIMITED WARRANTY. Sun warrants to you that for a period of ninety (90) days from the date of purchase, as evidenced by a copy of the receipt, the media on which Software is furnished (if any) will be free of defects in materials and workmanship under normal use. Except for the foregoing, Software is provided "AS IS". Your exclusive remedy and Sun's entire liability under this limited warranty will be at Sun's option to replace Software media or refund the fee paid for Software.

4. DISCLAIMER OF WARRANTY. UNLESS SPECIFIED IN THIS AGREEMENT, ALL EXPRESS OR IMPLIED CONDITIONS, REPRESENTATIONS AND WARRANTIES, INCLUDING ANY IMPLIED WARRANTY OF MERCHANTABILITY, FITNESS FOR A PARTICULAR PURPOSE OR NON-INFRINGEMENT ARE DISCLAIMED, EXCEPT TO THE EXTENT THAT THESE DISCLAIMERS ARE HELD TO BE LEGALLY INVALID.

5. LIMITATION OF LIABILITY. TO THE EXTENT NOT PROHIBITED BY LAW, IN NO EVENT WILL SUN OR ITS LICENSORS BE LIABLE FOR ANY LOST REVENUE, PROFIT OR DATA, OR FOR SPECIAL, INDIRECT, CONSEQUENTIAL, INCIDENTAL OR PUNITIVE DAMAGES, HOWEVER CAUSED REGARDLESS OF THE THEORY OF LIABILITY, ARISING OUT OF OR RELATED TO THE USE OF OR INABILITY TO USE SOFTWARE, EVEN IF SUN HAS BEEN ADVISED OF THE POSSIBILITY OF SUCH DAMAGES. In no event will Sun's liability to you, whether in contract, tort (including negligence), or otherwise, exceed the amount paid by you for Software under this Agreement. The foregoing limitations will apply even if the above stated warranty fails of its essential purpose.

6. Termination. This Agreement is effective until terminated. You may terminate this Agreement at any time by destroying all copies of Software. This Agreement will terminate immediately without notice from Sun if you fail to comply with any provision of this Agreement. Upon Termination, you must destroy all copies of Software.

7. Export Regulations. All Software and technical data delivered under this Agreement are subject to US export control laws and may be subject to export or import regulations in other countries. You

agree to comply strictly with all such laws and regulations and acknowledge that you have the responsibility to obtain such licenses to export, re-export, or import as may be required after delivery to you.

8. **U.S. Government Restricted Rights.** If Software is being acquired by or on behalf of the U.S. Government or by a U.S. Government prime contractor or subcontractor (at any tier), then the Government's rights in Software and accompanying documentation will be only as set forth in this Agreement; this is in accordance with 48 CFR 227.7201 through 227.7202-4 (for Department of Defense (DOD) acquisitions) and with 48 CFR 2.101 and 12.212 (for non-DOD acquisitions).

9. **Governing Law.** Any action related to this Agreement will be governed by California law and controlling U.S. federal law. No choice of law rules of any jurisdiction will apply.

10. **Severability.** If any provision of this Agreement is held to be unenforceable, this Agreement will remain in effect with the provision omitted, unless omission would frustrate the intent of the parties, in which case this Agreement will immediately terminate.

11. **Integration.** This Agreement is the entire agreement between you and Sun relating to its subject matter. It supersedes all prior or contemporaneous oral or written communications, proposals, representations and warranties and prevails over any conflicting or additional terms of any quote, order, acknowledgment, or other communication between the parties relating to its subject matter during the term of this Agreement. No modification of this Agreement will be binding, unless in writing and signed by an authorized representative of each party.

JAVA™ DEVELOPMENT TOOLS FORTE™ FOR JAVA™, RELEASE 2.0, COMMUNITY EDITION SUPPLEMENTAL LICENSE TERMS

These supplemental license terms ("Supplemental Terms") add to or modify the terms of the Binary Code License Agreement (collectively, the "Agreement"). Capitalized terms not defined in these Supplemental Terms shall have the same meanings ascribed to them in the Agreement. These Supplemental Terms shall supersede any inconsistent or conflicting terms in the Agreement, or in any license contained within the Software.

1. **Software Internal Use and Development License Grant.** Subject to the terms and conditions of this Agreement, including, but not limited to Section 3 (Java(TM) Technology Restrictions) of these Supplemental Terms, Sun grants you a non-exclusive, non-transferable, limited license to reproduce internally and use internally the binary form of the Software complete and unmodified for the sole purpose of designing, developing and testing your [Java applets and] applications intended to run on the Java platform ("Programs").

2. **License to Distribute Redistributables.** In addition to the license granted in Section 1 (Redistributables Internal Use and Development License Grant) of these Supplemental Terms, subject to the terms and conditions of this Agreement, including, but not limited to Section 3 (Java Technology Restrictions) of these Supplemental Terms, Sun grants you a non-exclusive, non-transferable, limited license to reproduce and distribute those files specifically identified as redistributable in the Software "README" file ("Redistributables") provided that: (i) you distribute the Redistributables complete and unmodified (unless otherwise specified in the applicable README file), and only bundled as part of your Programs, (ii) you do not distribute additional software intended to supercede any component(s) of the Redistributables, (iii) you do not remove or alter any proprietary legends or notices contained in or on the Redistributables, (iv) for a particular version of the Java platform, any executable output generated by a compiler that is contained in the Software must (a) only be compiled from source code that conforms to the corresponding version of the OEM Java Language Specification; (b) be in the class file format defined by the corresponding version of the OEM Java Virtual Machine Specification; and (c) execute properly on a reference runtime, as specified by Sun, associated with such version of the Java platform, (v) you only distribute the Redistributables pursuant to a license agreement that protects Sun's interests consistent with the terms contained in the Agreement, and (vi) you agree to defend and indemnify Sun and its licensors from and against any damages, costs, liabilities, settlement amounts and/or expenses (including attorneys' fees) incurred in connection with any

claim, lawsuit or action by any third party that arises or results from the use or distribution of any and all Programs and/or Software.

3. Java Technology Restrictions. You may not modify the Java Platform Interface ("JPI", identified as classes contained within the "java" package or any subpackages of the "java" package), by creating additional classes within the JPI or otherwise causing the addition to or modification of the classes in the JPI. In the event that you create an additional class and associated API(s) which (i) extends the functionality of the Java platform, and (ii) is exposed to third party software developers for the purpose of developing additional software which invokes such additional API, you must promptly publish broadly an accurate specification for such API for free use by all developers. You may not create, or authorize your licensees to create, additional classes, interfaces, or subpackages that are in any way identified as "java", "javax", "sun" or similar convention as specified by Sun in any naming convention designation.

4. Java Runtime Availability. Refer to the appropriate version of the Java Runtime Environment binary code license (currently located at http://www.java.sun.com/jdk/index.html) for the availability of runtime code which may be distributed with Java applets and applications.

5. Trademarks and Logos. You acknowledge and agree as between you and Sun that Sun owns the SUN, SOLARIS, JAVA, JINI, FORTE, STAROFFICE, STARPORTAL and iPLANET trademarks and all SUN, SOLARIS, JAVA, JINI, FORTE, STAROFFICE, STARPORTAL and iPLANET-related trademarks, service marks, logos and other brand designations ("Sun Marks"), and you agree to comply with the Sun Trademark and Logo Usage Requirements currently located at http://www.sun.com/policies/trademarks. Any use you make of the Sun Marks inures to Sun's benefit.

6. Source Code. Software may contain source code that is provided solely for reference purposes pursuant to the terms of this Agreement. Source code may not be redistributed unless expressly provided for in this Agreement.

7. Termination for Infringement. Either party may terminate this Agreement immediately should any Software become, or in either party's opinion be likely to become, the subject of a claim of infringement of any intellectual property right.

For inquiries please contact: Sun Microsystems, Inc. 901 San Antonio Road, Palo Alto, California 94303

AMENDMENT NO. 1 TO
BINARY LICENSE AND REDISTRIBUTION AGREEMENT

This Amendment No. 1 (the "Amendment") to Binary License and Redistribution Agreement is entered into by and between Sun Microsystems, Inc. ("Sun") and Hungry Minds, Inc. ("Publisher") effective as of the date signed by Sun below ("Effective Date").

WHEREAS, Sun and Publisher are parties to that certain Binary License and Redistribution Agreement (No. 90610) dated _____, 2001 (the "Agreement"); and

WHEREAS, the parties desire to amend the Agreement as set forth herein.

NOW, THEREFORE, the parties hereby agree as follows:

1. Additional Software. The following is hereby added to Exhibit A of the Agreement:

   "Software: Sun's Java 2 Platform, Micro Edition, Wireless Toolkit 1.0.1
   Website: http://java.sun.com/products/j2mewtoolkit/download.html
   Per Unit Royalty: $0 US
   End User License Agreement: Exhibit C–3"

2. Additional Publications. The Publications listed below are hereby added to Exhibit B of the Agreement.

   Title: Peer–to–Peer Application Development
   Author: DreamTech Software Team
   ISBN: 0764549049

   Title: WAP, Bluetooth and 3G Programming: Cracking the Code
   Author: DreamTech Software Team
   ISBN: 0764549057

3. Notice of Publication. As of the Effective Date of this Amendment, Publisher may add Publications to Exhibit B of the Agreement by providing a written "Notice of Publication" to Sun, prior to the date of publication, which references the Agreement and contains the following information: (i) Publisher's name and address, (ii) title of Publication, (iii) name(s) of author(s), (iv) ISBN number, (v) expected date of publication, and (v) Software to be distributed with the Publication. All other terms and conditions of the Agreement will continue to apply to all Publications so added.

4. Binary Code License. Exhibit C–3, attached hereto, is hereby added to the Agreement.

5. Product Names. The first paragraph of Exhibit D is hereby amended to read in its entirety as follows:

"Product Names: The CD–ROM label may refer to the Software as follows: (i) Java™ 2 Software Development Kit Standard Edition version 1.3 for Windows, (ii) Forte for Java, release 2.0, Community Edition for All Platforms, and (iii) Java 2 Platform, Micro Edition, Wireless Toolkit 1.0.1."

6. <u>Effect of Amendment</u>. Except as expressly provided herein, all other terms and conditions of the Agreement shall remain in full force and effect.

IN WITNESS WHEREOF, this Amendment has been signed by authorized representatives of the parties as of the Effective Date.

SUN MICROSYSTEMS, INC.   HUNGRY MINDS, INC.

By: _____   By: _____
Printed Name:_____   Printed Name:_____
Title:_____   Title:_____
Date:_____   Date:_____

<u>**EXHIBIT C–3**</u>
Java(TM) 2 Micro Edition Wireless Toolkit 1.0.1

JavaTM 2 Micro Edition Wireless Toolkit
Evaluation and Binary Code License Agreement

SUN MICROSYSTEMS, INC. ("SUN") IS WILLING TO LICENSE THE JAVATM 2 MICRO EDITION WIRELESS TOOLKIT SOFTWARE TO LICENSEE ONLY UPON THE CONDITION THAT LICENSEE ACCEPTS ALL OF THE TERMS CONTAINED IN THIS LICENSE AGREEMENT AND ANY PROVIDED SUPPLEMENTAL LICENSE TERMS (COLLECTIVELY "AGREEMENT") CAREFULLY BEFORE OPENING THE SOFTWARE MEDIA PACKAGE. BY OPENING THE SOFTWARE MEDIA PACKAGE, YOU AGREE TO THE TERMS OF THIS AGREEMENT. IF YOU ARE ACCESSING THE SOFTWARE ELECTRONICALLY, INDICATE YOUR ACCEPTANCE OF THESE TERMS BY SELECTING THE "ACCEPT" BUTTON AT THE END OF THIS AGREEMENT. IF YOU DO NOT AGREE TO ALL THESE TERMS, PROMPTLY RETURN THE UNUSED SOFTWARE TO YOUR PLACE OF PURCHASE FOR A REFUND OR, IF THE SOFTWARE IS ACCESSED ELECTRONICALLY, SELECT THE "DECLINE" BUTTON AT THE END OF THIS AGREEMENT AND THE INSTALLATION PROCESS WILL NOT CONTINUE.

1. License to Use. Sun grants you a non–exclusive and non–transferable license for the internal use only of the accompanying software and documentation and any error corrections provided by Sun (collectively "Software"), by the number of users and the class of computer hardware for which the corresponding fee has been paid.

2. Restrictions. Software is confidential and copyrighted. Title to Software and all associated intellectual property rights is retained by Sun and/or its licensors. Except as specifically authorized in any Supplemental License Terms, you may not make copies of Software, other than a single copy of Software for archival purposes. Unless enforcement is prohibited by applicable law, you may not modify, decompile, or reverse engineer Software. Customer acknowledges that Products are not designed, licensed, or intended for use in the design, construction, operation or maintenance of any nuclear facility. Sun disclaims any express or implied warranty of fitness for such uses. No right, title or interest in or to any trademark, service mark, logo or trade name of Sun or its licensors is granted under this Agreement.

3. Limited Warranty. Sun warrants to you that for a period of ninety (90) days from the date of purchase, as evidenced by a copy of the receipt, the media on which Software is furnished (if any) will be free of defects in materials and workmanship under normal use. Except for the foregoing, Software is provided "AS IS". Your exclusive remedy and Sun's entire liability under this limited warranty will be at Sun's option to replace Software media or refund the fee paid for Software.

4. DISCLAIMER OF WARRANTY. UNLESS SPECIFIED IN THIS AGREEMENT, ALL EXPRESS OR IMPLIED CONDITIONS, REPRESENTATIONS AND WARRANTIES, INCLUDING ANY IMPLIED WARRANTY OF MERCHANTABILITY, FITNESS FOR A PARTICULAR PURPOSE OR NON–INFRINGEMENT ARE DISCLAIMED, EXCEPT TO THE EXTENT THAT THESE DISCLAIMERS ARE HELD TO BE LEGALLY INVALID.

5. LIMITATION OF LIABILITY. TO THE EXTENT NOT PROHIBITED BY LAW, IN NO EVENT WILL SUN OR ITS LICENSORS BE LIABLE FOR ANY LOST REVENUE, PROFIT OR DATA, OR FOR SPECIAL, INDIRECT, CONSEQUENTIAL, INCIDENTAL OR PUNITIVE DAMAGES, HOWEVER CAUSED REGARDLESS OF THE THEORY OF LIABILITY, ARISING OUT OF OR RELATED TO THE USE OF OR INABILITY TO USE SOFTWARE, EVEN IF SUN HAS BEEN ADVISED OF THE POSSIBILITY OF SUCH DAMAGES. In no event will Sun's liability to you, whether in contract, tort (including negligence), or otherwise, exceed the amount paid by you for Software under this Agreement. The foregoing limitations will apply even if the above stated warranty fails of its essential purpose.

6. Termination. This Agreement is effective until terminated. You may terminate this Agreement at any time by destroying all copies of Software. This Agreement will terminate immediately without notice from Sun if you fail to comply with any provision of this Agreement. Upon Termination, you must destroy all copies of Software.

7. Export Regulations. All Software and technical data delivered under this Agreement are subject to US export control laws and may be subject to export or import regulations in other countries. You agree to comply strictly with all such laws and regulations and acknowledge that you have the responsibility to obtain such licenses to export, re–export, or import as may be required after delivery to you.

8. U.S. Government Restricted Rights. If this Software is being acquired by or on behalf of the U.S. Government or by a U.S. Government prime contractor or subcontractor (at any tier), then the Government's rights in the Software and accompanying documentation shall be only as set forth in this license; this is in accordance with 48 C.F.R. 227.7202–4 (for Department of Defense (DOD) acquisitions) and with 48 C.F.R. 2.101 and 12.212 (for non–DOD acquisitions).

9. Governing Law. Any action related to this Agreement will be governed by California law and controlling U.S. federal law. No choice of law rules of any jurisdiction will apply.

10. Severability. If any provision of this Agreement is held to be unenforceable, this Agreement will remain in effect with the provision omitted, unless omission would frustrate the intent of the parties, in which case this Agreement will immediately terminate.

11. Integration. This Agreement is the entire agreement between you and Sun relating to its subject matter. It supersedes all prior or contemporaneous oral or written communications, proposals, representations and warranties and prevails over any conflicting or additional terms of any quote, order, acknowledgment, or other communication between the parties relating to its subject matter during the term of this Agreement. No modification of this Agreement will be binding, unless in writing and signed by an authorized representative of each party.

For inquiries please contact: Sun Microsystems, Inc. 901 San Antonio Road, Palo Alto, California 94303